Computing and Control for the Water Industry

WATER ENGINEERING AND MANAGEMENT SERIES

Series Editors: **Professor Bryan Coulbeck**
Professor of Water Control Systems
De Montfort University, Leicester, UK
and
Dr Bogumil Ulanicki
Research Director of Water Software Systems
De Montfort University, Leicester, UK

1. Performance in Water Distribution: A SYSTEMS APPROACH
Sérgio Teixeira Coelho

2. Computing and Control for the Water Industry
Edited by **Roger Powell** *and* **K S Hindi**

Computing and Control for the Water Industry

Edited by

Roger Powell
Director of Water Operational Research Centre
Brunel University, UK

K S Hindi
Professor of Engineering Systems
Brunel University, UK

RESEARCH STUDIES PRESS LTD.
Baldock, Hertfordshire, England

RESEARCH STUDIES PRESS LTD.
15/16 Coach House Cloisters, 10 Hitchin Street, Baldock, Hertfordshire, England, SG7 6AE

Marketing:

NORTH AMERICA
Taylor & Francis Inc.
325 Chestnut Street, Philadelphia, PA 19106, USA

EUROPE & REST OF THE WORLD
Research Studies Press Ltd.
15/16 Coach House Cloisters, 10 Hitchin Street, Baldock, Hertfordshire, England, SG7 6AE

Distribution:

NORTH AMERICA
Taylor & Francis Inc.
47 Runway Road, Suite G, Levittown, PA 19057 - 4700, USA

ASIA-PACIFIC
Hemisphere Publication Services
Golden Wheel Building, 41 Kallang Pudding Road #04-03, Singapore

EUROPE & REST OF THE WORLD
John Wiley & Sons Ltd.
Shripney Road, Bognor Regis, West Sussex, England, PO22 9SA

Library of Congress Cataloging-in-Publication Data

Computing and control for the water industry / edited by Roger Powell, K.S. Hindi.
p. cm. -- (Water engineering and management series ; 2)
Includes bibliographical references and index.
ISBN 0-86380-230-3 (hardbound : alk. paper)
1. Water--Distribution--Mathematical models. 2. Water-supply--Management--Data processing. I. Powell, Roger, 1957- II. Hindi, K. S. (Khalil S.) III. Series.
TD482.C66 1999
628.1'44'015118--dc21 98-53238
CIP

British Library Cataloguing in Publication Data
A catalogue record for this book is available from the British Library.

ISBN 0 86380 230 3

Printed in Great Britain by SRP Ltd., Exeter

Editorial Preface

This series of books is intended to present reviews of recent developments and associated research, and the application of that work, to engineering, operation and management of water systems.

The basic methods of engineering, operating and managing such water systems are well established and well documented. However, the increasing availability and application of computer based methods has had a revolutionary effect on these traditional methods. Significant advances have been made, and are continuing, in such broad areas as: Information technologies, Operational modeling, and Optimal decision strategies.

Very efficient and effective SCADA and GIS systems are now available; these can collect, store and organize large quantities of data. Water companies have taken advantage of these systems to achieve comprehensive information coverage and integration. In turn, this has enabled the development and application of more sophisticated engineering software.

This second book in the series is representative of such advances, and contains contributions from leading experts in the areas of:

- Hydraulic modeling, including simulation, estimation, optimization and design.
- Water quality modeling.
- Water system reliability.
- Information integration within water companies.
- Applications of advanced software technologies.

The material is expected to be of significant interest to practitioners and researchers in the subject area.

The book is based on the proceedings of the Brunel University International Conference, Computing and Control for the Water Industry. This event is a continuation of the series of conferences which started at De Montfort University in 1981.

Bryan Coulbeck
Bogumil Ulanicki
December 1998

List of Authors

Andersen, J.H.
Water Operational Research Centre, Brunel University, Uxbridge, Middlesex UB8 3PH, England

Arnold, E.
Technical University of Ilmenau , Department of Automation and Systems Engineering, PO Box 100565, D-98684, Ilmenau, Germany

Atkinson, R.
School of Engineering, University of Exeter, North Park Road, Exeter EX4 4QF, England

Banyard, J. Director of Investment and Technology
Severn Trent Water Ltd., 2297 Coventry Road, Birmingham, B26 3PU

Barrett, R.J.
United Water Idaho, 8248 West Victory Road, PO Box 7488, Boise, ID 83707-1488, USA

Boulos, P.F.
Montgomery Watson, 301 North Lake Avenue, Suite 1200, Pasadena, CA 91101, USA

Bounds, P.L.M.
Water Software Systems, De Montfort University, The Gateway, Leicester LE1 9BH, England

Brdys, M.A.
Control and Estimation Group, School of Electronic and Electrical Engineering, University of Birmingham, Edgbaston, Birmingham B15 2TT, England

Burgess, A.
South West Water Services Ltd., Peninsula House, Rydon Road, Exeter EX2 7HR, England

Burrows, R.
Department of Civil Engineering, University of Liverpool, PO Box 147, Liverpool L69 3BX, England

Cameron, R.W.
United Water Idaho, 8248 West Victory Road, PO Box 7488, Boise, ID 83707-1488, USA

Cazottes, N.
SAFEGE Consulting Engineers, Parc de l'Ile, 15/27 Rue de Port, BP727-92007, Nanterre Cedex, France

Cembrano, G.
Institut de Robòtica i Informàtica Industrial, Universitat Politècnica de Catalunya, Consejo Superior de Investigaciones Científicas, Edifici Nexus, Gran Capità, 2-4, 08034 Barcelona, Spain

Chen, K.
Control and Estimation Group, School of Electronic and Electrical Engineering, University of Birmingham, Edgbaston, Birmingham B15 2TT, England

Coelho, S.T.
LNEC, National Civil Engineering Laboratory - Av. Brasil 101, 1799 Lisbon, Portugal

Cook, S. Managing Director
Tynemarch Systems Engineering Ltd., Abinger House, Church Street, Dorking, Surrey RH4 1DF, England

Coulbeck, B.
Water Software Systems, De Montfort University, The Gateway, Leicester LE1 9BH, England

Creasey, J.D.
WRC Engineering, Frankland Road, Blagrove, Swindon, Wiltshire SN5 8YF, England

Dukan, S.
Suez-Lyonnaise des Eaux, CIRSEE, 38 rue du President Wilson, 78230, LePecq, France

Evans, E.P.
Sir William Halcrow & Partners Ltd., Burderop Park, Swindon, Wiltshire SN4 0QD, England

Fotoohi, F.
Suez-Lyonnaise des Eaux, CITI, France

Fowler, M. Project Manager
Tynemarch Systems Engineering Ltd., Abinger House, Church Street, Dorking, Surrey RH4 1DF, England

Franke, R.
Technical University of Ilmenau, Department of Automation and Systems Engineering, PO Box 100565, D-98684, Ilmenau, Germany

Fritsch, P.
Technical University of Ilmenau, Department of Automation and Systems Engineering, PO Box 100565, D-98684 Ilmenau, Germany

Gallego, A.
School of Civil Engineering - UPC, Gran Capitan s/n, 08034 Barcelona, Spain

Gomez, M.
School of Civil Engineering - UPC, Gran Capitan s/n, 08034 Barcelona, Spain

Green, A. Client Services Manager
Stoner Associates Europe, 2800 The Crescent, Birmingham Business Park, Birmingham B37 7YL, England

Green, A.P.E.
Sir William Halcrow & Partners Ltd., Burderop Park, Swindon, Wiltshire, SN4 0QD, England

Halhal, D.
School of Engineering, University of Exeter, North Park Road, Exeter EX4 4QF, England

Hoggart, T.M.
Sir William Halcrow & Partners Ltd., Burderop Park, Swindon, Wiltshire SN4 0QD, England

Hopfgarten, S.
Technical University of Ilmenau, Department of Automation and Systems Engineering, PO Box 100565, D-98684 Ilmenau, Germany

Jamieson, D.G.
Department of Civil Engineering, University of Newcastle, Newcastle upon Tyne NE1 7RU, England

Jarrige, P.A.
SAFEGE Consulting Engineers, Parc de l'Ile, 15/27 Rue de Port, BP727-92007, Nanterre Cedex, France

Jowitt, P.W.
Civil and Offshore Engineering Department, Heriot-Watt University, Riccarton, Edinburgh EH14 4AS, Scotland

Kapelan, Z.
School of Engineering, University of Exeter, North Park Road, Exeter EX4 4QF, England

Levi, Y.
Suez-Lyonnaise des Eaux, CIRSEE, 38 rue du President Wilson, 78230, LePecq, France

Linke, H.
Technical University of Ilmenau , Department of Automation and Systems Engineering, PO Box 100565, D-98684, Ilmenau, Germany

Maier, S.H.
Water Operational Research Centre, Brunel University, Uxbridge, Middlesex UB8 3PH, England

Morris, G.D.
Asys2000 Limited, Ridgeway House, 9 Trinfield Avenue, Exmouth, Devon EX8 3JU, England

Nace, A.
Suez-Lyonnaise des Eaux, CITI, France

Orr, C-H.
Montgomery Watson, 301 North Lake Avenue, Suite 1200, Pasadena, CA 91101, USA

Piriou, P.
Suez-Lyonnaise des Eaux, C.I.R.S.E.E., 38 rue du President Wilson, 78230, LePecq, France

Powell, R.S.
Water Operational Research Centre, Brunel University, Uxbridge, Middlesex UB8 3PH, England

Puta, H.
Technical University of Ilmenau, Department of Automation and Systems Engineering, PO Box 100565, D-98684 Ilmenau, Germany

Quevedo, J.
Department Enginyeria de Sistemes, Automàtica i Informàtica Industrial, Edifici d'Automàtica - TR11, Universitat Politècnica de Catalunya, Campus de Terrassa, Rambla Sant Nebridi, s/n., 08222 Terrassa, Spain

Rance, J.P.
Water Software Systems, De Montfort University, The Gateway, Leicester LE1 9BH, England

Rodellar, J.
School of Civil Engineering - UPC, Gran Capitán s/n, 08034 Barcelona, Spain

Savic, D.A.
School of Engineering, University of Exeter, North Park Road, Exeter EX4 4QF, England

Sterling, M.J.H.
Water Operational Research Centre, Brunel University, Uxbridge, Midddlesex UB8 3PH, England

Tabesh, M.
Department of Civil Engineering, University of Liverpool, PO Box 147, Liverpool L69 3BX, England

Tagg, A.F.
Thames Water Utilities, Environment and Quality Directorate, Nugent House, Reading RG1 8DB, England

Tanyimboh, T.T.
Department of Civil Engineering, University of Liverpool, PO Box 147, Liverpool L69 3BX, England

Thurley, R.W.F.
School of Engineering, University of Exeter, North Park Road, Exeter EX4 4QF, England

Tocqueville, L.
SAFEGE Consulting Engineers, Parc de l'Ile, 15/27 Rue de Port, BP727-92007, Nanterre Cedex, France

Todini, E.
Department of Earth and Geo-Environmental Sciences, University of Bologna, Via Zamboni 67, 40136 Bologna, Italy

Ta, T.
Thames Water Utilities Ltd., Spencer House, Manor Farm Road, Reading, RG2 0JN, England

Ulanicka, K.
Water Software Systems, De Montfort University, The Gateway, Leicester LE1 9BH, England

Ulanicki, B.
Water Software Systems, De Montfort University, The Gateway, Leicester LE1 9BH, England

Villon, P.
University of Technology of Compiègne, Compiègne, France

Walters, G.A.
School of Engineering, University of Exeter, North Park Road, Exeter EX4 4QF, England

Wang, C.G.
Department of Civil Engineering, University of Newcastle, Newcastle upon Tyne NE1 7RU, England

Wang, C.
Water Operational Research Centre, Brunel University, Uxbridge, Middlesex UB8 3PH, England

Whiter, J.
Thames Water Utilities Ltd., Spencer House, Manor Farm Road, Reading, RG2 0JN, England

Woodward, C.A.
Thames Water Utilities Ltd., Group Research & Technology, Spencer House, Manor Farm Road, Reading, RG2 0JN, England

Contents

Introduction

This book is based on the proceedings of the third International Conference on Computing and Control for the Water Industry held at Brunel University, England in September 1997. Papers were presented by a representative cross-section of the community of practitioners and academics at the cutting edge of design, implementation and operation of computer-based methods for all aspects of the water business.

The objectives of the conference were:

- To facilitate continued co-operation of academic institutions and industry.
- To examine the current state-of-the-art of computing and control techniques applicable to the water industry.
- To provide a forum for discussion and dissemination of ideas on applied computing and control for the water industry.
- To present the recent developments in research.
- To present the users' experience of latest techniques.

The topics included:

- Steady state and transient analysis; modelling and simulation.
- Operational management, scheduling and control.
- Resource management and allocation.
- Quality modelling, management and control.
- Monitoring and estimation.
- Information and decision support systems.
- Performance, security and reliability assessment.

As with most industries, the water industry is undergoing a process of continual change, driven, in part, by the promise of greater control of all aspects of its business arising out of the steady growth in information technology.

The water industry was one of the first to recognise the benefits in computer technologies. Over the last three decades, computers have given the industry supervisory control and data acquisition (SCADA) systems, geographical information systems, relational databases for the storage of asset data and sophisticated customer billing systems, to name but a few. These technologies have grown in number and sophistication. For example, many companies now have very large amounts of telemetered data arriving in central control rooms every second.

However, the complexity of the tasks of design and operation of water and sewerage systems is often greatly underestimated. Paradoxically, the water industry itself is sometimes guilty of failing to recognise the shear difficulty of designing and running its plant in the way it would like. It is easy to draw parallels between the water industry and the process industry or the electricity industry. There are many processes that are tricky to model mathematically but few are as complex as the predominantly biological processes used in the water industry such as sewage treatment or water treatment. For instance, water treatment is itself both a localised process and a distributed one. When water leaves the treatment works the reaction of disinfectants with biological material continues in the reservoirs and out into the distribution system.

Even the relationship between flow and pressure is highly non-linear and many analysts conveniently ignore the differences in the regimes of laminar, transition and turbulent flow. Data are gathered from transducers and, in a quest to gain information and ultimately knowledge from these data, they are superimposed on mathematical models containing descriptions of continuous and discontinuous elements grouped together by a model of the topology of the system. The models for the elements (valves, pumps, pipes, aqueducts, etc.) can give rise to computational problems and are often simplifications of more complicated underlying phenomena. Assumptions about the network topology are sometimes incorrect. Furthermore, the greatest culprit of all in this emerging picture of uncertainty is demand. Many analytic packages are demand driven; if the demand data are wrong then so are the answers.

Another example is the operational management of water distribution systems containing pumps and reservoirs. Operations staff must schedule each set of pumps over a period of one or more days to meet the forecasted demand, minimise the energy costs, fully exploit the reservoirs, ensure the treatment works can cope, ensure the security of supply is sufficient and that every node is always supplied with water at or above the statutory minimum pressure. Most systems are interconnected, which means that every change of flow in one area can affect the flows and pressures throughout the system. Furthermore, as well as deciding which pumps to run and when to run them (so that the electricity tariffs are exploited to the full) one has also to ensure that they operate as close as possible to their own optimal efficiency points whilst they are running. Other constraints, such as minimising wear and tear from frequent pump switching and water quality considerations must also be taken into account. If there were no storage in the system (as is often the case in electrical power distribution systems), this problem would be reasonably manageable, but when one adds storage, the number of options becomes overwhelmingly large. Computer programs that can perform such scheduling tasks quickly enough for on-line usage, for non-specific systems, are exceedingly difficult to design.

It is small wonder then that the promises of information technology in the context of computer control have, all too often, not been realised. There is, therefore, much still to do and it is hoped that through a process of evolution and, perhaps, revolution these problems will diminish to acceptable levels.

The ultimate goal of full computer integrated control is reachable. The merging of data in their different forms may no longer be necessary as technologies exist that allow different sources of data to be handled by the same applications. Thus GIS, asset data, mathematical models and SCADA data could be handled in a common way. Soon algorithms will process on-line data against this wealth of stored knowledge and build up realistic pictures of all the flows, pressures and quality parameters in large supply and distribution systems in real-time. But, like weather forecasts that cannot predict exactly where it is going to rain, there will be limits to the fine detail provided. Nevertheless, this real-time database of validated information will be available for advanced operational management and control; it will then be possible to make high-level decisions about operating the plant and planning maintenance and to leave the details (optimising cost, quality and security) to the computers.

It is hoped that this book will make a contribution that is a step on the road to full computer control for the water industry.

Dr. R. S. Powell *and* Professor K. S. Hindi
December 1998

Section 1

Risk Assessment and Reliability

CHAPTER 1

Performance Analysis in Water Distribution

S.T.Coelho *and* P.W.Jowitt

Abstract

The level of service provided by water supply and distribution systems is one of the key issues facing the water industry today. However, measuring the performance and assessing the level of service provided by a water distribution network are not straightforward tasks, given the multiple factors and viewpoints involved, and the lack of a unified approach or a single clear-cut definition of performance. This chapter addresses the engineering side of the problem, by using a flexible framework based on an array of performance indices. The Performance Evaluation System developed is a technical analysis tool, designed to shift the focus of management and operations of water systems to a wider, more rigorous, performance-oriented view. It is based on a system of penalty curves, flexible enough to accommodate individual sensitivities and interpretations. The methodology allows for a rapid gain in sensitivity to the network's behaviour, providing a standardised means of diagnosis, and is a valuable aid for planning, design, operation and rehabilitation of water distribution systems.

1. Introduction

The ability of an existing or planned water supply and distribution system to perform adequately – that is, to appropriately fulfil its intended purpose – under the widest possible range of likely operating conditions, particularly those that are expected to occur during its working life, is a crucial system characteristic. The likely performance of a distribution system is not often assessed in its relevant globality or even explicitly defined in water supply engineering, which traditionally approaches its tasks from a relatively fragmented perspective and has difficulty in formulating its methods for the complete range of operating conditions that are in reality met by the systems.

Traditional engineering design is based on minimisation of cost factors provided some simplistic hydraulic constraints are respected. Optimal operation will look at pumping or disinfection efficiency, again subject to some simple constraints of a hydraulic or water quality nature. Leakage control concentrates mostly on excess pressure reduction, without much concern for the remaining performance of the system, and so on. This diversity of objectives makes it difficult for the water engineer to address the overall performance of a water supply and distribution system at any one moment in a balanced manner. However, the tendency in the water industry itself, driven by a market-oriented need to provide customers with the best level of service at the lowest possible cost while satisfying the regulatory framework, is progressively to take into consideration and deal at the same level with all the different aspects of water distribution that may be subject to informed or not-so-informed scrutiny.

The systematic use of network analysis models is certainly one path towards the solution of the problem. However, the type of results returned by such models can be complex and far from intuitive, frequently making their interpretation difficult and less than objective when comparing between different situations. The present work aims to contribute to bridging this gap, by using a standardised method for the assessment of performance in order to focus on a variety of aspects of water systems' operation and behaviour.

The framework required must be able to define some sort of system which, for a certain domain relevant to the technical management of a water network, classifies its activity according to a scale of merit with regard to the level of service provided, to a particular notion of technical performance, or more generally to an analysis or design objective ([1], [2], [3]). The principal requirements for such a methodology are: flexibility, in order to accommodate easily the different sensitivities, interpretations or objectives of the analysis; a certain degree of standardisation in order to facilitate a multi-disciplinary approach; and a quantitative, numerical base.

2. A Performance Assessment Framework

The system for performance assessment in water distribution used here is centred around indices based on the analysis, from specific viewpoints, of the network's characteristics or behaviour. The method is thoroughly described by Coelho [1] and developed from earlier work [4, 5]. A very brief overview follows.

The method is defined by three types of entities (Fig.1):

• The numerical value of a *network property or state variable*, which is deemed to be expressive of the particular aspect being scrutinised. The tool of choice for providing the values of state variables, for any given state or scenario of interest, is network analysis with all its associated models, including water quality models. It must be noted that the methodology is valid whatever the source of the values for the state variables. If network analysis is utilised, its assumptions and simplifications are by necessity inherited by the present method. One further aspect to note is that the accuracy of the methodology is limited by the accuracy of the original information about the network's state variables. Whatever the source of the data, the method is essentially based on a performance-oriented interpretation of the source. The method can hardly compensate for poorly calibrated models or other sources of inaccuracy, even though it can be used as an aid to gaining sensitivity to the origins of such errors.

• A penalty curve which plots the values of a performance index credited to the state variable or network property, at network element level, over a given range. The performance index varies between a no-service and an optimum-service situation, and the curves are supposed to penalise any deviation from the latter. The basic idea is primarily related to the concept of level of service, hence the "no-service to optimum service" classification. The curves are arbitrary in nature and can be applied in a number of ways, depending on the specific analysis or diagnosis procedure the analyst has in mind — in essence, the decision variable is rated for a given purpose over an operative range. This is where the methodology's flexibility resides, although there is every advantage in keeping the curves' shapes as simple as possible. The convention adopted here uses a 0 to 4 scale, with the following meanings: 4 - optimum service, 3 - adequate service, 2 - acceptable service, 1 - unacceptable service and 0 - no service.

• A network operator which allows the performance values at element level to be aggregated across part or all of the network. As an example, W might simply be an average across the network, but other types of operator may be used, such as weighted

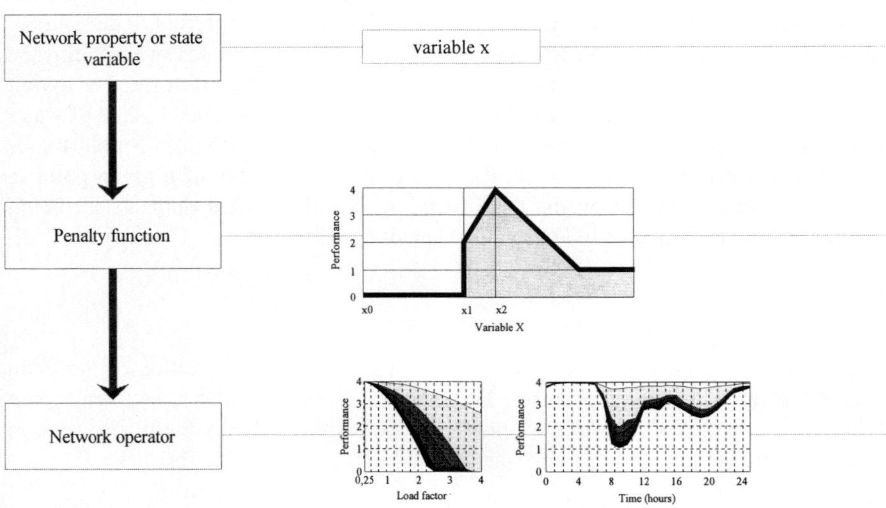

Figure 1. Performance assessment approach

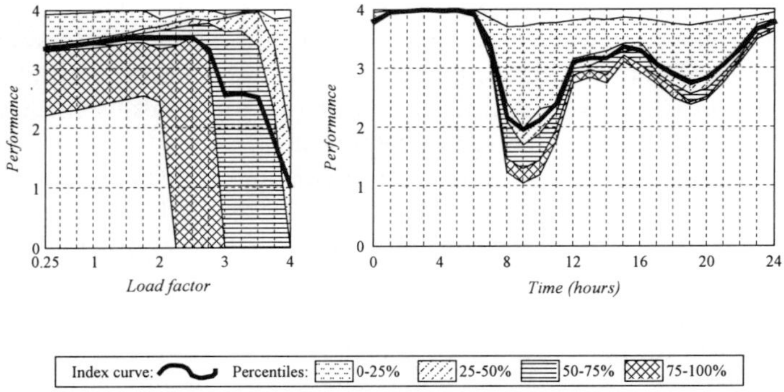

Figure 2. System graph and extended period simulation graph

averages or those which focus on maximum or minimum values. In fact, the type of operator depends on the objective of the analysis. For most water quality parameters, the regulatory approach would look for the single worst case across the network, in which case the generalising operator would be the 0% or 100% percentile (i.e. the minimum or maximum value). However, for the same parameters, a designer analysing different alternatives might be more interested in other percentiles or weighted averages as a general approach.

Hence, this method yields values of performance evaluation for every element of a network as well as for the network as a whole. There is a global value which is achieved through a particular operator in order to represent the performance assessment of the network, and conversely, a population of elementary values which lends itself to a basic statistical treatment. The two are combined together graphically in diagrams where performance is plotted against a series of operational conditions, typically either a range of demand loads (system graph) or a 24-hour simulation (extended-period simulation graph). The main curve represents the global performance, whereas the shaded areas are 25% percentile bands which, for the system graph, should be read as follows: if (x,y) are the co-ordinates of a given point in the P% percentile curve, it means that for a load factor of x, the percentage of water delivered with a performance index smaller or equal to y is P% (Fig.2). Similarly, for an extended period simulation graph, if (t,y) are the co-ordinates of a given point in the P% percentile curve, it means that at time t, P% of the total demand are being supplied with a performance index smaller than or equal to y.

3. Performance Domains and Penalty Curves

The first step in the application of the above methodology is a selection of the main areas of water systems' performance. The considerations that follow, concerning not just this selection but also the development of the corresponding penalty curves over the appropriate variables, summarise the work described by Coelho [1].

3.1 Hydraulic performance

The first and most obvious domain concerns the hydraulic behaviour of the network. The processes of conceiving, designing, building and running a water supply system are primarily driven by the need to satisfy a given set of demand points with sufficient flow of water at usable pressure levels. That has always been the prime motivation of engineers and designers, and central to the regulatory environment of most countries.

Hydraulic performance measures considered here concern pressure and velocity considerations, and result from traditional design and operational criteria which are relatively straightforward to relate to in terms of quantifiable performance.

The pressure-related measures stem from two basic assertions: for a network to perform well from a hydraulic point of view, pressure at every supply point must fall between a maximum and a minimum requirement, typically around 20 m and 80 m, respectively; and the head surface across the network should not be subject to great fluctuations over time (water distribution legislation and company practice normally consider a figure of 30 to 40 m as the maximum allowable variation). The resulting penalty curves are shown, respectively, in Figs. 3 and 4. In terms of a network operator, and since both measures are mostly consumption-oriented, a weighted average with the nodal demands as weights is used across the network.

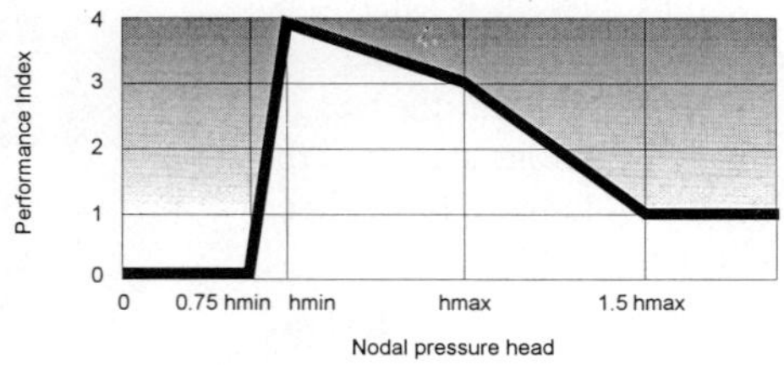

Figure 3. Penalty curve for pressure

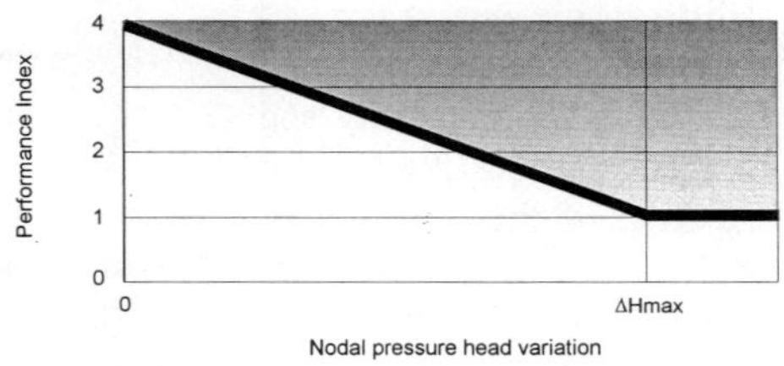

Figure 4. Penalty curve for pressure fluctuation

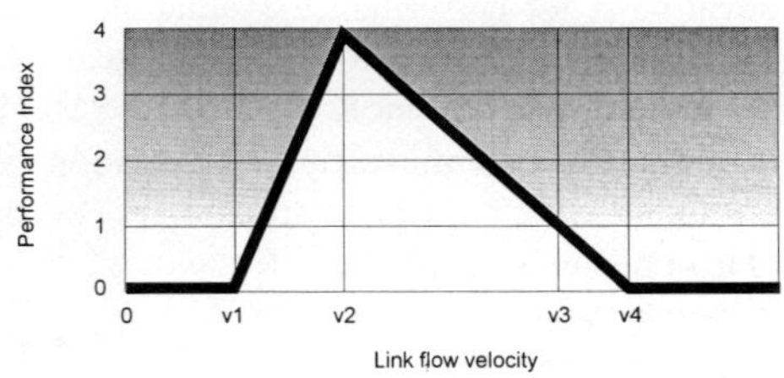

Figure 5. Penalty curve for velocity

Most network designers and managers prefer to keep a check on flow velocities. Very high values may have negative structural consequences on the pipes, or represent extreme and undesirable hydraulic regimes. On the other hand, very low velocities may induce excessive deposit or even stagnation of flow. The second type of hydraulic performance index is therefore a velocity measure applied to link flow. It is based on a simple but plausible classification, developed from the perception of water network managers according to the penalty curve in Fig.5. The suggested reference velocity is V_{ref}= 0.5 m/s. In the figure, the following values are used: $V_1 = 0.5\ V_{ref}$, $V_2 = V_{ref}$, $V_3 = 2.0\ V_{ref}$, $V_4 = 3.0\ V_{ref}$

The generalising function to be applied in this case is less intuitive than in the pressure-based nodal measures. Again a weighted average seems correct, but what weights to use may be arguable. In order to incorporate both the length and the cross-section, the pipe volume has been chosen.

3.2 Water quality performance

Water supply and distribution companies are naturally also required to deliver wholesome water and must meet service standards relating to the potability and aesthetic aspects, not just for the sake of their customers' health, but also as a matter of acceptability. Potable water must meet restrictions on its microbiological contents, as well as on the concentration values of chemical, biochemical and physical substances carried with it. Water quality is therefore the second major area of concern as the accomplishment of a system is tested.

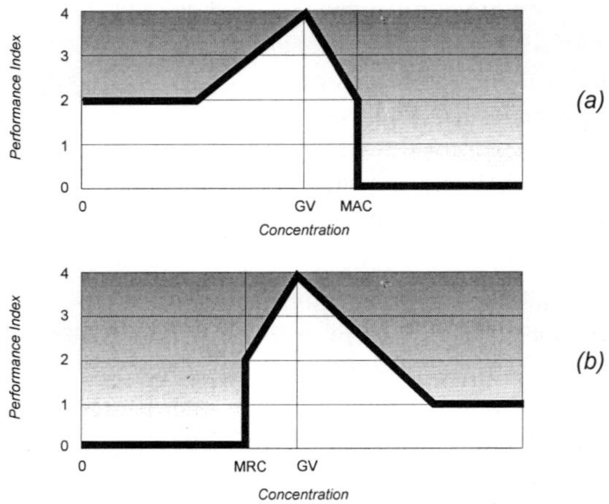

Figure 6. Penalty curves for (a) unwanted substance and (b) essential parameter, using GV

Water quality standards, usually expressed in terms of Guide Values (GV) provide an ideal basis for performance evaluation in the terms employed here. Figure 6 shows a possible configuration for penalty curves. The optimum situation is the GV, to which a value of 4 is assigned. The MAC (Maximum Allowable Concentration) or MRC (Minimum Recommended Concentration) values are at the adequacy limit (2), and beyond them a no-service situation (0) occurs. Conversely, the shape of the curve on the opposite side of the GV depends very much on the particular parameter and on the nature of the GV. In case (a), achieving concentrations much below the GV often increases the treatment costs so much that it becomes undesirable, hence the arbitrary drop shown in the figure to merely acceptable, at 2. This would be an example of a multi-constrained penalty curve, looking at both quality and cost. In actual fact, the Guide Value happens to be simply zero for many undesirable substances, which solves that problem. In case (b), values

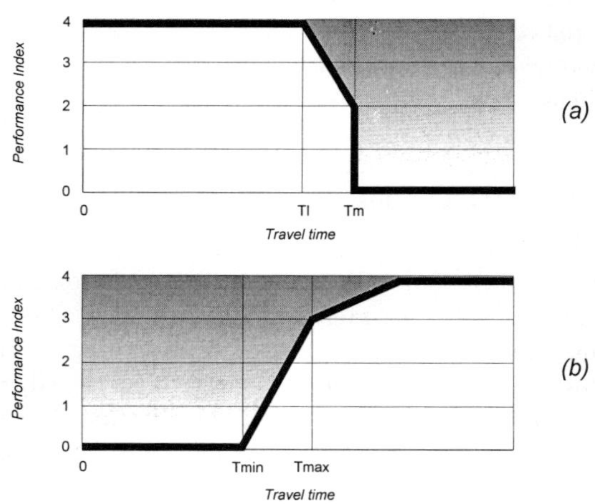

Figure 7. Penalty curves for (a) water age and (b) reaction to incident

above the GV may often correspond to increased treatment costs or imply undesirable side effects. A good example of that is chlorine residual, which will be illustrated later.

Travel time is the other product of water quality models that lends itself to a straightforward performance assessment treatment. Figure 7 shows penalty curves corresponding to two different applications of travel time as a performance assessment variable. The first is the straightforward water age case, where a certain time limit will be defined and the network will be tested for compliance with that limit. The penalty curve is a very simple one, grading any travel time below the limit (Tl) as optimum and allowing a certain tolerance above that, defined through a maximum time (Tm), to drop down to the acceptable level. Above that, it is a no-service situation.

The second case curve (b) refers to a much more specific situation which illustrates a very "topological" application of travel times, that of testing the effect of a contamination incident. In this case, travel time is graded against the response capabilities of the water utility. The longer the travel time to a particular node, the more likely a consumer supplied by it will be warned in time.

3.3 Reliability Performance

The preceding topics correspond to some of the most palpable aspects of the performance of a water distribution system, both for the designer or technical manager and for the consumer. Generally speaking, those aspects represent the very objective of a water utility: to satisfy all demands with sufficient and wholesome water, at adequate pressure, and at the minimum possible cost.

In addition to finding out to what degree that objective is accomplished, the performance of a water supply and distribution system can also be measured by how consistently or reliably it actually does achieve it. Indeed, some authors associate the idea of performance of a water network mainly with its reliability ([7], [8]). Performance of a water supply and distribution does have a broader meaning in the framework of the present study, but it must certainly include some measure of the reliability of the system. Reliability of a network can also be said to be a potential performance measure, as opposed to the *operational* characteristics the two other fields cover. Reliability is more a property of the network than an everyday *modus operandi*. One of the reasons for this is the crucial role of the network layout in the level of reliability that the network can possibly offer. The layout is also the feature of an existing network that an engineer can do less about. Some approaches to reliability also consider reliability from the point of view of day-to-day operational scenarios.

The detailed analysis of reliability concepts and measures has shown that this is a domain where the performance evaluation system as described above may not exhibit the same level of applicability as shown in other areas. For the purposes of a quantifiable performance assessment method, it is appropriate to associate reliability of a network with its redundancy of supply, as shown by Coelho ([1]).

The existence of backup or alternate supply pathways constitutes redundancy in the distribution system. Reliability, in its most general sense, defines how well the system performs in meeting the demands placed upon it. It can therefore be said that redundancy, as it represents the presence of alternate supply paths through the network, and the associated ability to maintain adequate service with some components out of service, is a major contributor to reliability.

An entropy-based measure of redundancy has been developed by Tanyimboh and Templeman ([9], [10]) that would appear to be a good candidate to fit the above scheme ([1]). It is based on the postulate that the network flow distribution that maximises a suitably formulated entropy function *S* corresponds to the most uniform distribution of flows among all the paths of the network, in the sense that all the alternative paths of supply to a node (or demand from a node) carry equal fractions of the demand (or supply) at that node. There is every reason to believe that this distribution will take best advantage of the diversity of paths existing in a network. From the point of view of supplying demands, that diversity is only present as long as the network is not purely tree-type. Tree-type networks have zero diversity of supply, hence zero entropy of supply paths to a demand node.

The maximum entropy flow distribution is the most central, or most uniform, of all the distributions capable of satisfying the demands of the network. Indeed, Tanyimboh has worked on optimal design of networks based on the assumption that the magnitude of the possible changes to the values of the link flows of the network can be minimised by designing the network to carry maximum entropy flows. These possible changes always carry a heavy hydraulic penalty, as the headloss varies approximately with the square of the flow rate. Consequently, the closer the flow distribution is to a mid-point, the smaller the squared differences will be, and the smaller the 'wasted' headloss. An additional consideration is that minimising headlosses in this way will increase the capability of the network to withstand flows caused by exceptional or unexpected demands.

It is important, however, to recall that entropy-based measures do not effectively represent the hydraulics of the network, and as such are limited as a measure of redundancy to a mainly topological role.

Another important aspect is that reliability is traditionally and primarily associated with the continuity of supply and (or) the satisfaction of pressure and other hydraulic related requirements. It is therefore mainly concerned with network element failure or malfunction, or exceptional demand situations, as the main threats to stability.

However, recalling the primary objectives of good design, operation and management of water distribution systems — to supply sufficient quantities of potable water, at adequate pressure and at minimum possible cost — it seems reasonable to approach the reliability performance of a water network from a broader range of perspectives than the *mere* satisfaction of hydraulic or continuity-of-supply requirements. Among the remaining objectives which would benefit from the introduction or evaluation of reliability are those relating to water quality. Domains such as the propagation of a desired substance (e.g., chlorine residual or fluoride) and source utilisation (particularly with regard to the influence of good quality water over one that is less good, or the impact of a pollution incident) deserve to be looked at from the point of view of how reliable the network is likely to be, relative to the established objectives in each domain.

It is in the face of those several, sometimes conflicting, reliability requirements that the path-based formulations developed by Coelho ([1]) prove useful in application. S_n^{FS} or S_n^{FJ}, measure the uncertainty in the diversity of paths originating from, or leading up to, a particular network node *n*. For that reason, they are respectively associated with the uncertainty in flow-splitting and in flow-joining processes. Those two measures can be associated with different objectives in reliability analysis. The classical problem which consists of trying to enhance the capability of the network to reach a given demand node can be looked at with regard to path-based flow-joining entropy. On the other hand, flow-splitting analysis which measures the diversity of paths emanating from a given node is better suited, for example, to trying to protect the area of influence of a given node.

Reliability is fundamentally conditioned by the shape and layout of the network. Measuring reliability for the purpose of assessing the performance of a network cannot hope to have the same potential for comparison as some of the other measures analysed previously. It is difficult to compare different networks, by classifying them according to some universal referencing system. The best that can be hoped for is to analyse and compare different layouts which supply the same distribution of demand points, or to compare different ways of utilising the same layout to supply the same demand points. For both these objectives, the entropy measure does seem to be the best candidate to provide useful results.

The use of entropy-based measures does carry some benefits in that respect, namely the fact that they are dimensionless measurements – two networks with the same layout and flow directions, and with different but proportional demands and flows, will produce the same entropy values. Also, the fact that for each layout it is possible to define the optimal flow distribution according to an entropy maximisation criterion, provides both a way of grading any given flow distribution against that ideal, for a fixed layout, and comparing different layouts based on the optimal entropy values that each can achieve. Either is a fair means of comparison, and a suitable approach to the development of performance measures.

For those reasons, it seems appropriate to choose as performance evaluation variables for reliability/ redundancy the ratios between the entropy of flow distribution and the corresponding maximum possible (optimal) value, on a nodal or global basis. Two measures are thus obtained as follows:

(i) Entropy of supply paths to the node as a percentage of the network's optimal potential, $\dfrac{S^{FJ}}{S^{FJ}_{\max}}$.

(ii) Entropy of demand paths from the node as a percentage of the network's optimal potential, $\dfrac{S^{FS}}{S^{FS}_{\max}}$.

In terms of penalty curves, and apart from the optimum, which could presumably be associated with the maximum entropy flow distribution, any other level of service definition in this domain is arguable. To be consistent with the adoption of a redundancy-based measure, it would seem logical that the 'no-service' situation corresponds to zero path diversity, or zero entropy, generated at nodes with single supply or demand paths. For this convention to be adopted, one must bear in mind that nodes that have no supply/ demand paths to/from them are effectively omitted from the network (they do not contribute to the network entropy functions). Within these limitations, a possible penalty curve for $\frac{S^{FJ}}{S^{FJ}_{\max}}$ or $\frac{S^{FS}}{S^{FS}_{\max}}$ would be shown as in Figure 8.

Since it is possible for nodal entropy values to be greater than one (the maximum network entropy does not imply that all nodes maximise their individual entropies), the curve would be defined as optimal for values greater than or equal to one. This feature is the only real difference between using this penalty curve and the actual value of the variable, given the direct proportionality. However, the use of a penalty curve has the advantage of bringing the possibility of standardisation achieved in other areas to this domain, and that is the main reason why it is introduced here.

The problem of choosing a generalising function is, in this case, solved from the outset as the path-entropy expressions can be calculated for the whole network. The same penalty curve as above can be applied to the value of the variable $\frac{S^{FJ}}{S^{FJ}_{\max}}$ or $\frac{S^{FS}}{S^{FS}_{\max}}$ calculated for the whole network, which is a departure from the approach used previously of applying the generalising function to the nodal performance values. It makes more sense, in this case, to take advantage of the global entropy values, which, like the remaining nodal values, have a precise and significant meaning.

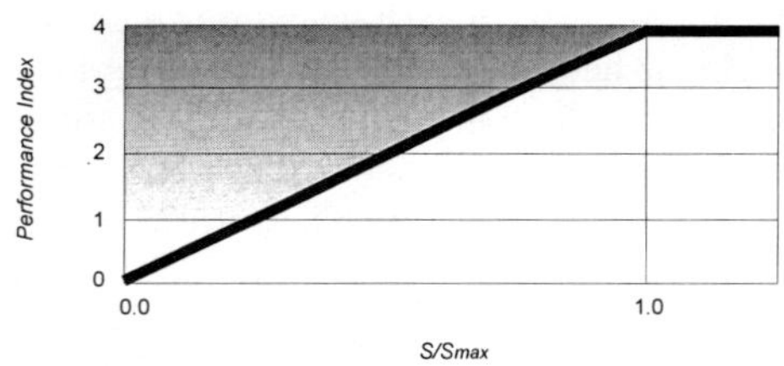

Figure 8. Penalty curve for entropy measure

4. Application Examples

4.1 Hydraulic performance

Town A is a residential area in a rural setting, with a distribution network serving about 9 000 people on a relatively hilly topography. It will be used to illustrate some of the hydraulic measures.

4.1.1 System analysis diagrams

The diagrams displaying the variation of the three performance indices for the system analysis are shown in Fig.9. Starting with the pressure index, it can be seen that the global performance curve follows a relatively typical pattern, with an ascending stretch in the upper values of the index levelling out smoothly before a descending limb that eventually drops to less acceptable values.

The ascending limb corresponds to a range of loads for which the system operates with pressures above the recommended minimum (briefly looking at the pressure penalty curve on Fig.3, the index values are to the right of the peak, working their way uphill as demands increase and available heads decrease). The global curve remains above 3 in this first stretch, which means that those pressures are still adequate and not excessive. However, part of the lower percentile (around 10-20% of the demand) is indeed below 3, corresponding to nodes with excessive pressure head.

As the demands keep increasing (and pressures decrease) the system index curve levels out and eventually starts to fall, when the available heads drop below the minimum required. The index curve for the system as a whole remains at very acceptable levels for loads up to 2.75 times the average. However, there are demand nodes in clear difficulty for loads above 2, as can be seen from the two lower dispersion bands. Above 3.6 the system no longer provides an acceptable level of service. The relatively narrow bands indicate a fairly homogeneous system up to a load of around 2. The hump on the index curve between 3 and 3.75 is probably caused by two areas with different behaviours at those load levels.

It can be noticed that the index curve drops below the 50% percentile for loads of 2 and above, corresponding to a skewed distribution of index values across the demand nodes domain. This will possibly mean that the problems may be localised or due to a small number of demand nodes.

The pressure fluctuation index shows a typical smooth behaviour, with acceptable values and good homogeneity for loads of up to around twice the average. The slope of the curve shows that the system will be moderately sensitive to changes in the load.

As for the velocity index, its steady growth throughout the whole domain means that, with respect to this criterion, the system is over designed, i.e., it displays low velocities for the entire range. Only above loads of 2.25 does the performance become acceptable on average, but the width of the dispersion bands reveals great heterogeneity.

4.1.2 Hour simulation diagrams

The diagrams showing the variation of the three performance indices over a 24 hour extended-period simulation are presented in Figs.10 to 12. The pressure index shows

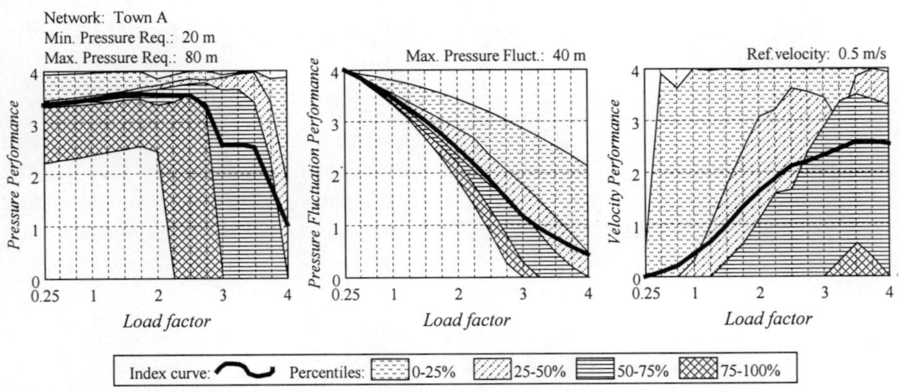

Figure 9. Town A system performance diagrams

an acceptable performance throughout the 24 hour period. Only the lower percentile band falls below 3, but its width is much greater than any of the other bands, probably indicating that the problem nodes are few and that localised changes in the system may significantly improve performance. The sudden drop at around 09:00 is due to low pressures occurring at a small number of nodes.

The pressure fluctuation index displays less acceptable behaviour during the morning working period, with the average curve bordering on a value of 2 and 75% of the demand below that. This is probably explained by the network's uneven topography and by the fact that it is partially supplied by another network with a significant head fluctuation of over 20 m throughout the day.

The velocity index merely represents the expected behaviour of the system diagram across the equivalent demand load range. In particular, it shows that night-time velocities are seriously low across the system, which may induce stagnation and sedimentation problems.

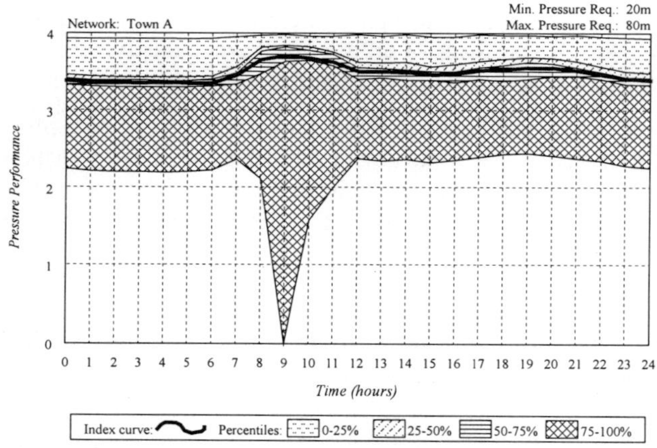

Figure 10. Town A extended-period performance simulation for pressure

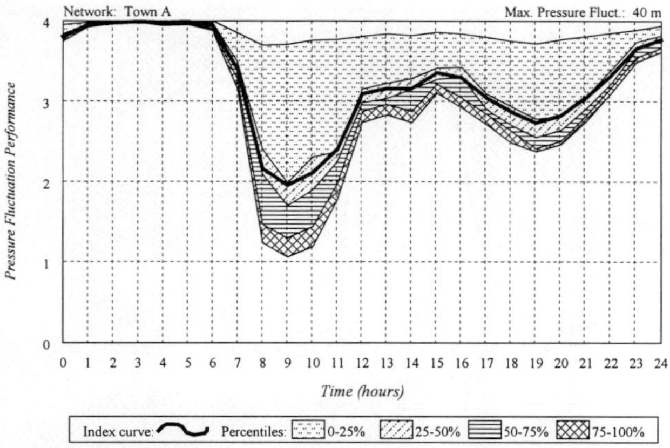

Figure 11. Town A extended-period performance simulation for pressure fluctuation

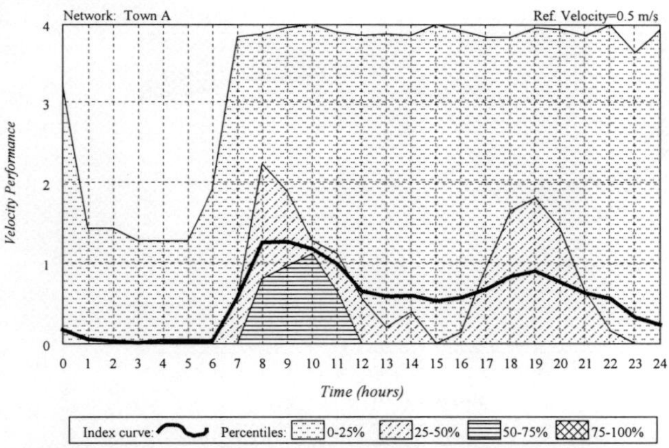

Figure 12. Town A extended-period performance simulation for velocity

4.2 Water quality performance

The network for the next example, Town B, supplies about 300 000 people in a densely populated, hilly, urban area. The network has an elongated shape and is supplied from a single source at one end. The extended-period simulation graphs in Figs. 13-14 illustrate the analysis of chlorine residual and travel time (the penalty curves are shown inset as some specific features are introduced relating to chlorine residual). The graphs show that the network would have areas with insufficient disinfection problems, probably corresponding to peripheral nodes with longer travel times in what is effectively a rather elongated-shaped network. A slight increase in the chlorine dosage at source produces the graph in Fig.15, where significant improvements can be seen.

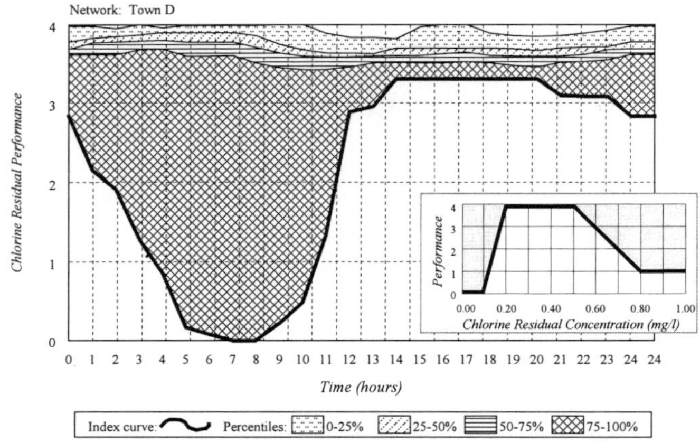

Figure 13. Town B extended-period performance simulation for chlorine residuals

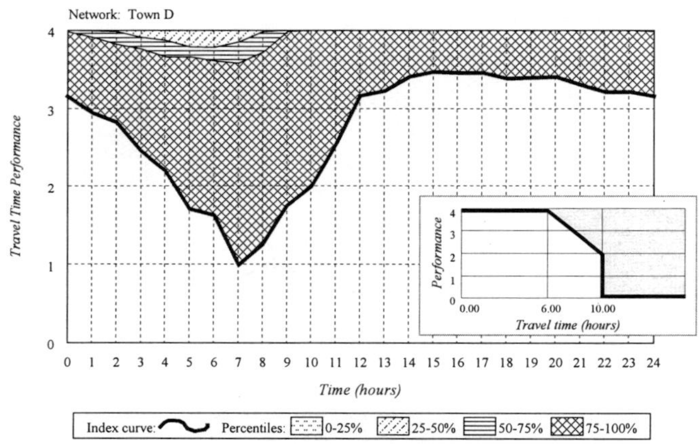

Figure 14. Town B extended-period performance simulation for water age

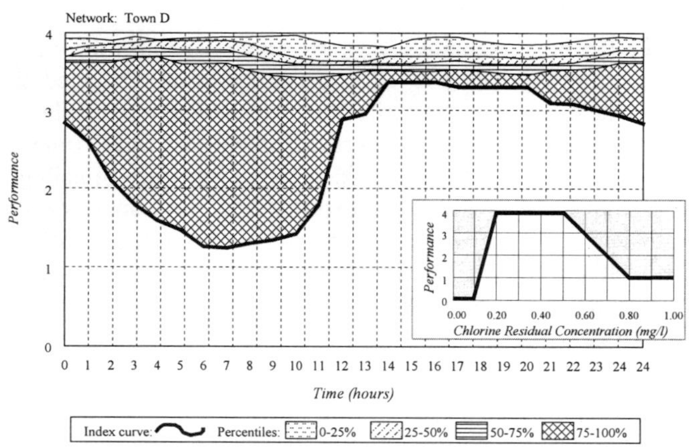

Figure 15. As per fig.13, with improved disinfection

4.3 Reliability performance

Figure 16 shows the entropy-based reliability performance measures, calculated for both flow-splitting and flow-joining, for a test network consisting of a square matrix of 4 by 4 nodes, with all vertical and horizontal links active, and supplied from one corner. A plausible hydraulic solution is taken as the basis for load factor 1, with demands at all nodes except the reservoir. The network seems to be operating at a reasonable fraction, around ¾, of its maximum redundancy potential, as given by both global entropy curves, similar to that expected. As the layout of this single-source network is symmetrical along its longitudinal axis (the diagonal defined by the reservoir and the furthest corner), and the pipe sizes favour a good spread of flow, there is a reasonable degree of uniformity of the flow solution.

This network has a substantial proportion of its hydraulic capacity still left at normal operating conditions. As the demand loads increase, so do the flows, but the flow distributions are proportional given that capacity. For proportional flow and demand distributions on a similar layout, the entropy values will be constant, and that property is one of the most noticeable features of the above diagrams.

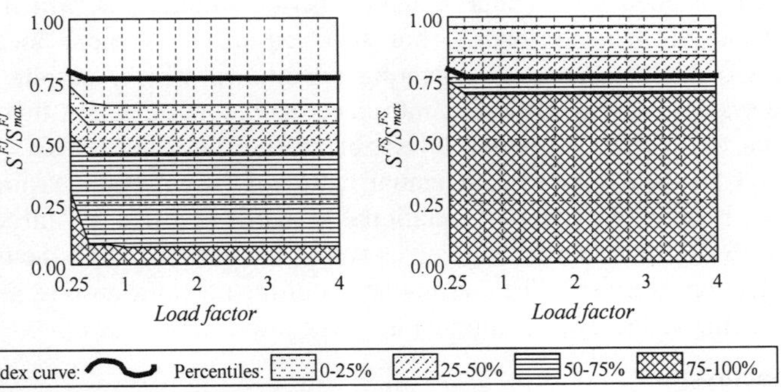

Figure 16. System graphs for test network

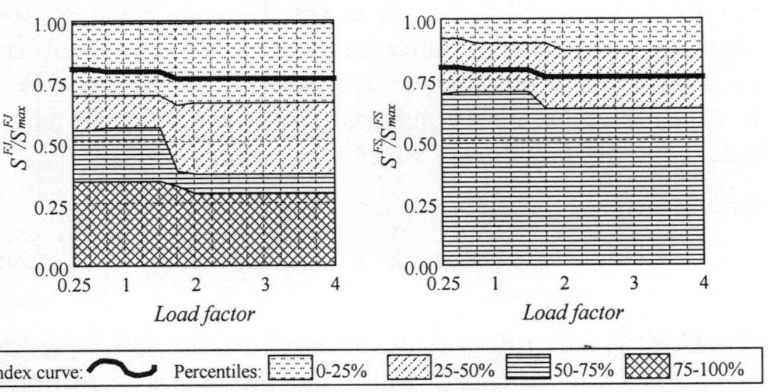

Figure 17. Reliability system graphs for the Town B network

The initial demand load, which corresponds to 0.25 of the average load, generates very small flows around the network, in many cases tending to zero for the degree of numerical accuracy used in the simulation. These actually correspond to a more uniform flow distribution, hence the slightly higher values produced. The width of the dispersion bands shows that increase is greater for certain sets of nodes (certain areas) of the network, than for the network as a whole, which makes sense.

Despite the global curves being forcibly the same, it can be seen that the flow-splitting processes in the network paths themselves, thus at the network nodes, generate higher entropy levels, or fulfil a greater part of their redundancy potential, than the flow-joining ones. This is to be expected from any single-source, multiple-demand-point network, as the flow-joining processes produce considerable more by flow-joining entropy than the (zero) flow-splitting entropy generated.

A second example of flow-splitting processes is shown in Figure 17 and concerns the Town B network. This system has a greater spread of entropy values, which is to be expected since there are quite a few branched sections generating zero flow-joining entropy, as well as elongated and well looped sections which are probably operating near their potential. This example is shown, however, to illustrate a different use of the performance curves. It has been seen in the previous network that the simple variation of demand loads may not be very expressive, for the flow distribution will tend to vary proportionally, which yields the same entropy values, as seen before.

The same will happen for 24-hour, extended-period simulations, which use an even narrower band of demand loads. For that reason, it is more meaningful and informative to study a range of operating conditions, which, despite being based around the system graph philosophy, introduce operational changes that are likely to be employed to face those demand levels, or need to be tested. This type of use is more in line with the exploratory, 'potential' nature of the entropy measure. In the case of the Town B network, a likely operational scenario is tested by introducing given pressure limits at pressure reducing valves across the network, with the objective of a leakage reduction exercise. The entropy levels of the network drop as a consequence of the flow being suddenly concentrated in fewer paths around the affected areas.

5. Conclusions

The Performance Evaluation System developed is a technical analysis tool, designed to shift the focus of management and operations of water systems to a wider, more rigorous, performance-oriented view. It is based on a system of penalty curves, flexible enough to accommodate individual perceptions and interpretations. The methodology allows for a rapid gain in sensitivity to the network's behaviour, providing a standardised means of diagnosis, and is a valuable aid for planning, design, operation and rehabilitation of water distribution systems.

6. References

1. Coelho, S.T. 1997. 'Performance in water distribution: a systems approach', Research Studies Press, England.

2. Alegre, H., Coelho, S.T. 1994. 'Hydraulic performance and reliability strategies', Short Course on Improving Efficiency and Reliability in Water Distribution Systems, Menendez Payo International University, 21-25 Nov. 1994, Valencia, Spain.

3. Hashimoto, T. 1982. 'Reliability, resiliency and vulnerability criteria for water resource systems performance evaluation'. *Water Resources Research*, Vol. 18, No.1, February 1982.

4. Alegre, H. 1988. 'Efficiency analysis of water distribution systems using pressure and stability ratios'. Proc. 17th World Conference of the International Water Suppliers Association IWSA, September 1988, Rio de Janeiro, Brasil.

5. Alegre, M.H., Coelho, S.T. 1992. 'Diagnosis of Hydraulic Performance of Water Distribution Networks', in *Pipeline Systems,* eds.Coulbeck & Evans, Kluwer Academic Press, UK.

6. Hashimoto, T. 1982. 'Reliability, resiliency and vulnerability criteria for water resource systems performance evaluation'. *Water Resources Research*, Vol.18, No.1, February 1982, 14-20.

7. Mays, L.W. 1993. 'Methodologies for reliability analysis of water distribution systems'. Proc. American Water Works Association 1993 Annual Conference.

8. Tanyimboh, T.T. 1993. 'An entropy-based approach to the optimum design of reliable water distribution networks'. PhD thesis, Civil Eng. Dept., University of Liverpool.

9. Tanyimboh, T.T., Templeman, A.B. 1993. 'Calculating maximum entropy flows in networks'. *Journal of the Operational Research Society*, Vol.44, No.4, pp.383-396.

CHAPTER 2

An Improved Source Head Method for Calculating the Reliability of Water Distribution Networks

T.T.Tanyimboh, M.Tabesh *and* R.Burrows

Abstract

In order to calculate the reliability of single-source networks, this chapter presents a new way of interpreting results of the traditional demand-driven network analysis as an approximation to pressure-driven simulation. This approach is useful because most network modelling software packages use the demand-driven analysis approach and are incapable of simulating pressure-deficient conditions properly. Furthermore, as far as pressure-driven analysis is concerned, many questions remain unanswered. The method proposed herein can be used to calculate the reliability of an entire water distribution network and/or that of the individual demand nodes. Using a sample network, it is shown that the method is much more accurate than previous formulations and retains the proven advantages of the source head approach to reliability calculation.

1 Introduction

For a long time, little attention was paid to the definition and quantification of reliability in the context of water distribution. Early research in the area was mostly concerned, initially, with the transfer of well-established approaches in other fields such as power transmission. It soon became clear that the uniqueness of water distribution networks required methods specifically developed for these networks. Despite initial uncertainty about the essence of water distribution network reliability, it has been established during the last five years or so that reliability should be a function of the ratio of actual flow delivered to the required flow.

For a while, it was believed that calculated reliability values for a distribution network could be raised artificially by reducing the flow to the parts of the network with insufficient pressure [1]. It was felt that this would make it possible to increase available flow in the remainder of the network. Furthermore, there were no satisfactory methods for quantifying partial failure. This was primarily due to the fact that algorithms for network analysis generally treated nodal outflows as constants with pre-determined values. Therefore, to enable like-with-like comparisons between different networks and avoid the above-mentioned uncertainties and difficulties, the source head approach to reliability calculation was developed using the notional source head for full satisfaction of all demands in a single-source network

[2–5; also see 6].

However, early results from pressure-dependent network analysis have shown that the consequences of insufficient pressure (i.e. insufficient flow) tend to be localised, with conditions elsewhere often being largely unaffected [7–9]. In other words, the spatial nature of the hydraulic performance of distribution networks should be recognised by reliability measures. Furthermore, the basic source head method (SHM) [2, 4–5] tacitly treated the source node as if it were a demand node whose demand is equal to the combined demand of the actual demand nodes of the single-source network. The modelling effects of lumping the demands in the above way have been detailed in [7] where it was concluded that such approaches generally provide approximate rather than accurate results. As such, the SHM can at best be expected to give reasonable estimates of reliability values. On the other hand, network models in which the demand nodes are considered individually are generally more accurate [7]. Therefore, unlike previous formulations, the present improved source head method (ISHM) uses the required source heads to satisfy the demands of individual nodes to estimate the available flow at those nodes.

The theoretical formulation of the ISHM approach to reliability analysis is based on pressure-driven network analysis principles [5]. However, its practical implementation depends on a novel interpretation and use of the traditional demand-driven analysis results. The aim of this chapter is to demonstrate a method of approximating nodal outflows and system reliability using demand-driven simulation and an evaluation of the required pressures at individual nodes. Using a much-studied sample network, it is shown that reliability values calculated using the proposed method (ISHM) are far more accurate than previous results and that all the previously identified advantages of the SHM including computational efficiency [4-5] are retained. An issue which has not received sufficient attention is the interdependency between the flows available at the demand nodes and its significance in system reliability calculations. This issue is also addressed in this chapter.

2 Nodal Outflow

The quantity of water which a distribution network can supply at adequate pressure is one of the principal factors determining the reliability of the system. Therefore, the relationship between actual nodal outflows and pressures should be incorporated in any realistic network reliability measure. Thus, following [5], for a single-source network the relationship can be approximated as

$$Q_j = Q_j^{req} \left(\frac{H_s - H_{s,j}^{min}}{H_{s,j}^{des} - H_{s,j}^{min}} \right)^{\frac{1}{n_j}} \quad H_{s,j}^{min} \leq H_s \leq H_{s,j}^{des};\ \forall j \tag{1}$$

in which: Q_j^{req} and Q_j, respectively, represent the demand and actual outflow at node j. H_s is the available source head. $H_{s,j}^{min}$ is the source head below which outflow at node j is zero or deemed unsatisfactory. $H_{s,j}^{des}$ is the source head above which the demand at node j is fully satisfied. n_j is an exponent whose value, usually between about 1 and 2 [1, 7, 10], can be determined by calibration.

To calculate the values of the Q_j a demand-driven analysis of the network is performed using the demands Q_j^{req}. This gives

$$H_{s,j}^{des} \approx H_s - H_j \tag{2}$$

in which H_j represents the head at node j. The value of $H_{s,j}^{min}$, the source head corresponding to zero outflow at demand node j can be found using pressure-driven simulation [7] or field tests. Inherently, however, the present formulation does not have the full capabilities of pressure-driven analysis. Therefore, $H_{s,j}^{min}$ is approximated using H_s^{min}, the source head above which outflow just begins at any node of the network. Thus $H_s^{min} = Min < H_{s,j}^{min}, \quad \forall j >$, which may be taken as the elevation of the lowest node.

3 Reliability Analysis

For any given source head, the available flow obviously depends on whether the system is in a reduced state or not. The components (pipes) of a distribution network can be unavailable for use due to failure/bursts and/or repair/maintenance, etc. It is commonly assumed that pipe bursts are not interdependent [11–12]. With this assumption, the probability $p(0)$ that no pipe is unavailable is

$$p(0) = \prod_{l=1}^{NL} a_l \tag{3}$$

in which a_l is the probability that pipe (link) l is available and NL is the number of links. A function for calculating the availability of individual pipes is given shortly. Also, the probability $p(N)$ that only N specified links are unavailable while the remaining $(NL - N)$ are available is given by

$$p(N) = p(0) \prod_{n=1}^{N} \frac{u_n}{a_n} \quad N = 1, ..., NL \tag{4}$$

in which u denotes the unavailability of a component.

Pipe availability can be taken as the ratio of the mean time between failures to the mean time between failures plus the mean failure, including repair, duration. This can be calculated as in [13] using

$$a_l = \frac{0.21218 D_l^{1.462131}}{0.00074 D_l^{0.285} + 0.21218 D_l^{1.462131}} \quad l = 1, ..., NL \tag{5}$$

in which D_l is the diameter of pipe l in inches (1 in. = 25.4 mm).

For any given normal or subnormal configuration, nodal reliability can be defined as the ratio of the available flow to the required flow, i.e.

$$r_j(N) = \frac{Q_j(N)}{Q_j^{req}} \quad N = 0, ..., NL; \; \forall j \tag{6}$$

in which $r_j(N)$ is the nodal reliability with N specified pipes unavailable and $Q_j(N)$ is the available flow when the N specified pipes are unavailable (Eq. (1)). Using Eq. (6) and taking all network configurations into consideration, the reliability R_j of the node is given by the expectation of the nodal reliabilities for the various configurations, i.e.

$$R_j = p(0) \sum_{N=0}^{NL} \left(r_j(N) \prod_{n=1}^{N} \frac{u_n}{a_n} \right) \quad \forall j \tag{7}$$

If no more than two simultaneously unavailable links are considered, then the reliability is given by

$$\begin{aligned} R_j &= \frac{1}{Q_j^{req}} \left(\sum_{l=0}^{NL} p(l)Q_j(l) + \sum_{\substack{l=1 \\ m:m>l}}^{NL-1} p(l,m)Q_j(l,m) \right) \\ &= p(0) \left(r_j(0) + \sum_{l=1}^{NL} r_j(l)\frac{u_l}{a_l} + \sum_{\substack{l=1 \\ m:m>l}}^{NL-1} r_j(l,m)\frac{u_l}{a_l}\frac{u_m}{a_m} \right) \quad \forall j \end{aligned} \tag{8}$$

in which: $p(l)$ and $p(l,m)$ are the respective probabilities that only pipes l and both l and m, together, are unavailable. Similarly, $r_j(l)$ and $r_j(l,m)$ are the respective nodal reliabilities with pipe l and both pipes l and m simultaneously unavailable. $Q_j(l)$ and $Q_j(l,m)$ are the respective available flows at node j with pipes l, and both l and m, together, unavailable. The nodal unreliabilities, U_j, can be determined from Eqs. (8) by simply replacing the available flow, Q_j, by the shortfall in supply, $(Q_j^{req} - Q_j)$. The values of nodal reliability, R_j, and unreliability, U_j, given by the above equations are lower bounds because the terms for three or more simultaneous link failures are not included. Thus an upper bound to nodal reliability is given by $1 - U_j$ which, together with the lower bound of Eq. (8), can be used to determine the point in the summation of Eq. (7) beyond which further terms need not be included for a given accuracy.

The reliability, R, of the network as a whole can be determined in a similar way by simply writing Eqs. (6–8) without the subscript j. To this end,

$$Q_{req} = \sum_{j=1}^{J} Q_j^{req} \tag{9}$$

$$Q = \sum_{j=1}^{J} Q_j \tag{10}$$

in which Q_{req} and Q are, respectively, the sum of the nodal demands and available flow and J represents the number of demand nodes.

Finally, the damage tolerance, T, of the system [2, 4–5] can be calculated as

$$T = \frac{R - r(0)p(0)}{1 - p(0)} \tag{11}$$

in which $r(0)$ represents the system reliability (Q/Q_{req}) with all components available. The damage tolerance of individual nodes can also be calculated in a similar way if required.

4 Appraisal

The advantages of the source head approach (SHM), namely simplicity, sensitivity and computational efficiency have previously been demonstrated [4–5]. The main aim of the following appraisal is to show the present improved source head method (ISHM) is a great deal more accurate than the previous SHM formulation. The present demonstration is based on the network of Figure 1. This simple symmetric four-loop network has previously been used by a number of researchers to demonstrate several aspects of design and reliability [4–5, 11, 14–16] and, as such, is well known.

The designs upon which the present appraisal is based were taken from [11]. These designs represent a progression in that they were obtained by generating minimum cost designs respectively satisfying a progression of specified levels of reliability, including a maximum hydraulic gradient limit of 0.01. Pipe data for the 16 designs are given in Tables 1 and 2. These designs were selected because successive designs in the progression are virtually identical. Consequently, by using these designs, it is relatively easy to judge whether any reliability indicator is consistent and, therefore, reliable. Also, as shown shortly, the hydraulic performance of the designs cannot be properly simulated using demand-driven analysis because there is insufficient pressure in the system to drive the required flows.

Pipe	Diameter (mm)							
1-2, 1-4[a]	250	250	250	250	250	250	250	250
2-3, 4-7	175	175	180	180	180	185	185	185
2-5, 4-5	145	145	145	145	145	145	145	145
3-6, 7-8	115	115	115	120	125	125	130	135
5-6, 5-8	100	105	105	105	105	105	105	105
6-9, 8-9	100	100	100	100	100	100	100	100
Cost[b] ($ 10^6)	0.255	0.257	0.259	0.261	0.263	0.266	0.268	0.270
Design	1	2	3	4	5	6	7	8

Table 1. Pipe Data (Designs 1–8)

[a] All designs are symmetrical about the line joining nodes 1, 5 and 9; all length = 1000m, C value = 130. [b] From Fujiwara and Tung (1991)

The hydraulic performance of the designs has previously been assessed [5] in terms of the required source head to fully satisfy demands throughout the network (demand-driven analysis) with individual pipes isolated in turn. Also, the actual nodal outflows were calculated for a range of values of the source head (pressure-driven analysis [7]). It was concluded that, in terms of hydraulic performance, the designs do constitute a gradual and smooth progression. Because the layout of the designs does not change, their mechanical reliabilities can be compared using $p(0)$, the probability that no component is unavailable. The $p(0)$ values are shown in Table 3 along with the required source heads, $H_s(0)$, for full satisfaction of the total demand of the network with all pipes available. The total flow supplied at adequate pressure [7] for the available source head of 100m for the fully connected network is also shown. Table 3 shows that the designs are deficient and provides further evidence that the designs form a good progression.

Reliability and damage tolerance values were calculated using the improved source head method (ISHM) with $H_s^{min} = 0m$, $n_j = 2$ and $H_s = 100m$. The results are reported in Figure 2 and Table 4 where SHM values are also shown for comparison. The approximations to actual system flow given by the ISHM are compared to the SHM in Table 5 and shown graphically in Figure 3. Corresponding values for individual nodes and their respective reliabilities are given in Tables 6 and 7, respectively.

Fortran 77 programs were written for the network analysis (Newton-Raphson method) and the reliability calculations. The programs were run using a PC with a Pentium processor (75 MHZ, 8 MB RAM). The total CPU time to simulate all combinations of up to two isolated pipes and calculate the system and nodal reliability values including damage tolerance was less than 5 seconds per design.

Pipe	Diameter (mm)							
1-2, 1-4[a]	250	250	250	250	250	255	255	255
2-3, 4-7	190	190	190	190	190	190	190	190
2-5, 4-5	145	145	145	150	150	150	155	155
3-6, 7-8	135	140	140	140	140	140	140	140
5-6, 5-8	105	105	110	110	115	115	115	120
6-9, 8-9	100	100	100	100	100	100	100	100
Cost[b] ($ 10^6)	0.272	0.274	0.276	0.278	0.280	0.283	0.285	0.287
Design	9	10	11	12	13	14	15	16

Table 2. Pipe Data (Designs 9–16)

[a] All designs are symmetrical about the line joining nodes 1, 5 and 9; all length = 1000m, C value = 130. [b] From Fujiwara and Tung (1991)

5 Discussion

It is clear from Table 4 and Figure 2 that the present method (ISHM) gives significantly higher values of reliability and damage tolerance than the previous formulation (SHM). The reason for the difference is that the ISHM gives more accurate values of flow delivered at adequate pressure than SHM (Table 5). While the SHM underestimates the actual flow delivered by about 25%, the ISHM overestimates it by only about 5%. As shown in Tables 3 and 6, the shortfall in supply due to insufficient pressure is localised around nodes 6, 8 and 9 while supply elsewhere is not affected. Therefore, by considering the demand nodes individually, the ISHM recognises the spatial characteristics of the distribution sytem. As such, the ISHM has successfully addressed the main weakness of the previous network-wide required source head approach which often underestimated the quantity of actual flow delivered. In particular, the present analysis clearly shows that the reliability value given by the original SHM is in reality an approximation to the reliability of the most critical node — node 9 in the present example (cf. Table 4: SHM and Table 7: node 9). Also, it is worth observing that there is good correlation between the available flow values of the approximate SHM and ISHM methods and the more accurate head-driven simulation method (HDSM) as demonstrated graphically in Figure 4.

A major advantage of the ISHM (unlike SHM) is its ability to provide nodal reliability values. These are shown in Table 7. For comparison, the system reliability values are also shown in Table 7 along with the arithmetic and demand-weighted means of the nodal reliabilities. It can be seen that the nodal means are different from the real reliability value of each network (also see [17]) though the weighted means are remarkably similar to the true values. An important reason for these differences is that the nodal outflows (and, hence, their reliabilities) are not mutually independent [2, 7–9]. This issue was addressed herein by first calculating nodal outflows, the sum of which was then used to calculate system reliability [2]. This way, double counting was avoided.

6 Conclusions

Using various parameters it has been shown that the designs appraised herein form a good progression in terms of hydraulic performance and reliability. They would therefore be suitable as a test bed for any reliability measures proposed in future. In the past, one of the major difficulties with research into reliability analysis has been the lack of results against which rigorous comparisons could be made.

In order to ensure fair reliability comparisons between different water distribution systems, the present formulation retains the requirement that demands be fully satisfied throughout the network, and this is achieved using demand-driven simulation to determine nodal pressures corresponding to those demands. The available flow at individual nodes is then found using an approximation to the relationship between nodal outflow and pressure. By so doing, the proposed (ISHM) method allows for spatial variations in the performance of the distribution network. This leads to much improved estimates of system reliability compared to the previous (SHM) formulation. Thus the ISHM has successfully addressed the main weakness of the source head approach to reliability calculation. Furthermore, it has the advantage that nodal reliability values can also be computed for any nodes of particular interest.

Finally, it has been shown that the reliability value of a distribution network is not equal to the arithmetic mean of the respective nodal reliability values. Surprisingly, however, the demand-weighted mean which reflects the relative importance of the nodal demands turned out to be very close to the true reliability of the system for the examples considered. Further investigation is required to assess the significance of this.

Acknowledgment

The authors gratefully acknowlege the financial support of the Ministry of Culture and Higher Education of the Islamic Republic of Iran for the PhD programme of Mr M Tabesh.

References

1. Wagner JM, Shamir U and Marks DH (1988). 'Water distribution network reliability: simulation methods.' *J. Water Resources Planning and Management,* ASCE, 114(3), 276–294.
2. Tanyimboh TT (1993). *An Entropy-based Approach to the Optimum Design of Reliable Water Distribution Networks,* PhD Thesis, University of Liverpool, England.
3. Tanyimboh TT and Templeman AB (1993). 'Optimum design of flexible water distribution networks.' *Civil Engineering Systems,* 10(3), 243–258.
4. Tanyimboh TT and Templeman AB (1995). 'A new method for calculating the reliability of single-source networks.' In *Developments in Computational Techniques for Civil Engineering,* Topping BHV (ed.), Civil-Comp Press, 1–9.
5. Tanyimboh TT and Tabesh M (1997). 'The basis of the source head method of calculating distribution network reliability.' In *Proceeding of the 3rd International*

Conference on Water Pipeline Systems, The Hague, 13–15 May 1997, BHR Group, 211–220.

6. Bao Y and Mays LW (1990). 'Model for water distribution system reliability.' *J. Hydraulic Engineering,* ASCE, 116(9), 1119–1137.

7. Gupta R and Bhave PR (1996). 'Comparison of methods for predicting deficient-network performance.' *J. Water Resources Planning and Management,* ASCE, 122(3), 214–217.

8. Tanyimboh TT and Tabesh M (1997). Discussion of 'Comparison of methods for predicting deficient-network performance.' *J. Water Resources Planning and Management,* ASCE, (accepted for publication).

9. Bhave, PR (1991). *Analysis of Flow in water Distribution Networks,* Technomic Publishing Co., Lancaster, Pa.

10. Chandapillai J (1991). 'Realistic simulation of water distribution system.' *J. Transportation Engineering,* ASCE, 117(2), 258–263.

11. Fujiwara O and Tung HD (1991). 'Reliability improvement for water distribution network through improving pipe size.' *Water Resources Research,* 27(7), 1395–1402.

12. Su Y, Mays LW, Duan N and Lansey KE (1987). 'Reliability-based optimization model for water distribution systems.' *J. Hydraulic Engineering,* ASCE, 114(12), 1539–1556.

13. Cullinane JM, Lansey KE and Mays LW (1992). 'Optimization-availability-based design of water distribution networks.' *J. Hydraulic Engineering,* ASCE, 118(3), 420–441.

14. Awumah K and Goulter I (1992). 'Maximizing entropy-defined reliability of water distribution network.' *Engineering Optimization,* 20(1), 57–80.

15. Goulter IC and Coals AV (1986). 'Quantitative approaches to reliability assessment in pipe networks.' *J. Transportation Engineering,* ASCE, 112(3), 287–301.

16. Fujiwara O and de Silva AU (1990). 'Algorithm for reliability-based optimal design of water networks.' *J. Environmental Engineering,* ASCE, 116(3), 575–587.

17. Fujiwara O and Ganesharajah T (1993). 'Reliability assessment of water supply systems with storage and distribution networks.' *Water Resources Research,* 29(8), 2917–2924.

Design[a]	$Q(0)^a$ (m^3/s)	$H_s^{req}(0)^b$ (m)	$p(0)$	$H_{s,6}^{req}(0)^c$ (m)
1	0.171951	277.6	0.993972	120.3
2	0.173044	270.5	0.994049	113.2
3	0.173323	268.6	0.994072	111.3
4	0.174264	260.4	0.994129	103.1
5	0.174327	253.2	0.994182	<100
6	0.174653	251.4	0.994204	<100
7	0.175417	245.1	0.994251	<100
8	0.176089	239.6	0.994296	<100
9	0.176424	237.8	0.994316	<100
10	0.177033	232.9	0.994357	<100
11	0.177137	230.1	0.994427	<100
12	0.177361	229.0	0.994461	<100
13	0.177711	226.3	0.994524	<100
14	0.178042	224.8	0.994535	<100
15	0.178263	223.7	0.994568	<100
16	0.178822	221.2	0.994625	<100

Table 3. Hydraulic performance and mechanical reliability indicators

[a] All 16 designs are deficient: $Q < Q_{req}$ and $H_s^{req} > H_s$ for full network.

[b] Equivalent to the head loss from the source to node 9 with all demands fully satisfied.

[c] Nodes for which required source head exceeds available source head are 6 ($\equiv$ 8) and 9.

Design	Reliability		Damage tolerance	
	ISHM	SHM	ISHM	SHM
1	0.861656	0.599357	0.765560	0.467538
2	0.869717	0.607279	0.771899	0.475736
3	0.871875	0.609345	0.773837	0.477353
4	0.882139	0.618897	0.781304	0.485405
5	0.887809	0.627596	0.788458	0.492750
6	0.888510	0.629896	0.790451	0.494583
7	0.890974	0.638008	0.796639	0.501566
8	0.893189	0.645301	0.802303	0.507660
9	0.893933	0.647755	0.804397	0.509659
10	0.895975	0.654495	0.809053	0.515393
11	0.897178	0.658447	0.813000	0.520590
12	0.897678	0.660079	0.814811	0.522373
13	0.898856	0.663961	0.818552	0.527498
14	0.899551	0.666243	0.820327	0.529177
15	0.900050	0.667877	0.822270	0.530997
16	0.901213	0.671701	0.826098	0.536022

Table 4. Values of system reliability and damage tolerance

Design	Fraction of total demand satisfied			Error[b] (%)	
	SHM	ISHM	HDSM[a]	SHM	ISHM
1	0.600156	0.862239	0.826290	-27.40	4.35
2	0.608066	0.870303	0.831543	-26.87	4.66
3	0.610132	0.872460	0.832883	-26.74	4.75
4	0.619686	0.882734	0.837405	-26.00	5.41
5	0.628385	0.888390	0.837808	-25.00	6.04
6	0.630685	0.889082	0.839274	-24.85	5.93
7	0.638796	0.891519	0.842946	-24.22	5.76
8	0.646091	0.893710	0.846175	-23.65	5.62
9	0.648594	0.894445	0.847785	-23.50	5.50
10	0.655285	0.896468	0.850711	-22.97	5.38
11	0.659220	0.897650	0.851211	-22.56	5.46
12	0.660846	0.898140	0.852287	-22.46	5.38
13	0.664712	0.899298	0.853969	-22.16	5.31
14	0.666996	0.899986	0.855560	-22.04	5.19
15	0.668625	0.900475	0.856622	-21.95	5.12
16	0.672434	0.901619	0.859308	-21.75	4.92
Mean Error				-24.01	5.30

Table 5. Fractions of total demand satisfied by fully connected network
[a] Head-Driven Simulation Method [7]. [b] % of corresponding HDSM value

Node	Proportion of nodal demand satisfied					
2–5, 7	1.000	1.000	1.000	1.000	1.000	1.000
6, 8	0.912	0.940	0.985	1.000	1.000	1.000
9	0.600	0.608	0.620	0.646	0.661	0.673
Design	1	2	4	8	12	16

Table 6. Fractions of nodal demands satisfied by fully connected network (ISHM)

Node	Reliability				
2, 4	0.999879	0.999882	0.999888	0.999897	0.999908
3, 7	0.999653	0.999677	0.999690	0.999723	0.999764
5	0.999775	0.999792	0.999810	0.999828	0.999848
6, 8	0.910446	0.983533	0.999096	0.999311	0.999476
9	0.599358	0.618898	0.645302	0.660079	0.671701
Mean	0.927373	0.947234	0.955308	0.957221	0.958731
Weighted Mean	0.861644	0.881441	0.893187	0.897678	0.901002
System	0.861656	0.882139	0.893189	0.897678	0.901213
Design	1	4	8	12	16

Table 7. Reliabilities of individual nodes

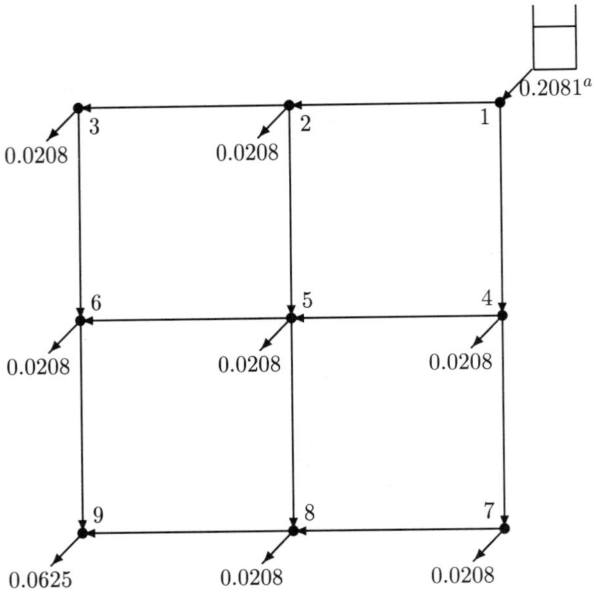

Figure 1. Sample network
[a] Flows are in m^3/s; node elevations are all 0 m; source head = 100 m.

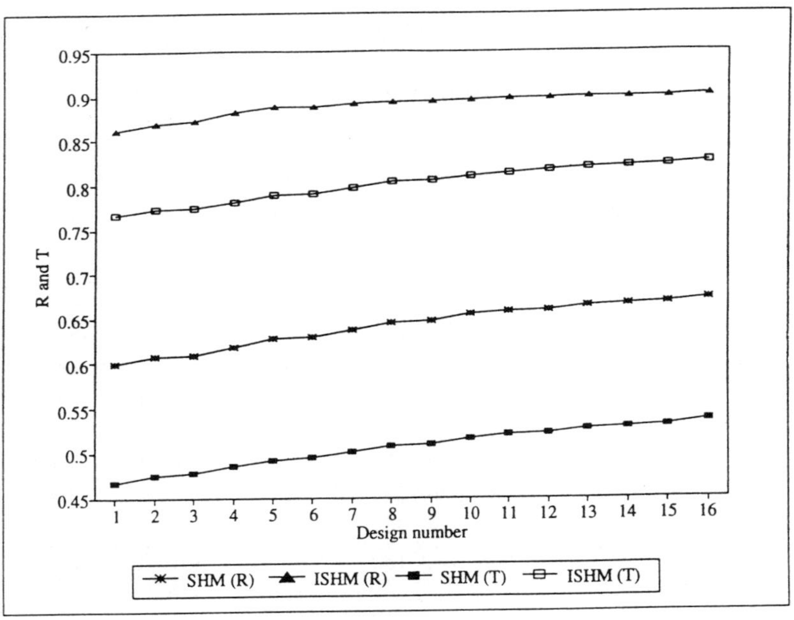

Figure 2. Network reliability and damage tolerance values

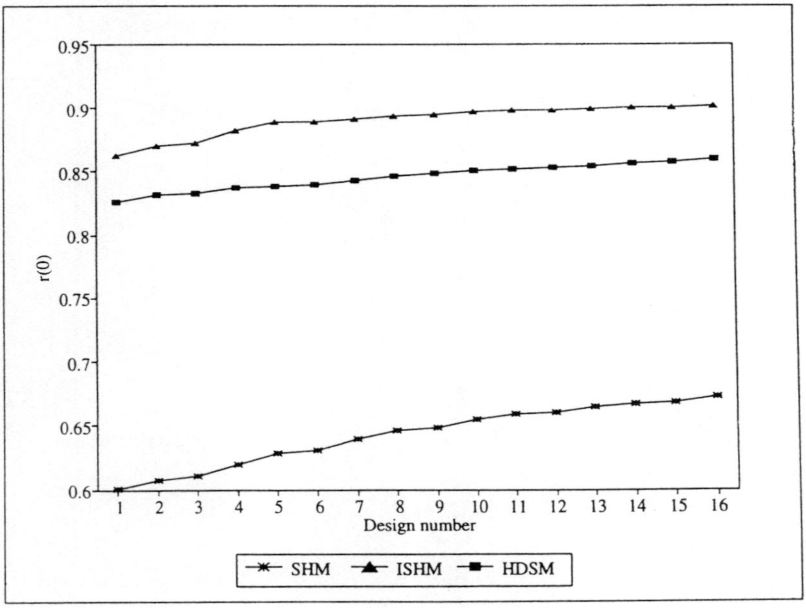

Figure 3. Fractions of total demand satisfied by fully connected networks

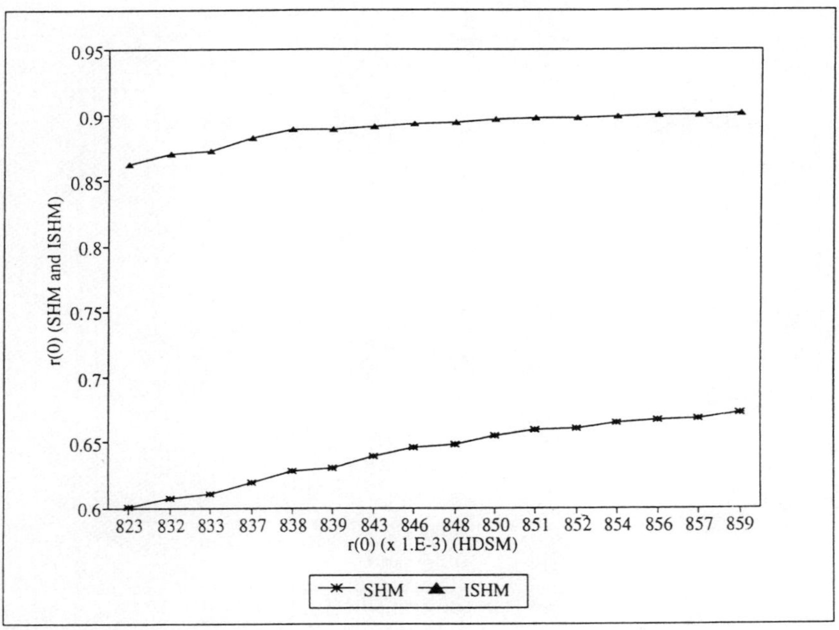

Figure 4. SHM and ISHM fraction of total demand against HDSM value

CHAPTER 3

Risk Analysis Related to Water Mains Bursts

C.A.Woodward, T.Ta *and* J.Whiter

Abstract

A predictive GIS model for bursts of water mains of diameter over 300 mm is being developed with the aim of reducing the costs of mains breaks and developing a more robust rehabilitation strategy. The causes of water mains bursts include ground mobility, traffic loading, corrosivity, weather conditions, pipe material and pipe age. Data on a number of different factors causing water main fracture is being collated and is being used to analyse past fractures in order to deduce a burst probability score for each water main. The consequences of large water main bursts include the threat to public safety, threat to supply, damage to property and traffic disruption Spatial data on the consequences of bursts is being collated and input into the GIS model. Hydraulic models have been used to simulate bursts throughout the network and the maximum possible water flow rates have been predicted. Digital elevation data, enhanced by information from sewer manhole surveys are being used to predict the likely extent of resulting flooding and this is being combined with information on property type etc. to produce a consequence score for each length of water mains (Burst Reach). Probability and consequence scores will be combined to produce an overall risk score for each main. This chapter focuses on the estimation of the extent and location of areas at risk of flooding (Floodable Areas).

1. **Introduction**

Thames Water Utilities Limited (1-WUL) are responsible for the operation and maintenance of approximately 30,000 km of water mains. Most of these pipes were installed by a variety of predecessor organisations and many are over a 100 years old The system has been expanding more or less continually over the last century with a variety of different types of pipe being laid over the years as manufacturing methods have changed and new materials have become available. The majority of pipes now owned by TWUL are either cast iron, ductile iron or steel. These pipes vary not only in the quality and thickness of metal used but also in the jointing systems employed and in the internal and external linings that have been applied to prevent corrosion. Pipes are laid to a variety of standards, in a variety of different types of soil and convey waters with a range of corrosivities.

Fractures in water mains over 300 mm in diameter (about 10% of the total length) in the area supplied by Thames Water occur at about the rate of 120 a year. The potential threat to public safety and the costs of repair, reinstatement and compensation claims running into more than £1,000,000 for major incidents, makes the study of mains fractures essential.

Until recently there has been limited understanding as to why mains fractures occur. A number of different factors such as ground movement, rapid changes in air temperature, traffic loading etc. have been suggested as causes However, the degree to which each factor has an influence on mains failure has not been established. By achieving this, the frequency of burst mains can be reduced through priority planning of the replacement and rehabilitation programme.

2. **Overview of GIS based model for burst water mains risk assessment**

A GIS based model for the London Water supply area is under development that will identify potential high risk mains based on demographic and other spatial data as well as hydraulic network models of the water distribution and drainage systems The model is being designed to answer the following simple questions for each water main over 300 mm in diameter:

- How likely is it that a burst will occur?
- How much water will be released?
- Where will the water go?
- What are the potential consequences?

The probability of a burst occurring can be determined by an analysis of past fractures against the suspected causal factors. Hydraulic modelling allows maximum possible burst flow rates to be determined. Digital elevation data and drainage capacity data allow us to predict where the water will flow and which postcode areas will be affected. Postcode based data such as the presence of basements, property values and building use allow the consequences to be quantified. Thus the model will allow both risk and consequence 'scores' for each trunk main to be determined.

The GIS model holds many layers of information including the TWUL trunk main network, Ordnance Survey (OS) Landline data, sensitive street and road reinstatement class polygons, postcode area polygons, digital elevation data, and soil type polygons Burst main causal and consequence parameters are attached as attributes to the appropriate entities.

The OS Landline data are used as background information only, to allow other coverages to be displayed over a recognisable map background.

Many sensitive street and road reinstatement class polygons have been digitised by the company as part of its commitment to meeting the requirements of the New Roads and Street Works Act. These polygons clearly identify the street boundaries so that it is a simple matter to determine what length of main lies under the road. Where these polygons are not available, street boundaries are estimated by buffering around the relevant Meridian road centre line. These data are being used in conjunction with traffic density estimates, to test the hypothesis that mains laid beneath overloaded streets are more likely to fracture than those in lightly loaded roads or in the verge.

Soil type polygons have been supplied by SSLRC at Cranfield. They classify soils according to their corrosivity and according to the likelihood of their causing a water main to fracture due to ground movement.

Traffic loading data are based on a node and link traffic planning model, holding the co-ordinates of the ends of the lengths of road to which the counts apply but not the detailed routing of the roads. Part of the model building has involved identifying the appropriate area of land to which a particular traffic loading should apply (i.e. the exact route of the real road represented by each arc in the model).

Digital elevation data obtained from the Ordnance Survey has been enhanced by addition of manhole cover levels which are maintained by the company to facilitate sewer maintenance and drainage area modelling. Use of this data to predict the fate of flood water released from a burst main will be the subject of future study.

The water main network comprises locations of pipes of a diameter of 300 mm and above, nodal areas*, valve positions and burst locations. Pipe attributes include diameters, operating pressures and, where known, age and material.

Bursts are simulated every 50m on all mains using hydraulic network models to determine the maximum water release rate which will become an attribute of the length of main on either side of the burst. Nodal area attributes include the number of domestic and industrial customers, critical and key customers as well as water consumption levels. This information allows calculations to determine the number of customers threatened with loss of supply or low pressure following a burst. The position of valves and attribute information such as size and type allow the likely time to isolate the burst to be estimated, based on the number and sizes of the valves to be closed.

Postcode area polygons are derived from 'Enhanced postcode centroids' supplied by C.A.C.I. Postcode attributes include total rateable value of domestic premises, 'insurance reserve' for commercial property.

3 Estimation of burst flow rates

The companies' hydraulic network models were used as the basis for estimation. These strategic planning models were developed over a number of years. A variety of different consultants assisted in the development of models of the various pressure zones and the standards of calibration and documentation varied from model to model. Generally, models included all mains of 300mm diameter and above plus any smaller mains considered to be 'hydraulically important'. produced to run under GINAS – which, at the time when the earlier models were produced, did not have a graphical interface, making the recording of nodal co-ordinates seem unnecessary.

The models were all converted to run under Piccolo and a substantial programme of enhancement was undertaken to render the models suitable for use in this application. This involved identification of node locations (where they were not already known), de-simplification (where this was needed to allow the relationship between real and model pipes to be established) and changes to boundary conditions (e.g. a fixed head

---

* Points of intersection of two or more pipes and the ends of mains are known as nodes. Hydraulic models calculate the flows in pipes and the pressures at nodes. They also assume that all customers are supplied from nodes. A nodal area encloses the properties deemed to be supplied from the relevant node

reference used to simulate an infusion from another zone may be adequate under normal diurnal demand variation but appears to give unrealistic levels of support in the event of a burst simulation).

Burst simulation was affected by:

a) Splitting a model pipe to create a node at the burst simulation point.

b) Creating a fixed head reservoir attached to the new node (head set equal to ground level, estimated by linear interpolation between the elevations of the end nodes of the original pipe).

c) Running the model in steady state simulation mode.

In order to generate results for the whole of the network, Safege were contracted to provide tools to facilitate the automatic generation of bursts at intervals along each pipe in the model and at each reasonable node in the model, to run the simulations and to save the appropriate results. (This work will be the subject of a separate study in the near future).

4. Estimation of Floodable Areas

4.1 Assignment of burst flow rates

While bursts have been simulated effectively at discrete points on the network, the results are being applied to lengths of main in the GIS model. These lengths of main are referred to as 'Burst Reaches'. The burst reaches are easy to define on the Piccolo model but their equivalent lengths of main on the real network (and hence the GIS model) are harder to identify. This work is currently in progress.

When GIS burst reaches have been defined, the burst flow rate data (together with information on the areas likely to be affected by loss of pressure), will be attached to them. These values will be used to estimate floodable areas for bursts occurring anywhere within the reach.

4.2 Estimation of capacity- of Road/Drainage system to convey water away from burst location

Observations of the fate of water from a number of large water mains bursts have revealed that large amounts of water can be conveyed away from the site of a burst by the road network. Flooding is likely to occur in the immediate vicinity of the burst but the depth of water in the road decreases rapidly with distance from the scene as velocity increases.

For a burst occurring within a road, the amount of water that can be conveyed away from the burst's site without local flooding is determined by the width and depth of the road and its gradient.

The 'depth' of the road is a function of the height of its curbs and its camber. It is generally level in the direction perpendicular to its centre line although the line itself may not be horizontal. In this case it is possible to ignore flows except those parallel to the road centre line and to treat the flow from the burst as if it were dispersed across the carriageway (Figure 1).

Ignoring friction effects

$$H = z + h\cos\theta + \frac{v^2}{2g}$$

and $$Q = A_w v$$

Where

$H =$	Initial energy head (m)
$\theta =$	Slope of road
$z =$	Elevation (m)
$h =$	Height of water (m)
$v =$	Velocity of water ($m.s^{-1}$)
$g =$	Acceleration due to gravity ($m.s^{-2}$)

To estimate the initial energy head, we have chosen to use H = 100mm as this is the approximate height of a curb.

For simulation of the situation close to the burst we use the bank full equation after Williams (1978)

$$Q_{Channelfull} = 4.0A_w^{1.21}(\sin\theta)^{0.28}$$

Where A_w = Cross sectional area of flowing water (m^2)

and $A_w = wh$ where w = width of road (m)

This equation is used to calculate the maximum burst flow rate that could be contained within the roadway at the point of discharge of $Q_{Channelfull}$ or to estimate h where h<0. 1

$$Q_{Channel} = min(Q_{Channelfull}, Q)$$

It can be seen that Williams' equation requires a value for the slope of the road and for the road's cross sectional area. These values are estimated as follows:

a) Slope of Road

Where manhole cover level data is available for the road in question, it is generally the best available indicator. Where a 15m buffer around the relevant centre line is found to contain at least one manhole on either side of the burst, the gradient between the pair of closest manholes is taken Otherwise, a triangular irregular net (TIN) of the region is constructed using ordnance survey digital elevation data together with manhole cover level data and the gradient of the road centreline is estimated from the resulting digital terrain model.

b) Cross Section of Road

Where the burst location falls within a known road polygon (the company has digitised the outlines of road sections that have been designated as sensitive by the local authorities and/or which have special reinstatement requirements), the road width can be estimated by measuring the length of the line joining the two sides of the polygon and constructed perpendicular to the road centre line and passing through the burst location. Where the burst is not inside a known road polygon, the width of the road is estimated on the basis of its 'class' as given by its Meridian centre line.

The curb heights and camber details are not available for specific stretches of road. They are observed to be quite variable, without any obvious pattern. On the basis of limited observation, the following general assumptions have been made. They will be refined if and when better data becomes available.

The depth of the curbs is assumed to be 100mm.

The road camber is assumed to take the form of an isosceles triangle, being 75rnm higher at the centre than at the curb (Figure 2).

This gives Cross Section $A_w = 0.1w - 0.075\frac{w}{2} = 0.0625w\,(\text{m}^2)$

Thus: $Q_{Local\_Flooding} = \max(Q - 4(0.0625w^{1.21}(\sin\theta)^{0.28}, 0) = \max(Q - Q_{Channelfull}, 0)$

Preliminary investigations indicate that this equation performs reasonably well for bursts occurring under the carriageway, 10m or more from a junction. For bursts at a junction, the water-carrying capacity of all the roads should be taken into account. It is proposed that this should be done by adding the capacities of all roads sloping away from the burst location, giving

$$Q_{Local\_Flooding} = \max(Q - Q_{Channelfull\_1} - Q_{Channelfull\_2} \cdots - Q_{Channelfull\_n}, 0)$$

4.3 **Drainage capacity and open channel flow**

Road drainage systems are designed to deal with rainfall which, even when taking the form of localised storms, is a diffuse source by comparison to a water main burst. The sewers or road drains are designed to cope with flows entering from a large number of road gullies simultaneously. Widespread, intense rain may cause the road drains to surcharge but this is unlikely to be the result of a burst water main which, while it may completely submerge a number of road gullies, will only enter the drainage system at a rate determined by the capacity of those gullies.

There are a variety of different designs of gully and their selection and location is normally left to the professional judgement of an engineer. All that can be said with total confidence is that the gullies are designed to deal with the drainage requirements associated with the highest likely local rainfall rate (short term). This is typically taken to be 100mm.hr^{-1} for the South East of England, however, observations of the results of large water mains bursts indicate that actual capacities are some 10 - 20 times greater than this. It is believed that this is due to allowance being made for blocked gullies, the need to allow for runoff from other paved areas and a degree of conservatism in design.

Since there is no possibility within the GIS model of knowing the capacities of the gullies or exactly where they are located, an average drainage rate of 2000mm.hr^{-1} is assumed for all roads. Thus the maximum total area of road which can be covered in water is 1800 $Q_{channel}$ m^2.

Once water has left the immediate vicinity of the burst, it will continue to accelerate down the road until:

a) It disappears into the drainage system.

b) It bleeds off into a side road.

c) It comes to a bend in the road.

d) It comes to the end of the road.

e) It reaches the bottom of the hill.

Case a) will occur wherever there are $1800Q_{channel}/w$ m of straight road with no gradient inflections and no side roads.

In cases b), c) and d), it is likely that the flow will be split with some water going straight on, due to its inertia and some being diverted. A flow split will have to be estimated and road born flows tracked until the condition for case a) is satisfied.

In case d) localised flooding will occur at a rate of $\left(\frac{1800}{w} - L\right)Q_{channel}$ ($m^3.s^{-1}$)

where L = Distance from burst location to bottom of hill(m).

4.4 **Fate of flood water**

In the above argument, any water not entering the drainage system of the roads is regarded as flood water, without regard to its eventual fate. In the general case, it is intended that this flood water will be assigned an area whose size will be a linear function of the volumetric flow rate and whose shape will be determined by local topography.

There are, however, two cases that are believed to be significant enough to warrant special treatment. These are

a) Rivers, streams, canals, surface drains and other watercourses.

b) Railway lines in cuttings.

In both cases, flooding of property will be avoided and small amounts of water can be handled without problems. In the case of railways, however, large amounts of floodwater are likely to carry debris onto the line and cause delays even though the depth of water is not great enough to cover the clinker base of the tracks.

The GIS model contains data on the locations of these features and it is possible to assume that water reaching them will be dispersed harmlessly. All other flood water will be assumed to do damage in proportion to the fraction of each post code area covered, i.e.,

Total Damage = ($Value_{PCA1}$ * $Area_{PCA1}$ / Flooded $Area_{PCA1}$) + ($Value_{PCA2}$ * $Area_{PCA2}$ / Flooded

$Area_{PCA2}$) + … + ($Value_{PCAn}$ * $Area_{PCAn}$ / Flooded $_{AreaPCAn}$)

4.5 **Case studies**

The arguments developed above are based on the findings of a number of case studies following recent water mains bursts in the London area The algorithms and relationships proposed have been calibrated and tested against observations. It is likely that some of the ideas presented will be refined in the light of findings from further case studies and it is most probable that calibration values will change. The three case studies presented here are believed to be typical of their kind but have been chosen to illustrate specific features.

4.5.1 Case Study 1

In case 1, the burst occurred on a 30-inch diameter in a main road of width 18m, close to a junction with a single side road. The main road runs along the base of a valley so that all side roads run up hill away from away from it. The valley floor has an incline of 5.0 degrees at the burst location. The maximum possible burst flow rate was calculated to be 320ml.d^{-1} (3.704 $m^3 .s^{-1}$) and flow level and pressure sensors indicated that the actual burst flow rate was of that order.

The local topography was such that properties set back from the road had ground floors set significantly above the level of the road. Nevertheless, basements existed that could have suffered major damage as a result of a small rise in water level.

In the event, virtually all the water remained between the curbs although a very small amount of flooding did occur in one property on the Northern side of the road, just down stream of the burst location, indicating that me water release rate was close to the maximum capacity of the road at that point (the bank full capacity).

Substituting gives $Q = 4 \times (0.0625 \times 18)^{1.21} \times \sin(1.54)^{0.28} = 1.676\,\mathrm{m^3/s}$ as the likely actual peak flow rate.

There were a number of side roads along the length of main road that was flooded but very little water went up them as they were all up hill. There were no bends or changes of slope in the affected stretch of road so the total extent of flooding (area of road) was 285m * 18m = 5130 m giving an effective drainage rate of 1.676*3600/5130 = 1.176 m^3/m^2/hr based on the assumption that the burst flow rate was equal to the calculated bank full capacity of the road or 3.704*3600/5130 = 2.60 m^3/m^2/hr based on the maximum possible rate.

4.5.2 Case study 2

Case 2 is more complex. Here the road in which the burst occurred ran from south east to north west and was almost level at the burst site, which was near the edge of a small plateaux. The ground sloped away from the road quite sharply to the northeast and rose gently to the south-west. A number of road gullies was found to be blocked immediately after the event.

Figure 3 shows the layout of the area around the burst, with elevation data. Figure 4 adds the burst location and the flooded area. It can be seen that floodwater spread a considerable distance in both directions along the main road. Very little water spread into the side road to the south of the burst but a considerable amount of water mounted the curb and flooded property in the immediate vicinity of the source. The slope of the ground was such that the properties concerned had a floor which, while it was at basement level at the front, was at ground floor level at the rear. Water did not reach any great depth in these houses but rather flowed through them in sufficient volume to cause significant damage to the properties behind.

A large amount of water flowed into the side road to the north east of the burst but, by the time it reached the bend in the road, its volume had been reduced to the point where very little water failed to negotiate the change in direction. Flooding of property to the north of the side road was attributed primarily to water flowing through the houses, down the rear access road and crossing the street.

The broken main was 36 inches in diameter and hydraulic models indicated that the maximum possible burst flow rate would be 230Ml/d (9600 m^3 /hr). Flow and level sensors indicated that the actual flow rate was probably somewhat less than this (c.a. 5000 m^3/hr). This lower figure is consistent with the fact that the burst in this case was the result of corrosion and water could only escape through a relatively small hole in the pipe wall. The bank full equation predicts a road capacity of about 4860 m^3/hr, giving a predicted local flood water flow rate of 4740 m^3/hr and estimated actual value of 140 m^3/hr.

The total area of road covered by flood water was not measured accurately in this case but was subsequently estimated to be about 7000 m^2, giving an effective drainage rate of 0.69 to 1.37 m^3/m^2/hr. These figures are much lower than those estimated for case study 1, consistent with the idea that the blocked road gullies found after the incident were either blocked prior to the burst or became so quickly thereafter.

Case study 3

Figures 5 and 6 show the layout of the area and the extent of flooding. Once again, the floodwater has primarily followed the roads but property has been affected in the immediate vicinity of the burst. In this case, secondary flooding has occurred at the bottom of the hill, near to the point where the main road begins to ascend to go over the railway / canal to the south-east. Some water has found its way into the side road to the north of the area of secondary flooding and this water has followed the roads remaining between curbs till reaching the canal.

This event has not yet been analysed to determine the actual or predicted burst flow rates, however, it does demonstrate the potential significance of side road flows and of changes in slope and of water courses.

5. **Conclusion**

This chapter has briefly described the development of a GIS based model for TWUL's London Water Supply area containing spatial information relating to the causes and consequences of large water main bursts. Analysis of causal factors and past burst records will allow burst probability scores to be determined for each water main.

Hydraulic models and digital elevation data allow areas affected by flooding to be predicted and case studies have indicated that the algorithms proposed can give reasonable accuracy in predicting both the extent and the location of flooding.

Flood predictions combined with spatial consequence data will lead to a consequence score for each length of water main. Combining probability and consequence scores will lead to an overall risk score for each water main. Implementation of this risk model will lead to a reduction both in disruption to customers and in the costs associated with water main failures through a more effectively targeted replacement programme.

References

1. GINAS IV (Graphical and Interactive Network Analysis Software), De Montfort University, Leicester.

2. Piccolo potable water distribution system modelling software Version 3.53, Safege C.E., Parc de Llle, - 15/27, Rue du Port, B.P.727-92007 Nanterre CEDEX - France.

3. WS Atkins. Trunk mains risk assessment report for TWUL (1996).

4. Whiter J. and Woodward C. A., AGI '96, 24-26 September 1996, Birmingham, U.K.

Acknowledgement

The authors gratefully acknowledge the considerable contribution of past and present members of the bursts project team.

The views expressed in this chapter represent those of the authors and are not necessarily those of Thames Water Utilities Limited.

Figure 1.

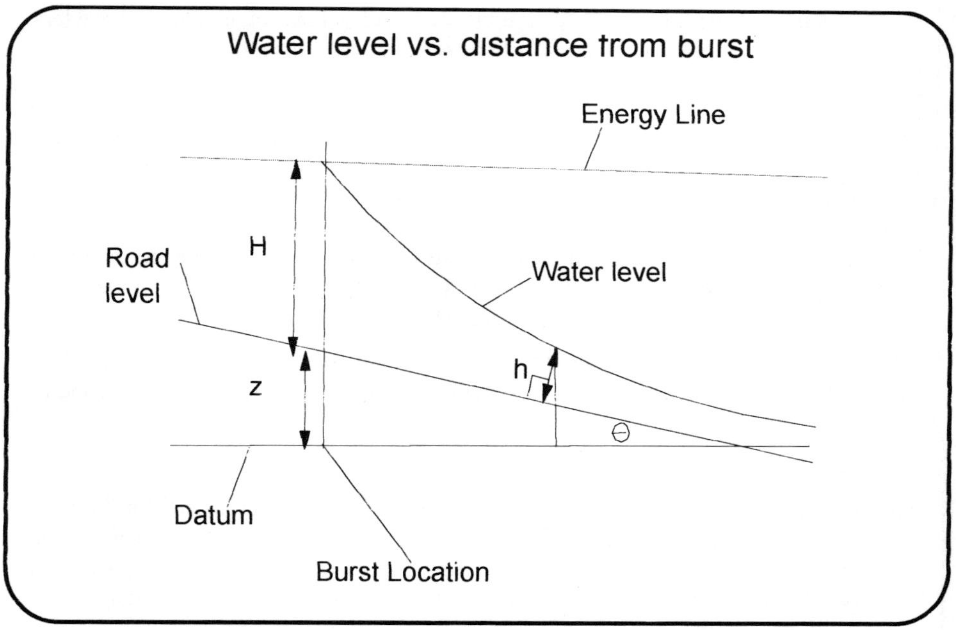

Figure 2.

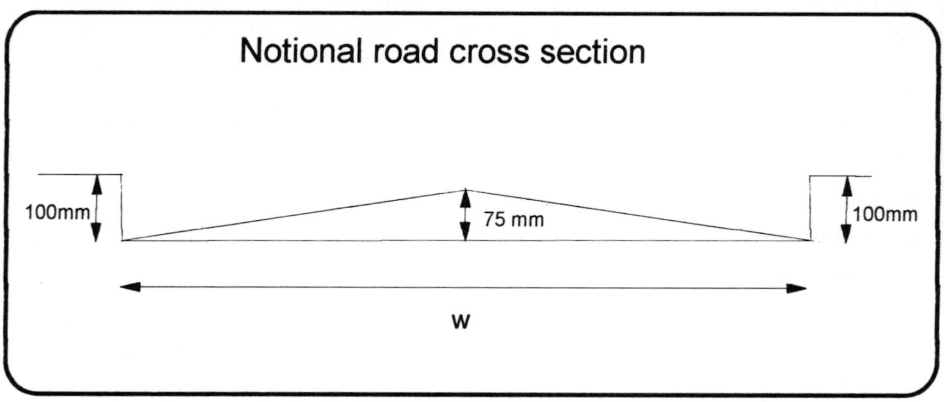

Figure 3. Case study 1. - Topographical plan.

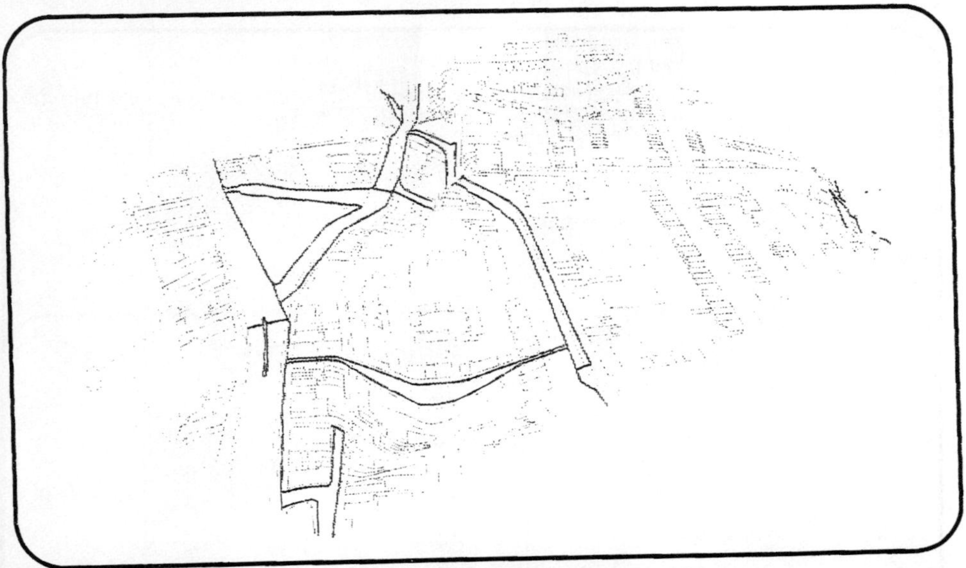

Based upon Ordnance Survey material on behalf of The Controller of Her Majesty's Stationery Office,
© Crown Copyright Licence No MC 88821M001

Figure 4. Case study 1 - Burst location and flooded area

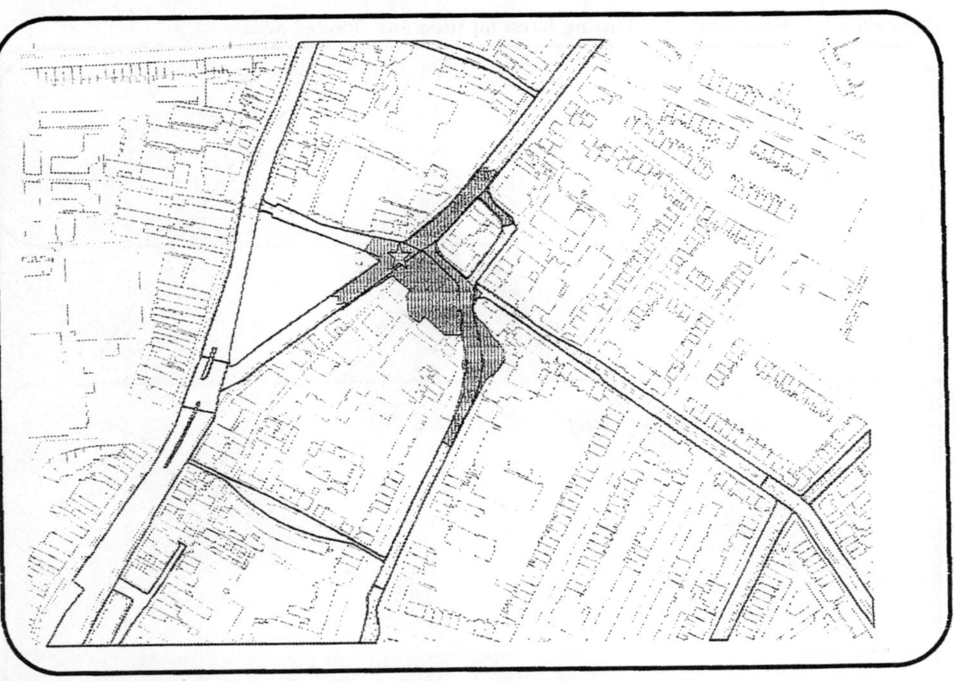

Based upon Ordnance Survey material on behalf of The Controller of Her Majesty's Stationery Office,
© Crown Copyright Licence No MC 88821M001

Figure 5. Case study 3 - Topographical plan

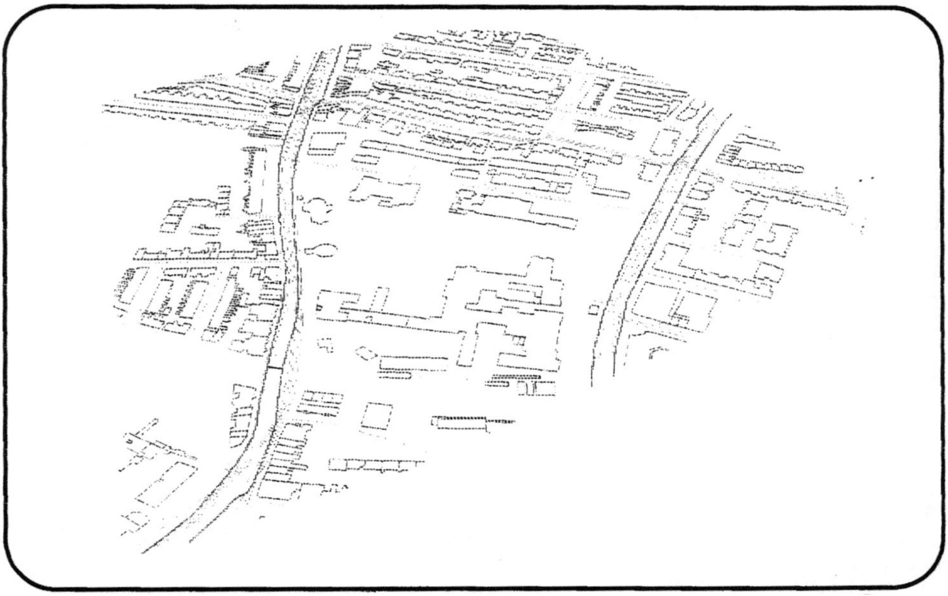

Based upon Ordnance Survey material on behalf of The Controller of Her Majesty's Stationery Office,
© Crown Copyright Licence No MC 88821M001

Figure 6. Case study 3 - showing burst location and flooded area

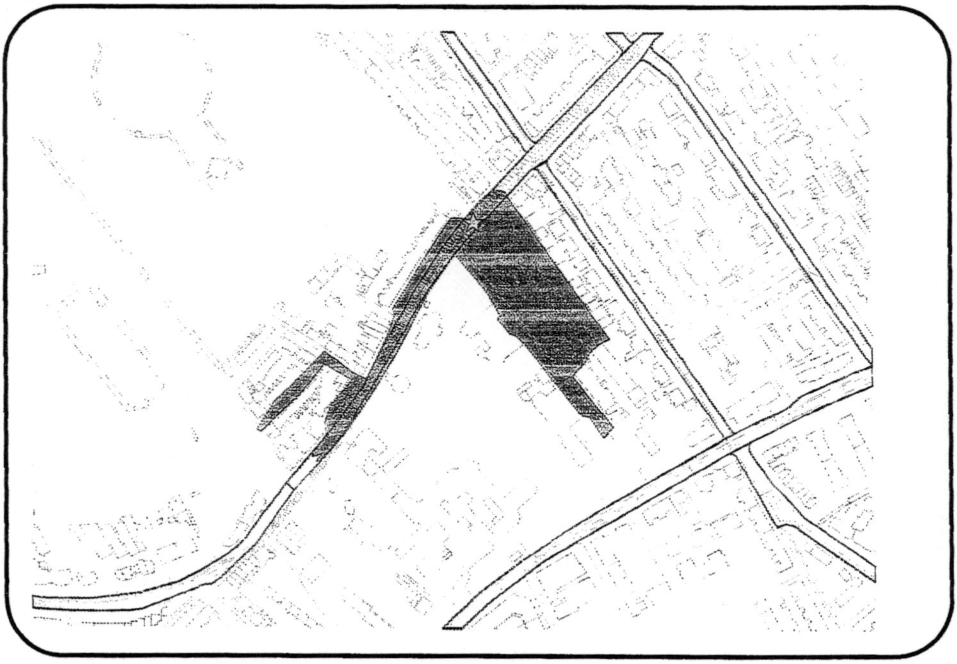

Based upon Ordnance Survey material on behalf of The Controller of Her Majesty's Stationery Office,
© Crown Copyright Licence No MC 88821M001

CHAPTER 4

Quantitative Risk Analysis for Ranking Security of Supply Investment Schemes

S.Cook, J.Banyard *and* M.Fowler

Abstract

In the framework of Severn Trent's objectives of meeting levels of service commitments within acceptable cost targets, a risk-based methodology was required to assist the investment decision-making process concerning security of supply schemes (such as reservoir replacement, source capacity increases or network flexibility improvements). A methodology has been developed which involves consequence modelling of potential failure events, Monte Carlo simulation and operational optimisation, to provide a quantitative assessment of the risk of unplanned interruptions to supply inherent in a water supply system and a means of evaluating the risk-reduction achieved by alternative investment scheme combinations. As described in two case studies, the methodology is continuing to be applied successfully in assisting Severn Trent to locate areas of risk, identify and prioritise schemes, and determine an appropriate balance between capital expenditure and security of supply risk.

1. Introduction

Decisions on investment in schemes to improve security of supply involve consideration of a number of criteria. Given the increasing financial pressures on UK water companies having large but limited capital budgets, it is no longer acceptable for these criteria to be based on an informal assessment of the investment benefits and an approach to decision-making is sought which is objective and can be audited. The use of quantitative risk analysis (QRA) to measure the potential improvement in security of supply following investment meets these requirements and is increasingly being viewed as an important decision-support tool for identifying and prioritising investment.

This chapter describes a QRA methodology developed for Severn Trent Water to support investment decision-making, primarily addressing security of supply issues but in fact applicable to more general water supply problems. Typical investment schemes to resolve security of supply problems include improving redundancy (both transmission routes and source capacity) and increasing storage. QRA can also be used, however, to quantify the risk-reduction benefit of operational measures to improve security of supply such as reducing failure response and repair times or operating at higher storage levels.

A key advantage of QRA over more subjective risk analysis methods is the ability to quantify the benefits of operational measures and investment in improving security of supply. These may be compared with the costs of risk-reduction measures to provide a direct cost/benefit measure that may be made across different systems or different types of schemes competing for funds.

2. Definition of Risk

In any risk analysis, the meaning of risk requires precise definition so that it may be interpreted correctly. Risk is considered to be a combination of the tendency to fail and a measure of failure consequences, alongside a definition of what are undesirable outcomes of failure and the scope of circumstances which might give rise to these outcomes.

2.1 Failure Tendency

A suitable measure of tendency is the probability of occurrence of a nominated number of failure occurrences in a given period. This is a quantitative measure of tendency on a universal scale, independent of system characteristics, making comparison of risks within and between systems possible.

2.2 Failure Outcome

For security of supply risk analysis, the outcome of concern is an unplanned interruption to water supply for any number of customers and for any period of time.

2.3 Failure Consequence Measures

Suitable consequence measures for security of supply failures are the number of properties experiencing an interruption and the duration of that interruption. Although these are both obvious measures, other measures may be of concern; for example, the number of sensitive customers affected or the frequency with which particular customers are affected. Whereas these are customer-oriented measures and naturally of concern to a water supply company, the commercial consequences of failure will also be of substantial interest. These are termed "business consequences" and are related to compensation payments, guaranteed standards payments, insurance payments and issues related to public profile such as share price, market position and overseas earnings. The degree to which this range of customer-oriented and business consequences is taken into account in any risk analysis will depend upon perceptions as to what is important and upon the extent to which these consequences can be quantified. This issue is revisited in Case Study 1 (Section 5.1).

2.4 Scope of Failure Events

The scope of failure events which could give rise to the failure outcomes should be determined using methodical approaches such as fault tree and event tree analyses. It is also necessary to recall the overall role of risk analysis here as one of aiding the process of investment decision-making and as a consequence relate quantitative measures of risk at least to those factors that are influenced directly by investment.

In the case of security of supply, faults which could give rise to unplanned interruptions may arise out of major asset failure (e.g. trunk mains bursts, treatment works failure), minor asset failure (e.g. distribution main burst, local valve failure), human error, third-party failure (e.g. power supply), communications system failure and so on. Other, non fault-related failure modes are also possible including inadequate yield and inadequate transmission capacity. In fact, these conditions are all similar in the sense that they relate to insufficient system resources to satisfy demand caused by loss of part of the system or excessive demand or both.

2.5 Definition

Taking into account the foregoing, a suitable quantitative definition of risk for security of supply failures which includes the basic consequence measures is proposed as:

$$\text{probability}(N\{F,T,P^*,D^*\}>N^*) \qquad (1)$$

$N\{F,T,P^*,D^*\}$ = number of unplanned interruptions to supply in period T, arising from component failure F, affecting a population $\geq P^*$ for a duration $\geq D^*$

where: N^*,P^* and D^* are chosen to suit the purposes of the risk analysis.

N^* should be selected either arbitrarily to allow comparison of risks or specifically to reflect management decisions on what is considered to be an (un)acceptable frequency of supply interruptions. For example, if N^* is set to zero, then risk is quantified as the probability of any number of unplanned interruptions to supply within the chosen analysis horizon.

P^* and D^* can be varied both to provide points on a risk surface and to match specific levels of service; for example, the DG3 reporting requirements.

T is the time period over which risk is to be assessed and is chosen to match the investment planning horizon (e.g. 25 years).

Whilst the above definition is effective for the quantification of risk for a given failure, its multi-dimensional nature makes comparison of risk, either between failure events or between pre- and post-investment scenarios, less straightforward. To simplify the consideration of risk and provide a means of comparing investment schemes, a “Risk Index” is defined as follows:

Risk Index(F,T) = number of man-hours interruption to supply expected in period T as a result of failure F

Under the assumption of fixed T, the risk index is a scalar measure of risk for each failure event and can be used to rank failures in order of seriousness and to measure the effectiveness of risk-reduction investment. Where failure events are independent, the risk index may be summed over events to give a measure of overall system risk.

The above definitions of risk can be extended or re-framed to include additional factors (e.g. sensitive customers) where these are considered important. Equally, the risk index can be modified to include only losses of supply that exceed a given magnitude, should this prove to be a requirement.

3. Quantification of Risk

The approach to quantifying risk involves a number of steps as follows.

3.1 Preliminary Hazard Identification (PHI)

In contrast to the scope of failure events (above) PHI involves the identification of specific events or failures of the system which are expected to result in a significant unplanned interruption to supply and which may be addressed by investment. Various techniques are available to assist including the use of fault trees, event trees, expert panels and historical event analysis. The outcome of PHI is a list of events or scenarios for which risk is to be quantified. These are known as "primary failure events".

3.2 Failure Event and Duration Modelling

For each primary failure event, the probability of the event occurring during the chosen period is determined following statistical modelling of event occurrence. Similarly, statistical models for failure event duration are developed to account for uncertainty in failure detection, response, repair and recommissioning times. Sources of data for the identification of these models include local and generally available databases on asset and system failures and repairs, together with knowledge gleaned from direct operator experience of failures.

3.3 Failure Consequence Modelling

In most cases, the security of supply consequences of a failure will depend, amongst other things, on the way in which the system is operated during the failure. Determining the "best" operational response to failures requires a knowledge of the status of the system at the time of failure, an estimate of the demand likely to be exerted, an estimate of the duration of the failure and an understanding of the behaviour of the system. The approach taken to consequence modelling recognises that for many practical situations, the dependency on these uncertain conditions means that choosing the best system operation cannot easily be framed in a set of rules or procedures which can be encoded simply into a consequence model. Accordingly, operation of the system during failure and the resultant failure consequences are determined by framing a formal optimisation problem in which the objective function is a measure of satisfaction of customer demand, behaviour of the system is given by a water allocation model and the prevailing conditions (demands, usable storage etc.) are treated as random variables sampled from distributions based on statistical models identified using historical data.

In practice, consequence modelling proceeds as a Monte Carlo simulation as follows:

- A primary failure event is chosen.
- The failure is modelled in the water allocation model, for example by removing the failed component or reducing its capacity or similar.
- The date of the failure is sampled.
- Demands are sampled from identified distributions taking into account the date of the failure.
- Storages in the system are sampled from identified distributions taking into account the date of the failure.
- A feasibility check is performed to determine if the demands can be fully met simply from local resources and if so, the system is assumed not to be at risk of failure.
- Otherwise, an optimisation is performed to determine the operation of the system under failure which minimises the impact of unplanned interruptions to supply.

- The duration of the failure event is sampled and the population affected and the duration of the loss are recorded.
- The above process is repeated many times for each primary failure.

The output of the Monte Carlo Simulation consequence modelling for each primary failure event is a set of population/duration data pairs that can be represented as a joint frequency distribution of population suffering an interruption to supply and duration of interruption.

3.4 Risk Determination

The statistical models of event occurrence identified earlier are combined with the failure consequence frequency distribution to produce, for each primary failure event, estimates of the probability of failure in the form given by expression (1).

4. Investment for Risk Reduction

Where investment resources are limited and in any case for efficiency, an attractive criterion for determining investment priorities is the effectiveness of investment in reducing the risk of security of supply failures. Other criteria are possible but not considered here; for example, directing investment towards those areas exhibiting the highest actual risk or highest perceived risk.

In choosing to direct investment according to its risk-reduction effectiveness, the first task is to identify areas in the supply system which have an unacceptably high risk of failure. The results of the QRA can be used at this stage to rank primary failure events in order of descending risk index. This provides a simple measure of relative risk and could be used to focus attention on schemes which will be expected to deliver major reduction in risk. Note that care must be exercised in interpreting the risk index as it is a sample statistic from a frequency distribution which should be reviewed itself for a more comprehensive statement of risk.

Identifying areas of unacceptable risk presumes a level of acceptable risk which must be decided upon by those responsible for water supply. In the extreme, this level may be set such that no risk is acceptable reflecting a cautious approach in which all sources of risk are considered to attract investment.

For each primary failure event resulting in an unacceptably high risk of unplanned interruptions, investment schemes are devised which are considered to reduce the risk to or near to an acceptable level or, in principle, to meet any other criterion. For each scheme, the quantitative risk analysis is repeated with the effects of the scheme taken into account to determine the post-investment level of risk. Depending on the scheme, these effects may manifest themselves as a reduction in the primary failure event probability, a change in the water allocation model configuration, a change in the failure event duration distribution and so on. The risk analysis must also be repeated for sensible combinations of schemes where the risk-reduction effects of two or more schemes compound.

The results from these re-analyses, together with scheme cost estimates, can be used to assess the effectiveness of investment in reducing risk and thereby prioritise investment. The simplest approach involves ordering schemes and combinations of schemes according to reduction in risk index per £ invested in the scheme. This enables inefficient schemes to be identified so that they may be either discounted or reviewed to determine the cause of their inefficiency.

A second approach is to select the scheme or combination of schemes which gives the maximum reduction in total risk index for any given level of investment. This enables the best combination of schemes to be chosen for any given maximum investment and helps determine the level of investment beyond which a unit reduction in total risk index becomes increasingly costly. Figure 3 from Case Study 1 is an example of this approach which shows total risk index against maximum investment and gives an indication of the specific schemes which are most effective in reducing risk at each cost level. Note that as investment increases, different combinations of schemes are identified as being most effective and that a scheme included at low investment levels will not necessarily be included as investment increases. Note also that the shape of the curve indicates how the unit cost of risk-reduction increases significantly as the curve flattens defining the region in which investment is much less effective.

5. Case Studies

Two case studies are presented illustrating how Severn Trent have used quantified risk analysis to assist in capital investment decision-making. The first involves a strategic, high-level study reviewing the prioritisation of a large number of schemes across the Severn Trent Region. The second concerns more detailed analysis of a number of reservoirs to assess appropriate storage volumes with respect to security of supply.

5.1 Case Study 1

As part of their overall water supply strategy review, which includes initiatives on resource risk, resource management and optimised system operation, Severn Trent identified potential security of supply capital schemes with a total value of around £150m. Tynemarch were commissioned to develop and apply a quantified risk analysis methodology to aid scheme prioritisation, involving identifying and ranking security of supply risks, and evaluating and prioritising associated schemes.
The Severn Trent strategic system is shown in

Figure 1. The system is characterised by water treatment works, supplied by two principal rivers - the Severn and the Trent - and impounding reservoirs in the Elan and Derwent Valleys, with connectivity provided by the 'Grid' system of aqueducts and trunk mains. A set of strategic reservoirs on the Grid enhance the security for District-based demand.

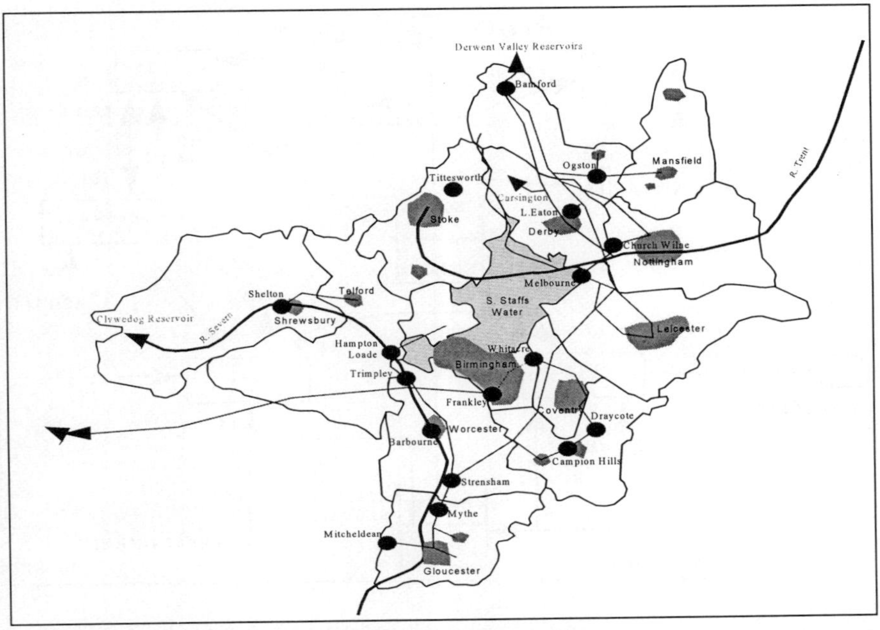

Figure 1. Severn Trent Strategic Water Supply System

Potential hazards were first identified through expert panel meetings, network analysis modelling and judgement, and included mains failures, surface asset failures, pollution incidents and electricity supply failures. Probability and duration data were collected from a multitude of sources, including Severn Trent historical records, expert panels (through questionnaires and interviews), previous reports and databases, in combination with literature reviews, in-house databases and public databases. Mathematical models were created where necessary, for example, to simulate river pollution events, based on information about discharge sites, past closures, river travel times, pulse attenuation data and so on.

A high-level allocation model of the strategic network was generated for consequence modelling (section shown in Figure 2). Key aspects of the strategic system in terms of the consequences are incorporated including production limits, Grid transfer capacities and strategic storage capability.

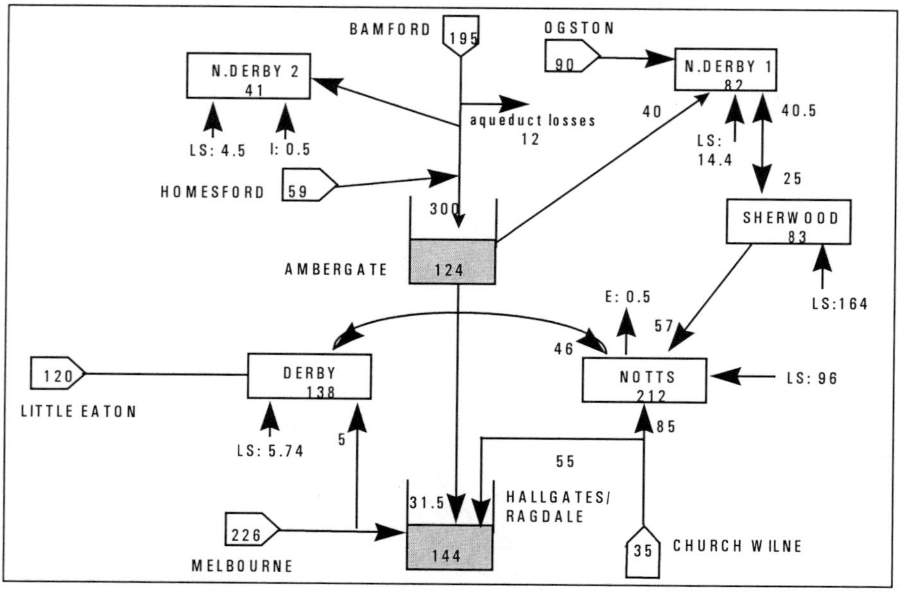

Figure 2. Section of Strategic System Allocation Model

A methodology was established for summarising information about District demands and reservoir storage based on "population/duration curves" describing the population affected against time under zero District inflow, through consideration of the local storage, demands and operational capability. The curves are applied in consequence modelling together with the modelled inflows to determine the resultant population affected and duration of effect in each District.

The chosen objective function used to simulate operational response is:

$$\text{Min} \sum_{i=1}^{N} \frac{p_i}{t_i}$$

where: N is the total number of population/duration curve steps

p_i is the population affected by a supply interruption in each step

t_i is the time following failure occurrence after which p_i is affected

The results of the risk analysis enabled ranking of failure events in the Region according to risk index. Subsequently, a degree of manual sorting of the schemes was carried out and areas requiring greater focus identified. One significant result was that a number of events which might have intuitively been regarded as being associated with low risk, owing to their low probability, were identified as carrying relatively high risk due to their potentially extremely severe consequences. As a result, a number of additional schemes were identified increasing the total value under general consideration to around £230m.

Further risk analysis was carried out with alternative schemes and sets of schemes in place to establish the impact of alternative schemes on the risks and to generate the risk index/cost graph (Figure 3). Scheme numbers are identified beside each significant reduction in risk. There are a number of important features to note on this graph, including:

- The level of risk drops rapidly initially and is halved at an investment of around £8m.
- Further risk reduction is achieved at a lower rate for higher investment levels with step-drops in risk where risk-effective schemes come into effect.
- About 10% of the overall level of risk is not affected by any schemes at any level of investment up to £50m.

The graph has been found to be an invaluable aid to decision-making, both in terms of assessing the level of investment required and identifying which schemes generate the most cost-effective reduction in risk. For example, many proposed schemes considered worthwhile on a subjective assessment of risk actually deliver little risk-reduction benefit and would represent a poor investment if executed.

Sensitivity analysis was used in combination with the risk/cost graph to identify how variations in underlying failure data might affect the results, particularly for rare events for which failure data are scarce. It was found that, even for 200% and 50% variations in the probabilities of significant failures for example, there was little change to the results.

Further results are being produced to review additional measures of quantifying risk, such as estimated business cost to provide a direct "cost versus cost" basis on which to assess investment options. This business cost is established from historical records on failure costs and a theoretical consideration of the direct costs (such as compensation payments) and indirect costs (such as share price falls or loss of further business). An example of the expected type of output is indicated in Figure 4, showing failure cost (£/year) against scheme cost, and sum of failure and scheme cost against scheme cost for which the lowest point indicates a cost minimum and potentially suitable point for investment.

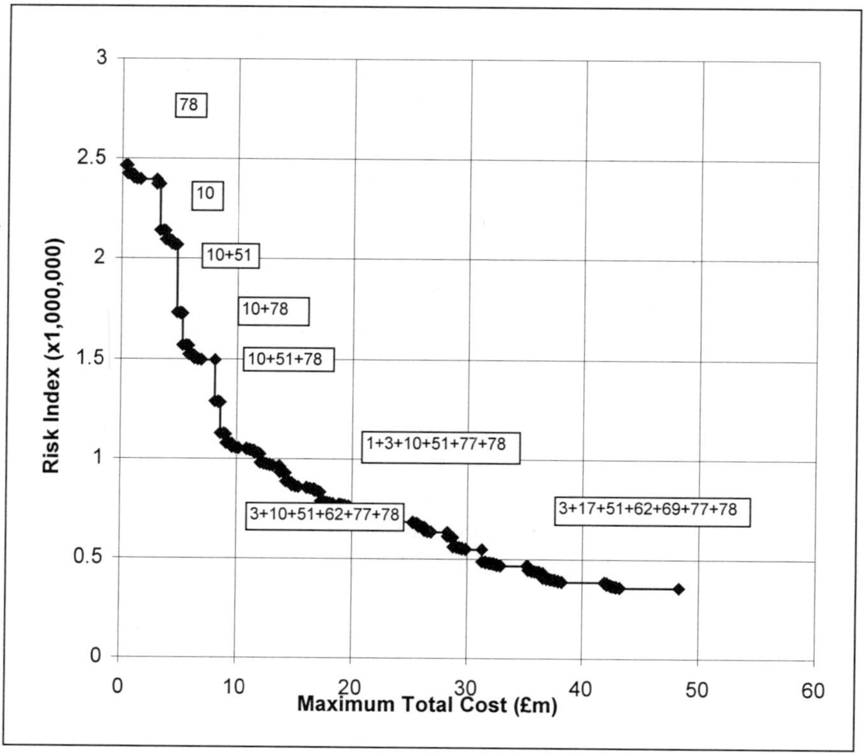

Figure 3. Variation in Risk with Capital Expenditure

The results have helped Severn Trent to focus attention on cost-effective schemes and currently the methodology is being applied by the client to assess different options for the identified schemes. Maintenance and use of the QRA methodology is carried out by Severn Trent Water using software tools provided, ensuring further successful application of the methodology.

5.2 Case Study 2

Tynemarch were commissioned to carry out detailed risk analyses of three important reservoirs within the Severn Trent area due for replacement or refurbishment to assess the security of supply risks associated with alternative replacement or additional storage options. One of the schemes relates to the provision of temporary storage whilst refurbishment of a strategic reservoir is carried out. The total value of potential options in the studies ranges from £3m to £12m. The studies evaluated other schemes in addition to changes in reservoir storage, such as increased network flexibility via new mains, or by reduced source optimisation to increase prevailing buffer storage.

The studies required generally greater detail of modelling than at the strategic level, owing to the lower ratio of failure duration to reservoir empty times under consideration. For example, in the failure analysis, data were obtained as described in Case Study 1, but lower duration failures were also of concern such as short-term power failures.

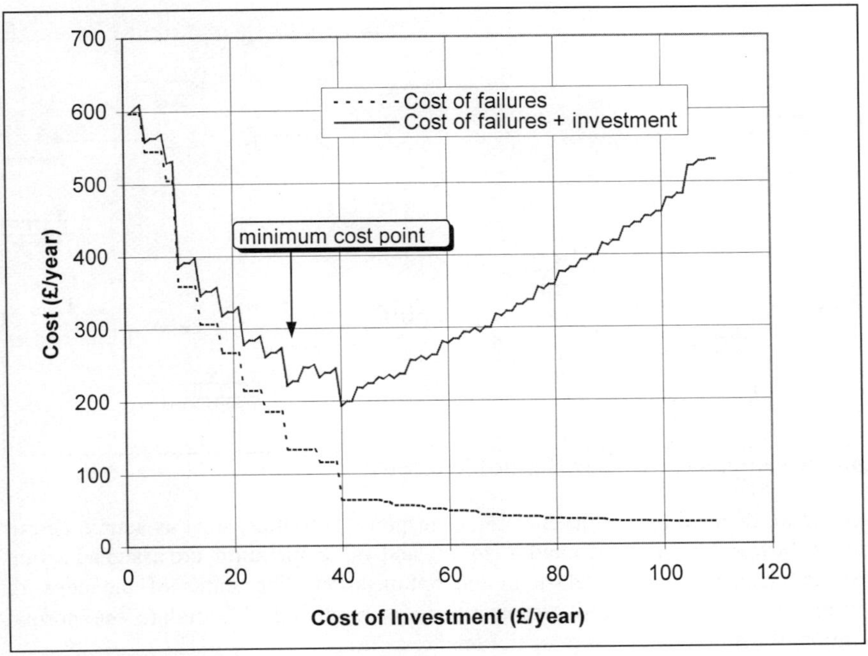

Figure 4. Cost of Failure Against Cost of Schemes

In consequence modelling, an allocation model is used as illustrated in Figure 5. All storage, demands and sources are explicitly modelled. Links between these nodes are modelled with their relevant maximum carrying capacities. These links can either represent actual mains or, as shown here, the summarisation of all available links between each node.

A timestep approach was used in the optimisation to reflect the more detailed approach required. A single optimisation is carried out for each Monte Carlo trial, and results are obtained for the flows, reservoir levels, demands and population affected in each timestep. As in the strategic study, the optimiser aims to minimise the populations affected as a result of a failure event and to maximise the time until failure occurs, based on the objective function:

$$\text{Min} \sum_{i=1}^{N} p_i \left(N - i + 1\right)$$

where: p_i is population affected in timestep i

N is the total number of timesteps

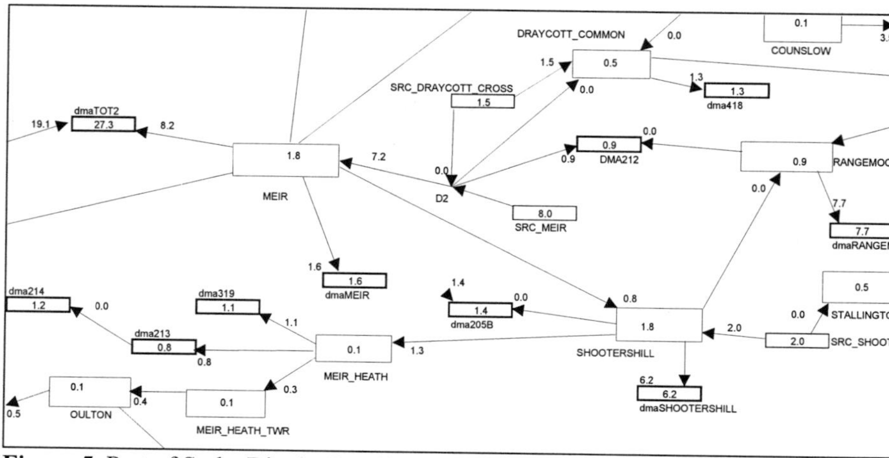

Figure 5. Part of Stoke District Detailed Risk Model

In this more detailed approach, operational response activities, such as source output changes, flow propagation, demand re-zoning and valve operation, are assigned action times and incorporated as delays in the optimisation. The status of the network between point of failure and response time is modelled to simulate the normal operation of the network prior to operational response.

One significant outcome of consequence modelling has been the collection of knowledge from operations and the definition of actual operational capability based on experience. Furthermore, the modelling has focused attention on areas where there is uncertainty of network capability, providing an impetus for testing prior to actual failure.

These studies are currently in progress, with the objective of identifying the variation in risk with alternative reservoir storage volumes and other schemes. Initial results indicate that storage requirements at all three reservoirs are significantly lower than were expected, indicated by levels of risk not falling with increasing reservoir storage. In some areas, alternative schemes provide far more cost-effective reductions in risk.

These results will subsequently be used in connection with the storage needs for factors other than risk, such as pumping head and demand variations, to determine the overall storage requirement.

As a result of this work, Severn Trent are wishing to expand the detailed models to encompass other areas of the Region for further risk analysis, and are looking to develop the models to provide operational response assistance in the event of an actual network failure.

6. Closing Remarks

All water utility companies are anxious to improve customer service but at the same time have limited but large capital budgets available. QRA provides a logical route to prioritising expenditure aimed at delivering the biggest benefit to the largest number of people for each pound spent.

Significant cost savings can be made by carrying out a detailed QRA study to identify and prioritise required capital expenditure. Where schemes have high costs as in the case studies described above, such detailed analysis can identify significant savings which can be justified objectively and subjected to scrutiny through sensitivity analysis.

The case studies presented demonstrate that subjective decision-making cannot be relied upon to deliver efficiency in investment and that the use of conventional wisdom alone would lead to wasteful use of limited capital. QRA provides an opportunity to optimise investment decisions, freeing up cash to be spent on solving level of service problems rather than over-engineered solutions.

Acknowledgements

The case studies described in this chapter were commissioned by Severn Trent Water Limited, and the authors wish to thank Tony Stead and Graham Woodhouse of Severn Trent Project Planning and Promotion for their continuing involvement and commitment.

Section 2

Simulation, Control and Optimisation

CHAPTER 5

A Unifying View on the Different Looped Pipe Network Analysis Algorithms

E.Todini

Abstract

Following an overview of the methods used for the steady-state flow analysis of water distribution networks, a very general formulation of the problem is provided together with a discussion on the convergence of the algorithms employed in the search for the solution. For the sake of simplicity, the problem of analysing a looped-mesh network is defined on the absence of pumps, valves and other concentrated dissipation devices, which may, however, be introduced without affecting the substance of the results. After showing that the problem can be formulated as the solution of a system of equations, partly linear and partly non-linear, the chapter goes on to analyse various available methods based on the linearisation of the original system. The most widely used algorithms for the analysis of looped networks, which are practically all based upon the application of iterative Newton-Raphson schemes, and can be distinguished according to the space of the state variables used as unknowns, are analysed and compared in terms of their efficiency and their robustness. An extremely simplified example is then used to demonstrate the assertions made.

1. Introduction

The analysis of a looped water distribution network, operating under pressure and in steady flow conditions, can be accomplished once the topology of the network, the geometry of the pipes, the discharges delivered at the nodes and the head value of at least one node are known.

Historically, the search for the most efficient algorithm, or rather the one which offers the most rapid convergence, has the lowest computational requirements and is the most "robust", i.e. able to reduce the number of cases in which the search for the solution fails, stretches over a period extending from the application of local linearisation methods in the 1930s [2] right down to the present day and the development of global linearisation techniques, i.e. techniques applied to all the equations in the system simultaneously.

Probably the most comprehensive approach to the problem is the one set out by Collins et al. [4], entailing definition of the "content" model, i.e., definition of a functional in terms of discharge flowing through the branches of the network, or of its dual model (the co-content) in terms of head values at the nodes. The network analysis problem is accordingly reduced to the search for the minimum of the functional (either in terms of discharge in the branches or in terms of head at the nodes) which is performed by means of numerical least-squares techniques such as those proposed by Collins et al. [4] and by Contro and Franzetti [5], or alternatively by solving the system of equations in terms of the discharge and head values, as shown by Todini and Pilati [17].

This second way of addressing the problem is in effect much more traditional since, historically, the study of water supply networks proceeded directly from the setting of continuity equations at the nodes and steady flow equations in the branches of the network, thereby arriving at a system that is partly linear and partly non-linear, the solution of which produces the discharge and head values.

The search for the minimum solution of the content model by means of mathematical programming algorithms is particularly laborious, given the large number of variables present in real cases; therefore an efficient search for the solution of the analysis problem can be performed by the application of numerical techniques for the linearisation of the equations of the system derived from the content model.

Given the convexity of the content functional, which guarantees the existence and the uniqueness of the solution, linearisation of the non-linear equations can be performed efficiently by means of the Newton-Raphson gradient techniques, reducing the problem to the iterative solution of a system of linear equations, and accordingly a variety of algorithms have been developed which differ from each other in terms of the unknowns used in the differentiation of the original system.

Basically, four different algorithms are available in the literature, which characterise the solution algorithm, according to the unknowns selected:

1) All the pipe discharges Q, totalling n_p the number of pipes, and all the head values at the nodes H, totalling n_n the number of nodes, giving rise to the algorithm which is referred to as the Newton-Raphson Global algorithm [G] [17]; [13]; [15].

2) The pipe discharges Q, totalling n_p in number, causing the head values at the nodes H to disappear by means of appropriate linear transformation, giving rise to the algorithm known in the literature as the Linear Theory algorithm [LT] [18].

3) The loop discharge quantities $Q^{\#}$, totalling n_l the number of closed loops, after appropriate linear transformation to re-project the original problem on the closed loops, giving rise to the algorithm referred to as the Newton-Raphson Loop algorithm [L]. Specifically, this algorithm can be seen as an extension of the Cross method from local (loop by loop and iterative) to simultaneous (all the loops at the same time) [7]; [8].

4) The head values at the nodes H, totaling n_n in number, causing the reach discharges Q to disappear by means of appropriate non-linear transformation, giving rise to the algorithm which is referred to as the Newton-Raphson Head algorithm [H] and is known in the literature as the Newton-Raphson Nodal algorithm [11]; [16]; [12].

These algorithms share the common characteristic of having to solve a system of linear equations several times in order to arrive, iteratively and by means of successive approximations, at the solution of the original system of partly linear and partly non-linear equations. However, the size of the linear system to be solved and the information that has to be provided to formulate it or to identify a first-attempt solution required to initiate the iterative process vary according to the method chosen.

Todini and Pilati [17] have shown that the Linear Theory and Newton-Raphson Loop algorithms can be obtained by a simple linear transformation of the more general Newton-Raphson Global algorithm (once the original system has been differentiated with respect to all the discharge quantities Q and all the head values H in order to perform the Taylor series expansion). They also showed that although this latter algorithm apparently leads to the solution of a larger size system of equations (N_P+N_N), in reality it translates into the search for solutions of a system of equations of size N_N, thus offering considerable computational advantages compared with the Linear Theory algorithm. Using the Newton-Raphson Global algorithm, considerable simplifications can be gained in the description of the network, which at the same time can accept closed or open loops, as well as in the fact that a first-trial solution is not required (as is the case with the Linear Theory algorithm), but is automatically calculated at the first step, while the Newton-Raphson Loop algorithm produces the smallest linear system matrix to be solved at each iteration.

Different considerations apply to the Newton-Raphson Head at Nodes algorithm, since it is derived from a non-linear transformation of the variables of the original system that modifies its functional links. The transformation to non-linearity form lies at the root of a series of problems with the Newton-Raphson Head at Nodes algorithm, which have already been reported in the literature by Lamm and Wolla [9], Lemieux [10], Donachie [6], Mignosa [12] and which can be summarised as follows:

- Marked dependence of the convergence rate on the initial solution.
- Slowness or absence of convergence on the solution, or only at the cost (which, however, slows down convergence compared with the other methods).

These two problems can be reduced by applying a relaxation coefficient at each Newton-Raphson step, as proposed by several authors [16]; [9]; [10]; [6]; [12].

2. A GENERAL MATHEMATICAL FORMULATION

Following the formulation given in Todini and Pilati [17], in very broad terms and, as has been said, without considering - for the sake of simplicity though without compromising the substance of this chapter - such special devices as pumps, valves and other dissipation elements [14], and assuming that a monomial expression is used to define head loss along the ith pipe of the network, such as:

$$f_i(Q_i) = \beta_i Q_i |Q|^{n_i - 1} \tag{2.1}$$

where:

β_i is a head loss coefficient which depends on the roughness, diameter and length of the pipe

n_i is the exponent which takes account of the flow regime and of the dependence of the roughness coefficient on discharge, and which has a value of approximately 1 for laminar flow and approximately 2 for turbulent flow.

A network comprising n_p pipes with unknown discharge, n_n nodes with unknown head and n_0 nodes with known head can be described by the following system of equations:

$$\begin{bmatrix} A_{pp} & A_{pn} \\ A_{np} & 0 \end{bmatrix} \begin{bmatrix} Q \\ H \end{bmatrix} = \begin{bmatrix} -A_{p0} H_0 \\ q \end{bmatrix} \tag{2.2}$$

where:

$Q^T = \left[Q_1, Q_2, \cdots, Q_{n_p}\right]$ is the $\left[1, n_p\right]$ vector of the unknown pipe discharges

$H^T = \left[H_1, H_2, \cdots, H_{n_n}\right]$ is the $\left[1, n_n\right]$ vector of the unknown nodal heads

$H_0^T = \left[H_{01}, H_{02}, \cdots, H_{0n_0}\right]$ is the $\left[1, n_0\right]$ vector of the known nodal heads

$q^T = \left[q_1, q_2, \cdots, q_{n_n}\right]$ is the $\left[1, n_n\right]$ vector of nodal demands

In equation (2.2) A_{pp} represents an $\left(n_p, n_p\right)$ diagonal matrix whose elements are defined as $A_{pp}(i,i) = \beta_i \left|Q_i\right|^{n-1}$, while $A_{pn} = A_{np}^T$ and $A_{p0} = A_{0p}^T$ are topological incidence sub-matrices, of size $\left[n_p, n_n\right]$ and $\left[n_p, n_0\right]$, respectively, derived from the general topological matrix $\bar{A}_{pn} = \left[A_{pn} \vdots A_{p0}\right]$ of size, $\left[n_p, n_n + n_0\right]$, the definition of which is the following:

$$\bar{A}_{pn}(i,j) = \begin{cases} 1 & \text{if flow of pipe } i \text{ enters node } j \\ 0 & \text{if pipe } i \text{ is not connected with node } j \\ -1 & \text{if flow of pipe } i \text{ leaves node } j \end{cases} \tag{2.3}$$

If all the n_i equal 1, as in electrical circuits, the solution of the system (2.2) is immediate since it consists solely of linear equations. However, the exponents n_i are always greater than or equal to 1, and in general, since a turbulent regime is assumed, they are approximately equal to 2. It is therefore necessary to solve a system of non-linear equations and the most general problem takes the form of an iterative search for the solution of the linearised system by Taylor series expansion [17], i.e.:

$$\begin{bmatrix} NA_{pp} & A_{pn} \\ A_{np} & 0 \end{bmatrix} \begin{bmatrix} dQ \\ dH \end{bmatrix} = \begin{bmatrix} dE \\ dq \end{bmatrix} \tag{2.4}$$

with N an $\left(n_p, n_p\right)$ diagonal matrix whose elements are defined as $N(i,i) = n_i$.

The solution of the problem is therefore obtained iteratively by solving the following system of linear equations at each step:

$$\begin{bmatrix} dQ \\ dH \end{bmatrix} = \begin{bmatrix} NA_{pp} & A_{pn} \\ A_{np} & 0 \end{bmatrix}^{-1} \begin{bmatrix} dE \\ dq \end{bmatrix} \tag{2.5}$$

where the differentials may be approximately substituted for in discrete form as:

$$dQ = Q_k - Q_{k+1}$$
$$dH = H_k - H_{k+1}$$
$$dE = A_{pp} Q_k + A_{pn} H_k + A_{p0} H_0$$
$$dq = A_{np} Q_k - q$$

starting from an initial guess solution for $k = 0$, k being the index of the iteration step, which does not necessarily have to satisfy the equilibrium or congruence conditions.

Thus, the solution provided by the Newton-Raphson Global algorithm, which allows the value of the unknowns at the (k+1)-th step to be calculated as a function of the known value at the (k)-th step, is[17]:

$$\begin{aligned} [H_{k+1}]_G &= -\left(A_{np} N^{-1} A_{pp}^{-1} A_{pn}\right)^{-1} \left[A_{np} N^{-1}\left([Q_k]_G + A_{pp}^{-1} A_{p0} H_0\right) + \left(q - A_{np}[Q_k]_G\right)\right] \\ [Q_{k+1}]_G &= \left(I - N^{-1}\right)[Q_k]_G - N^{-1} A_{pp}^{-1}\left(A_{pn}[H_{k+1}]_G + A_{p0} H_0\right) \end{aligned} \quad (2.6)$$

Apparently, therefore, it is a case of solving, several times, a system of linear equations of a size equal to all the unknowns involved, i.e. the n_n head values at the nodes and the n_p pipe discharges. In reality it is easy to verify that equation (2.6) requires, at each step, the solution of a system of linear equations of size n_n equal to the number of unknown head values at the nodes [17].

If one defines the loop incidence matrix M_{pl} as the (n_p, n_l) matrix with the following properties:

$$M_{pl}(i,k) = \begin{cases} 1 & \text{if flow of pipe } i \text{ flows clockwise in loop } k \\ 0 & \text{if pipe } i \text{ does not pertain to loop } k \\ -1 & \text{if flow of pipe } i \text{ flows anti-clockwise in loop } k \end{cases} \quad (2.7)$$

by making appropriate use of topological properties which join nodes, branches and loops in a network, namely $A_{np} M_{pl} = 0$ and $A_{0p} M_{pl} = 0$, it is possible to re-project the system of equations given by (2.2) onto vector bases different from the original base of size $n_p + n_n$. In this way one arrives first at the formulation of the Linear Theory algorithm where, by making the unknown head values at the nodes disappear:

$$[Q_{k+1}]_{LT} = [Q_k]_{LT} - [dQ_k]_{LT} = [Q_k]_{LT} - \begin{bmatrix} M_{lp} N A_{pp} \\ A_{np} \end{bmatrix}^{-1} \begin{bmatrix} M_{lp} A_{pp} [Q_k]_{LT} \\ A_{np}[Q_k]_{LT} - q \end{bmatrix} \quad (2.8)$$

and expressing the problem as a function of the sole pipe discharges, the solution of a system of linear equations of size n_p is obtained. By means of a further linear transformation given by $[dQ_k]_L = M_{pl}\left[dQ_k^{\#}\right]_L$ it is then initially possible to formulate the problem in terms of the n_l unknown loop discharges $\left[Q^{\#}\right]_L$ and thereby arrive at the solution of a problem whose size is equal to the number of independent loops n_l, which is generally much smaller than the number of pipes and the number of nodes, to give:

$$[Q_{k+1}]_L = [Q_k]_L - [dQ_k]_L = [Q_k]_L - M_{pl}\left(M_{lp}\, N\, A_{pp}\, M_{pl}\right)^{-1} M_{lp} A_{pp} [Q_k]_L \quad (2.9)$$

With respect to the last two algorithms [LT] and [L] described above, it is useful to point out that they are directly derived by means of linear transformations from the more general [G] algorithm, and therefore, apart from rounding errors, they will follow exactly the same succession of solutions, as will also be demonstrated by means of the numerical example below. In addition it is important to note that the rapidity of convergence is virtually independent of the initial solution, and that, as far as the first two methods are concerned, this initial solution does not necessarily need to be balanced at the nodes.

The issue becomes more complex in the case of the $[H]$ algorithm, since the non-linear link between the functions and the unknowns; this time the n_n head values at the nodes is of the type:

$$g(H) = \Delta H^{1/n} \quad (2.10)$$

Following the derivation given in [1], the non-linear system of equations to be solved in this case is expressed in terms of the nodal head as:

$$G_H\{H\} = 0 \quad (2.11)$$

Accordingly, the aim is to show that, in this case, the iterative method derived by several authors [9, 12, 16] from the application of the Newton-Raphson procedure is no longer the best in that it generates an alternating type of convergence. What is obtained is:

$$[H_{k+1}]_H = [H_k]_H - [dH_k]_H = [H_k]_H - J_H\{H_k\}^{-1} G_H\{H_k\} \quad (2.12)$$

where $J_H\{H_k\}$ is the Jacobian of $G_H\{H\}$ with respect to H at iteration step k.

It is easy to show that in the $[H]$ scheme, there is an alternating convergence with positive and negative corrections, as has been reported by various authors [6]. This process is dampened and convergent (albeit very slowly because of the alternation) if the actual solution is sufficiently large in absolute value, whereas there is practically no convergence at all if the solution is very close to zero.

The explanation lies in the fact that whereas in the case of the preceding algorithms the non-linearity consisted of a functional link of the unknowns with an exponent n greater than 1, and therefore the derivatives are still non-linear functions of the unknowns with exponent $(n-1)$ greater than zero, in the case of the system of non-linear equations from which the $[H]$ algorithm is originated, the derivatives have a functional link with head differences of the type $(1/n-1)$ which is unquestionably negative and tends to generate over-corrections at each gradient step. It is because of this over-abundance of the corrections generated by the form of the derivatives that it is also necessary to start the search procedure at a point not too distant from the actual solution, creating a greater dependence of the number of iterations on the value of the first-attempt solution.

The modified $[H]$ scheme proposed by several authors [16]; [9]; [10]; [6]; [12], which will be denoted as $[H]^{\#}$ is given in equation (2.13):

$$[H_{k+1}]_{H^\#} = [H_k]_{H^\#} - [dH_k]_{H^\#} = [H_k]_{H^\#} - \vartheta \times J_{H^\#}\{H_k\}^{-1} G_{H^\#}\{H_k\} \qquad (2.13)$$

where ϑ is a relaxation coefficient smaller than one. It will be shown that the performance of the [H#] algorithm is definitely better than the original $[H]$, both in terms of convergence (although it is still slow if compared to the other three, namely $[G]$, $[LT]$ and $[L]$) and in terms of the independence from the initial solution.

3 NUMERICAL EXPERIMENTS

Verification of these assertions was conducted by numerical simulation based on an extremely simple network scheme (5 nodes and 7 pipes) to show that they are independent from the loop complexity. In Figure 1 the schematic representation of the network is shown, while Table 1 shows the relevant data required to make the computational analysis.

The tests performed were:

1 - Network analysis performed using the different algorithms starting with the same initial solution.

2 - Network analysis performed using the different algorithms starting with 100 initial solutions generated at random around the true solution of the problem.

The algorithms compared were the five discussed above, namely $[G]$, $[LT]$ and $[L]$, $[H]$ and $[H]^\#$. For applying the latter, an optimal value for the relaxation coefficient was used, which was found to be $\vartheta = 0.7$.

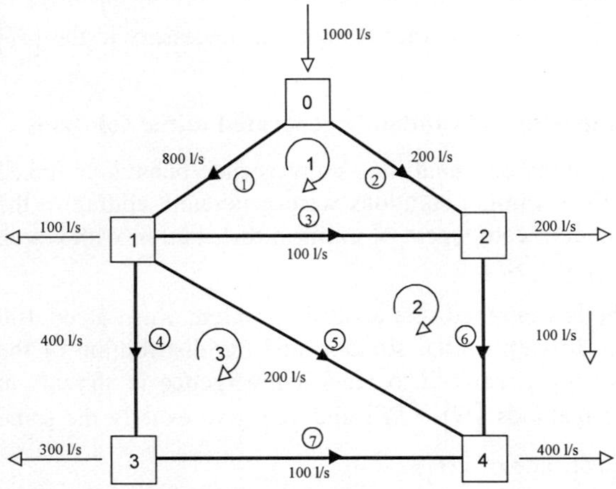

Figure 1 - Schematic representation of the looped pipe network

PIPES	Q [l/s]	β [$sm^{-5}\ 10^6$]	NODES	q [l/s]	H [m]
1	800	1.5625 10^{-4}	0	-1000	100
2	200	0.5 10^{-4}	1	100	99
3	100	0.01	2	200	98
4	400	0.125 10^{-4}	3	300	97
5	200	0.75 10^{-4}	4	400	96
6	100	0.02			
7	100	0.01			

Table 1 - Data relevant to the test case

3.1 Network analysis starting with the same initial solution

Figures 2 to 5 show the trend in the head values at the nodes. Figures 7 to 9 show the corresponding results in terms of nodal discharges and Figures 10 to 16 show the pipe flow discharges, all calculated at the various Newton-Raphson iteration steps.

In all the figures, the solid line represents the behaviour of the $[H]$ algorithm, the dashed line the behaviour of the $[H]^{\#}$ algorithm, while the dotted line describes the identical behaviour of the other three algorithms, namely $[G]$, $[LT]$ and $[L]$.

From the figures, superiority in terms of stability and of rate of convergence of the latter three is quite evident: the final solution is reached with the required accuracy in 7 steps against the 24 of the $[H]^{\#}$ scheme and the 60 iterations necessary in the $[H]$ scheme.

3.2 Network analysis starting with 100 randomly generated initial solutions

With a view to generalising this study and analysing convergence behaviour linked with the initial solution, 100 different initial solutions were generated, adding to the true solution of the problem a random component of uniform distribution with a zero average and falling within a range of ± 50 m.

Next, for each of the five methods examined, the analysis problem was solved 100 times, starting each time with a different initial solution and the distribution of the histogram of the number of iterations required to reach convergence is shown in Figure 17. Once again the three methods $[G]$, $[LT]$ and $[L]$ give exactly the same results and perform better than $[H]^{\#}$ and of $[H]$.

These experiments indisputably show the greater dependence of the $[H]$ method on the initial solution with a wide spread of the number of iterations that can reach 110 iterations, even in the case of the extremely simple network analysed.

A marked improvement in behaviour can be seen when using the $[H]^{\#}$ algorithm using the optimal value for ϑ: the number of iterations now centres around 23-24 iterations with a modest dispersion between 22 and 25; however, it should be stressed that the optimum parameter for one network is not necessarily the optimum for another.

Finally one should appreciate the optimal performance of the other three algorithms $[G]$, $[LT]$ and $[L]$ that shows a narrow histogram around 6 with a minimum dispersion of 5 to 7 iterations.

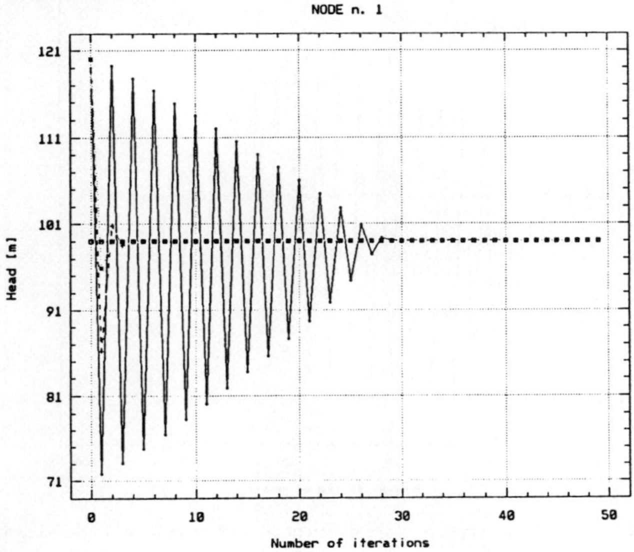

Figure 2 Node 1 convergence of the different algorithms in terms of nodal head H
[H] Solid line
[H#] Dashed line
[G] = [LT] = [L] Dotted line

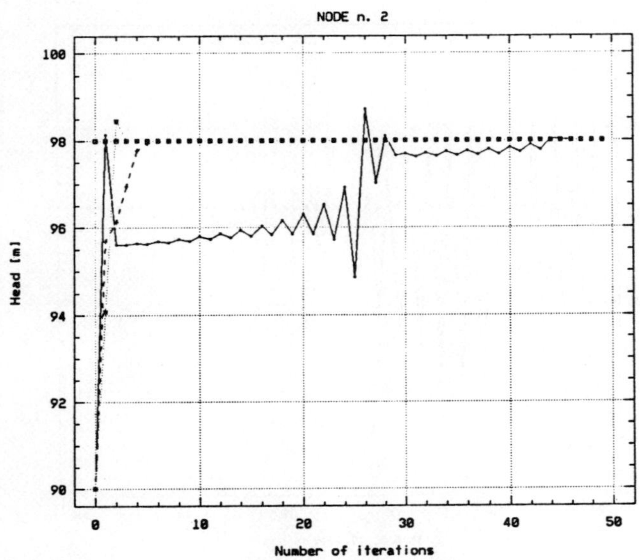

Figure 3 Node 2 convergence of the different algorithms in terms of nodal head H
[H] Solid line
[H#] Dashed line
[G] = [LT] = [L] Dotted line

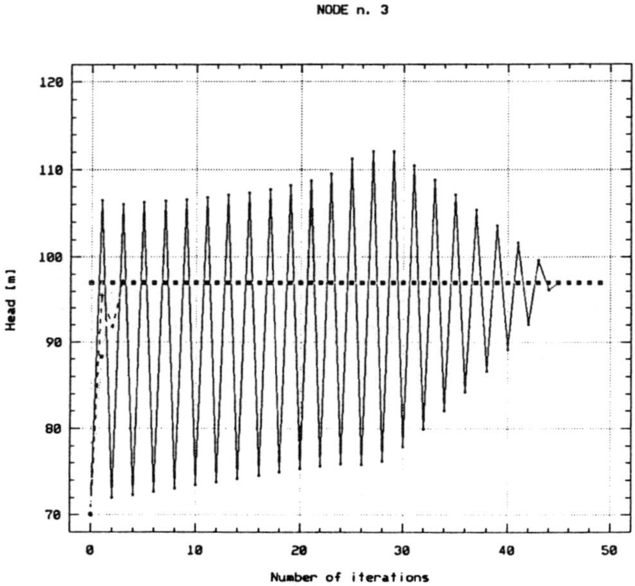

Figure 4 Node 3 convergence of the different algorithms in terms of nodal head H
[H] Solid line
[H#] Dashed line
[G] = [LT] = [L] Dotted line

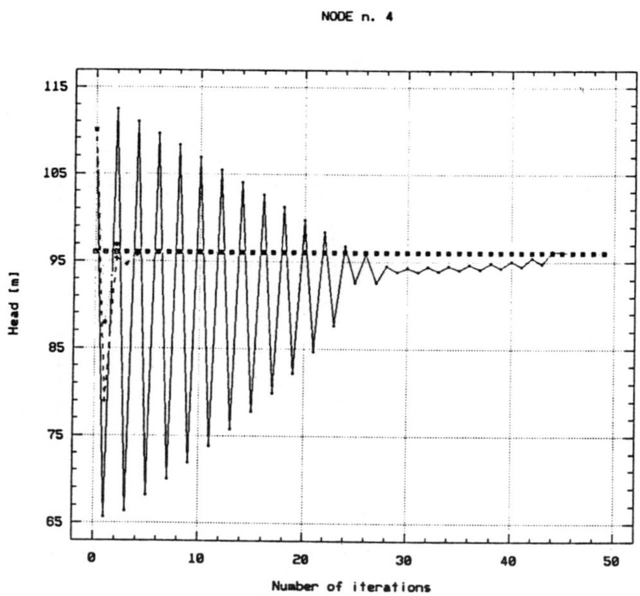

Figure 5 Node 4 convergence of the different algorithms in terms of nodal head H
[H] Solid line
[H#] Dashed line
[G] = [LT] = [L] Dotted line

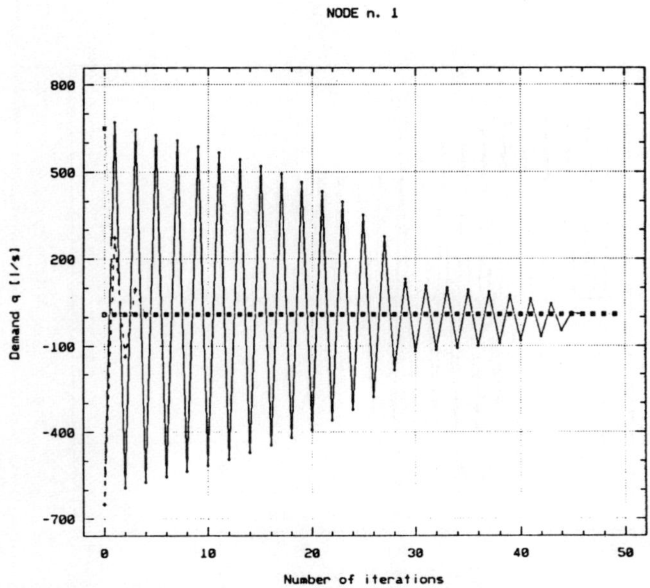

Figure 6 Node 1 convergence of the different algorithms in terms of nodal discharge q

[H] Solid line

[$H^{\#}$] Dashed line

[G] = [LT] = [L] Dotted line

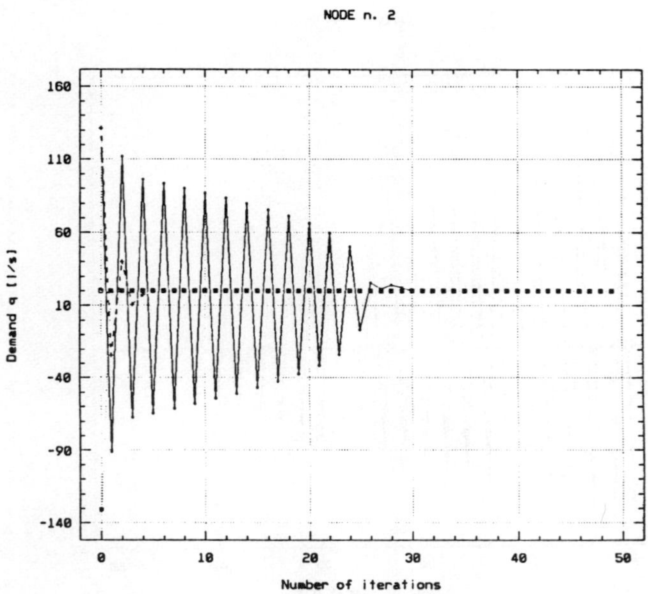

Figure 7 Node 2 convergence of the different algorithms in terms of nodal discharge q

[H] Solid line

[$H^{\#}$] Dashed line

[G] = [LT] = [L] Dotted line

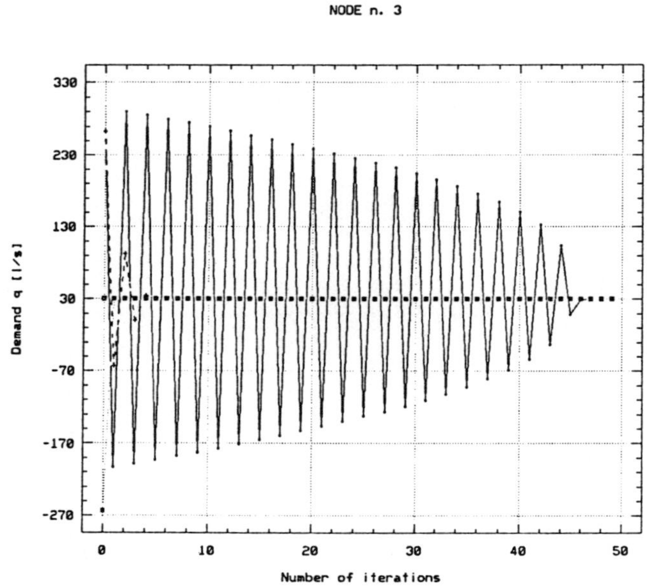

Figure 8 Node 3 convergence of the different algorithms in terms of nodal discharge q
[H] Solid line
[$H^{\#}$] Dashed line
[G] = [LT] = [L] Dotted line

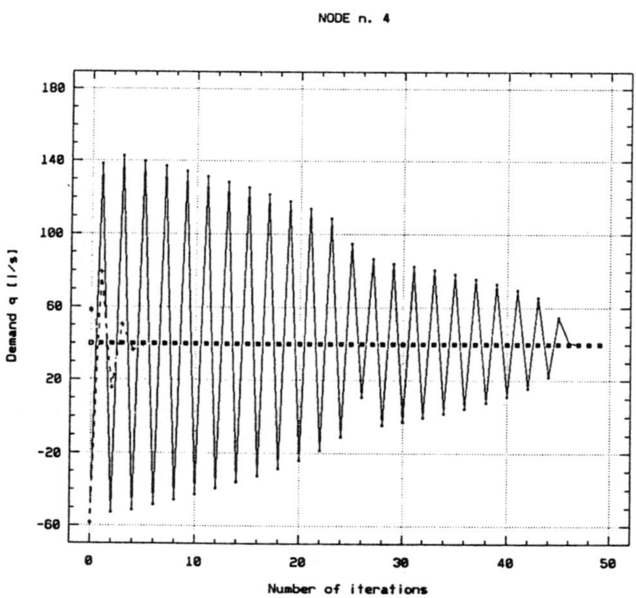

Figure 9 Node 4 convergence of the different algorithms in terms of nodal discharge q
[H] Solid line
[$H^{\#}$] Dashed line
[G] = [LT] = [L] Dotted line

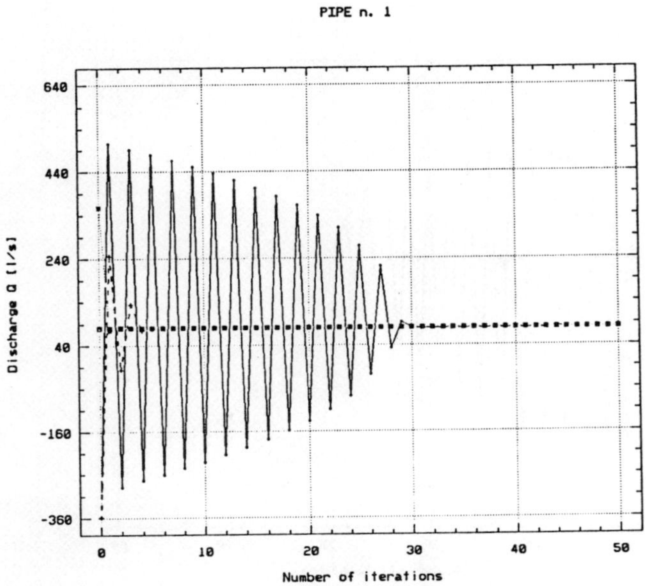

Figure 10 Pipe 1 convergence of the different algorithms in terms of pipe discharges Q

[H] Solid line

[H#] Dashed line

[G] = [LT] = [L] Dotted line

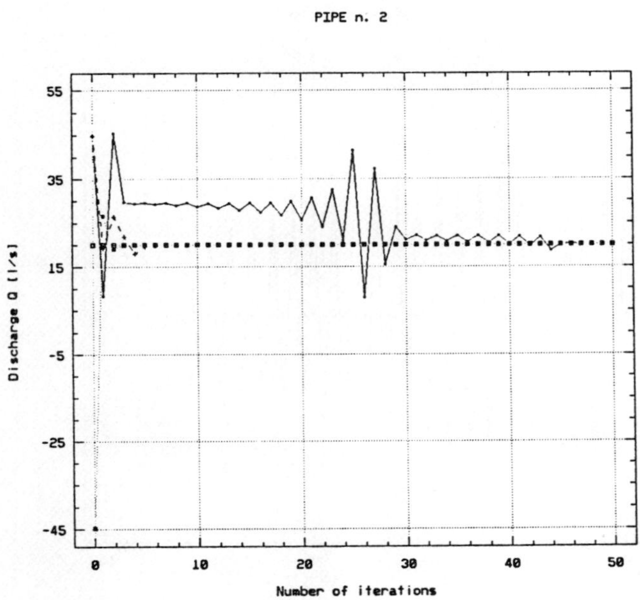

Figure 11 Pipe 2 convergence of the different algorithms in terms of pipe discharges Q

[H] Solid line

[H#] Dashed line

[G] = [LT] = [L] Dotted line

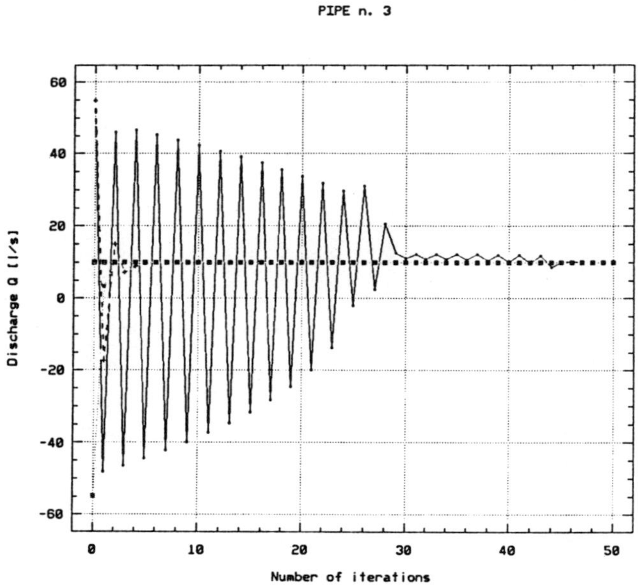

Figure 12 Pipe 3 convergence of the different algorithms in terms of pipe discharges Q
[H] Solid line
[H#] Dashed line
[G] = [LT] = [L] Dotted line

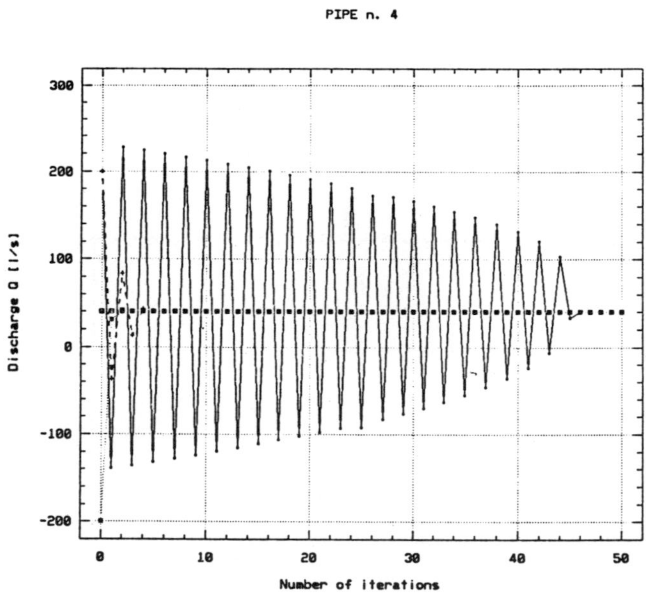

Figure 13 Pipe 4 convergence of the different algorithms in terms of pipe discharges Q
[H] Solid line
[H#] Dashed line
[G] = [LT] = [L] Dotted line

PIPE n. 5

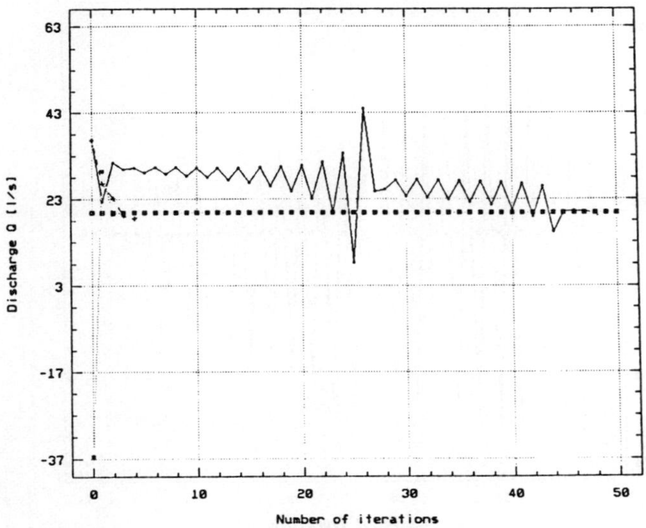

Figure 14 Pipe 5 convergence of the different algorithms in terms of pipe discharges Q

[H] Solid line

[H#] Dashed line

[G] = [LT] = [L] Dotted line

PIPE n. 6

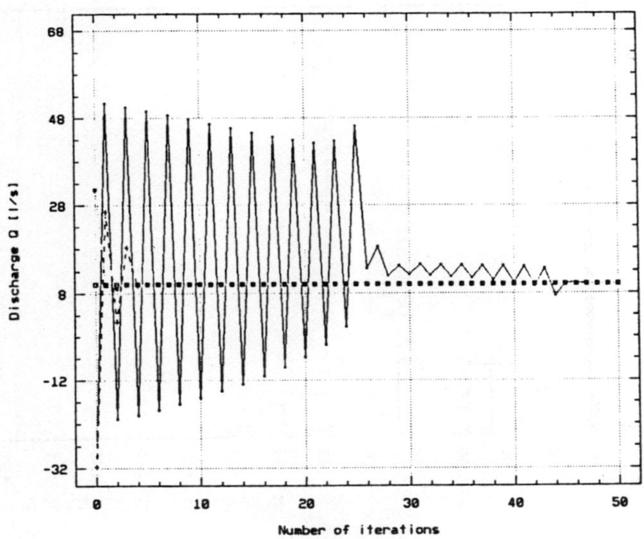

Figure 15 Pipe 6 convergence of the different algorithms in terms of pipe discharges Q

[H] Solid line

[H#] Dashed line

[G] = [LT] = [L] Dotted line

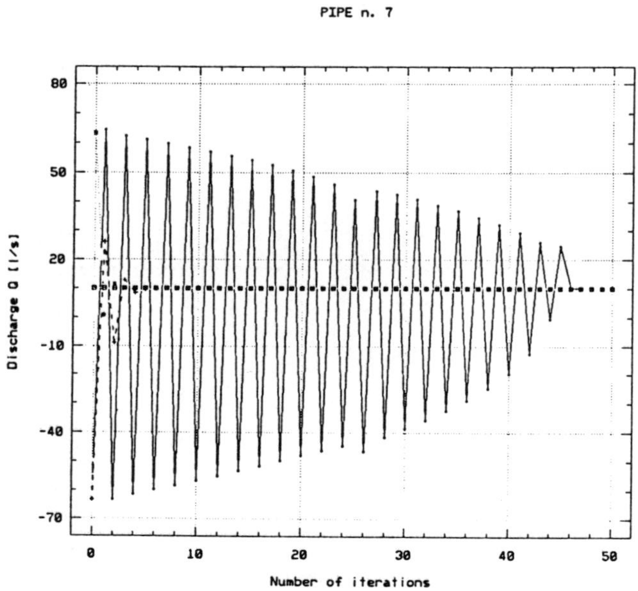

Figure 16 Pipe 7 convergence of the different algorithms in terms of pipe discharges Q
[H] Solid line
[H#] Dashed line
[G] = [LT] = [L] Dotted line

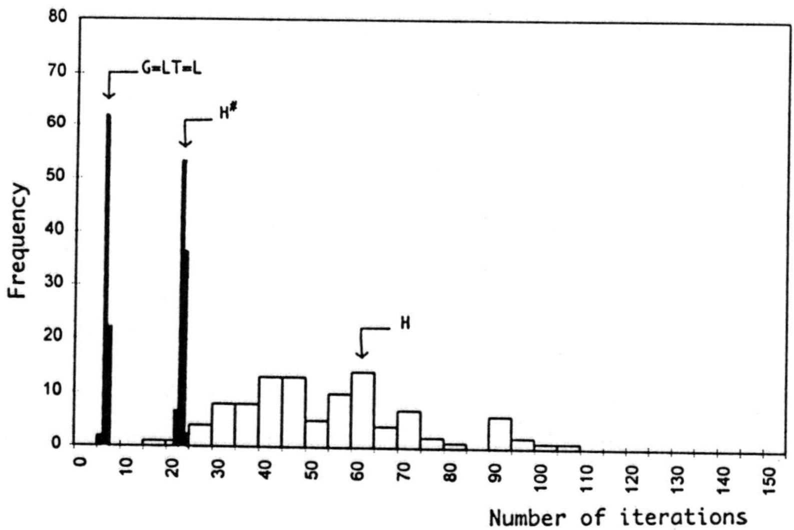

Figure 17 Frequency histograms of the number of iterations necessary to reach convergence from randomly generated initial guess solutions

4. Conclusions

The findings of the theoretical analysis performed by comparing five of the most frequently used Newton-Raphson methods for the analysis of closed loop water distribution networks are confirmed by the numerical simulations conducted using an extremely simple network scheme.

The numerical tests show that the first three methods, i.e. the Newton-Raphson Global, the Linear Theory and the Newton-Raphson Mesh methods are absolutely identical, in terms of convergence. Moreover, the tests show the inherent inadequacy of the Newton-Raphson Head at Nodes method, which generates a poorly conditioned problem because of the functional link with the unknowns, while improved results, although still poorer than those obtainable with the previous three, can be reached with its relaxed version.

Thus, the final choice is between the Global method and the Mesh method, since the Linear Theory method, which produces a system of linear equations with a larger non-symmetrical matrix is not efficient in computational terms.

Given that the Loop algorithm produces the smallest size system matrix it is the belief of the author that it is the one to be preferred, provided that the need for a balanced initial guess solution can be overcome and that the input data requirements remain the same as for the Global method. This implies the need for developing a pre processor of the topological network matrices (the incidence matrices) to automatically produce the linear transformations necessary to reduce the original problem to its Loop formulation, and the automatic derivation of the balanced first guess solution, in a manner similar to what was advocated by Carpentier et al. [3].

References

[1] Artina S. and Todini E. (1990): “Sulla convergenza dei metodi di verifica delle reti di distribuzione idrica a maglie” (in Italian), IDROTECNICA n. 4: 185-192.

[2] Cross H. (1936): "Analysis of flow in networks of conduits or conductors", Bulletin no.286, University of Illinois Engineering Experimental Station, Urbana Illinois, USA.

[3] Carpentier P., G. Cohen and Y. Hamam (1987): "Water Network Equilibrium Variational Formulation and Comparison of Numerical Algorithms", from Computer Applications in Water Supply, Volume 1 (System analysis and simulation), John Wiley & Sons.

[4] Collins M., L. Cooper, R. Helgason, J. Kenningston and L. LeBlanc (1978): "Solving the pipe network analysis problem using optimization techniques", Management Science, Vol. 24.

[5] Contro R. and S. Franzetti (1983): " A new objective function for analysing hydraulic pipe networks in the presence of different states of flow", Meccanica.

[6] Donachie R.P. (1974):"Digital Program for Water Network Analysis", Journal of the Hydraulics Division, ASCE, Vol.100: 393-403.

[7] Epp R. and A. G. Fowler (1970): "Efficient Code for steady-state flows in networks". Journal of the Hydraulics Division, ASCE , Vol. 96, No. HY1

[8] Kesavan H.K. and M. Chandrashekar (1972): " Graph-theoretic models for pipe network analysis". Journal of the Hydraulics Division, ASCE , Vol. 98

[9] Lamm C.F and M.L. Wolla (1972): "Computer Analysis of Water Distribution Systems": Part I - Formulation of Equations, Journal of the Hydraulic Division, ASCE, Vol. 98: 335-344; Part II - Numerical Solution, Journal of the Hydraulic Division, ASCE, Vol. 98: 447-460.

[10] Lemieux P.F. (1972): "Efficient Algorithm for Distribution Networks", Journal of the Hydraulics Division, ASCE, Vol.98, pp.1911-1920.

[11] Martin D.W. and G. Peters (1963): "The application of Newton's method to network analysis by digital computers" IWES Journal.

[12] Mignosa P. (1987): "Sui problemi di verifica delle reti di distribuzione idrica complesse". Idrotecnica, n.2:257-273.

[13] Salgado R., E. Todini and P.E. O' Connell (1987): "Comparison of the gradient method with some traditional methods for the analysis of Water Supply and Distribution", from Computer Applications in Water Supply, Volume 1 (System analysis and simulation), John Wiley & Sons.

[14] Salgado R., E. Todini and P.E. O' Connell (1988): "Extending the gradient method to include pressure regulating valves in pipe networks", International Symposium on Computer Modelling of Water Distribution Systems, Lexington, Kentucky USA.

[15] Salgado R. (1988): "Computer modelling of water distribution networks using the Gradient Method", Ph.D. Thesis, University of Newcastle Upon Tyne, UK.

[16] Shamir U and C. D. D. Howard (1968): "Water distribution network analysis". Journal of the Hydraulics Division, ASCE , Vol. 94, No. HY1.

[17] Todini E. and S. Pilati (1987): "A gradient method for the solution of looped pipe networks", from Computer Applications in Water Supply, Volume 1 (System analysis and simulation), John Wiley & Sons.

[18] Wood D.J. and C. O. A. Charles (1972): "Hydraulic network analysis using linear theory". Journal of the Hydraulics Division, ASCE, Vol. 98, No. HY7.

CHAPTER 6

Hydraulic Modeling for Water Distribution Systems

C-H.Orr *and* P.F.Boulos

Abstract

Model automation requires proper coordination and integration of modeling capabilities and information management. This chapter discusses some of the central issues in the integration of sophisticated solution modules with planning, design, and implementation of an advanced hydraulic modeling information system. The chapter also discusses the concerns in model development and its extended applications. Overall considerations are targeted for both water system management and operations.

1. Introduction: Information and Modeling

The water utility industry is under increasing pressure to reduce costs and expand services within a framework of reducing capital, shortages in water supply availability, and continuously aging infrastructure. Coupled with the rapid surge in regulatory activities and public demand for improved quality services, faster response times, and cheaper charging rates, water utilities are confronted with the challenge of dealing with competing objectives of achieving more with less resources. Whilst the capital allocation for a water utility covers a broad range of facilities, the water distribution system itself often necessitates the largest capital investment. Since water distribution systems generally account for more than 80 percent of the capital associated with water utility investment, there is much to be gained by more efficient planning, management, and control of these systems.

In the recent years, hydraulic network models have already become an integral component in water distribution systems planning, operations, and management. Water utility personnel today use network models to solve a variety of hydraulic problems. Through their analytical nature and predictive capabilities, these models provide a powerful tool for making informed decisions to support many organizational decisions, programs, and policies from both short-term operational applications to longer term management planning. Hydraulic modeling has become essential for optimizing the use of existing facilities, ensuring proper levels of services, reducing operating costs, determining future facility requirements, and addressing water quality distribution issues.

Network modeling requires a large amount of data from various sources, including: network infrastructure, facilities available, operations rules, consumer characteristics and respective consumption patterns, fire-flow requirements, energy consumption and corresponding energy and power charging rates, and water quality data from both source sampling to laboratory test results. Such a large number of data sets is often difficult to assemble and manage. Modern water utilities have adopted advances in computing technologies and have been engaged in development and implementation of various databases for these types of data. A number of information systems have emerged and been applied successfully in their respective application areas, such as Consumer Information System (CIS), Geographic Information System (GIS), Supervisory Control and Data Acquisition System (SCADA), Maintenance Management System (MMS), and Laboratory Information System (LIMS). The desirable optimal water distribution management model is a decision support platform which not only integrates the various sources of data information with the hydraulic modeling capabilities, but also makes the best use of these available data and predictive modeling results in the support of planning, operations, and management of the utility systems. Such an integrated network modeling management environment must provide considerable flexibility in handling and managing a large amount of data from diversified sources, and it should also be supported with user-friendly decision support tools for effective information manipulation and extraction. So far, this effort has seen limited success.

Whilst highly sophisticated numerical algorithms and models have been proposed for use in water distribution network analysis and optimization, less success has been experienced with regard to the development of an integrated modeling environment and application of such a platform in the solution of engineering problems. Such limited acceptance has primarily been caused by the lack of comprehensive data integration among various information sources and modeling packages. It is further limited by the lack of appropriate information display and efficient data manipulation facilities at a user-friendly level, amenable to general water utility operation. Without the support of these fully integrated data and information management tools, numerical modeling packages often do not reflect the context in which water distribution decisions are made by practicing engineers and system planners. Water utilities are currently seeking more effective information management solutions that will share enterprise-wide information from the common organizational databases. An immediate objective for modern hydraulic model development is to implement an automated, computerized method of transferring the data from a variety of data sources to the network model, and to integrate such data resources with modeling capabilities in effective decision support for decision making in utility water distribution.

Information systems have adopted both computer technologies and data management advances to greatly facilitate and automate many of the data compilation and management duties critical in effective network modeling. Central to information management is a data storage and management system. Relational databases and associating relational database management systems (RBDMS) have been widely used in the water utility industry to maintain demand consumption data, network asset data, and system operation data. Such data management information systems effectively eliminate data duplication and data redundancy. In addition, they also provide an organized means of access to organizational data and greater flexibility in data modeling for engineering applications.

A great deal of much needed information for network modeling is already embedded within many existing information systems. A GIS or Computer Aided Design (CAD) system can be used to effectively store and retrieve geographically based information in water map forms, with associated descriptive system facility information. These systems enable the model input and output data to be developed and displayed in a graphical format consistent with the geographical details, generation of accurate data, verification of data integrity, and production of high quality engineering maps. MMS maintains information on pertinent pipelines, pumps, valves, storage tanks, and other water system facilities. The respective operational characteristics of these components can be retrieved for model construction and asset management. CIS contains an information source on individual consumer types, billing records on customer consumption characteristics, and reports of service level status. This amount of information can be extracted for demand modeling as well as performance assessment. A SCADA system compiles both real-time and historical operational data for local facility sites. Such information is useful to define the loading conditions in temporal format for zonal and system demands, and boundary conditions for tank and reservoir water levels, pump status, valve settings, etc., all of which is essential for both basic modeling needs and real-time system assessment. The SCADA output for pressure and flow measurements can also be used in model calibration for both off-line and on-line applications. LIMS provides a centralized repository for laboratory information management for water quality measurements and characteristics pertinent to the distribution system. Such water quality information can be used in conjunction with the hydraulic model performance to assess adequacy of the system quality, which is becoming one of the fundamental concerns to the utilities swamped with waves of stringent regulatory control measures.

Since these information systems constitute the primary data source required for network modeling applications, significant benefits can be gained from integration to leverage information and streamlining water distribution operation and management activities. This integration will minimize cost, improve data application efficiency and accuracy, and increase productivity. In addition, integration of these data resources with numerical models can lead to additional useful information management modules, such as an energy management system in developing optimal operating policies, a hydrant flow testing database for system assessment and model calibration, etc.

Today's open system architecture in computer model development allows for comprehensive multi-level integration. Integrating information management systems with network models, however, can be a significant undertaking. Multi-level integration necessitates a great deal of high-level implementation effort, and the data exchange process must be inherently generic to the various information system databases. In addition, the graphical user-interface must also be intuitive and comprehensive, allowing seamless communication between the various systems. Recently, a number of small-scale integration models have been proposed for use in surface-water modeling, ground-water modeling, storm-water drainage modeling, water quality modeling, and water distribution analysis and design. The developed models were largely customized to perform specific modeling applications and were predicted on an external interface or through direct integration of a GIS, a CAD, or a graphical package to a numerical simulation model. Explicit interface with other information systems is not discussed. A tightly integrated database-oriented model geared towards water distribution network management has yet to gain wide spread acceptance.

This chapter focuses on the concept and development of an advanced management model for water supply and distribution systems. The developed model is called H2ONET [1] and is based on optimizing information flow in conjunction with a full network simulator. Through the linking of a digital mapping and information system to a common database, the model has the ability to freely exchange spatial and operational data and performs all necessary network modeling and management operations. The integrated model provides a powerful platform for water distribution systems management and has been successfully applied to a large number of utility systems throughout the United States and a number of other countries in different continents. The methodology employed is also suitable to other modeling applications in the field of water resources.

2. Basic Methodologies

A number of numerical modules are featured in the modern day hydraulic modeling environment to provide necessary capabilities for a range of application objectives, including but not limited to: strategic planning, design, analysis, operations, control, management, etc. Central to these numerical modules is the hydraulic simulation module. Other desirable modules include the water quality module, energy management module, fire-flow modeling module, etc. In the following, basic methodologies of these modules are outlined.

2.1 Hydraulic Simulation Module

Water systems are modeled as networks of nodes and links. Nodes represent junctions of connections, locations of consumer demands, and supply and storage reservoirs. The nodes are connected in pairs by physical link elements, such as pipes, pumps, and valves.

Demand consumption of different types, such as domestic, commercial, governmental, industrial, office buildings, schools, hospitals, parks and recreation areas, etc., is allocated to individual nodes. Total consumption for a given node $D_i(t)$ for any particular time instant t is described as:

$$D_i(t) = \sum_{demand\_type=1}^{m} d_{demand\_type}(t) \tag{2.1}$$

where $d_{demand\_type}(t)$ = the demand level for the given demand type at the specified time instant. The total system consumption $D_{Total}(t)$ at any particular time instant t is therefore given by:

$$D_{Total}(t) = \sum_{i=1}^{n} D_i(t) \tag{2.2}$$

The primary objective of the water system service is to provide these demands at an adequate pressure level from the available sources and storage through the system pipe, pump, and valve network facility infrastructure.

Network link elements are described by their respective hydraulic characteristics, which are typically non-linear, characterized by:

$$\Delta H_{ik} = f_j(Q_j) \tag{2.3}$$

where ΔH_{ik} = the head difference between nodes i and k, and Q_j is the link flow for the particular link element j. A simplified pipeline hydraulic expression is represented as:

$$\Delta H_{ik} = R_j^{0.54} Q_j \tag{2.4}$$

after the popular Hazen-Williams modeling formulation, where R_j represents the hydraulic conductance. The head increase ΔH_j for pump j can be described by:

$$\Delta H_j = f_j(Q_j, s_j) \tag{2.5}$$

where s_j = speed setting for variable speed pumps. Hydraulic expressions for valves vary according to the modeling of individual valve types.

Most of the applications require an extended time simulation over a given time period, such as 24 hours. The simulation model essentially solves a set of hydraulic balancing conditions between supply and consumption, which are governed by the flow continuity equation at individual nodes i:

$$D_i + \sum_{j=1}^{n} Q_{j(i)} = 0 \tag{2.6}$$

with n link connections, where $Q_{j(i)}$ = flow at link j connected to node i by the energy head equation for any closed network loop e:

$$\sum_{e=1}^{m} \Delta H_e = 0 \tag{2.7}$$

with m link branches, and by the mass conservation principle at individual storage tanks k:

$$\frac{dH_k(t)}{dt} = f_k(Q_k(t)) \tag{2.8}$$

where $H_k(t)$ = change in water levels at individual storage tanks, $Q_k(t)$ = net flow into or out of the tank k at time t, $f_k(.)$ = storage volumetric characteristic and is equivalent to $(1/A_k)$ for regular shaped storage tanks with cross-sectional area A_k. A set of simultaneous equations is then formulated. Various numerical techniques have been developed for the effective solution of the above formulations. Recent implementations have adopted the numerically more efficient Hybrid Method [2],[3]. The basic result set from the solution of the above formulation includes pressure head at individual nodes, link flows at individual link elements, and the new storage levels at individual tanks. This result set provides the basis to derive additional result information, such as nodal pressure, pipe velocity, etc.

2.2 Water Quality Simulation Module

Water quality module is used to simulate the fate of a dissolved substance flowing through the water network over time. The simulation module is typically represented by a one-dimensional transport model, in which instantaneous and complete mixing of material is assumed. Mixing for pumps and valves is assumed to be instantaneous, with an identical concentration between the incoming and outgoing flows. The model is focused on the system pipes. It tracks the fate of the dissolved substance constituent based on individual pipe flow velocities obtained from the hydraulic simulation.

The underlying principle is governed by the mass conservation equation for each pipe. Change in the constituent volumetric concentration $C_j(t)$ for pipe j at time t is described by:

$$\frac{\partial C_j(t)}{\partial t} = \frac{Q_j}{A_j}\frac{\partial C_j(t)}{\partial x} + \Theta(C_j(t)) \tag{2.9}$$

where A_j = constant pipe cross-sectional area, x = the pipe distance along the flow direction, and $\Theta(.)$ = function of the constituent reaction rate for the given pipe. Constituent reaction can occur both within the bulk flow of the pipe and with material along the pipe wall for certain substances, such as chlorine. First order kinetics have been applied to model the constituent reaction function as:

$$\Theta(C_j) = -K C_j \tag{2.10}$$

for pipe j, where K = overall first order decay rate constant, which itself can be expressed as a function of the bulk reaction rate constant, the mass transfer coefficient between bulk flow and pipe wall, and the wall reaction rate constant.

The mass balance principle given in Eq.(2.9) leads to a set of differential/algebraic equations, which can be solved using Lagrangian time-driven or event-driven methods or Eulerian finite-difference or discrete-volume methods [4]. The Lagrangian methods track movements of different water segments of variable sizes along each pipe until a new condition based on either fixed time interval or when a water segment reaches the pipe boundary. Eulerian methods assume equally spaced segments for individual pipes and compute the water transport at fixed time intervals. In particular, the Lagrangian event-driven method is found to be able to provide reliable and efficient means of modeling the water quality transport problem [5]. Dispersive transport can be accounted for using procedures as described in [6]. The solution set constitutes the temporal and spatial distribution of constituent concentration throughout the entire network over the extended time simulation period.

This basis of water quality modeling can be extended to model water age and to perform source tracing. Water age is modeled as substances with zero decay rates. New water entering the system is assigned the age of zero. Water age at a given node can also be interpreted as the time of travel to that particular node. Source tracing is modeled with a the zero reaction term. The source contribution is typically expressed as a percentage with source node concentration value constantly set at 100%. Both water age and source tracing provide another means to assess the water quality distribution in time and space within the given network.

2.3 Energy Management Module

In addition to the hydraulic and water quality performance for the given water network, energy consumption and its effective management is also a concern for system operation. Energy consumption is primarily based on supply and distribution pumping. The pumping power requirement is a function of the hydraulic head and flow of the given pump. The useful water power $P_{u(j)}$ of pump j is described by:

$$P_{u(j)} = \frac{\gamma\, Q_j\, \Delta H_j}{11.827} \quad \text{(in KW)} \tag{2.11}$$

where γ = specific gravity, Q_j = pump discharge flow, and ΔH_j is the pump head increase. The overall pump input power requirement P_j for pump j can then be expressed as:

$$P_j = \frac{P_{u(j)}}{e_j} \quad \text{(in KW)} \tag{2.12}$$

where e_j = the total or overall pump efficiency and is a function of the hydraulic efficiency e_h for the measure of hydraulic friction losses, the mechanical efficiency e_m for the measure of mechanical friction losses, and the volumetric efficiency e_v for the measure of leakage losses, imperfect valve action, etc.

The hydraulic head-flow characteristics of a given pump are described by Eq.(2.5). In general, the overall pump efficiency e_j for pump j can also be expressed as a function of pump discharge flow as:

$$e_j = f_j(Q_j) \tag{2.13}$$

As the discharge flow Q_j is a function of pump speed factor s_j for variable speed pumps, the overall efficiency e_j also becomes an implicit function of s_j.

There are typically two different types of electricity charges associated with water pump operation: the energy unit charge and the maximum power demand charge. Both of these electricity charges can be associated with a time dependent charging rate tariff, which is typically divided into varying peak, normal, and off-peak time periods, etc., each with a different charging rate.

The energy charge is the total operating cost based on individual charging period energy consumption over the duration of the simulation. Essentially, the energy unit charge $M_{u(j)}$ for pump j over U charging periods within the simulation time domain can be modeled as:

$$M_{u(j)} = \sum_{u=1}^{U} \left[m_u \cdot \sum_{k=1}^{K} P_{k(j)}\, \Delta t_k \right] \tag{2.14}$$

where m_u = the energy unit charging rate for the uth charging period, $P_{k(j)}$ = pump power output at the equivalent k^{th} hydraulic time step within the given charging period and Δt_k is the kth hydraulic time step duration within the given u^{th} charging period. The energy unit cost computation is accumulative. Useful information, such as energy cost on per unit volume of water delivered, can easily be derived.

The maximum power demand charge is a penalty charge based on the maximum KW power demand consumption within each demand charge period. The charge is imposed for an extended period, typically a month. For modeling with a shorter time duration, this demand charge term is often modeled as the equivalent cost for that particular simulation period only. The maximum demand cost is computed based on individual charging periods of the same charging type, such as peak time and off-peak time. Essentially, the maximum demand charge $M_{d(j)}$ for pump j over D charging periods within the simulation time domain can be modeled as:

$$M_{d(j)} = \frac{1}{T}\sum_{d=1}^{D}\left\{m_d \cdot \max\left[P_{k(d)(j)}\right]\Big|_{k=1,\dots,K} \cdot \Delta T_d\right\} \tag{2.15}$$

where m_d = the maximum demand charging rate for the dth type charging period, $P_{k(d)(j)}$ = the power demand output at the equivalent k^{th} hydraulic time step for the combined charging period of type d, ΔT_d = combined simulation time period for the same d^{th} type of charging rate within the total simulation period and T = the total billing time period, such as a month.

Modeling of the pump energy and demand costs provides a direct means of measuring the operating costs associated with individual pump sources and/or operational policies. Electricity cost is a major cost factor in the operation of water supply and distribution systems. Attempts have been made in the provision of optimal scheduling control to make more effective use of the cheaper charging periods through intelligent management of system storage and pumping capacity. A successful on-line implementation of such an optimal control scheme in the automation of a city supply system is described in [7].

2.4 System Flow Management Module

Fire-flow simulation is important in the master planning stage for system design. It is also useful for system fire assessment during the normal operating stage and for model calibration. For the purpose of safety protection in drinking water quality, the system-operating condition should be maintained above a threshold pressure level. This is particularly important under the fire fighting condition when the system is under additional demand stress at given locations. The fire-flow management module provides an effective tool for the assessment of system adequacy. In particular, it provides information for: residual pressure under the fire-flow demand, available flow to maintain the minimum pressure at the fire-flow location, and the design flow obtainable at the fire-flow node whilst maintaining the minimum system design pressure at any given critical node.

Three methods have been widely used in conducting computer-modeling analysis of system fire flow. The basic procedure is a manual method based on trial and error. Fire-flow amount is adjusted incrementally at the given node until the corresponding pressure approaches to the system level. The second approach is based on alternating the system configuration by means of introducing a virtual pipe with negligible resistance connecting the fire-flow node of interest to a fictitious source node with a pressure head set at a required system pressure level for the fire-flow node. Whilst the first approach suffers from the burden of lengthy computation with less than accurate results, the second approach suffers the major drawback of fundamentally alternating the network topology.

An explicit numerical approach has been recently introduced [8, 9]. The technique is based on solving the pipe flow equation for the virtual pipe connecting the fire-flow node to a fictitious fixed head reservoir under three different conditions:

1. A static condition where the normal flow Q_s applies to the node, resulting in a pressure head of H_s.
2. A fire-flow condition where Q_a is the available flow at the pressure head of H_a.
3. An intermediate demand flow condition of Q_t with a corresponding pressure head of H_t.

Under these conditions, the available fire flow Q_a at the designated hydrant node location with targeted system pressure head of H_a can be computed from:

$$Q_a = Q_t \left[\frac{H_s - H_a - c(H_t - H_a)}{H_s - H_t} \right]^{\frac{1}{n}} \tag{2.16}$$

where $n = (n \in [1.85, 2.0])$ is the pipe flow exponent depending on the appropriate pipe head-flow relationship, and c = iterative correction factor and is given by:

$$c = \left(\frac{Q_s}{Q_t} \right)^n \tag{2.17}$$

The fire-flow model described by Eq.(2.16) can be applied to extended time period conditions, in which the available fire flow is evaluated for each hydraulic time instant over the fire-flow period as required by the Fire Department. The dynamic nature of this assessment provides a direct measure of the system adequacy for both pumping and storage capacities in times of fire. Multiple fire-flow conditions can also be evaluated simultaneously. The modeling technique can also be extended to evaluate a hydrant performance curve at the fire-flow node of interest. Such a hydrant curve provides the head-flow relationship between the available flow within the available range of fire-flow pressure.

3. Implementation

Different approaches have been adopted in the design and implementation of software systems. Recent developments in the computer industry have provided much improved power in usability and computability. The changes in these capabilities are rapidly altering the software design and development philosophy, from traditional stand-alone solution-centric applications to system integration and data-centric applications. Selected topics are discussed in this section regarding the basic framework in the development of a modern hydraulic modeling package.

3.1 Basic Software System Architecture

Modern engineering software systems are typically composed of three major software components for: a numerical solution module, a graphical user interface module, and a data management module. The numerical solution module is the kernel to the entire system application. It is focused on providing both an accurate representation of the system model and an efficient solution to the system problem. The graphical user interface module is the shell of the application, providing the application environment for user interaction. It is focused on providing both direct and effective visual information to the users and easy control to manipulate the application data and options. The data management module is the system information repository joining and supporting both the numerical solution and the user interface modules. It is focused on effective and systematic management of the system data needs, serving different requirements based on various user and application schemas.

Essentially, there are two implementation schemes for engineering applications with comprehensive database support and graphical user interface interaction. These are: the embedded scheme and the coordinated scheme. The primary distinctions between these schemes can be found in the use of data in each case and the degree of coupling among individual modules. The embedded scheme is a tightly coupled implementation with modeling data directly embedded together with application data management and interface application. All modules share the same copy of primary data within the application environment. The coordinated scheme decouples the use of data among individual application modules. The data management module through interaction with the user interface module maintains data sets. The numerical model module is supported by data extraction from the database environment.

Tightly coupled implementations enjoy increased efficiency for smaller applications, whereas well managed decoupled implementations enjoy better flexibility and system maintainability, especially for more sophisticated applications. Recent developments in hydraulic modeling packages are in favor of the latter approach. Fig.3.1 illustrates the basic software system architecture for an advanced hydraulic modeling package implementation.

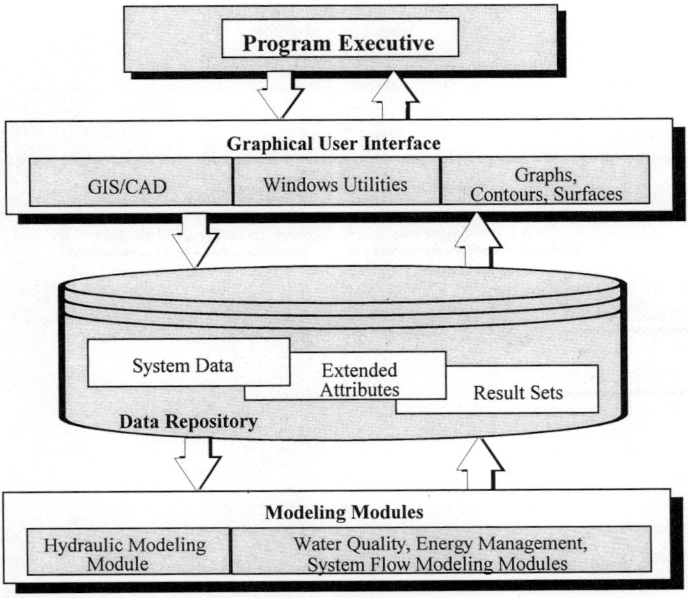

Fig.3.1 Basic modeling software system architecture

The implementation philosophy is based on the coordinated scheme. An advanced graphical platform is used as the primary display and user interaction environment. A separate database management module is incorporated to maintain and support all data application needs. System modeling computation is coordinated with the database for model input data extraction and model result output organization. Overall the application management module closely linked with the graphical user interface platform manages the system application.

As described in Section 2, a range of modeling modules is supported within the modeling environment. Central to all these modeling facilities is the hydraulic simulation module. Other computational modules, such as water quality modeling, energy management modeling, fire-flow modeling, etc. are based on the given hydraulic solution sets. A hierarchical class structure for these computational models is shown in Fig.3.2 in which the system flow class is further exposed for illustration purposes. Such a hierarchical structure is well suited for the object-oriented methodology [10], in which additional computational modules are organized as the derived classes from the top-level hydraulic modeling class. Each of these computational classes has its own implementation derived from the common hydraulic solution functionalities at the hydraulic modeling level. Further discussions in the object-oriented modeling analysis and design are beyond the scope of this chapter.

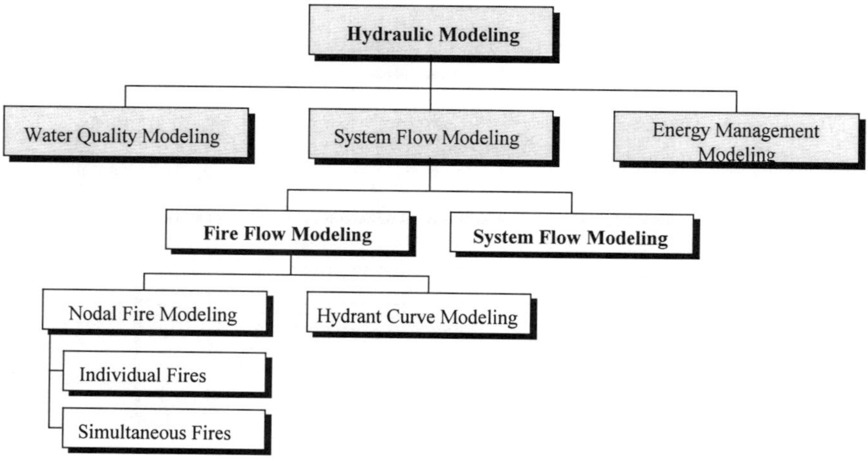

Fig.3.2 System modeling hierarchy

Data requirements for hydraulic modeling are relatively standard. Many of these applications are implemented around the file interface with the hydraulic modeling data sets. Communication between the modeling module and the data management and user interface environments are typically based on a set of input data and result files. Data are extracted from the data management module to form a separate system data input file for the hydraulic model. Computed results are returned as a hydraulic result file in a pre-defined format. Result evaluation can then be coordinated among the user interface and data management modules with this hydraulic result file. Data for other computational modules are managed as optional additional data sections or implemented as supplementary data file input. Similarly, solution results from the advanced modeling options can be returned in conjunction with the hydraulic result set as optional result sections, or returned as supplementary result files.

Traditionally, the graphical user environment was implemented based on standard graphical library standards, such as GKS, PHIGS, GINO, etc. Windowing environment standards such as Windows, Motif, etc., have now been widely accepted, with their respective sets of graphical primitive functions. Advanced hydraulic modeling applications require more sophisticated graphical capabilities and data management support. The use of Geographical Information System (GIS) and Computed Aided Design (CAD) facilities has greatly enhanced the user interface environment. Display of background street maps and exact geographical representation of system facilities can now be well catered for with implicit support from a full set of display attribute functions, such as thickness, size, color, etc. Integrating these enhanced graphical information platforms with comprehensive windowing utilities, such as tabbed dialog data editing facilities, spreadsheet data manipulation, time-series graph display, two-dimensional contours and three-dimensional surfaces, renders the overall user environment a powerful visual information management system.

Relational data technologies have been widely adopted in the data processing community. All current modeling data needs and corresponding result sets are primarily in the numerical format and can easily be implemented using proper relational relationships.

For instance, network components can easily be defined by a set of Node Table, Link Table, Reservoir/Tank Table, etc., in which each component is assigned a unique primary key field. Data tables can be joined based on these primary key fields. Further linkages can be established to enhance the data attribute descriptions beyond the basic modeling needs. The combined modeling data, enhanced data attributes, and modeled result set then provide a comprehensive data information repository from which whole range of data queries can be applied to support various application schemas.

Modeling data are extracted from individual data tables to form a modeling set. Modeling results are returned to the data environment in a pre-defined file format. Snap-shot of the result data can be incorporated into the database result fields. Extended result data can be extracted from the data repository as required. Data queries can be coupled with the user interface to enhance the application capability. Typical applications include: highlighting system facilities based on queries on system data attributes, model result, or both; selection of sub-systems, such as pressure zone division; highlighting system performance, such as spread of water quality with time from a given source in an animated manner, etc. Such informative displays provide direct and effective user focus.

An illustration of the software application is shown in Fig.3.3

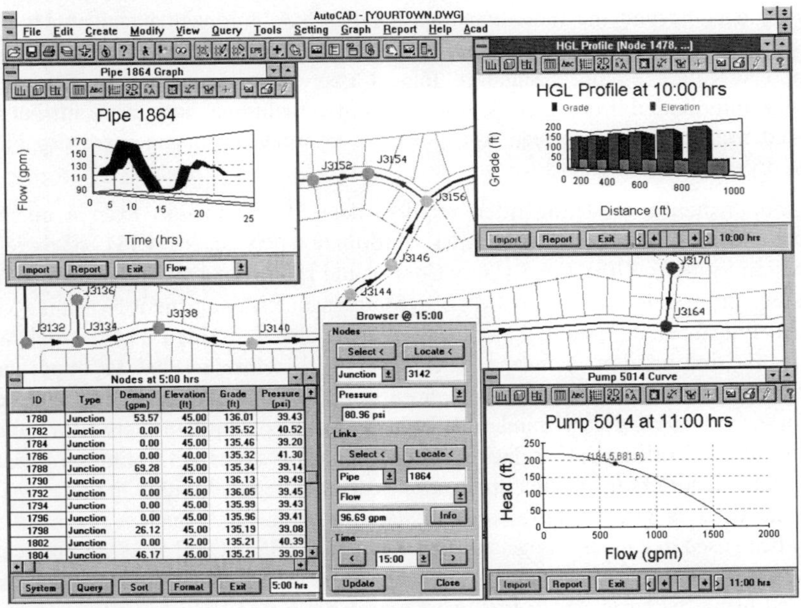

Fig.3.3 Hydraulic modeling application with H2ONET.

The overall application is under the control of the Program Executive. The particular module is closely implemented with the graphical user interface as the latter provides first level interaction with the users. The module is responsible for coordinating various activities among the graphical user interface, the data management environment, and the modeling applications. The coordinated implementation scheme not only greatly enhances the maintainability of the resulting software package but also allows for flexibility and adaptability to changes in user requirements, computing technologies, and research and development works.

3.2 System Model Management and Maintenance

Data have been central to analytical software applications. Several issues have been of concern when using engineering software. These include:

- Effective use of available data within current system definition.
- Data exchange with external applications.
- Selection of sub-systems for system applications.
- Support and maintenance of different operating condition sets.

Current implementation adopts a coordinated architecture, with modeling and user interface components decoupled from the data management module. A relational database management system is incorporated as the central information repository environment for modeling, user interaction, and graphic presentation. The data management module only selects relevant information to support individual data processing activities. Such a data-centric approach has the much-desired flexibility in managing data beyond the modeling requirements. Additional data attributes can be easily added to respective data relational tables, thus enhancing the available information for application processing. Standard logical query statements are used to retrieve necessary information from this central repository, including both data attributes and simulated results. All these lead to a powerful information management capability to support diversified user needs.

Successful hydraulic modeling often requires derived information from a number of different sources, including Customer Information Systems (CIS), Geographical Information Systems (GIS), Supervisory Control and Data Acquisition System (SCADA), Laboratory Information System (LIMS), Maintenance Management Systems (MMS), [11]. Analytical results from hydraulic modeling are also desirable for other applications. An effective information exchange mechanism is therefore needed to import and/or export the required information among various applications. An open data architecture with non-proprietary industry-standard storage and data exchange formats allows the user to access the network modeling data in other software systems with minimal translation effort. Data identifiers from other applications can be integrated within the relational data tables and used as primary keys to facilitate data exchange. Such a mechanism has already been used in data exchange among a number of GIS, SCADA, MMS applications. In addition to data field exchange between databases, data exchange can also be facilitated using the basic ASCII text and Comma Separated Values (CSV) formats, and through the standard Windows clipboard to interface with a range of productivity applications.

It is often desirable to focus modeling works on a portion of an established system model, such as separate pressure zones, main trunk supply system, network skeletonization, etc. These sub-systems are part of the same model and share the same system components with the overall system description. Creation of parallel system projects will inevitably lead to system redundancy and difficulties in model maintenance. Sub-system modeling is essentially an extraction mechanism allowing users to select sub-networks from the overall network definition based on a number of criteria, such as pressure zone, different node/link identifications, pipe size, etc. Extraction procedure is based on queries to the central database and can be derived within the application environment in a number of ways, including direct graphical selection, system facility queries, etc. The extracted model forms a higher level abstract view of the original model without departing from the original modeling environment. Modeling applications can then continue from the extracted level. Such a capability enables system sub-modeling from the overall network model, without creating separate sub-system models. Network extraction can also be saved to separate extraction sets for future use, thus greatly simplifying system model maintenance.

Demand loading and control action represent two areas of operational conditions that concern both design and operations. Various demand loading factors are used for different purposes. In the planning stage, demand forecasting is performed in the evaluation of long term demand trends. For design purposes, demand loading factors for average day, maximum day, peak hour, peak hour on maximum day, etc. are typically used. Demand level also varies during the week, from Monday to Friday and during the weekend, and is also subject to seasonal variation. All these factors should be taken into consideration for daily operation control. Managing a range of demand loading factors has often proved to be one of the most demanding tasks in network modeling applications. A demand management module has been incorporated to provide an organized means to categorize individual demand application cases. Different demand loading conditions can be easily defined as independent sets of demand scenarios, which can then be called upon depending on the application needs.

Operational control involves selection of appropriate pump combinations and valve settings to achieve hydraulic balance, to maintain service levels, and to ensure acceptable water quality standard. Hydraulic modeling has provided a useful means to simulate various operational strategies in assessing the system responses under a range of operational profiles. Different pump and valve control policies are applied for individual cases. Such simulation works have proved to be very helpful in the training of operation to cope with operational control from routine daily application to emergency system breakdowns and fire fighting. Traditionally, such experience is incorporated into a set of operation rules used as a reference knowledge base. An operational control management module has been incorporated to enable easy management of such control and operational knowledge. Established control strategies can be saved as various operational control scenarios, and recalled upon individual needs. All these model management utilities have much improved the model maintenance effort in the support of various model applications and different operational conditions.

3.3 System Model Control

In hydraulic modeling, control implies the change of operating status on the network link elements. The most common types of control include: change of the link status between Open and Closed; and change of setting values such as pump speed, valve factors, etc. Traditionally, these controls are governed by basic hydraulic events, such as water levels, pressures, and flows at individual tanks, nodes, links, respectively and/or by simple time events, such as time instants along the simulation time horizon. The switching modes on the link status are activated whenever any such control statements are satisfied for the particular controlled link element. Other implementations have also incorporated time dependent switching values for hydraulic event.

With modeling applications becoming ever more sophisticated, there is a need to improve the control statements for more advanced types of control activities. An attempt of such control implementation has been discussed in [12], in which a set of control statements based on hydraulic and time events are combined together in the logical AND mode with corresponding action sets for positive and negative assertions. This effort represents a major advance towards rule-based type control operation in water network analysis. Such a scheme is further developed here with more comprehensive logical operations and assertion statements, thus extending basic rule-based control into higher level rule-based logical control for water operation.

The rule-based logical control implementation is based on the standard format of the logical statements used in major computer languages. The Conditional Statements are governed by the following keywords: *If*, *Elseif*, *Else*, and *Endif*. Each Conditional Clause governed by the keywords *If* and *Elseif* is referred to as an Assertion Clause and is used in the assertion of the overall logical condition. *Else* is the last conditional keyword to be applied when all preceding conditional clauses are asserted negative. *Endif* is a syntactic keyword used to terminate the overall logical control statement. The Predicate Clause is defined as the basic conditional description for a particular hydraulic or time event condition. Each Assertion Clause is composed of logical combinations of a series of Predicate Clauses using the binary and unary logical operators *And*, *Or*, and *Not*. Also defined for each of these conditional statements is a set of Action Clauses, to be applied when the given conditional clause is asserted positive. Nesting of the conditional statements is not considered in order to distinguish the Assertion Clause from the Action Clause definitions. A typical logical control statement structure is illustrated below:

```
If ( Assertion Clause )
  begin
    Action Clause
    ...
    Action Clause
  end
Elseif ( Assertion Clause )
  begin
    Action Clause
    ...
    Action Clause
  end
Elseif ( Assertion Clause )
  ...
Else
  begin
    Action Clause
    ...
    Action Clause
  end
Endif
```

in which examples of the Assertion Clause are illustrated as:

```
(( Predicate_Clause_1 And Predicate_Clause_2) Or (Predicate_Clause_3))
( Not( Predicate_Clause_1 ) And (Predicate_Clause_2))
```

Typical Predicate Clauses are composed of four key components: qualifier, network element, operator, and value. Supported qualifier types include: Current, Historical Time, and Rate of Change, describing, respectively, the network data value for the assertion to be derived from the current simulated result, the historically simulated result, and the current rate of change of the given network data. The data attribute value or hydraulic result item for a particular network element, such as Node, Tank, Pipe, Pump, and Valve defines the network element field. Typical network element data supported in the logical assertion include: elevation, grade, pressure, demand, time to fill tank level, time to drain tank level, etc. for respective nodes; flow, hydraulic grade difference, head loss, velocity, status, setting, diameter, etc. for respective links; and general system information, such as total system demand, simulation time, etc. Logical operators, such as *Equal To*, *Not Equal To*, *Greater Than*, *Smaller Than*, *Greater Than or Equal To*, *Smaller Than or Equal To* are supported for numerical value field; whereas symbolic operators *Is* are used for the predefined logical symbol field, such as logical values for Open and Closed, Value_Rising and Value_Falling, etc.

Control actions are considered for both link status for all links and potential link settings for all pumps and valves. Typical Action Clauses are composed of three key components: network element, control data type, and new control value assignment. The network link elements are identified by their respective type identifier references. Control data type includes definitions for the link status or setting. New assignment is governed by the new status condition or by an appropriate new setting value. Each Assertion Clause is associated with a set of Action Clauses. The Action section following each Assertion Clause defines the set of appropriate Action Clauses for individual controlled links. Keywords such as *Begin* and *End* are used to indicate the beginning and ending of such statement section definition.

From a structural point of view, a logical control statement is composed of multiple conditional sections joined by the conditional keywords *If*, *Elseif*, *Else*. Each of these conditional sections has its own logical Assertion Clause and an associated Action Clause set. Each Assertion Clause is composed of a number of Predicate Clauses joined by logical operators *And*, *Or*, and *Not*. Both Assertion Clause and Predicate Clause statements are described by their respective regular structural patterns with well-defined data fields. They can easily be represented by regular data class structures.

On the other hand, the Assertion Clause is described by arbitrary logical combinations of any number of Predicate Clauses. Under these circumstances, it is no longer appropriate to represent such descriptions using regular data class structures. A logical data representation is required. Since all Predicate Clauses are joined by binary operators *And*/*Or*, the resulting logical clause can be best represented by a binary tree. With potential qualification using the unary operator *Not* on individual Predicate Clauses, the binary tree can be considered as a 2nd degree logical tree. Fig.3.4 illustrates a 2nd degree tree structure for a logical statement of:

```
(Not PC1 And PC2) And ((Not(PC3 Or PC4) Or (PC5 And PC6))
```

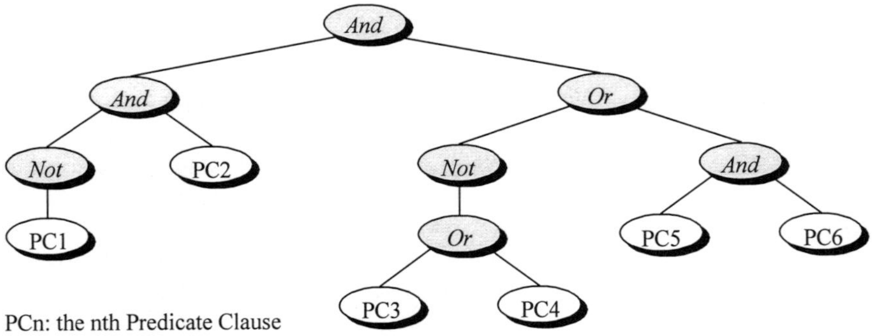

Figure 3.4 The 2nd degree logical tree for an illustrated Assertion Clause

in which the nodes are represented by either the Predicate Clauses or governing logical operators. The leaves of the logical tree are filled by Predicate Clauses, whilst the root of the tree is governed by a logical operator. Predicate Clause nodes at child levels are joined by appropriate logical operators at their respective parent levels. The logical relationship can therefore be assessed by traversing the given logical tree in any of the standard pre-order, post-order, in-order, or level-order manners, depending on individual implementation criteria.

Evaluation of the logical control rules is performed using the top-down approach. At appropriate simulation time steps, the logical control set is retrieved. Each logical control rule is expanded into individual assertion statements, which are then asserted accordingly with the following action set. In essence, this is a multi-level execution. The pseudo-code logic of its implementation in C/C++ style is illustrated below, with indentation indicating respective levels of action:

```
//
//
//  ** Process Logical Control Rule Set **
//
get Logical_Control_Rule_set;
//
for ( each Logical_Control_Rule in the Logical_Control_Rule_set )
 {
  get corresponding Assertion_Clause_set;
//
//
//  -- Manage the Assertion Clause Loop -
//
  for ( each Assertion_Clause in the Assertion_Clause_set )
   {
//
//  Assert the Assertion_Clause
//
    Assert the given Assertion_Clause
     {
      get individual logical tree_node_element;
      while ( tree_node_element is not empty )
       {
```

```
          if ( tree_node_element = operator) get Predicate_Clause_operands
          for ( each Predicate_Clause_Operands ) // 1 for unary operations
            {
             get Predicate_Clause_elements;
             check data/result conditions;
             return assertion status, either True or False;
            }
          apply logical operation for corresponding operands;
          process overall Assertion_Clause status, either True or False;
         }
      }
//
//  Perform consequential action
//
     if ( Assertion_Clause == true )
      {
       get corresponding Action_Clause_set;
       for ( each Action_Clause )
        {
         get Action_Clause_elements;
         carry out the action, by changing status/setting;
        }
      }
    }
//
 }
```

In the above illustration, the data object elements are highlighted in the *italic* format, whereas the program function keywords are highlighted using the **bold** style. Comment statements follow the // C++ standard for clarity. Statement sections are paired in the C/C++ open and closed braces {}.

During the implementation, various Action Clauses may apply to the same controlled links, leading to potential conflicts in the resulting status setting for the given links. Different schemes may be applied in resolving such conflicts, ranging from basic Last-In, First-In schemes to user defined Priority Schemes. Both the First-In and Priority schemes require a buffer list to store intermediate information. The Last-In scheme is the most straightforward in its implementation.

The logical control scheme provides the fundamental basis of knowledge management for system control. The control rules are defined using combinational logic, traditionally derived from operational experience. The potential to derive such operational control rules under the current implementation and its extension to interface with an established knowledge base environment would seamlessly integrate the knowledge base and expert system technologies [13, 14] directly with conventional hydraulic modeling as shown in Fig.3.5. Further coupling with a SCADA interface for on-line data update would lead to automation in system operations and control not only in the traditional manner but also in real-time environment. Such extension is again outside the scope of this chapter.

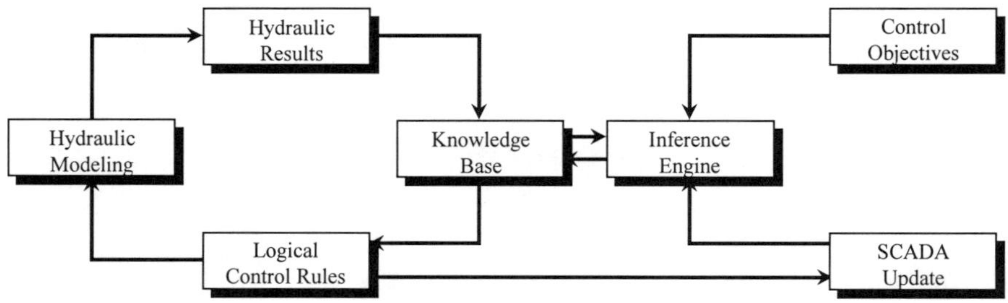

Figure 3.5 Hydraulic modeling and knowledge based systems

4. Applications

Hydraulic models have been widely used for a number of purposes in the recent years, from planning, design, system analysis, to operations control. Successful applications in these areas rely on development of a hydraulic model to accurately represent system behavior. Hydraulic modeling follows a logical progression of events from: collection of baseline data, construction of a facility model, allocation of demands, model set-up, field data acquisition, model calibration, to system evaluation and applications, as shown by the flow diagram in Fig.4.1.

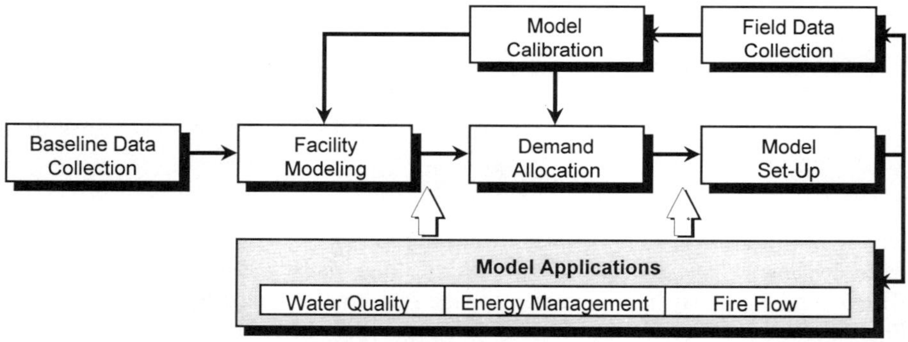

Figure 4.1 Model construction and application process

4.1 Model Development

Baseline information of a given water utility system can generally be derived from a set of engineering water system base maps. The maps typically contain detailed information on pipeline locations, sizes, and materials. They also contain geographical locations for other system facilities, including reservoirs, underground water wells, pump stations, pressure regulating and control valves, etc. This information can be used in conjunction with data gathered and assimilated from other sources, such as geological surveys, to form the baseline information set necessary to develop the facility model.

With the GIS/CAD based graphical environment, the geographical representation of all physical facilities can be digitized into the model. Background street maps, including main roads and landmarks, can also be superimposed for easy reference. System facilities are defined using respective modeling elements. Junction nodes are assigned at both ends of a link. They are used to represent facility installations, pipe junctions, locations where pipes change characteristics (such as size, material, installation age, etc.), and demand locations. Tanks, reservoirs, pipes, pumps, and valves are represented directly using corresponding modeling equivalents. Each of these components is assigned a unique identification key within its data set domain. Such unique identification keys are used in all database applications to distinguish individual components and are used to join pertinent relationships. With appropriate numbering and/or reference schemes, these facilities can be labeled according to different criteria, such as pressure zones, etc. Data attributes, such as pipe diameter, material and age, are entered individually using standard Windows dialog boxes and/or edited as a group using spreadsheet type utilities. Pipe length can be computed automatically based on the digitized map. Valve settings can often be obtained from operations records, whereas pump tests can be performed to obtain the respective pumping characteristics. Nodal elevation information can be obtained from the base maps or derived from geological survey maps. For larger systems, it may be decided to leave out smaller pipes if they do not form part of a hydraulic loop nor connect to the neighboring service areas.

4.2 Demand Allocation

Demand allocation has often been one of the more difficult tasks in successful hydraulic modeling. Demand data are normally defined in both base levels and temporal formats to support static and extended period simulation. Generally, spatial demand levels for typical days are first estimated for all demand nodes. Temporal variations are then adjusted based on representative consumption profiles for individual consumption categories. Knowledge of demand values is typically derived from billing records and estimates of consumer classes in the evaluation of baseline demand levels, and telemetered system flows in the evaluation of temporal changes.

Fundamentally, demand types are divided into a number of classes, such as residential, commercial, industrial, governmental/offices, schools, recreational, and irrigational. Each of these major classes are further divided into a series of sub-classes, such as single-family, multi-family, high density family dwelling classes for residential consumption, etc. Each of these classes has its own unique water needs and share similar demand characteristics within the same class. Therefore, categorization on consumer classes is instrumental in the estimation of appropriate demand values. In addition, it is also customary for the water utilities to document the respective water consumption levels for each demand class as part of the statistical evaluation and regulatory agency requirements. Demand class data are typically derived from consumer population information and local land use characteristics. Census population data have been widely used in defining demand classes and demand distribution. Land use categorization has been part of standard City planning activities and such information can be used to evaluate demand coefficients in terms of each land use category and corresponding land area acreage.

Existing practices in demand allocation involve a series of data evaluation activities: from evaluation of system production level, flow balance between production and storage, division of consumers into a number of demand classes, to estimation of individual demand class population and demand land use coefficients. Large water users such as major industries, schools, parks, golf courses, etc. are identified from billing records and modeled directly with individual demand nodes. Remaining demand nodes are then modeled based on their respective areas of influence from individual demand classes. The population technique can be used to superimpose the estimated population zone over individual demand junction boundaries, whereas the land use technique is used to superimpose the land use boundaries over the demand junction boundaries. To effectively model demand allocation based on these techniques, it then becomes essential to automate an estimation procedure to evaluate the degree of influence from individual demand classes.

In water network modeling, each demand node can be assigned a particular area coverage. Independent of this demand-area assignment, each demand categorization is also associated with its respective area of influence, such as derived from land use representation. Superimposing these areas of influence from the demand categorization over the demand node coverage, it becomes possible to derive the resulting area of influence of individual demand classes upon the given demand node, as given by:

$$D_n = \sum_i a_i D_i \tag{4-1}$$

in which D_n is the demand level for node n, a_i is the percentage area coverage for the ith demand class at the given node, and D_i is the base demand of the particular demand class. Fig.4.2 illustrates a land use division with respect to model demand junction nodes.

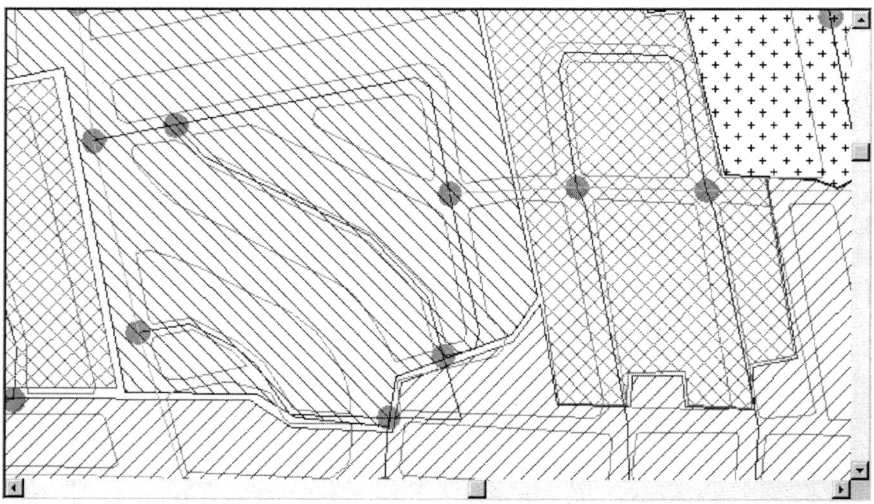

Figure 4.2 Land use areas and demand nodes.

In computational geometry terms, area coverage from both the demand node and demand classes is represented by graphical polygons. The areas of influence between individual polygons are derived from the respective overlapping areas among these polygons. The graphical representation of the demand node areas for the entire system can be viewed from the top master graphical layer, whereas demand type categorization, such as land use areas, etc., can be represented by additional secondary layers. The problem of finding areas of influence can then be described as one of evaluating the degrees of influence of the polygons at the master layer by individual polygons from the secondary layers. Various techniques from polyline tracing and line clipping on intersecting edges between two polygons, pixel based pseudo-screen rendering, to sophisticated vector scan approach in conjunction with multi-dimensional cross-linked list data structure are considered in [15]. With areas of influence and percentages of contribution from individual demand categories found for each node, the base level demand can be evaluated by comparing the relative ratios between the areas of contribution to the total category demands.

In modeling applications, all junction nodes are evaluated for demand allocation consideration. Only those junction nodes appropriate for water demand allocation are categorized as demand junctions. These demand junctions are assigned respective demand polygons, which are selected based on pressure zone boundaries and their proximity to other junctions. These demand polygons are then combined with geographical water use data based on population, land use, existing structures, etc. to enable calculation of the base line water demand evaluation for individual demand junctions. Application experience has demonstrated that such a demand allocation procedure has consistently provided reliable base level demand definitions. Coupled with the representative diurnal demand characteristics from telemetered readings and historical records, demand data can be reliably assigned with individual demand junctions.

4.3 Model Set-Up

Although facility modeling is developed based on static condition, engineering applications often require models to be setup to support extended period simulation, typically 24 hours. Most existing systems are operated under a set of control rules regarding both the pumping strategies and reservoir storage policies. Typically, pump operation can be based on pressure levels and/or operational times during the day. The pump operation is then turned On or Off according to the preset pressure levels and/or times of the day. Conventionally, pumps are turned On when the system pressure is falling and/or when the time has reached the peak demand hours. Pumps are then turned Off when the system pressure is rising and/or when the time has reached the low demand hours. Other considerations, such as energy management criteria, may lead to controlled pumping policies according to the system storage capacity and varying electricity-charging rates for the pumps.

In addition to pumping control, diurnal demand patterns also need to be setup, typically for individual demand categories, from single-family residential, multi-family residential, commercial, light industry, heavy industry, office, school, park and recreation, to irrigation uses. Different categories of consumers at different locations display different water usage characteristics. Development of proper diurnal demand patterns may involve local field surveys and detailed studies.

4.4 Calibration

Hydraulic modeling based on system facilities and historical data often does not give the most accurate representation of the current system operation. A calibration process is used to refine modeling component values to achieve a more accurate representation. The general events in the hydraulic calibration process include:

- Setup the base hydraulic model.
- Perform field-tests on representative days.
- Collect field-test data, typically flows and pressure values.
- Update the hydraulic model with the field test operating conditions.
- Compare corresponding hydraulic model results with field test data.
- Adjust the model parameters where appropriate to achieve better match.

A hydraulic model is considered calibrated for a given set of system conditions if the predicted flows and pressure values from the model match the field data observations with reasonable accuracy.

Some of the most common calibration indicators include:

- Reservoir storage levels : Reservoir storage has often been used to provide a direct indicator for modeling adequacy. The objective is to achieve comparable storage levels during a 24 hour operation.
- Pressure at selected nodes : Nodes downstream from production pumps and nodes with critical pressure levels, such as those from major consumers, are often targeted for field measurement. Nodes with fire hydrants are also chosen for calibration purposes with specially conducted hydrant flow tests.
- Flows at selected links : Pump flow measurement is readily available and therefore is commonly used for system calibration. Other link flow measurements, such as sub-area supply records and main trunk flows, are also often used.

Typical model input data for calibration consideration include: roughness coefficients for the system pipelines, demand allocation, and hydraulic data on many of the system facilities, such as pump and well head-flow characteristics, etc. Normally, static calibration process for selected test hours is performed on adjusting the pipeline roughness coefficients, typically based on information on the pipeline age and material. Demand allocation may require extended period consideration with their diurnal patterns. They are often adjusted under the extended period conditions. The reservoir storage levels, pressure levels, and supply flows are then used as indicators for calibration adequacy. Although over the years various attempts based on numerical algorithms, optimization schemes, and artificial intelligence have been applied with varying degrees of success, such modeling tools for calibration have yet to be developed for regular use.

4.5 Model Applications

With reasonably calibrated hydraulic model, the model can then be used in a number of system evaluation and management applications, such as water quality analysis, energy cost optimization, fire-flow assessment, etc.

Water quality modeling is based on the corresponding hydraulic results. Its capabilities have been applied in evaluation of contaminant tracking throughout the system over an extended period in time, water age and source contribution evaluation at individual nodes, and determination of how water and constituents propagate within the system. Such analytical results can be effectively used in a number of ways, including [16]: prediction of water quality degradation problems, determination of disinfectant residuals, evaluation of water quality aspects in distribution system and storage reservoirs, prediction of disinfectant/disinfection by product growth, design of water quality sampling and flushing programs, siting of rechlorination facilities, optimization of disinfection processes, analysis of blended water properties and management of multi-quality source networks, planning the repair and rehabilitation of existing systems, etc. In addition, water quality modeling can also be used to assess operational alternatives to satisfy contaminant control under regulatory agency requirements.

Energy management can be applied in both the design and operation system. During the design stage, the module enables engineering decisions to select the most cost effective pumping facilities to satisfy both the system hydraulic requirements and efficiency objectives. During the operation stage, the module enables assessment of various pumping policies and selection of appropriate pumping sources to achieve the cost savings based on varying electricity tariffs and storage capacity available. An illustration of the energy management application is shown in Fig.4.3.

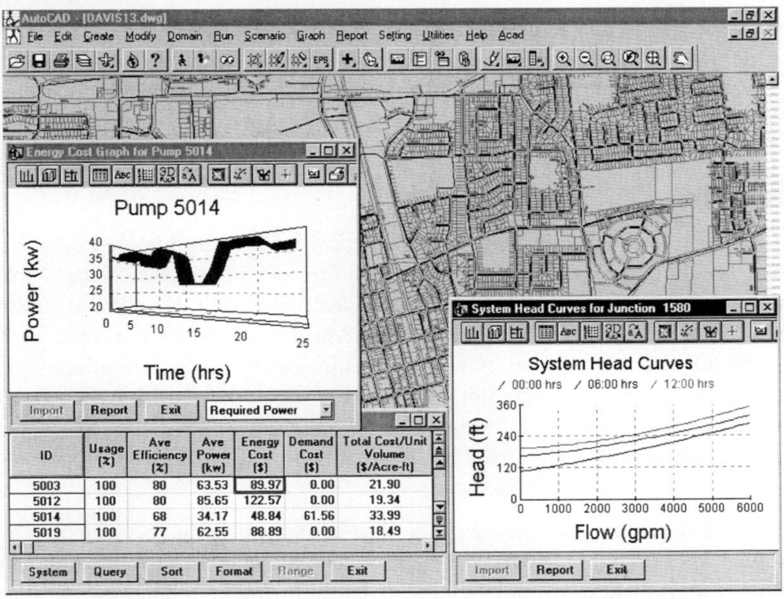

Figure 4.3 Energy Management module from H2ONET.

Fire fighting demands can have a significant impact on the sizing design of a distribution system. These additional demands create extra, localized stress on water systems and may induce undesirable areas of low pressures. Both design concerns and regulatory requirements call for adequate design of the distribution to be able to deliver the fire flows whilst being able to maintain the required minimum system pressure. Application of the fire-flow model provides an efficient and reliable approach to assess system impacts under these emergency conditions. An illustration of the fire-flow application is shown in Fig.4.4.

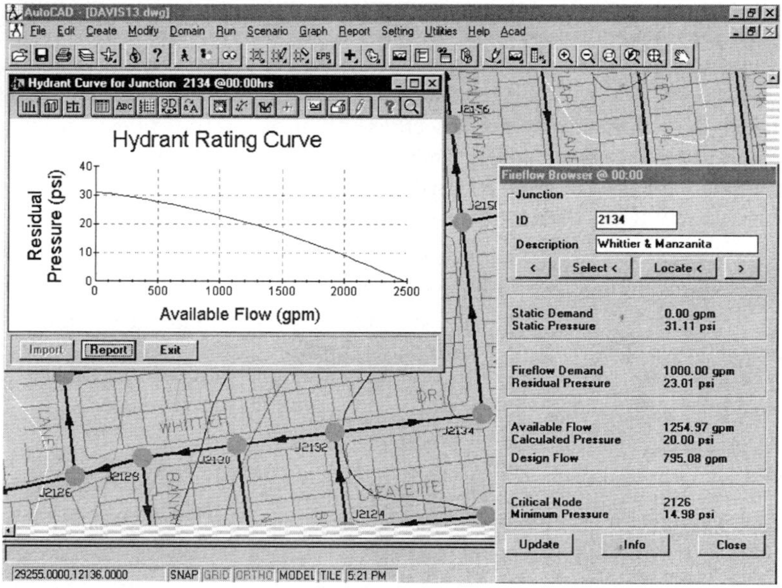

Figure 4.4 Fire Flow module from H2ONET.

5 Conclusions

The current trend in the water utility industry is growing towards automation by adopting appropriate modern technologies. Automation considerations are being applied in information management, customer services, engineering design, operational control, and management decision support. Primary objectives are to improve system operation, system performance, and system reliability within the resource limitations available. Hydraulic modeling and its integration with an information framework have proved to be fundamental towards this goal. Information is becoming invaluable in this computer age. The key to success is automation of the use of available information to support decision making in a timely and effective manner.

The implemented hydraulic modeling system has been applied successfully by numerous water utilities as an essential decision support tool allowing direct integration of the information management environment with advanced hydraulic modeling functionalities. The use of a central information repository with open and effective data sharing has enabled information consolidation with network system models and management objectives. Automation in information management provides free flow of knowledge in a consistent and readily available format to allow greater confidence and better understanding of the common objectives among the water utility management teams.

The benefits of integrated information and modeling systems are numerous. Some immediate advantages include: elimination of the laborious and time consuming process of working with voluminous data; elimination of the risks of maintaining multiple and often duplicate data definitions and the associated problems in maintaining data integrity; better visual comprehension from massive data and result information. The resulting model system greatly enhances the ability of water utilities to conceive and evaluate effective and economical water distribution system management and operational alternatives. Direct access to an integrated environment will optimize operations and maximize efficiencies of all water utility divisions in the challenging times ahead. The integrated model will prove useful to any water utility attempting to optimize engineering productivity and performance.

Acknowledgments

Chun-Hou Orr would like to express his deepest personal gratitude to his wife Cathy for her endless understanding and encouragement. He would also like to thank his two daughters Rebecca and Jennifer for the time he has taken away from them on this work.

References

[1] 'H2ONET Users Manual', 1997, MW Soft, Inc., 300 North Lake Avenue, Suite 1200, Pasadena, CA 91101, USA

[2] Rossman, L.A., 1994, 'EPANET Users Manual', EPA-600/R-94/057, U.S. Environmental Protection Agency, Risk Reduction Engineering Laboratory, Cincinnati, Ohio, USA

[3] Todini, E. and Pilati, S., 1987, 'A Gradient Method for the Analysis of Pipe Networks', in B. Coulbeck and C.H. Orr, '*Computer Applications in Water Supply*', RSP, Letchworth, England, pp.1-20

[4] Rossman, L.A. and Boulos, P.F., 1996, 'Numerical Methods for Modeling Water Quality in Distribution Systems: A Comparison', *ASCE J. Water Resources Planning and Management*, Vol.122, No.2, pp.137-146

[5] Boulos, P.F.; Altman, T.; Jarrige, P.A.; and Collevati, F.; 1995, 'Discrete Simulation Approach for Network Water Quality Models', *ASCE J. Water Resources Planning and Management*, Vol.121, No.1, pp.49-60

[6] Axworthy, D.H. and Karney, B.W., 1996, 'Modeling Flow Velocity/High Dispersion Flow in Water Distribution Systems', *ASCE J. Water Resources Planning and Management*, Vol.122, No.3, pp.218-221

[7] Orr, C.H.; Parkar, M.A.; and Tennant, S.T.; 1990, 'Implementation of On-Line Control Scheme for City Water System', *ASCE J. Water Resources Planning and Management*, Vol.116, No.5, pp.708-726

[8] Boulos, P.F.; Rossman, L.A.; Orr, C.H.; Heath, J.E.; and Meyer, M.S.; 1997, 'Fire Flow Computation with Network Models', *J. American Water Works Association*, Vol.89, No.2, pp.51-56

[9] Boulos, P.F.; Orr, C.H.; Heath, E.; Ro, J.; Meyer, M.; Hill, R.; and Moore, M.; 1997, 'Direct Calculation of Fire Flows with Water Distribution Network Models', *Proc. 4th International Conference on Computer Methods and Water Resources*, Byblos, Lebanon, June 16-18, 1997

[10] Orr, C.H.; Alegre, H.; and Coelho, S.T.; 1995; 'Object-Oriented Design and Development of Hydraulic Modeling Tools', *Proc. AWWA 1995 Annual Conference*, Anaheim, June 22-28, 1995, pp.343-367

[11] Gotoh, K.; Jacobs, J.K.; Hosoda, S.; and Gerstberger, R.L. (Eds.); 1993; 'Instrumentation and Computer Integration of Water Utility Operations', American Water Works Association Research Foundation, Denver, USA

[12] Grayman, W.M. and Rossman, L.A., 1994, 'Integrating a Network Model with an Expert System', *Proc. American Water Works Association Computer Conference*, Los Angeles, Calif. USA, April 10-13, 1994, pp.553-561

[13] Martin, J. and Oxman, S., 1988, 'Building Expert Systems', Prentice-Hall

[14] Buchanan, B.G. and Shortliffe, E.H., 1984, 'Rule-Based Expert Systems', Addison-Wesley

[15] Altman, T.; Orr, C.H.; Heath, J.E.; and Boulos, P.F.; 1997; 'Automated Calculation and Distribution of Water Demands in Distribution Network Models', *Proc. American Water Works Association Computer Conference*, Austin, Texas, USA, April 13-16, 1997, pp.219-231

[16] Vasconcelos, J.J.; Rossman, L.A.; Grayman, W.M.; Boulos, P.F.; and Clark, R.M.; 1997; 'Kinetics of Chlorine Decay', *J. American Water Works Association*, Vol.89, No.7, pp.54-65.

CHAPTER 7

Optimization in Water Networks

G.Cembrano *and* J.Quevedo

1. Introduction

Optimization in water networks refers to the problem of improving the management of water resources in a supervisory control system, in order to achieve specific operation goals. Water networks are generally composed of a large number of interconnected pipes, reservoirs, pumps, valves and other hydraulic elements which carry water to demand nodes from the supply areas, with specific pressure levels to provide a good service to consumers.

The hydraulic elements in a network may be classified into two categories: active and passive. The active elements are those which can be operated to control the flow and the pressure of water in specific parts of the network, such as pumps, valves and turbines. The pipes and reservoirs are passive elements, insofar as they receive the effects of the operation of the active elements, in terms of pressure and flow, but they cannot be directly acted upon.

A supervisory control system in a water network generally includes a telemetry system which periodically updates information from a selected set of passive elements and from most of (ideally all) the active elements. This information is generally composed of pressure and flow readings, as well as the status of the active elements, and it reflects the instantaneous operation condition of the water network. It also includes the mechanisms to actuate the active elements in the network and to control their performance. However, it is not always obvious how to derive appropriate control strategies for the active elements, in order to achieve efficient use of the resources and to meet the specific pressure and flow needs in the whole network, at all times.

Optimization in water networks deals with the problem of generating control strategies in advance, to guarantee a good service in the network, while achieving certain management goals, which may include one or more of the following, according to the needs of a specific utility: minimization of cost, including supply and power for pumping operations; maximization of water quality, in terms of dissolved materials and residence time; minimizing deviations of pressure and/or flow values from specific desired levels for leak prevention, etc.

The implementation of optimization procedures may prove an extremely efficient measure to contribute to the correct management of water resources and to improve the service to consumers, as well as to reduce operational costs, as has been shown in several water utilities around Europe. In the context of a European project (WATERNET, ESPRIT IV, No. 22.186), the authors are currently attempting to develop a general framework for optimization which can be used by a large class of water utilities. For this purpose, this chapter attempts to show how optimization problems may be posed for different types of water utilities, according to their physical characteristics and the necessary modeling assumptions. In section 2, the interaction of the optimization procedure with a general supervisory control system is outlined, section 3 deals with the problem of optimization in water utilities and section 4 is concerned with the factors influencing the computational complexity of the optimization problems arising in water management. In section 5, some representative examples of optimization in European water utilities are discussed, and, finally, the objectives of the WATERNET project in the area of optimization are presented in section 6.

2. Optimization in a Supervisory Control System

The optimization module interacts with the real network through the SCADA (Supervision Control and Data Acquisition) system, and must receive information about the current state of the network, in terms of

- Reservoir levels.
- Status of pumps and valves.
- Last demand readings.
- Pressure and/or flow readings at selected points.

The demand forecasting module, associated with the optimization module, contains a model of the demands which can generate forecasts of future demands, based on a record of a number of past values thereof. The demand information from the SCADA system is used to update the past-demand record and a forecast of the demand in the next period is performed. The demand forecasts are usually obtained with a horizon of the order of 1 day and the hourly data are obtained by modulation with appropriate demand patterns for each day in the week.

The optimization module contains a hydraulic model of the network which allows the test of the effect produced by a control action (flows in the active elements) on the network, in terms of:

- Reservoir levels.
- Pressure and/or flow readings at selected points.

The optimization procedure selects optimal control actions by searching in the space of possible controls and evaluating different alternatives, as described later in this chapter. The optimal control values are then sent through the SCADA as setpoints to the local controllers in the remote stations. The control procedures in the remote stations will then seek to regulate the control elements to follow the desired setpoint. Optimization updates are performed regularly during the day. The general scheme of interaction with the supervisory control system is shown in Fig. 1.

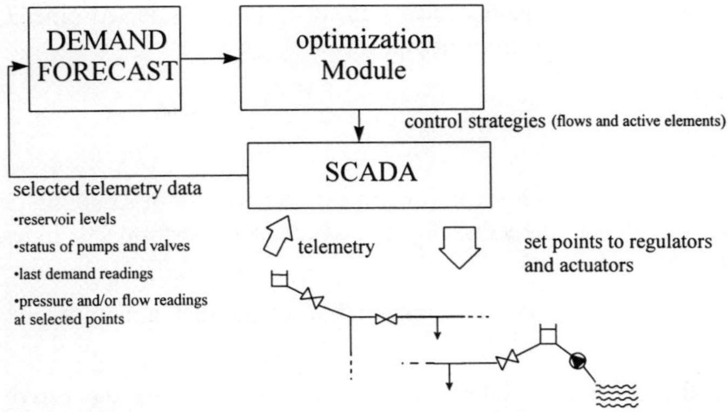

Figure 1. General scheme of supervisory control and optimization

3. Posing Optimal Operation Problems

The function of the optimization module in a supervisory control system is to generate control strategies for the controllers of the active hydraulic elements.

In water utilities, where the planning of reservoir storage is not a problem, optimization is an instantaneous problem, dealing with the obtention of the optimal values for the current setpoints in the controllers of the active hydraulic elements. In water networks where storage in reservoirs must be planned ahead to meet future demands with specific pressure levels, optimization involves the generation of controller strategies over a time period, called the optimization horizon, which may be of the order of 1 day for a common case of water distribution utility.

In both the instantaneous and the dynamic case, the generation of control actions must be performed with a mathematical procedure involving optimizing (maximizing or minimizing) an expression of the desired management goals, called the performance index. In general, a performance index may contain:

1. Terms related to the cost of water supply, treatment and elevation.

2. Terms related to the water pressure (or head) in specific key consumption or supply nodes of the network.

3. Terms related to the water quality in specific pipes of the network, for example, as defined by concentration of dissolved materials and residence time.

Then, a general performance index may be expressed as follows: for the instantaneous case,

$$P = \sum_{i=1}^{I} f(u_i) + \sum_{j=1}^{J} g(p_j) + \sum_{l=1}^{L} h(q_l)$$

where

P is the instantaneous value of the performance index

$f(u_i)$ is a function of the flow across the ith active hydraulic element, I being the total number of active hydraulic elements

$g(p_j)$ is a function of the pressure the jth selected key node, J being the total number pressure-observation points

$h(q_l)$ is a function of the quality measurement in the lth selected pipe, L being the total number of quality-measurement pipes

For the dynamic case,

$$J = \sum_{k=0}^{N-1} P^k \Big|$$

where N is the optimization horizon (in terms of the number of sampling periods) and the superindex k refers to the values of the instantaneous performance index at the kth time period.

Performance optimization must take into account that a number of important constraints exists:

- **On the control variables**, such as the flows across the active hydraulic elements. Pumps and valves have specific ranges of flow for correct operation.
- **On other variables**, such as the levels in the reservoirs. These include capacity and operational limits on water minimum and maximum allowed levels. Similar restrictions may be in order in certain selected pipes.

The optimization process consists of searching the space of *admissible control actions* to obtain the minimum (or maximum) value of the performance index, while producing only *admissible states* of the network, as measured in the reservoir levels (and possibly, flows on selected pipes).

It is important to note that the performance index can only be minimized with respect to the control variables (flows across active hydraulic elements), since these are the only variables which may be acted upon. However, the value of the index also depends on variables which are not directly controlled, but must be evaluated for each control action. Similarly, the constraints apply both on directly controlled variables and on other variables referred to as passive elements, which cannot be operated directly. These conditions contribute to the mathematical complexity of the optimization problems in water systems.

4 Complexity of the Optimization Problem

The computational complexity of the optimization problem is affected by a number of important factors in the real network and in the modeling assumptions. The main factors and their influence on the optimization complexity are: the size of the network, in terms of number of active elements; the reservoirs requiring planning and the key pressure/flow evaluation nodes.

The size of the optimization problem depends on the number of active hydraulic elements to be optimized, on the number of passive elements which reflect the state of the network, such as reservoirs and pressure- or flow-evaluation nodes, and also, most importantly, on the optimization horizon. Instantaneous optimization problems pose few computation-time problems, while the dynamic problems with optimization horizons of 24 hourly intervals, which are common in many water utilities in Europe, impose a very high computational burden on non-trivial networks. This is so because of the combinatorial nature of the problem of searching the space of controls for a number of interacting active elements in a 24-step horizon.

4.1 Type of Hydraulic Elements Involved

The type of hydraulic elements affects the design of the strategy optimization programs in that it determines the type of variables to be used to express flows and pressures. This is important since very efficient methods exist for optimizing vast classes of continuous-variable problems, especially as it is possible to use derivatives and gradients. Conversely, the methods of integer programming required to optimize problems with integer or binary variables are mainly of a combinatorial nature: they cannot make use of the gradient concepts. They are, therefore, very slow and not necessarily guaranteed to converge. Then, it is usually preferred to work with continuous approximations of the values of the variables involved in the optimization as follows:

- Valves: A valve allows any value of the flow in its operational range. Therefore, a continuous variable can be used to represent the value of the flow through a valve.
- Fixed-speed Pumps: For a specified value of the downstream pressure or the head increase within the operational range of the pipe, only one value of the flow is possible according to the characteristic equation. Therefore, the instantaneous value of the flow through a pump cannot be realistically modeled using continuous variables. However, the volumes through the pump in specified periods, as required for dynamic optimization, may achieve any desired (feasible) value through pulse-width modulation, i.e., by operating the pump only a portion of the period.
- Batteries of fixed-speed pumps: disposing of a number of fixed-speed pumps usually allows for a modulation in the flows, which makes it easier to model the flow as a continuous variable.

4.2 Type of Hydraulic Model

Another factor which influences the complexity of the optimization problem is the type of model used to test the effect of the control actions on the network, since it affects the time required for each control action to be tested by the optimizer.

Flow-only models and, in particular, those models where only control variables are required to compute the change in the state of the network produced by a control action allow for very fast evaluation of control actions.

Flow and pressure models, where a number of pressures and/or flows in passive elements are required to compute the change in the state of the network produced by a control action, impose longer execution times for each control action test. The problem is easier when explicit equations exist to compute the pressures and/or flows in passive elements, in terms of the control variables. If this is not the case, an iterative simulation procedure must be run for each evaluation of a control action and this situation may be extremely time-consuming.

4.3 Type of Optimization Equations

The availability and computational complexity of optimization methods vary according to the form of the equations involved. In particular, for continuous variables:

- Problems with linear performance indexes and linear constraints have fast and efficient solution methods based on the SIMPLEX method.
- Problems with quadratic performance indexes and linear constraints have fast and efficient methods based on gradient techniques, which are guaranteed to converge in a number of iterations equal to the dimension of the optimization space.
- Problems with other non linear convex performance indexes and linear constraints may be solved using the same methods as above, without the guarantee of converging in a number of iterations.
- More general problems with convex performance indexes and nonlinear constraints defining a convex space may be efficiently solved with gradient-based techniques.
- Nonconvex problems pose serious difficulties, as there is no guarantee that only one extremum (minimum or maximum) exists. In these cases, random-search and heuristic-search methods may be used, but these usually have very long convergence times and the solution is not guaranteed to achieve a global extremum.

For integer or binary-variable problems, the optimization problems are of a combinatorial nature. Search and pruning methods are available, such as the branch-and-bound algorithm, which are efficient in some specific cases with small dimensionality.

4.4 Topology

Topology is a key factor to be analyzed when studying a water network for optimization purposes. In particular, the topology determines how an action in a certain element of a water network affects the rest of the network. For example, in some simple tree-like networks an action at the end of a final branch may not affect the rest of the network at all, while in a mesh-like network, a more global influence of the actuation of most of the hydraulic control elements is to be expected. This situation is usually an important factor to be considered when selecting more or less de-centralized schemes for the supervisory control system in general and for the control strategy optimization in particular.

Star-structure water networks generally contain one large source (usually with an associated reservoir) from which water is supplied to a number of local small distribution areas, each of which may contain one reservoir, as shown in Fig. 2.

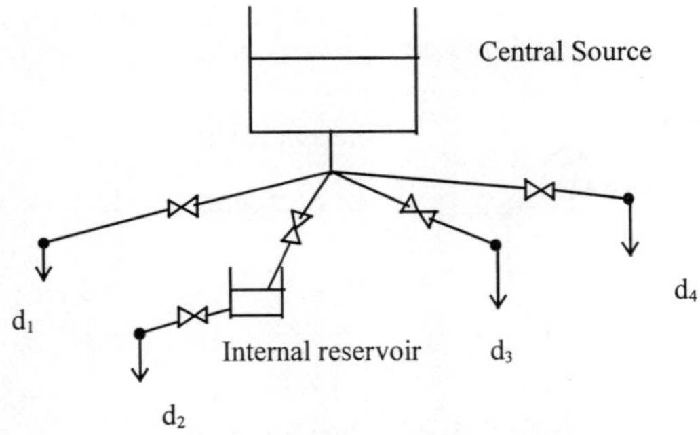

Figure 2. Star topology

The special characteristics of this network allow the use of spatial decomposition techniques for optimization, which reduces the mathematical complexity of a large problem to an iterative solution of a number of simple problems. Note, in particular, that the sense of the flows is fixed, from the central source to the demands.

Tree-structure water networks generally have one large source (and usually, an associated reservoir) from which water is supplied to a small number of intermediate locations, where it is stored and/or pumped to the demand, as shown in Fig. 3.

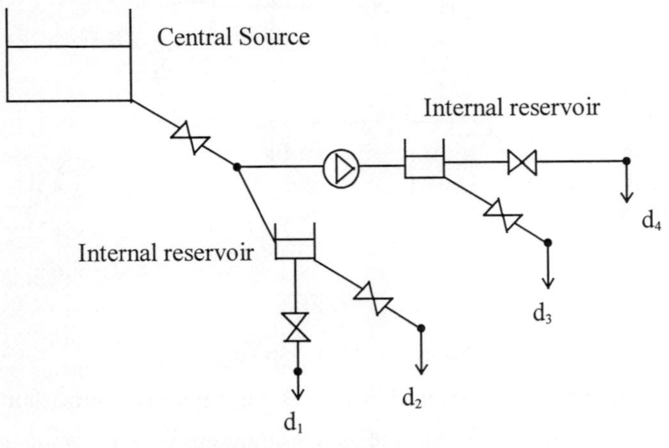

Figure 3. Tree topology

Note that here too, the sense of the flows is defined, from the source to the demands.

A cascade water network is a special case of a tree-structure network where there is only one branch, as shown in Fig. 4.

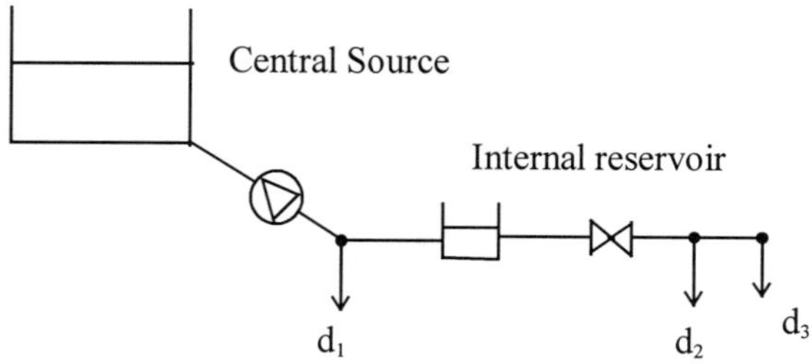

Figure 4. Cascade topology

A mesh-structure network usually contains several sources (e.g. with associated reservoirs) and is highly interconnected so that the demands can be supplied from more than one source and, in general, with different operation patterns, so that the sense of the flows is not fixed in some of the valves and pipes: see Fig. 5.

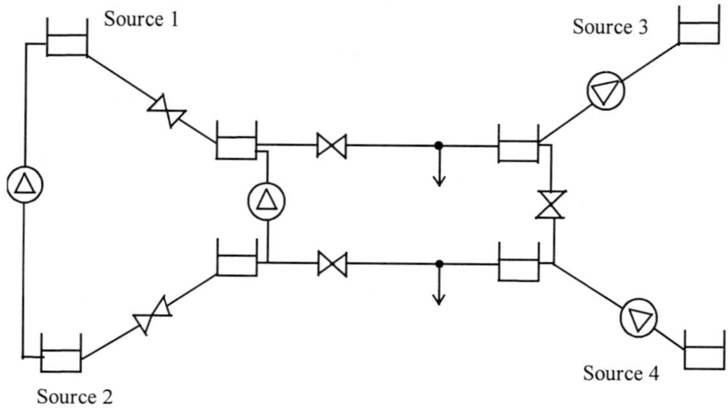

Figure 5. Mesh topology

5. Some Representative Examples of Water-Management Optimization

A number of large European utilities already use optimization programs to generate 24-hour strategies in advance to minimize costs while maintaining a good service to consumers. Several types of optimization procedures have been used, but most of them employ either dynamic programming or convex non linear programming techniques. In most cases, the size of the optimization problems involved makes it necessary to derive special methods, since direct application of the techniques does not produce acceptable computation times.

Fallside and Perry (1975) derived a hierarchical price-decomposition algorithm for the optimization of the Severn-Trent Water Authority network. The solution of the subproblems used a linearization around an operating point to reduce the mathematical complexity. The method was implemented in the Cambridge area, but it did not achieve completely satisfactory results in the long run.

A more general scheme of hierarchical-decomposition optimization in water networks was proposed by Coulbeck (1977) and tested in simulation for several UK networks.

In Barcelona, Solanas (1974) derived a successive approximation dynamic programming algorithm for the Barcelona network, which was later improved and tested in simulation (Solanas and Montoliu, 1987).

In the U.S., Murray and Yakowitz (1979) developed differential dynamic programming techniques which allowed use of the dynamic programming approach to the optimization of a relatively small simulated water network.

In the 1980s, one of the most relevant applications was the real implementation of the interaction prediction method developed by Carpentier (1983), in the network of Paris Sud of the French Company Lyonnaise des Eaux. This method was also based on the use of dynamic programming techniques and it made specific use of the star structure of the distribution network.

Later on, a non linear programming technique was developed for the Barcelona network, which made use of optimal control concepts (Cembrano et al., 1988), and an improvement thereof was implemented in the real network in 1990 (Griño and Cembrano, 1989). The Barcelona network is very interconnected and has a mesh-structure, which makes the use of decomposition techniques inefficient.

In the 1990s, Brdys (1992) considered the problem of optimizing the configuration of fixed-speed pumps in the water networks of Leicestershire and Yorkshire. He studied a class of cascade hydraulic systems in two cases: one with weak and the other with strong hydraulic interactions. Spatial and time decomposition were used in combination with branch-and-bound mixed-integer programming techniques to solve the optimization problems of the two areas. The method was implemented successfully by the Yorkshire Water Authority (Brdys, 1994).

6. Perspectives of Optimization Research in the WATERNET project

The WATERNET project is concerned with the development and dissemination of advanced techniques and tools for water management and planning, including modeling through learning and knowledge acquisition, simulation and state-estimation, optimization, quality analysis and management, and distributed-information-system design.

In the area of optimization, the project aims at demonstrating the benefits of introducing optimization in a variety of water utilities. In particular, two specific cases are being treated in detail, which correspond to the end-user partners in the consortium, Servicios Municipalizados de Agua de Sintra (P) and Wasserbedrijf Rotterdam (N).

The optimization procedures produced in the WATERNET project will incorporate aspects that have so far been mostly avoided for their computational complexity, such as the use of hydraulic models and pressures for the optimization and interaction with the state estimation and alarm management procedures to validate and correct optimization results. It is envisaged to achieve a demonstrator of the project with full capabilities in June 1998.

Acknowledgments

This work has been partly supported by the UE and the Spanish Board for Research and Technology (CICYT) under the contract ESPRIT IV, No. 22186 and TAP97-0869-CE and by the University and Research Commission of the 'Generalitat de Catalunya' ref. 1995-SGR-00474.

The author J. Quevedo is member of CERCA (Collective for the Study and Research of Control and Automation) and of LEA-SICA (European Associated Laboratory of Intelligent Systems and Advanced Control).

References

[1] Brdys, M. A. 1992. 'An algorithm for optimal scheduling of a class of cascade water supply systems', Optimal Control Applications and Methods, Vol. 13

[2] Brdys, M. A., Ulanicki, B. 1994. 'Operational control of water systems: Structures, algorithms and applications', Prentice Hall International, UK

[3] Carpentier, P. 1983. 'Décomposition et aggregation dans la conduite optimale d'un grand reseau de distribution d'eau', PhD. Thesis. École Nat. de Mines de Paris.

[4] Fallside, F., Perry, P.F. 1975. 'Hierarchical optimization of a water supply network', Proc. of the IEEE, 1222

[5] Murray, D. M., Yakowitz, S. J. 1979. 'Constrained differential dynamic programming and its application to multireservoir control', Water Reseources Research, 155

[6] Solanas, J. L. 1974. 'Mando en tiempo real de un sistema de suministro de agua', PhD. Thesis, Univ. Politècnica de Catalunya, Spain

[7] Solanas, J. L., Montoliu, J. M. 1987. 'Optimal operation of water systems', in Computer Applications in Water Supply Volume 2, B. Coulbeck and C. H. Orr eds., Research Studies Press, UK

[8] Cembrano, G., Brdys, M., Coulbeck, B., Orr, C. H. 1988. 'Optimization of a multireservoir water network using a conjugate-gradient technique', in Lecture Notes in Control and Information Science, Vol. III A. Bensousan and J. L. Lions eds., Springer Verlag, Berlin.

[9] Griño, R. and Cembrano, G., 1991.Technical Report 'Optimización en linea de estrategias de control de la red de distribución de agua abastecida por la SGAB mediante la metodología de flujos sobre redes, Instituto de Cibernética', Abril, IC-DT-1991.02.

CHAPTER 8

The Use of Continuous Decision Variables in an Optimising Fixed Speed Pump Scheduling Algorithm

J.H.Andersen *and* R.S.Powell

Introduction

It is well known that the optimal pump-scheduling problem is difficult to solve. This chapter describes a new pump scheduling method and its application to a large operational water distribution network. The network in this study comprises a wide range of network elements, including 10 pump stations with 22 pumps (20 schedulable, 2 unschedulable) and 15 reservoirs. All the pumps are of fixed speed, i.e. they can be switched on or off during the 24 hour optimisation horizon. The time axis is also discretised into 1 hour major steps, hence the problem becomes a discrete non-linear optimisation problem. This optimisation problem is furthermore constrained by upper and lower reservoir bounds and by required target levels.

By introducing a continuous control variable for deciding the number of active pumps in a pump station, a considerable shortcut over traditional integer programming methods may be achieved. Indeed, several authors have tried this approach. Ulanicki and Orr [3] use a time distribution function for allocating fractional time periods to each discrete control decision over the fundamental time step. The continuous equivalent control variables become the fractional durations of the discrete pump configurations. However, this greatly increases the number of variables in the problem. A straightforward translation of a continuous control value to fractional pumping periods for fixed speed pumps (FSPs) may lead to an undesirably large number of pump switches. Furthermore, the translation may upset the feasibility of the solution with respect to reservoir and pressure constraints. In the literature, few comments are offered on the translation procedure; it is commonly assumed that the number of pumps involved in a pump station is large enough to be approximated by the real value of a continuous decision variable. However, the decision is often binary. For instance, in a pump station with a duty/standby pump configuration, only one pump may be switched.

One or more pumps in a pump station may be grouped into a single pumping operation. In ordinary language, a pump station may contain several such groups, pumping into different branches of the network. However, for our purposes a pump station comprises only the possible pumps for a single branch direction, some of which may be inactive. Any combination of active pumps in the pump station is a possible control decision, hence the pump selection problem is combinatorial in nature. In practice, however, only a limited number of pump combinations are relevant. A general rank ordering of different combinations was considered by Zessler and Shamir [5]. In this chapter, we consider the combinations consisting of the successive parallel additions of pumps in a predetermined sequence such that the most efficient pumps are selected first.

The cost of electricity is subject to a tariff at each pump station. The tariffs have a strong daily variation, especially during the winter season. It is clear that there is an opportunity for cost savings by scheduling the pumping at the cheap tariff times. However, excessive pumping carries a high marginal cost due to a progressive non-linear network response. This suggests the existence of an optimal schedule that balances the marginal cost increase with the tariff reductions, subject to the reservoir level constraints. The reservoirs act as buffers, enabling cost-efficient scheduling.

Ormsbee and Lansey [2] make a distinction between the use of implicit or explicit control variables for controlling pump stations. With implicit control, the primary control variable may be the external flow from the pump station. The pump configuration is then adapted to this external variable. With explicit control variables, the individual pumps are controlled directly.

The pump scheduling cost function

The electricity cost of pumping over the time-discretised scheduling period can be written as:

$$C = E \cdot \Delta t \cdot \sum_{t=1}^{NT} \sum_{i=1}^{NS} T_{t,i} \left(\sum_{j=1}^{u} \frac{q_{t,i,j} \, \Delta h_{t,i,j}}{\eta(q_{t,i,j})} \right) \tag{1}$$

where
NT = total number of time periods
NS = number of pump stations
$T_{t,i}$ = tariff at time period t for pump station i
$u_{t,i}$ = number of active pumps (during time period t in pump station i)
η = pump efficiency function
E = cost conversion factor
Δt = length of time period in hours
$q_{t,i,j}$ = pump flow for pump j at station i

The network

The distribution system that is the focus of this chapter can be partitioned into 12 sub systems (islands), see Fig. 1. These are supplied in a hierarchical fashion by cascades of pumps originating from the main treatment works at the top. Hence, the supply chain forms a tree structure originating from the treatment works at the root. The individual islands may have loops and various controlling elements. In this example, the total network consists of 587 nodes and 648 links with a daily demand of approximately 20 Megalitres. The complexity of the network is indicated by the presence of 19 pressure reducing valves (PRVs), 13 floatvalves (FLVs) and 3 checkvalves (CHVs). By the definition of the islands, it is essential that there should be at least one reservoir in each island to provide buffering for the scheduled pumps. However, the pumps shown may directly supply some demand nodes as well as filling the reservoirs. The system also has two additional pressure dependent pumps that are not buffered by reservoirs. These pumps cannot be scheduled and are therefore integrated into their particular islands as special hydraulic elements.

Fig.1 shows the island structure; each island (containing the network elements) is represented as a circle, and each schedulable pump station is represented by a triangle.

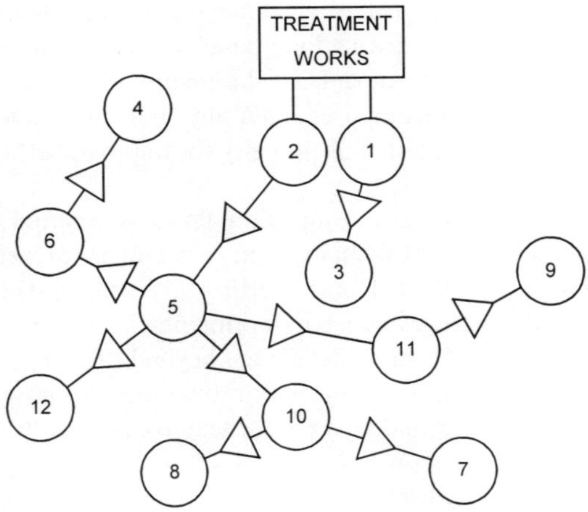

Figure 1.
Structure of the distribution system

The optimisation algorithm proceeds in two stages: in the first stage, the pumps are disconnected as elements and their flows are represented by nodal injections and demands, respectively, of equal magnitude. These flows are the continuous decision variables q_I; they correspond to an injection model of the pumps. The flows q_I must satisfy the following constraints:

1) Water budget constraints:

$$\sum_{t=1}^{NT} \sum_{j=1}^{u_{t,i}} q_{I\, t,i,j} = B_i \quad \text{for pump station } i \text{ (receiving island } i\text{).} \qquad (2)$$

The tree structure of the supply system allows all the 24 hour pump station (island) demand budgets B_i to be determined exactly from the downstream demands and the target reservoir levels. (Any reservoir surplus/deficit at the end of the optimisation period contributes to the demand budgets.)

2) Pump capacity constraints:

$$0 \leq \Delta h_{I\,t,i,j} \leq b_{i,j}\, q^2_{I\,t,i,j} + b_{i,j}\, q_{I\,t,i,j} + c_{i,j} \qquad (3)$$

3) Reservoir level constraints (expressed here as volume constraints):

$$V_r \min \ \leq V_{t,r} \leq V_r \max \qquad (4)$$

The reservoir volumes are determined from a network analysis algorithm. The reservoir flows are integrated over each time step; in the quasi-static approximation, constant flows are assumed during the time steps. However, a nearly full reservoir may require a fractional time step after which the reservoir is closed for the remainder of the time step. In this work we used a loop based simulation algorithm by Andersen, Powell [1]. Due to the injection models of the pumps used during this stage of the optimisation, the network decomposes naturally into disconnected islands. The network analysis algorithm exploits this property for improved efficiency.

The feasible, optimal solution to the injection flows is referred to as the *gradient solution*. This solution can be obtained in a number of ways by non-linear optimisation methods. Yu, Powell and Sterling [4] used a Generalised Reduced Gradient method (GRG). However, later developments resulted in a variant of the projected gradient method. The exact details are beyond the scope of this chapter; we assume that a solution method is available and the objective now is to interpret this solution so that the problem of finding a FSP schedule can be solved.

Interpretation of the gradient solution

The useful information in the gradient solution depends on the FSP configuration. In a duty/standby configuration, the only decision for the optimisation is to switch a single pump on or off. In normal operational conditions, the active pump flow will only vary a little; i.e. the pump is adapted to the network load. In this situation, the pump efficiency is almost constant and there is no issue of marginal costs. However, the gradient solution will be affected by progressive marginal costs, choosing the maximum pump capacity during cheap tariff times unless the capacity of the FSP is too large for efficient operation. Nevertheless, the gradient solution provides a feasible cumulative pump flow, which can be tracked by the FSPs. In a duty/assist mode the marginal cost information also becomes useful; by implication, the capacity of the main (duty) FSP is not too large for efficient operation.

Tracking the gradient solution

We consider now a single pump station in isolation. The FSP schedule is refined in two stages: schedule-A and schedule-B. The purpose of schedule-A is to establish the number of pumping hours for the duty and possible assist pumps (plus possibly higher pumps) without considering the pumping times in detail. This is done by tracking the cumulative flow of the gradient solution over the time horizon for the required island pumping. A full dynamic simulation is performed; the pumps are activated if the cumulative pumping falls behind the solution within a set error margin, and the pumping activity control is subject to reservoir level constraints. The output result of schedule-A is the total numbers ($n_{A\,1}\ldots, n_{A\,j}, \ldots$) of active pump times for each pump j in the pump station. The preferred pump times can now be found by rank ordering the values of the gradient solution island flow. Fig 2. illustrates an example where the duty pump is on at the 11 highest values and the assist pump is on at the 4 highest values of the gradient solution. (The duty/assist pump activity is shown as 'X' in Fig. 2.).

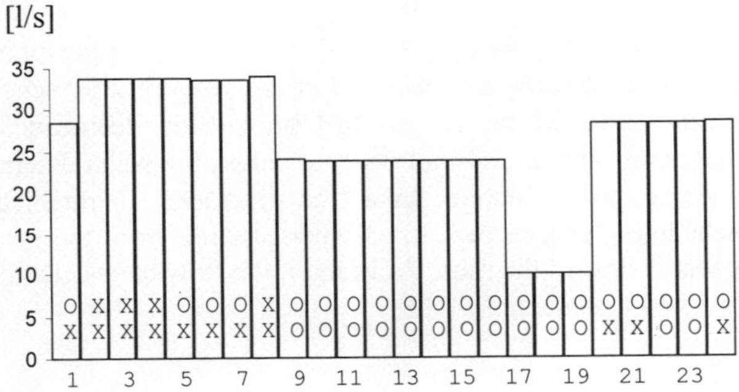

Figure. 2
Island 11 flow – Gradient solution

The rank ordering of the active pump times according to the gradient solution suggests the schedule as shown in (Fig. 2), but this is an idealised schedule. Although the gradient solution is feasible, the discretised FSP solution might not be. As a result of the rank ordering, a function giving the cumulative number of preferred pump times, $X_j(t)$ at time period t can be determined. The final adjustment to feasibility is carried out in schedule-B. In this schedule, the cumulative activity function, $X_j(t)$, is tracked subject to reservoir feasibility.

The function $X_j(t)$ for pump j in the station at time period t , for the idealised schedule (Fig. 2) is defined as :

$$X_j(t) = \sum_{t'=1}^{t} x_j(t') \tag{5}$$

where $x_j(t)$ is the corresponding indicator function, that is $x_j(t) = 1$ if pump j is on during time period t and $x_j(t) = 0$ otherwise.

In the tracking operation of schedule-B, another full dynamic simulation is performed. Feasible pumping activity is monitored by the cumulative activity function $\overline{X}_j(t)$ which is defined similarly to (5), but for the current simulation. As the dynamic simulation progresses forward in time, the pumping is activated by the condition: $\overline{X}_j(t) < X_j(t)$, provided that reservoir feasibility can be maintained.

If a pump is delayed due to a full reservoir in the line of flow with no alternative diversion, then the pump is activated at the earliest time after the event until the cumulative activity is restored. An emptying reservoir in line of a pump may force pumping even if the cumulative activity is ahead (of schedule). In this case, pumping will cease at the earliest time after the event. The main advantage of tracking the cumulative activity is that it allows for flexible adjustment to the FSP schedule in the event of infeasible reservoir levels. It should be stressed that the continuous gradient solution is already feasible, the adjustments are second order corrections due to the FSP translation.

Successive scheduling

In the above description for finding the FSP schedule, a single pump station was considered in isolation. When considering the entire network, FSP scheduling must be carried out in an organised fashion so that an already determined feasible FSP schedule for one pump station does not become unfeasible when determining the FSP schedule for another pump station. In a tree-structured (hierarchical) distribution system, safe scheduling can be performed when starting from the peripheral islands and moving upwards toward the root. At island i, the flow balance at a particular time t can be expressed by the equation:

$$Q_{t,k,i} - \sum_{j} Q_{t,i,j} - D_{t,i} = 0 \tag{6}$$

where $Q_{t,k,i}$ represents the flow into the island in the time period and $Q_{t,i,j}$ are the outflows to other islands. The flow $D_{t,i}$ accounts for the water consumed in the island by both consumer demands and by the reservoirs according to the optimised gradient solution.

At a peripheral island, there are no outflows so the inflow must balance the island demands. However, where the inflow is provided by a FSP, the exact balance may not be possible, nevertheless the FSP inflow balances the resulting island demand $\overline{D}_{t,j*}$ by definition. The FSP flow balance at a peripheral island is expressed symbolically using overbars:

$$\overline{Q}_{t,k*,i*} - \overline{D}_{t,i*} = 0 \tag{7}$$

Hence, moving upwards in the supply system for determining the FSPs activity in schedule-A or schedule-B, the outflows are always known. The FSP flow, $\overline{Q}_{t,k,i}$ for island i is determined by tracking the gradient solution (schedule-A) or by tracking the cumulative activity function (schedule-B). By definition, it satisfies the balance:

$$\overline{Q}_{t,k,i} - \sum_{j} \overline{Q}_{t,i,j} - \overline{D}_{t,i} = 0 \tag{8}$$

Again decomposition of the system is exploited. In a given time period t, the FSPs are gradually introduced into the network starting from the peripheral islands; by introducing the FSPs for island i, the upstream island k and all the downstream islands are connected as a network component. However, only this component needs to be in scope for the network analysis algorithm. The last FSPs to be introduced are near the treatment works; they connect the whole network, which branches out from the pump station. In the case study there are actually two independent branches from the treatment works, which could also have been treated as two independent optimisation problems.

Looped supply chain structure

The above mentioned water distribution system has a tree-structured supply chain, but with many loops inside each island. The tree structure is very convenient for the projected gradient optimisation method; the water budget constraints take the form of the linear system in equation (2). The method can, however, also be applied to a system containing loops in the supply chain. Just as in ordinary network analysis, each fundamental loop in the supply chain introduces an extra degree of freedom; the loop current (flow) becomes a new decision variable. This variable is time independent, corresponding to a change in water demand budgets for all the pump stations in the loop. Hence, equation (2) is replaced by:

$$\sum_{t=1}^{NT}\sum_{j=1}^{u_{t,i}} q_{I\,t,i,j} = B_i + w_\ell \quad \text{for pump station } i \text{ and supply chain loop } \ell. \tag{9}$$

The 24 hour demand budgets B_i are now relative to a suitable spanning tree for the supply chain and w_ℓ is the decision variable for the loop flow.

Moving the variable w_ℓ to the left-hand side of (9), the budget constraints appear again as a linear system. This means that an optimised gradient solution can be found by essentially the same projected gradient method. Using the spanning tree, this solution becomes the basis for the FSP tracking methods in schedule-A and schedule-B.

Results

The projected gradient scheme can be divided into major and minor iterations. The major iterations consist of the gradient calculation and its projections. Below those are a number of minor iterations for the line search, each of which includes a full 24 hour dynamic simulation for finding the reservoir levels and dealing with feasibility violations. An indication of performance is the convergence of the costs for the major iterations.

As shown in Table 1, the cost for the continuous solution by the projected gradient method decreases monotonously. However, this is not always the case for the FSP solution. This solution changes in discrete steps, the overriding aim being to find a feasible solution. The results suggest a limit of 2 or 3 iterations of the projected gradient before starting the final process for introducing the FSPs. These findings may well be influenced by the accuracy of the pump data and the demand profiles.

Table 1.

Gradient iteration No.	Continuous costs £	FSP costs £
0	440.33	490.98
1	435.09	431.94
2	432.95	419.99
3	431.66	419.89
4	421.41	428.67

The gradient solution for pumping into island No. 11 was shown in Fig. 2. Here, the effect of the variable tariff is clearly visible as 4 different tariff periods. Hence, the scheduling would be relatively straightforward if there were no reservoir constraint to consider. However, there is a particularly difficult constraint for this island in the form of a medium size reservoir (773 m^3) with no float-valve mechanism to stop the reservoir from overfilling.

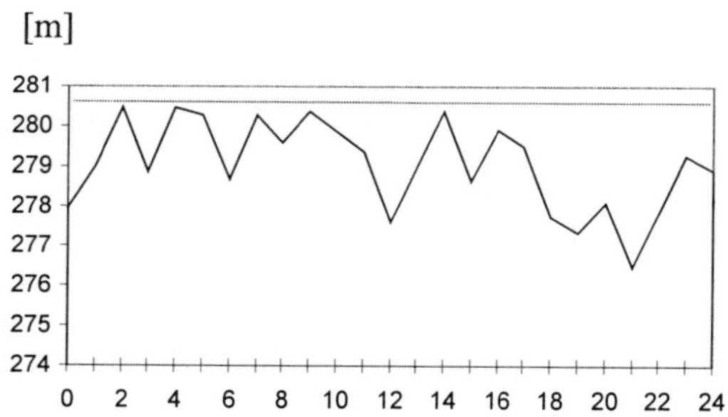

Figure. 3
D11 Reservoir profile

For the receiving reservoir in island No. 11, Fig. 3 shows the narrow band available for pumping during the early hours up to 8 am. The upward sloping curves indicate active pumping. The starting level at 278 m is a starting boundary condition. The strong downward slopes indicate strong demands that must be met by pumping, otherwise the reservoir can drop from the maximum security level (280.6 m) to minimum security level (273.6 m) in only 4 hours.

By dropping the starting level to 274 m, a more reasonable, less intermittent schedule is obtained, as shown in Fig 4.

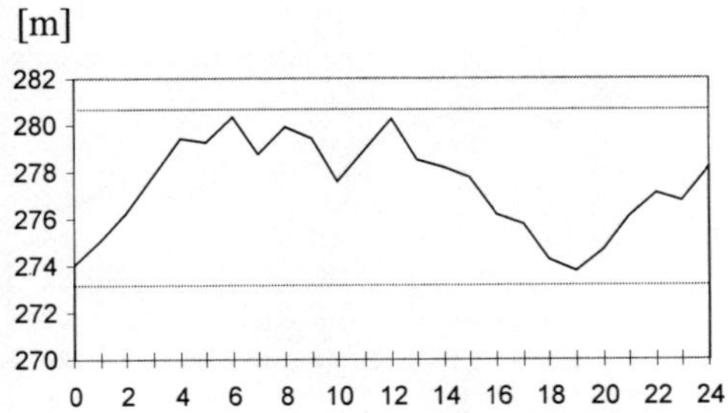

Figure. 4
D11 Reservoir profile – low start.

These reservoir profiles can be compared with the non-optimised starting profile in Fig. 5, although admittedly, in practice, some degree of manual scheduling makes this profile unrealistic.

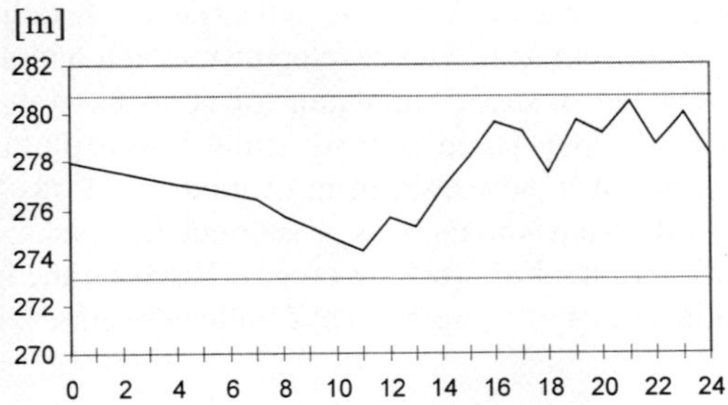

Figure. 5
D11 Reservoir profile – not optimised

The above examples for reservoir D11 are realistic, but are nevertheless not typical results. An example of a reservoir profile that indicates a schedule with contiguous pumping taking full advantage of the variable tariffs is shown in Fig. 6. The reservoir C12 is the receiving reservoir of island No.12; it appears that the reservoir is sufficient in size to enable the required time shifting.

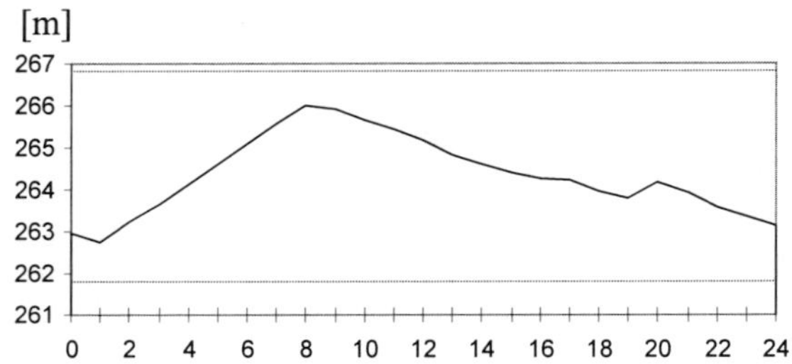

Figure. 6
C12 Reservoir profile

Conclusions

The difficulties in optimising (scheduling) a large water distribution system are related to the discrete combinatorial nature of the problem. It is also important, for the usefulness of software as a tool for operational management, that the methods employed are fast enough to be essentially interactive (i.e. a scheduling operation can be undertaken in just a few minutes). The development of the optimiser package has placed emphasis on detailed, realistic simulation of complex water networks , the speed being gained using a loop based network simulation exploiting the pipelined processor architecture, which is now used in most modern CPUs. The optimisation phase uses continuous decision variables as a shortcut heuristic, and optimisation principles are also built into the FSP tracking process based on the known properties of the increasing marginal costs of pumping in hydraulic networks.

References

[1] Andersen, J. H., Powell, R. S. 1997. 'An efficient loop-based algorithm for the analysis of water networks containing controlling elements', submitted to *Jour. of Water resources Planning and Management*, ASCE, April 1997.

[2] Ormsbee, L. E., Lansey, K. E. 1994. 'Optimal Control of Water Supply Pumping Systems' *Jour. of Water resources Planning and Management*, ASCE, Vol. 120, No. 2, pp 237-252

[3] Ulanicki, B., Orr, C. H. 1991. 'Unified approach for the Optimization of Non-linear Hydraulic Systems', *Jour. Optimisation Theory and Applications*, Vol. 68, No. 1, pp 161-179.

[4] Yu, G., Powell, R. S., Sterling, M. J. H. 1994. 'Optimised pump scheduling in water distribution systems', *Jour. Optimisation Theory and Applications*, Vol. 83, No. 6, No. 3 pp 463-488.

[5] Zessler, U., Shamir,U. 1989. 'Optimal operation of water distribution systems' *Jour. of Water resources Planning and Management*, ASCE, Vol. 115, No. 6, pp 735-751.

CHAPTER 9

Operational Network Modelling - Techniques for Updating Network Models with Telemetry Data

A.M.Green

Abstract

The operation and management of water distribution systems is under constant scrutiny, with ever more stringent regulations and heightened public awareness of water issues. During recent years, most water companies have installed company-wide telemetry systems to monitor and control mechanical and electrical assets in the water system, and provide a wealth of information on operational performance.

In parallel with this, these utilities are also investing in network models. With ever improving analysis software, such models are able to present essential information to the user in an easy, interpretable, friendly way. However, on a large scale, they are still being used mainly for traditional tasks such as forward planning, leakage analysis and system design.

The challenge now is to move the models into an on-line environment to allow them to be used for hourly decisions on the operation of the network - proactive network management.

1.0 **Introduction**

Since privatisation in the UK, the day-to-day business of water utilities is becoming an ever more public affair. The water utilities are now accountable to not only the regulatory bodies but also the public and the media. In this climate, utilities must manage and operate their water systems more efficiently, more effectively and with less risk. This must be achieved whilst also reducing costs and producing more profits for the shareholders.

In improving their operations, the utilities are adopting a range of technologies to improve the flow of information around the organisation and so improve decision making. Systems that are already in place in many utilities include Geographic Information Systems (GIS), Telemetry Systems (SCADA), Customer Information Systems (CIS) and Network Modelling Systems (NMS).

Whilst each one of these tools already provides useful information and benefits to the organisation, integrating them could yield even greater benefits and an associated reduction in costs through improved decision making.

The use and integration of GIS and CIS data for network model construction has been covered on a number of other occasions. This chapter will describe an approach to updating calibrated network models by using telemetry information and making these models available to support network management decisions. Some of the limitations of the approach will be considered as well as the viability of operating the models in this way.

2.0 **Background**

2.1 **Telemetry systems**

The first computer based telemetry systems were introduced as early as the 1970s. These early computers were extremely limited in computing power; frequently they were diskless systems and required paper-tape input. Since then we have seen a huge increase in the capabilities of computer hardware; what we considered a powerful machine a few years ago is now little more than a hand held electronic notepad.

This increase in computer power, combined with a similar decrease in cost, has enabled a dramatic leap forward in the capabilities and sophistication of telemetry software packages, and the applications that they can support. No longer limited to specified platforms, the wide variety of modern-day telemetry systems function on an equally wide variety of computer systems.

These developments, combined with developments in the fields of networking and communications, have allowed telemetry systems to evolve into a very user friendly operating tool. Operators can quickly and reliably access key data and control systems at remote sites. At the same time the data collected is stored and can be utilised in other parts of the organisation.

After two decades of significant developments, water companies are no longer looking at telemetry as a tool just for system operation, but as a tool to achieve more strategic corporate objectives.

2.2 **Network modelling**

Ever since its inception over 50 years ago, hydraulic modelling has been used to answer many questions about water distribution systems and it is now a well established tool in the majority of water utilities world-wide. Its use today bears little resemblance to the early methods applied; as the tools have developed over the years, so have the applications.

In the past network models were constructed and used by engineers to solve specific problems. These models were generally very simple, containing only the significant mains and attributes to describe each problem. This was partly due to the difficulty in accessing data, but also due to the limitations of software and hardware. Easy-to-use software combined with wider market availability allows more people from a variety of disciplines in the utility to benefit. Applications for hydraulic modelling are now company-wide from operations to engineering, customer service and forward planning departments.

By providing more information on the operational aspects and behaviour of a system, network analysis is seen as an important part of supply and distribution management. With utilities increasingly being forced to operate their systems within much narrower bands of acceptable performance in order to meet the often conflicting requirements for operating cost reduction, water quality, leakage control, system reliability and customer satisfaction, good analysis is essential.

The models for current operational applications are typically 'average day' models that are factored to reflect the current demand and operating scenarios. Whilst this analysis is still useful it does not reflect the current status of the network as required by operators for hourly decision support.

3.0 **Why Link the Systems?**

There are many reasons why a utility may want to link their telemetry system to their network modelling tool. Any particular decision to link the systems will typically depend on the ease of operation, size and complexity of the network in question. The benefits to be gained and the applications that can be applied will be much greater in a system where there is less network understanding or where the security of system supply is critical.

Telemetry linked network models can be divided into three categories: off line, on-line and real-time. Off-line simulation refers to the manual process of data transfer from a telemetry system to a hydraulic simulator; once there an operator controls the network analysis. On-line simulation refers to the ability to automatically transfer telemetry data to a hydraulic model and perform network analysis calculations at predefined intervals. Real-time simulation has a variety of connotations within the industry; in this context we shall describe it as a model that runs precisely in parallel with the real system, constantly feeding on telemetry information. Real-time models require vast quantities of data to drive the model and hence are of limited use in distribution systems. Also to run in real-time a transient simulator (rather than a steady-state or quasi-dynamic simulator) is required. Because we are concentrating on the latter we shall not cover real-time simulation in any more detail; literature on this topic is available [3,5].

A few examples of the applications of on-line and off-line models are given below.

3.1 **Off-line Applications**

3.1.1 **Operating strategies**

Data from the telemetry database (current or historic) could be used to drive a network model in an off-line mode if required. Taking data away from the on-line system would allow the operator to test various operating strategies and the information gained from this could then be used to improve system operation in the future.

3.1.2. **Incident analysis**

Incident analysis is similar in many ways to the previous example. Data from the telemetry database could be used to drive a model to find out what happened after an event. For example, in the aftermath of a pollution incident the priority is to clean the network and resume supply to the customers. A simulation using data from the time of the incident could be run to analyse and design a mains flushing program.

3.1.3. **Operator training**

An additional aspect of such an interface is the possibility to transfer simulated data and results back from the network for display on disconnected SCADA screens. This can be used as an excellent training tool to enable a new operator to see how a normal or emergency situation unfolds and how to interpret incipient signals so that he/she may take early preventive action.

3.2 **On-line Applications**

3.2.1. **Supplemental information**

Information from telemetry systems is only available where monitoring devices have been installed. A hydraulic model with current operating conditions imposed can calculate the state of the entire modelled network thus providing a more detailed picture of the system behaviour than is available from telemetry alone.

3.2.2. **Management of operational variations**

A network model that uses current system conditions to run the simulation can help system managers and operators look to not only at the whole system at the time in question but also to look forward in time. This can help operators to predict and hence take corrective action to prevent supply problems from occurring – proactive network management.

3.2.3. **Short and long term forecasting**

Similarly the predictive model could be used to look forward at a variety of future possible demand scenarios. Data collected over time in the telemetry system could be gathered and used to derive flow profiles for different days, weeks and seasons of the year. Based on the fact that water usage will follow fairly similar patterns given the day of the week, time of year and the weather, the predictive model could be refined to better forecast future demand.

3.2.4. **Incident prediction**

In a system emergency, for example, failure of pumps or a pollution incident, understanding how to ensure security of supply or to recover from the incident is critical. By running the simulation with present system conditions imposed, the extent of the incident can be quickly evaluated and appropriate action taken.

4.0 **Model/Telemetry Data Sharing**

The model/SCADA system interface requires three basic components: an accurate hydraulic model and modelling software, a SCADA system, and a method of transferring information between the two information systems. Each of these components is further addressed below.

4.1 **Hydraulic Model and Network Modelling Software**

An accurate, calibrated hydraulic model of all network facilities is a fundamental requirement. A network model file contains a complete hydraulic characteristic description of all network elements (e.g., pipes, pumps, reservoirs, valves, etc.) and their connectivity. It also contains a description of a specific water consumption distribution and pattern, as well as the operational data settings for a specific simulation (e.g., reservoir levels, status of pumps/valves, control scheme, etc.).

Network Modelling Software (NMS) must have the capability to import and export operational status data, which is the data component of interest for the SCADA data transfer.

Each operational facility in a model must be labelled with a unique name.

4.2 **SCADA System**

The SCADA system must be approached with a view towards identifying the required data to be monitored and potentially transferred. Firstly it is essential that all the key facility data are accessible in the SCADA system and that all values identified for transfer have a unique label (ideally the same as in the model). The SCADA system must also have some degree of programmability to permit the generation of a standard format data file (e.g., ASCII text, CSV, etc.) containing the operational data for the NMS.

4.3 **SCADA/Model Interface**

Perhaps the most critical link in the whole process is the interface between the SCADA system and the NMS. The process involves the development of a simple program that will extract the current values (most recent values of pressure, flow, status, etc.) from the SCADA database and write them to an exchange file of a certain structure.

The transfer of data between the SCADA system and the model focuses on the operational data only - a very small percentage of the network model data. Operational data consists of key operational states of non-pipe facilities, such as pump states, tank/reservoir levels, operational control valve positions. It also consists of corresponding monitored pressure and flow values, which are known as reference values. The operational values need to be set in the model to match the current condition in the network. The reference values are brought into the model so that the modeller can compare the simulated pressure and flow values to the recorded values for the new operating condition.

The focus of the interface therefore lies on establishing the correct correlation between the same data item in the SCADA system and the hydraulic model (i.e., ensuring that you are indeed transferring the level of reservoir X and not reservoir Y), and to implement the proper data validation checks to ensure that correct data is transferred. The key to this process is prudent labelling or development of a simple lookup table.

4.4 **Data Transfer**

From the hydraulic model perspective, data exchange means a network is first loaded into the simulator and then the operating conditions and reference values are replaced by reading in and superimposing new operational data.

The data can be passed over in one of two ways, manually or automatically, the method chosen depending on the application to which the telemetry-interfaced model is being used and the availability and frequency of the data.

4.4.1 **Manual**

Manual data transfer requires a trained operator to request the NMS to import the model data file and then the exchange file containing the telemetry data. The operator would then have to manually run the simulation making all the appropriate system decisions. Results and a log of the simulation events can then be returned to relevant users within the wider business environment.

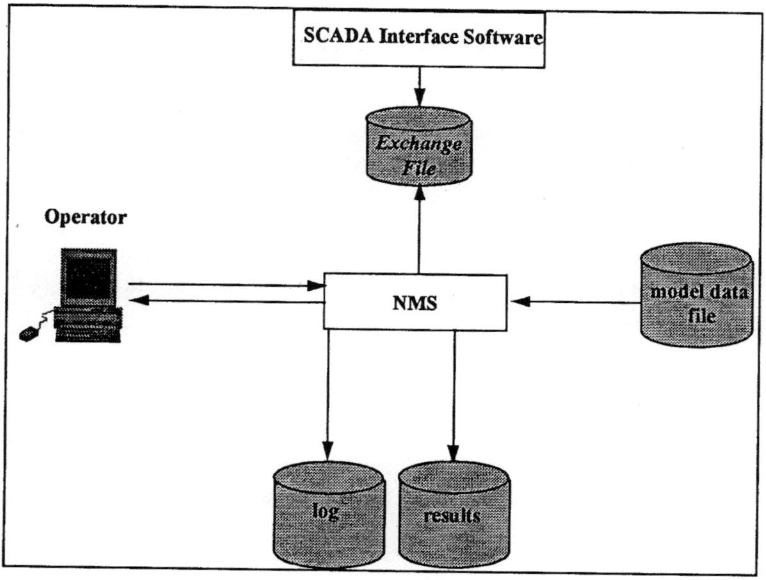

4.4.2 **Automated**

Automated transfer of the telemetry data would allow us to speed up the process somewhat and allow the simulation to operate on-line. In such a case the whole operation would be run by a program that we shall call the on-line module (OLM). At set intervals, the SCADA system will output an exchange file, and the OLM periodically checks for the existence of a new file. If a new file is not found the OLM will 'idle'; if a file is found the OLM will instruct the NMS to retrieve the model data file and import the current operating condition found in the new exchange file.

The OLM will then instruct the NMS to balance the network, compare the calculated results against predefined system conditions or rules and report on any anomalies. These anomalies could be sent directly to the operators screen or passed over by email. After concluding the reporting process the OLM instructs the NMS to display the graphic results and will 'idle' until another exchange file is generated.

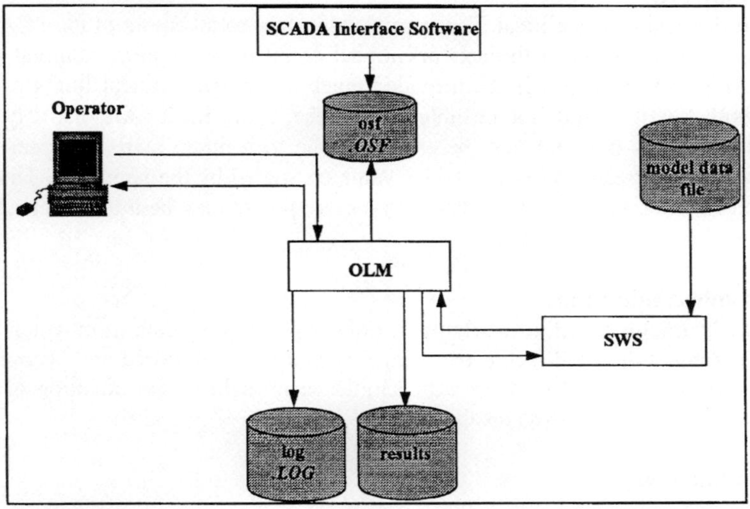

4.5 **Data Issues**

Availability of all data values is a key issue. Data are typically well monitored at key stations, but sometimes this is not the case for less frequently used stations. The hydraulic model will benefit from as many in-system pressure and flow values as can possibly be given. These data, even if not used to drive the simulation, can be used to validate that the updated model accurately reflects the current operating condition.

Frequently, however, there will be differences between the data reported by the telemetry system and those calculated by the hydraulic model. Upon commission of a telemetry interface, the hydraulic model must be calibrated in much the same way as an off line hydraulic model. From then on the model must draw its data from the telemetry system. Its accuracy is therefore highly dependent on the robustness and delivery of the data to the interface.

Unfortunately there will always be problems for a variety of reasons. Some situations that will directly affect the model are:

4.5.1 **Failure of a telemetry outstation**
For whatever reason (maintenance, damage, electrical failure etc.), a telemetry outstation may fail. However, the network analysis must continue.

Three of the most commonly used methods for continuing the simulation are:

- Continue using the last known good point.

- Continue by trending the last known good points.
- Continue if possible by omitting the missing piece of data.

4.5.2 **Data integrity**

Integrity of the data is also critical. For example, data can be taken out of the SCADA database as is. If this occurs, the network model could perform some nominal data error checking, for example: 'is the provided level within the physical limits of the tank levels?', but it would not be able to test the value itself. Alternatively, an abnormally high/low pressure may be extracted due to a pump start/stop transient, which would not correspond to the 'stable' value computed by the simulator. Thus, a comparison between the last three recorded pressure points may be a useful check to implement.

4.5.3 **Instrument calibration**

As with any hydraulic model, a simulation is only as good as the data from which it is derived. Instrument drift will occur over time and must be monitored and accounted for in any on-line model. Excessive drift should be brought to the attention of the operators and the instruments be recalibrated.

5.0 **Benefit Summary**

The successful implementation of the tools described in this chapter will impact and benefit many areas of network management. As with many IT based initiatives the costs incurred are often easy to identify, whilst the benefits are difficult to express in numerical terms. Those responsible for the safe and efficient operation of distribution networks will, however, recognise the benefits that have been identified to date. These include:

- Protection of the existing investment in network models by ensuring up-to-date model data and calibration.
- Improved system knowledge by simple, regular review of operating conditions.
- Comprehensive and efficient instrumentation maintenance schedules.
- Improved customer service through prediction and resolution of potential system problems.
- Improved incident response.
- Efficient communication between business functions within a company driven by the requirement to share data.

6.0 **Conclusions**

The techniques that we have discussed in this chapter describe the methodology utilised by a number of utilities to develop a telemetry interface to their network models. Whilst many companies have developed these systems as prototypes, there are some that have installations fully commissioned. With the concept of data transfer proven, most of these utilities are now in a period of review whilst reorganisation takes place and the new working practises installed are established.

Those companies that have not yet implemented telemetry linkages to their various corporate systems are in many cases ensuring that any new architectures will allow for such a development. As new telemetry systems are installed (or older ones refurbished and upgraded) the data transfer capability is usually a high priority in the specification. This confirms the trend in SCADA system design and implementation from their traditional role as alarm management systems to a wider IT environment where the need exists to present the data gathered by the system to a far larger user community.

While the implementation of this technology in most water companies is still the exception rather than the rule, the techniques are now proven and with the developments in the equipment, data transfer, network models and the interfaces, the installation of future systems should be cheaper, simpler and quicker.

References

1. Schulte A.M. & Malm A. 1993. Integrating Hydraulic Modelling and SCADA Systems for System Planning and Control. *AWWA Journal,* Vol. 85, No. 7: 62-66.
2. Joyner, M. & W.G. Wright 1996. Distribution Network Management - Norwich and Beyond. *AWWA Computer Conference,* Chicago, IL, April 21-24.
3. Wike, A. 1991. The Changing Significance of SCADA Information. *Proceedings of the 1991 American Gas Association Distribanon/lransmission Conference.*
4. Bonema, S., Elain, C., Mercier, M. & Tiburce, V. 1995 Linking SCADA With Network Simulation.
5. Wike, A. 1993. Simulation Applications Integrated With SCADA Systems. *Proceedings of the 1993 Australian Gas Association's SCADA Conference.*
6. Green, A. 1996. Hydraulic Modelling - Where is it Going?. *Knowledge, Data and Information 1996,* Buxton, UK, 3 April.
7. Cirugeda Garcia, M. 1997. Integrating a SCADA System with SWS Gas for the GasNatural Distribution System in Madrid, *TEAM Europe* 97, Birmingham, UK, 4-5 June.

CHAPTER 10

Automatic Predictive Control of the Exploitation of a Small Hydropower Scheme

M.Gómez, J.Rodellar *and* A.Gallego

Abstract

In this chapter, a control algorithm to operate small hydropower systems is presented. This algorithm is developed on the basis of a predictive control strategy, whose applications in other hydraulic systems, like irrigation canals, are well known. One of the main advantages of this system is that its parameters can be obtained from physical data of the hydropower system (penstock diameter and length, forebay area, etc.). The algorithm proposed is compared with a traditional PID regulator. In all cases, results are quite similar although the predictive controller can be more stable in front of some situations.

1. Introduction

The operation of hydropower schemes, such as the one illustrated in Figure 1, should guarantee maximum efficiency of the turbinated flows. Sometimes, variations of the circulating flow discharge in the diversion channel of a hydroelectric scheme modify the operating conditions, making it advisable to reduce or to increase the turbinated flow according to such variations. In order to obtain the maximum benefit, the height should be the greatest possible while avoiding spillings through the safety spillway and the flow should be that which permits the maximum volume of turbinated water, keeping in mind efficiency. A criterion of development could be to keep the maximum head, which means to keep the highest possible water level in the forebay. This would help to optimize the energy production.

The basic outline of the hydropower scheme studied is indicated in Figure 1. This chapter proposes the design of an algorithm for automatic control of the hydraulic system, based on a predictive control strategy. The objective is to maintain a desired constant water level in the forebay. The efficiency of the algorithm is evaluated by means of numerical studies with a hydraulic model simulating the behaviour of the channel. At the same time it is intended to compare the behaviour of the new control algorithm with other more classic controllers such as the PID.

2. Control Algorithm Development

In small hydropower schemes, generally installation is designed in such a way that, in the operating conditions of the turbine, the efficiency will be at maximum and should not oscillate too much according to the flow variations.

In order to maximize efficiency and energy production, the powerhouse includes some automatic controllers to regulate the turbine. Feedback controllers are the the most traditional and PID is the principal among them. PID controllers can be adapted to work with the relative error around a stationary workpoint as proposed by Betamio and Pinheiro [1]. This formulation can be very effective for small time steps. But this controller needs to know the values of some coefficients to operate, for instance, the proportional, integral or derivative gain coefficients (K_P, K_I and K_D). The estimation of these values can be made by means of numerical simulations of the system or through field tests in the hydropower plant. But sometimes, because some elements of the system are not well known (local losses in bends, distributors, regulators, etc) estimation of the values of the gaining constants cannot be precise enough.

In the field of Hydraulic Engineering, predictive control has been shown to be effective for regulation of irrigation channels, as it has been demonstrated in different studies [2]. Considering the predictive control formulation [3], different types of algorithms are proposed, according to the following issues:

- Control variable, which may be the opening of the turbine valve.

- Type of state of equilibrium, constant or variable with time.

- Type of outlined algorithm, equation in a first order difference equation or incremental formulation.

3. Control Algorithm Options: Basic Developments

Let's consider the scheme of Figure 2, composed of the forebay, penstock and the hydraulic turbine. It's one of the simplest small hydropower systems, and very common in Spain. Without any loss of generality, in order to simplify the hydraulic analysis, we consider at the final end of the penstock a local loss, representing the existence of a sluice valve, instead of the turbine. This assumption is reasonable for a Pelton turbine scheme, but for a Francis turbine scheme the characteristic curves of the turbine should be considered. In this case, the local energy loss should be understood as a simplified approach of the energy production of the turbine. The mass conservation applied to the forebay area can be expressed as,

$$Q_c - Q_t = A_f \frac{dH}{dt} \tag{1}$$

where Q_c is the discharge from the canal, Q_t is the turbinated discharge, A_f is the forebay area and H is the water height at the forebay. The turbinated discharge is a function of the geometry and losses, and can be expressed from the energy conservation equations as:

$$Q_t = \sqrt{\frac{H}{\frac{1}{2gA_p^2} - \frac{n_p^2 L_p}{A_p^2 (D/2)^{4/3}} - \Sigma \frac{k_i}{2gA_p^2} - \frac{K(a)}{2gA_p^2}}} \tag{2}$$

where L_p is the penstock length, D the penstock diameter, A_p the penstock section, n_p the Manning roughness coefficient of the penstock, k_i the local losses of the system and K(a) the equivalent local loss representing the turbine, associated to a specified valve opening (a). If we combine equations 1 and 2, we can write a nonlinear differential equation describing the process:

$$\frac{dH}{dt} = \frac{1}{A_f} Q_c - \frac{1}{A_f} \sqrt{\frac{H}{\alpha - \omega K(a)}} \tag{3}$$

where α and ω are a function of the physical data of the system. This is a nonlinear differential equation but in order to apply a control algorithm we need to work with a linear differential equation. We can consider an initial equilibrium state (steady state), characterized by a set of hydraulic values $\overline{Q}_c = \overline{Q}_t$, $\overline{H}$, $\overline{a}$ and $\overline{K(a)}$. These values agree with equations 1 and 2. Linearizing the differential equation (3) around the equilibrium state, neglecting second order terms, we obtain

$$\frac{d}{dt}(\Delta H) = \frac{1}{A_f}(\Delta Q_c) - \frac{\overline{Q}_t}{2\overline{H} A_f}(\Delta H) + \left[\frac{\overline{Q}_t}{(\alpha + \omega \overline{K}(a)) A_f} \omega \, \overline{K(a)} \right] (\Delta a) \tag{4}$$

where ΔH, ΔQ_c, Δa are the differences between H, Q_c, a and $\overline{H}$, $\overline{Q}_c$ and $\overline{a}$ equilibrium values. By simplifying the notation, we can rewrite the equation (4) in the form

$$\dot{y} = C\,y + D\,u + E\,v \tag{5}$$

where (y), is the output to be controlled (in our case the water level at the forebay ΔH), (u) is the control action (valve opening Δa) and (v) is an external perturbation (discharge coming from the canal ΔQ_c).

4. Predictive Model

Predictive control essentially relies on the use of a discrete–time model allowing prediction of the process output over a moving time horizon and computation of the control that makes the predicted output verify given performance criteria [3]. In the case considered in this chapter, based on eq. 5 describing the process, we can write the following predictive model, expressing the time variation of the water level in a discrete–time form, as:

$$\hat{y}(k+j|k) = \tau\,\hat{y}(k+j-1|k) + \beta\,\hat{u}(k+j-1|k) + \gamma\,\hat{v}(k+j-1|k) \tag{6}$$

where $\hat{y}(k+j|k)$ is the prediction made at instant k of the y value at time k+j, as a function of future values of u and v. Coefficients (τ, β, γ) can be expressed from the physical data of the system and the time step considered. k is the sampling instant and [k,k+λ] is a fictitious moving scenario used to predict the water level at the forebay. At every sampling time k, the model is redefined with the known values of y,u and v.

The predictive control strategy allows us to obtain the value of the control action $\hat{u}$(k|k), the first value of the control sequence over [k,k+λ], according to a performance criterion that should be specified. One such criterion could be to impose the condition that the water level in the forebay at instant k+λ is the desired setpoint value. If we write equation (6)in a recursive form from the time instant k to k+λ, we obtain:

$$\hat{y}(k+\lambda|k) = \tau^{\lambda} y(k) + \tau^{\lambda-1}\beta\hat{u}(k|k) + \tau^{\lambda-2}\beta\hat{u}(k+1|k) + ... + \beta\hat{u}(k+\lambda-1|k) +$$

$$\tau^{\lambda-1}\gamma\hat{v}(k|k) + ... + \gamma\hat{v}(k+\lambda-1|k) \tag{7}$$

We also assume that the control action (valve opening) is constant within the time horizon [k+1, k+λ]. Moreover, if we have no information concerning the perturbation (discharge from the hydroelectric canal, v), we will assume that it is approximately constant during the same time period. That is,

$$\hat{u}(k) = \hat{u}(k+1) = \hat{u}(k+2) = \ldots = \hat{u}(k+\lambda) \tag{8}$$

$$\hat{v}(k) = \hat{v}(k+1) = \hat{v}(k+2) = \ldots = \hat{v}(k+\lambda) \tag{9}$$

Finally, just imposing that $\hat{y}(k+\lambda|k)$ is zero in (7) and using (8) and (9), we obtain the control action as:

$$u(k) = \hat{u}(k|k) = \frac{-\tau^{\lambda}\, y(k) - (\tau^{\lambda-1} + \tau^{\lambda-2} + ... + 1)\gamma\, v(k)}{\beta\,(\tau^{\lambda-1} + \tau^{\lambda-2} + ... + 1)}$$

The term of discharge $v(k)$ is considered as a perturbation of the system and we can make different assumptions concerning its value. The control algorithm can adopt $v(k) = 0$ values, or $v(k)$ as an estimated/measured value. Control action will be different in both cases. In order to obtain a more stable control action, it would be recommended to include in the control algorithm an estimation of the discharge. The control action has another parameter: the length λ of the scenario to predict the water level at the forebay. The greater the λ value, the less intense the control action. The smaller the λ value, the more intense the control action.

5. Test Examples

One of the purposes of this work is to show the ability of the predictive control algorithm in comparison with the traditional controllers, in particular a PID controller. We will, therefore, analyse the behaviour of the predictive control algorithm and the PID for different operations in a hydropower scheme. We will follow the same examples presented by Betamio and Pinheiro [1]. We consider a 500 m long canal, with rectangular cross-section of 0.8 m width. The Slope is 0.0005 with a Manning roughness coefficient of 0.012. The forebay area is 50 m^2 and a safety spillway is located with a 1.2 m height over the forebay level, 5 m width and a discharge coefficient of 0.4. The penstock is 6 m long, with a 0.4 m diameter pipe and a 0.010 Manning roughness coefficient. The height between forebay and turbine is 6 m. System losses are estimated by a k_i=0.2 value.

The predictive control algorithm tested is designed for a λ=2 and a sampling time of 20 seconds. The PID controller parameters have been obtained by means of the ultimate sensitivity method, with a K_p=3.5, K_I=0.475 and K_D=17.5 values. More details are given in [4].

5.1. Test 1

We show the behaviour for a discharge variation at the upstream end of the canal, as shown in Figure 3, first a reduction and after an increase of discharge. The results are quite similar for both the PID and the predictive algorithm. Water level at the forebay is mantained in a level close to the initial setpoint value (Figure 4). Discharge evolution is presented in Figure 5 for both controllers. As a conclusion we may say that both provide good results.

5.2. Test 2

In this case (a decrease in the upstream discharge, Figure 6.a), some of the control algorithms can fail (for instance, Proportional controllers) because they do not recover the equilibrium state. They can establish another different equilibrium level, but not the initial one. In this case, again the predictive control algorithm and the PID recover the initial water level (Figure 6b).

5.3. Test 3

Case 3 describes an increase in upstream discharge (Figure 7a). In this case the PID had to be recalibrated (K_P=4.1, K_I=0.05 and K_D=52) in order to avoid some instabilities. Even with this set of parameters the PID controllers seem to be within the stability limits. The level results are shown in Figure 7b. Both controllers recover the initial water level but the PID produces more oscillations than the predictive controller.

6. Conclusions

The analysis and comparison of the results of the different types of controllers leads to the following conclusions:

Predictive controllers are an efficient alternative in the automatic control of hydropower schemes. Parameters of the predictive controller can be directly estimated from physical values of the system (forebay area, penstock length, diameter, etc.) and they do not show the adjustment problems as those of PID, whose parameters should be estimated from experience with the real system to control.

Most predictive controllers used are more stable than the PID controller In the presence of significant input disturbances.

If we have a PID controller that is well calibrated, it may not be necessary to substitute a predictive controller. However, in the case of new construction or automation, introducing a predictive controller is very convenient, since it reduces installation and calibration problems. The same can be said in the case of a reform in the canal or a variation of the operating conditions (increase of discharges), because the PID must be recalibrated, while the predictive controller need not be.

7. References

[1] Pinheiro, A., Betamio de Almeida, A. (1992). Water level regulation

in forebays of small hydropower schemes. in 'Unsteady Flow and Fluid Transients'. Ed. R. Bettes, J. Watts. Balkema. Rotterdam.

[2] Rodellar, J., Gómez, M., Bonet, L. (1993). On–demand operation of open-channel flow. Journal of Irrigation and Drainage Engineering. April. ASCE.

[3] Martín Sánchez, J.M., Rodellar, J., 1996. Adaptive Predictive control. Prentice–Hall.

[4] Gallego, A., 1996. Automatic control of the exploitation of a hydroelectric scheme. (in spanish). Minor Thesis. ETS. Ing. Caminos. UPC. Barcelona.

Acknowledgements

This work is partially supported by the Spanish Ministry of Education and Science, through the grant HID96-1417. Thanks are due to the School of Civil Engineering for their economic support.

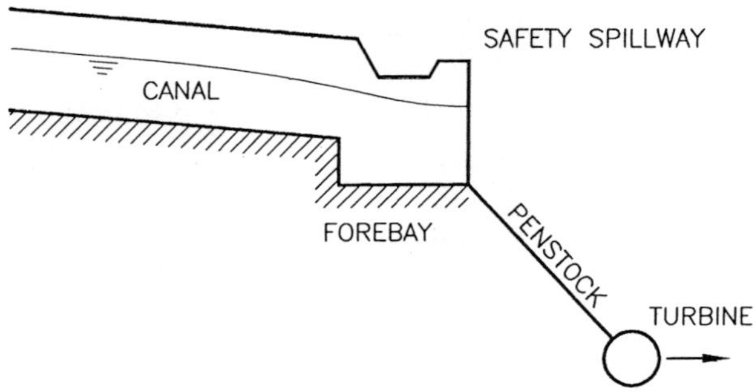

Figure 1. A small hydropower scheme

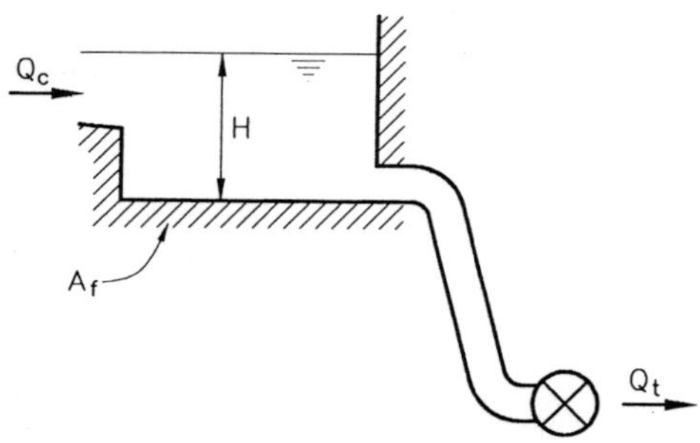

Figure 2. Forebay scheme: canal, forebay and penstock

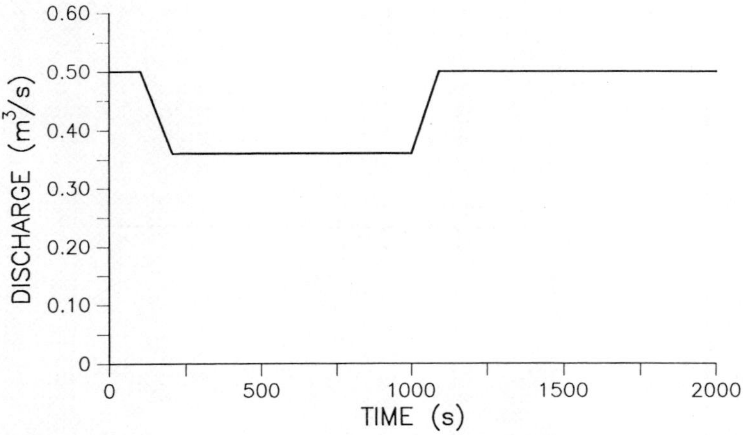

Figure 3. Test 1. Upstream discharge

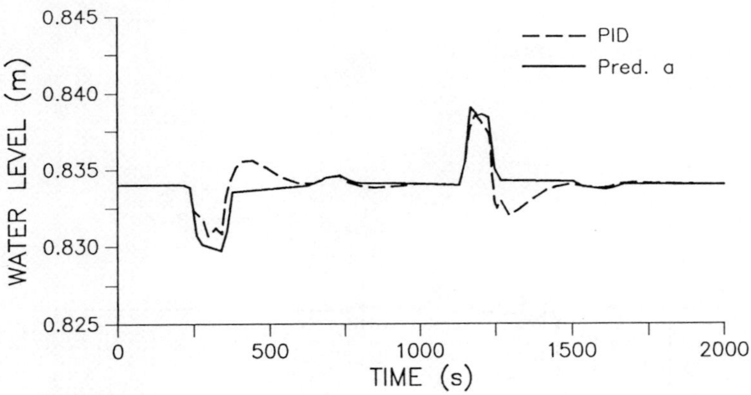

Figure 4. Test 1. Forebay water level evolution

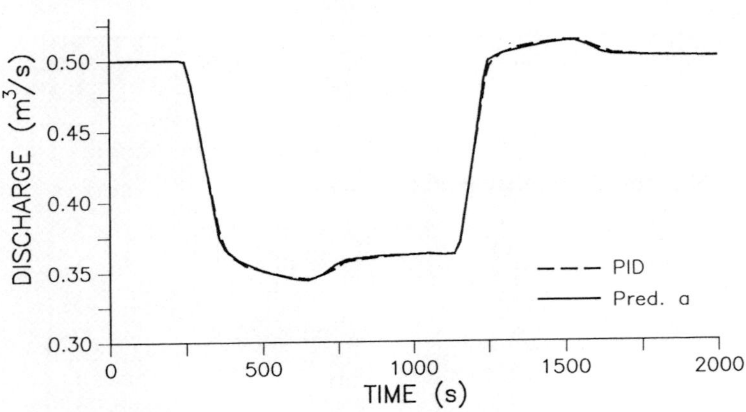

Figure 5. Test 1. Turbinated discharge evolution

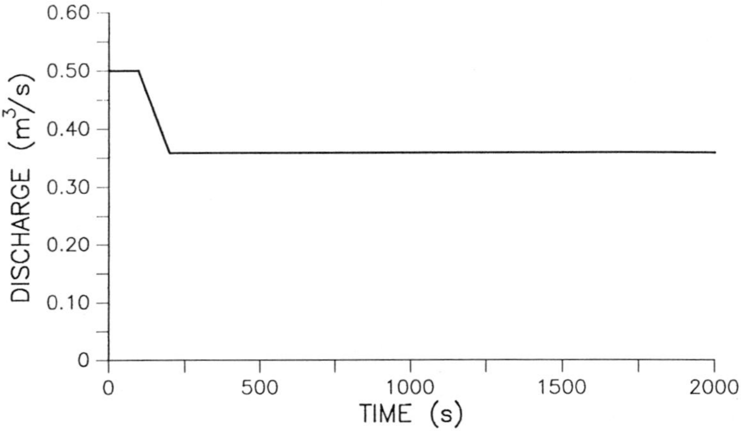

Figure 6a. Test 2. Upstream discharge

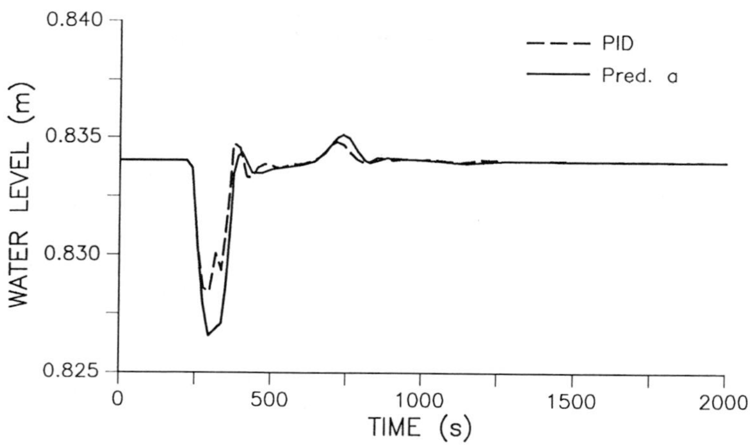

Figure 6b. Test 2. Forebay level evolution

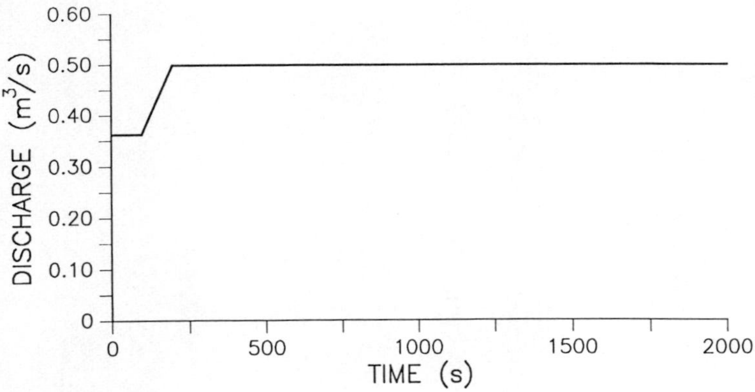

Figure 7a. Test 3. Upstream discharge

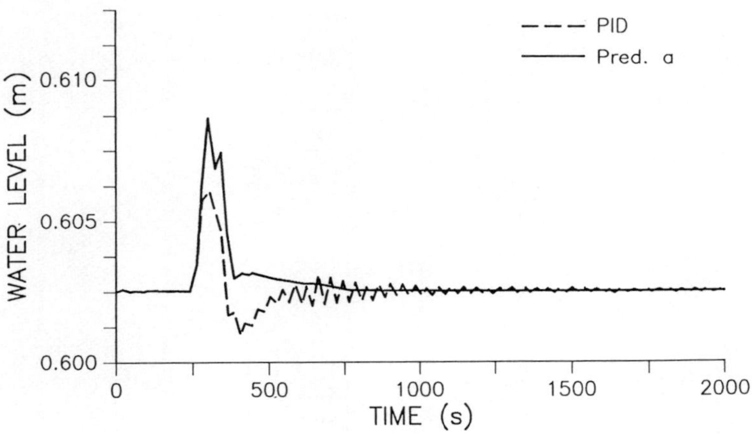

Figure 7b. Test 3. Forebay level evolution

CHAPTER 11

Operational Water Management of a Canal System

E.Arnold, H.Linke *and* R.Franke

1 Introduction

This chapter presents a decision support system for operational water management of a large navigable canal system.

The canal system under consideration is situated in northern Germany. It consists of three sections, each at a different height above sea level, with a total length of about 380 km. Five pump stations with a total electrical power of about 20 MW compensate for the water volume needed for raising and lowering ships at the locks between the canal sections.

The main purpose of such water management is to guarantee navigable water levels with minimum electrical energy (pump) costs. According to the dynamics of the system, operational management means a control horizon of several days with an update of the control decision every two hours.

Up to now, each pump station is controlled almost independently using local control rules and the operator's experience. The decision support system described here has been developed as part of a central process control system which is currently being installed.

Using similar techniques as for operational control of large drinking water supply systems and reservoir systems (see, e.g., [3], [14], [1]), the operational water management problem is formulated as an optimal control problem with a suitable control horizon. The pump and discharge flows are the decision variables of this optimal control problem.

Unfortunately, a process model based only on the volume balance equations of the individual sections would not reproduce the behavior of the system correctly. Strong wind, for instance, may cause local violations of navigable water levels because of the great length of the canal sections. Therefore, a model based on the numerical solution of the Saint Venant equations is used in order to reproduce such states of the canal and to be able to derive the correct control decisions.

Details of the process model and the numerical method for simulation are given in section 2.

In section 3, the discrete-time optimal control problem is stated and the sequential quadratic programming (SQP) solution procedure for the related nonlinear programming problem is outlined.

The decision support system provides optimal pump and discharge flows as control proposals to the operator. Due to differences between the model and reality, these control proposals have to be updated after some time, taking into account the real process behavior and actual predictions of the noncontrollable inputs, i.e. water demand of the locks, wind, and additional inflow. In that sense, a model-based predictive (or receding horizon) control strategy is developed (see, e.g., [8]). Details, including state estimation and constraint relaxation techniques are given in section 4.

2 Model

The process model has to describe the change of water level in space and time with sufficient accuracy. Besides the conservation of mass, the model has to reproduce long term effects of pump and discharge strategies as well as wind stress. Furthermore, the model has to be sufficiently smooth, in order to allow application of a derivative-based optimization algorithm.

The Saint Venant equations in their conservation form

$$\frac{\partial}{\partial t}\begin{pmatrix} A \\ Q \end{pmatrix} + \frac{\partial}{\partial \xi}\begin{pmatrix} Q \\ Q^2/A + P \end{pmatrix} = \begin{pmatrix} q \\ A\tau - gAS_f \end{pmatrix} \tag{1}$$

fulfill these model requirements, where A is the wet cross section of the canal, Q is the flow and P is the total pressure on A as a function of time t and position ξ. The lateral inflow is denoted by q.

The frictional slope S_f, which depends on the bottom structure, is described by the formulation of Chezy/Manning

$$S_f = \frac{n^2 Q|Q|}{A^2 {R_H}^{4/3}}, \tag{2}$$

where R_H denotes the hydraulic radius and n is the Manning roughness coefficient. Starting from first experiences with the simulation of the canal system, a quadratic formula was chosen for the wind stress τ. The Manning roughness coefficient and the wind stress coefficients have to be estimated from measurements and management data.

The Godunov method, which is based on the integral form of the underlying hyperbolic system and the solution of Riemann problems, is used for the numerical solution of (1). Each part of the canal system is therefore divided into equidistant cells with the states (A and Q) defined as the respective average over each cell.

In order to avoid difficulties with respect to the nonlinearity of the flux function (second term of (1)) a local linearization due to Roe [10] is used. The nonhomogeneous terms of (1) are handled by a decomposition with respect to the eigenvectors of linearized flux function [12]. The ends of each section of the canal system are considered as closed (solid wall condition). Therefore, all external influences on the volume balance (controllable and noncontrollable inflows) can be put together in the lateral inflow q, and the course of one dependent variable can be determined easily ($Q = 0$). The space discretization is chosen as 12 km with regard to the time restrictions for the computation of a new decision proposal. The discrete time step has to satisfy the Courant-Friedrichs-Lewy (CFL) condition and is fixed to 30 min according to an upper bound for the characteristic speed.

The validity of the model was first examined by comparative simulations with a high resolution model of the canal system (space discretization 200 m).

Further tests of the model – including the adaption of parameters like the Manning roughness coefficient and wind stress coefficients – were carried out on the basis of level and wind measurements, as well as lockage water and realized pump and discharge strategies from the last quarter of 1996. Fig. 1 shows the water level measurements and the simulated trajectories from estimated initial states at two locations of the western section of the canal system starting from 19/12/96 6.00 am. In this period of time the wind speed was up to 9 m/s, mainly from the east.

3 Optimal Control Problem

3.1 Problem formulation

The discretized Saint Venant equations of the canal model result in the discrete-time state equation of the process model

$$x^{k+1} = f^k(x^k, u^k, z^k), \quad k = 0, \ldots, K-1 \tag{3}$$

with k denoting the discrete time index, the control horizon K, the state variables (flow and water level of the cells) $x^k \in \mathbb{R}^n$, the control variables (pump and discharge flows) $u^k \in \mathbb{R}^m$, and predictions of the noncontrollable inputs (water demand of the locks, wind, and additional inflow) z^k.

A horizon K of 48 h is used for the optimal control problem to avoid fixing of the final water volume, which could lead to more expensive control strategies.

For this long time interval the difference between real and simulated system behavior might become significant enough to result in wrong control strategies as solutions due to unavoidable uncertainties in the wind predictions and in the model itself. Therefore, the optimization horizon is divided into two parts and a simple model based on the volume balance is used for the second part.

The operational control objectives, i.e. preserving navigable water levels with minimum pump costs, are expressed in the cost function and in additional restrictions. Therefore, the performance criterion J includes electrical energy costs for operation of the pumps as well as additional terms for evaluation of the final state.

$$J = F(x^K) + \sum_{k=0}^{K-1} f_0^k(x^k, u^k) \rightarrow \min! \tag{4}$$

The initial state x^0 of the system is fixed. Water level restrictions resulting from the demand for navigable water levels as well as pump flow constraints are formulated as bound constraints of the state and control variables, respectively. Additional constraints $c^k(x^k, u^k, z^k)$ arise from water volume bounds in the separate sections of the canal system.

$$\begin{aligned} x^0 &= x_0 && \\ x^k_{min} \le x^k &\le x^k_{max}, && k = 0, \ldots, K \\ u^k_{min} \le u^k &\le u^k_{max}, && k = 0, \ldots, K-1 \\ c^k(x^k, u^k, z^k) &\le 0, && k = 0, \ldots, K-1 \end{aligned} \tag{5}$$

3.2 Numerical solution method

The discrete-time optimal control problem (3)–(5) is solved as a large-scale, structured nonlinear programming problem in the state and control variables

$$\min_x \left\{ J(x) \;\middle|\; h(x) = 0,\; c(x) \le 0 \right\} \tag{6}$$

$$x = \begin{bmatrix} x^0 \\ u^0 \\ x^1 \\ u^1 \\ \vdots \\ x^{K-1} \\ u^{K-1} \\ x^K \end{bmatrix}, \qquad h(x) = \begin{bmatrix} x^0 - x_0 \\ f^0(x^0, u^0, z^0) - x^1 \\ \vdots \\ f^{K-1}(x^{K-1}, u^{K-1}, z^{K-1}) - x^K \end{bmatrix}$$

with equality constraints $h(x)$ resulting from the state equations (3), and inequality constraints $c(x)$ resulting from (5).

A sequential quadratic programming (SQP) algorithm is used to solve (6) numerically:

Step 1: Start with an approximation x to the solution vector, the Lagrange multipliers λ and y, and a positive definite approximation H to the Hessian matrix $\nabla^2_{xx}L$ of the Lagrangian

$$L(x,\lambda,y) \;=\; J(x)+\lambda^T h(x)+y^T c(x)$$

Step 2: Solve the quadratic programming problem

$$\min_s \left\{ \frac{1}{2}s^T H s + \nabla J(x)^T s \mid \right. \tag{7}$$

$$\left. \nabla h(x)s + h(x) = 0,\; \nabla c(x)s + c(x) \le 0 \right\}$$

to obtain the solution vector s^+ and the Lagrange multipliers λ^+ and y^+.

Step 3: Use s^+ as a search direction in which the next approximation x^+ is to be found

$$x^+ \;=\; x+\alpha s^+$$

and a step length parameter $0 < \alpha \le 1$ which sufficiently reduces a suitable line search function.

Step 4: Update the matrix H by a quasi-Newton update formula using the vectors $x^+ - x$ and $\nabla_x L(x^+,\lambda^+,y^+) - \nabla_x L(x,\lambda^+,y^+)$.

Step 5: Set $x \;:=\; x^+$, $\lambda \;:=\; \lambda^+$, $y \;:=\; y^+$ and go to step 2.

The required derivatives (gradient ∇J, Jacobians ∇h and ∇c) are obtained by automatic differentiation (see, e.g., [5]).

Because of the high dimension of the optimization problem (more than 2500 optimization variables and 1500 equality constraints) it is essential to take into account the sparsity structure of the problem in the solution procedure:

- The gradient ∇J and the Jacobians ∇h and ∇c are calculated taking into account the stage-wise problem formulation in equations (3) and (5).
- The block-diagonal structure of the Hessian $\nabla^2_{xx}L$ is preserved during the quasi-Newton update using a high-rank update scheme due to [2].
- Because of its advantageous numerical behavior, especially for the large-scale problem at hand, an interior-point method [13] is used for the solution of the quadratic programming problem (7).

The interior-point algorithm can be outlined as follows. An approximate solution (s^+, λ^+, y^+) of the system of necessary optimality conditions for (7)

$$\begin{aligned} Hs + \nabla J(x) + \nabla h(x)^T\lambda + \nabla c(x)^T y &= 0 \\ \nabla h(x)s + h(x) &= 0 \\ w = -\nabla c(x)s - c(x) &\geq 0 \\ y &\geq 0 \\ y^T w &= 0 \end{aligned} \tag{8}$$

is obtained by a Newton method. During the iterative procedure, the vector of slack variables w and the Lagrange multipliers y are restricted to $(w, y) > 0$ (interior points) and the complementarity condition in the last line of (8) is replaced by

$$y_i w_i = \mu \quad i = 1, \dots, \dim(c(x))$$

with a parameter $\mu \geq 0$, which is forced to $\mu \to 0$.

The main computational effort of the interior-point method as well as of the whole SQP algorithm is the solution of the linear equation systems, which is generating the Newton steps for (8). Here the sparsity structure of the problem is exploited again.

A block factorization method similar to the extended Riccati solution described in [1] allows for calculation of the Newton step in $\mathcal{O}(K)$ operations.

The algorithm uses numerical routines of the Meschach library [11]. Further details of the implementation of the large-scale nonlinear programming solver HQP are given in [4].

4 Receding Horizon Control

Calculation of the optimal control has to be repeated during operation of the system because of deviations in the noncontrollable inputs from the predictions, measurement noise, and model errors.

The optimal control is updated every two hours, starting from the actual state of the canal system and using current predictions of the noncontrollable inputs. The optimization horizon is shifted, and only the initial phase of each of the optimal control trajectories is proposed to be applied to the system (see, e.g., [8], [6]). This scheme is known as receding horizon control or model-based predictive control.

For $\hat{k} = 0, 1, \dots$:

Step 1: Get the actual state $x(\hat{k})$ from state estimation.

Step 2: Get actual predictions of the noncontrollable inputs $z^k(\hat{k})$, $k = \hat{k}, \ldots, \hat{k} + K - 1$.

Step 3: Calculate $u^k(\hat{k})$, $k = \hat{k}, \ldots, \hat{k} + K - 1$ from

$$\min_{u^k,\, k=\hat{k},\ldots,\hat{k}+K-1} \left\{ J = F(x^{\hat{k}+K}) + \sum_{k=\hat{k}}^{\hat{k}+K-1} f_0^k(x^k, u^k) \;\middle|\; \begin{array}{rcll} x^{k+1} & = & f^k(x^k, u^k, z^k(\hat{k})), & k = \hat{k}, \ldots, \hat{k} + K - 1 \\ x^{\hat{k}} & = & x(\hat{k}), & \\ x^k_{min} \le x^k & \le & x^k_{max}, & k = \hat{k}, \ldots, \hat{k} + K \\ u^k_{min} \le u^k & \le & u^k_{max}, & k = \hat{k}, \ldots, \hat{k} + K - 1 \\ c^k(x^k, u^k, z^k(\hat{k})) & \le & 0, & k = \hat{k}, \ldots, \hat{k} + K - 1 \end{array} \right\} \tag{9}$$

Step 4: Apply $u^{\hat{k}}(\hat{k})$ to the process.

The predictions of the noncontrollable inputs in step 2 are obtained from extrapolating lockage water demand data from the past and from the short-term weather forecast (wind).

Because of the fixed speed pumps, the desired real valued pump flows (step 4) of the pump stations cannot be implemented directly. The optimal pump flow trajectory has to be translated into a schedule containing the number of pumps and the run times of each pump.

4.1 Constraint relaxation

The feasibility of the optimization problem (3)–(5) is an obvious requirement for the computation of an optimal control strategy. Under wind stress or flood conditions with large additional inflows into the canal system, infeasibility with respect to the water level restrictions is possible.

Therefore, the water level restrictions are relaxed and replaced with penalty terms on their violation, see, e.g., [9].

For instance, the upper bound constraints $x^k \le x^k_{max}$ are replaced by

$$x^k - \eta^k \le x^k_{max}, \quad \eta^k \ge 0, \quad K = \hat{k}, \ldots, \hat{k} + K,$$

the objective function J is extended by an ℓ_1 penalty term

$$\sum_{k=\hat{k}}^{\hat{k}+K} \rho^T \eta^k$$

and the slack variables η^k are handled as free optimization variables.

The relaxed problem has a local minimum at the solution point of the original problem, provided this solution exists and the penalty coefficients ρ are sufficiently large. If there is no feasible solution of the original problem, the solution of the relaxed problem minimizes the violation of the original constraints in the ℓ_1 sense.

4.2 State estimation

The actual state of the system is reconstructed from water level measurements $\tilde{y}$ at discrete locations and model inputs over the last hours of the experimental period using a least squares method. The applied optimization criterion is

$$\tilde{J} = \frac{1}{2} \sum_{k=\hat{k}-\tilde{K}}^{\hat{k}} \left(y(x^k) - \tilde{y}^k\right)^2 \longrightarrow \min_{x^{\hat{k}-\tilde{K}}}! \tag{10}$$

with the water level $y^k(x^k)$ calculated by the model (3) within the discrete time horizon $k = \hat{k} - \tilde{K}, \ldots, \hat{k}$ and with known control decisions in this past period. The least squares criterion (10) is minimized with respect to the initial state $x^{\hat{k}-\tilde{K}}$, from which the actual state $x^{\hat{k}}$ can be found by forward simulation.

Sensitivity analysis is used to investigate the identifiability of both water level and flow under measurement noise.

The confidence intervals for the states at time $k = \hat{k}$ are used to evaluate the estimation results. Simulation runs with normally distributed measurement errors $N(0, (0.02\,\mathrm{m})^2)$ lead to confidence intervals of about $\pm 0.02\,\mathrm{m}$ for the levels and of $\pm 3\,\mathrm{m}^3/\mathrm{s}$ for the flow in the discrete cells.

With the help of simulations, a period of 6 h of the experimental period was determined to be sufficient for the estimation of the initial states. An extension of this period can compensate for the failure of measuring instruments.

The determination of non-measurable inflows at known locations by solving an extended estimation problem is not possible due to the high uncertainty of these estimated parameters.

4.3 Simulation test of the decision support system

Simulation results of the closed-loop behavior of the decision support system are shown in Fig. 2 for the northern section of the canal system. The volume balance of this section has to be controlled by the facilities at both ends, in Uelzen (connection to the top section of the canal system) and in Lueneburg. The simulation is based on wind measurements and lockage water demand between 11/12/96 and 15/12/96. Disturbance-free measurements and correct predictions of the noncontrollable inputs for the optimization horizon were assumed for the test. During the first 24 h of the optimization horizon, the Saint Venant equations were used to describe the process dynamics.

The dashed lines show optimal solution trajectories starting from 11/12/96 6.00 am. The actual state of the canal system at this time was reconstructed based on real level measurements. The volume of the northern section was handled by 'soft' constraints to avoid infeasible initial values. Because of the topography of the canal system the volume of this section only increases during the operating time of the locks. Therefore the discharge strategy in Lueneburg was necessary to reduce the volume first and subsequently to keep it within the bounds. The slight violations of the volume bounds result from the follow-up treatment of the continuous control strategy to obtain discrete valued pump and discharge flows. The related nonlinear programming problem (3)–(5) has 2787 decision variables, 1731 equality, and 2791 inequality constraints. The solution takes 8 SQP steps and 163 interior-point steps. The CPU time is about 9 minutes on a Sun Ultra SPARC 1/140 workstation.

The solid lines show the closed loop behavior of the decision support system. Each moment of updating is marked with a circle. The water volume restrictions are fulfilled, and the pumps are operated mostly during the night time. The use of a shifted optimization horizon leads to a changed control strategy, which is adapted every two hours to take into account the lockage water demand predicted for the following 48 hours.

In the period of time for which simulation results were presented in Fig. 1, strong wind from an eastern direction leads to a sloping water surface with local violations of the level restrictions in the western section of the canal system. Fig. 3 shows the course of the water level in Fuestrup at the western end of this section. A complicated discharge strategy (solid lines) is necessary to keep the water level within predetermined bounds. A comparative simulation, taking into consideration only the volume balance of the section, shows the course of the water level without control operations (dashed lines).

5 Conclusions

A decision support system for operational water management is presented in this chapter, which will be implemented as part of the process control system of a navigable canal system.

The main objective of operational management is to preserve navigable water levels in the individual canal sections with minimum pump costs. The problem is formulated as a (discrete-time) optimal control problem using a canal model based on the (discretized) Saint Venant equations.

Comparisons of measured and simulated water levels show that the model is suitable for the control objectives outlined in this chapter.

A special numerical solution method based on sequential quadratic programming with an interior-point solver for the linear-quadratic sub-problems is necessary for solution of the large-scale and structured nonlinear programming problems resulting from the operational water management problem with its underlying space and time discretization scheme.

The numerical effort is reduced to such an extent that the algorithm can be used in a model-based predictive (or receding horizon) control scheme: calculation of the optimal control is repeated every two hours, taking into account the actual state of the canal system and predictions of the noncontrollable inputs.

First simulation tests of the decision support system have been carried out successfully assuming disturbance-free measurements and exact predictions.

The optimal control trajectories show the expected behavior, i.e. under normal operating conditions, the night time is used for compensation of the lockage water due to the lower electrical energy tariff at night. Under wind stress or flood conditions, a combined pump and discharge strategy has to ensure the predetermined water levels of the canal sections.

Further work will be employed on an extended simulation test of the decision support system using real-world input data and an extended period of time.

Another direction of further research is the identification of noncontrollable and not directly measurable inflows from water level measurements and management data. The use of predictions of these inflows has the potential to improve the control decisions.

Acknowledgment

This work has been supported by the Bundesanstalt für Wasserbau, Karlsruhe, Germany.

References

[1] E. Arnold, P. Tatjewski, and P. Wołochowicz. Two methods for large scale nonlinear optimization problems and their comparision on a case study example of hydropower optimization. *J. Optim. Theory Appl.*, 81(2):221–248, 1994.

[2] H. G. Bock and K. J. Plitt. A multiple shooting algorithm for direct solution of optimal control problems. In *9th World Congress of IFAC*, volume 9, pages 242–247, Budapest, 1984.

[3] M. A. Brdyś and B. Ulanicki. *Operational Control of Water Systems: Structures, Algorithms and Application.* Prentice Hall, 1994.

[4] R. Franke and E. Arnold. Applying new numerical algorithms to the solution of discrete-time optimal control problems. In K. Warwick and M. Kárný, editors, *Computer-Intensive Methods in Control and Signal Processing: The Curse of Dimensionality*, pages 105–118. Birkhäuser, Basel, 1997.

[5] A. Griewank, D. Juedes, and J. Utke. ADOL-C: A package for the automatic differentiation of algorithms written in C/C++. *ACM Transactions on Mathematical Software*, June 1996.

[6] L. Kershenbaum, D. Q. Mayne, R. Pytlak, and R. B. Vinter. Receding horizon control. In D. Clarke, editor, *Advances in Model-Based Predictive Control*, pages 523–535. Oxford University Press, Oxford, 1994.

[7] R.J. LeVeque. *Numerical Methods for Conservation Laws*. Birkhäuser Verlag, 1992.

[8] M. Morari. Model predictive control: multivariable control technique of choice in the 1990s? In D. Clarke, editor, *Advances in Model-Based Predictive Control*, pages 22–37. Oxford University Press, Oxford, 1994.

[9] C. V. Rao, S. J. Wright, and J. B. Rawlings. Application of interior-point methods to model predictive control. Preprint ANL/MCS-P664-0597, Mathematics and Computer Science Division, Argonne National Laboratory, 1997.

[10] P. L. Roe. Approximate Riemann solvers, parameter vectors, and difference schemes. *J. Comput. Phys.*, 1981.

[11] D. E. Stewart. *Meschach: matrix computations in C*. University of Canberra, Canberra, Australia, 1992.

[12] T. Weiyan. *Shallow water hydrodynamics*. Elsevier Oceanography Series. Elsevier, 1992.

[13] S. J. Wright. Interior point methods for optimal control of discrete time systems. *J. Optim. Theory Appl.*, 77(1):161–187, 1993.

[14] W. W-G. Yeh. Reservoir management and operations models: A state-of-the-art review. *Water Resources Research*, 21(12):1797–1818, December 1985.

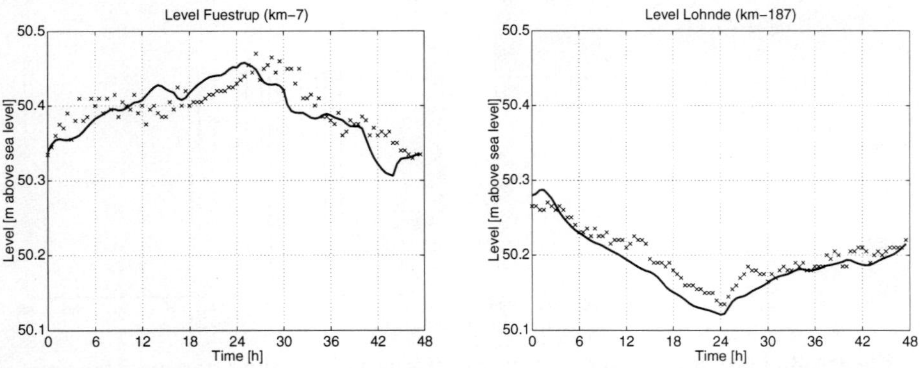

Figure 1. Measured (x-marks) and simulated (solid line) course of the water level at two different locations on the western section (total length 211 km)

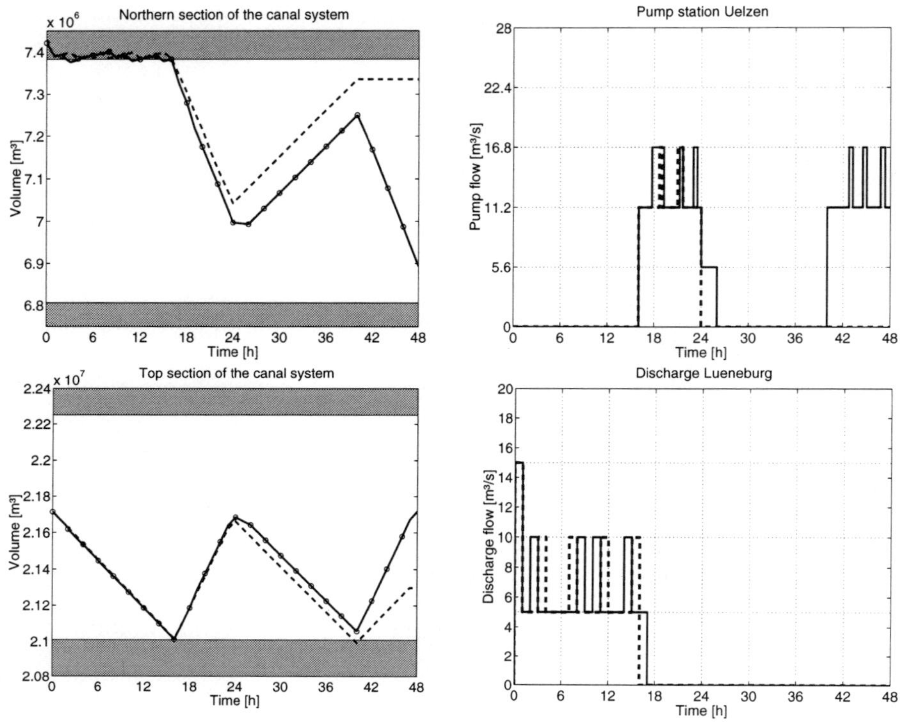

Figure 2. Closed loop behavior of the management system (starting 6.00 am)

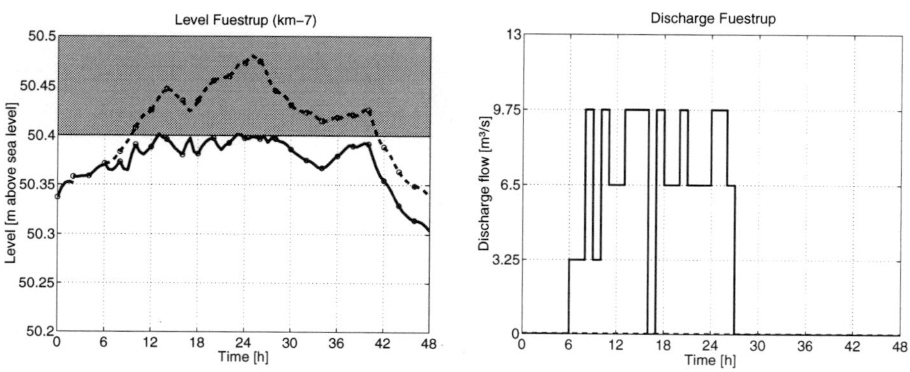

Figure 3. Level and discharge flow trajectories in Fuestrup (starting 6.00 am)

CHAPTER 12

Generalised Techniques for Optimisation of Water Networks

B.Ulanicki, B.Coulbeck *and* K.Ulanicka

1. Abstract

This chapter demonstrates that optimisation can significantly expand the scope of hydraulic analyses by solving inverse problems such as optimal scheduling, model calibration and design. A new generic optimisation approach based on a continuity assumption and the use of non-linear mathematical programming is proposed. This has been implemented to form a computer aided water network analysis facility. A high level of flexibility and functionality in solving optimisation problems has been achieved using the GAMS modelling language. Solution of a number of case studies has confirmed the advantages of the new approach. The method is illustrated by optimising a 4-reservoir, 4-pump station system. Overall the development is considered to be an important step towards creation of intelligent water network analysis systems.

2. Introduction

The chapter has four aims:

- To explain the role of optimisation in solving control and design problems.
- To discuss the importance of domain modelling languages, e.g. GAMS (Brooke *et al*, 1992) and LANCELOT (Conn et al., 1992).
- To propose an optimisation algorithm that can be used together with the modelling language to solve a wide range of optimisation problems for water networks.
- To compare some case-study results and produce example optimal schedules for the Yorkshire Grid system.

Computer Aided Water Engineering (CAWE) is evolving towards increased functionality and integration in the following sequence:

1. Independent applications packages for each type of analysis activity.

---

[1] This work was supported by EPSRC, Grant Ref: GR/K31923.

2. Integrated application modules with common task manager, common data store and common graphical user interface (GUI). Such modules enable co-ordinated execution and data exchange between different applications. While creation of a new application is a difficult task, its integration is comparatively easy.
3. Incorporation of modelling languages together with separation of modelling and execution activities (Figure 1). Special modelling languages ease the creation of new activities. Instead of a separate solver being required for each model, there can be a separate solver for each class of model (Figure 2). Integration is more complete because models are defined in the same language; development of new models is rapid and efficient.
4. Intelligent hydraulic analysis environment which will use various techniques, including simulation and optimisation, to answer general questions concerning engineering and operational tasks. This is for future development but such methodologies are already available for implementation (Russel and Norvig, 1995). Components of such systems will include a knowledge base, intelligent agents, a domain modelling language, and numerical solvers.

The chapter describes a third generation CAWE approach based on the GAMS modelling language. Water network analyses can be broadly categorised into direct tasks, such as simulation, and inverse tasks, such as pump scheduling. For the direct tasks the network input variables are pre-defined and the output variables must be determined, whereas for the inverse tasks the opposite, more difficult, problem occurs of deducing the input values. Water companies typically use network simulators for both types of task. However, use of a simulator for the inverse task can require an extended trial-and-error procedure. Starting from some initial assumptions repeated corrections are made to the input variables until the simulation output results are satisfactory. Optimisation techniques can solve such inverse problems directly and efficiently, and also have the potential to significantly enhance water network analyses. This latter case occurs when the input and output variables are each allowed to operate over ranges of practical values, and the optimisation method can then select the most cost effective solution from a multiplicity of feasible solutions. Such inverse problems for water networks, which can benefit from optimisation, are: pump scheduling (e.g. Yu and Powell, 1994), model calibration, component sizing (Ulanicki et al., 1993), etc.

3. Optimisation in water network analyses

Mathematical models of optimisation problems can be generally represented by a constraint set X and a cost function f that maps elements of X into real numbers. The set X consists of available decisions x, and the function $f(x)$ measures the cost of these decisions. An optimal decision is required, i.e. an $x^* \in X$, such that:

$$f(x^*) \leq f(x), \quad \forall x \in X. \tag{1}$$

The constraint set X is usually specified in terms of equality and inequality constraints:

$$\begin{aligned} h(x) &= 0; \\ g(x) &\leq 0. \end{aligned} \tag{2}$$

If the decision x is an n-dimensional vector of real numbers the problem is called a continuous mathematical programming problem. If some elements of the vector are discrete (e.g. integers) the problem belongs to a class of discrete mathematical programming. If the decisions are time functions then the problem belongs to the class of optimal control or dynamic optimisation. The computational complexity of discrete problems is exponential and is therefore much greater than for continuous ones, which are polynomial. In order to solve a practical problem it is necessary to prepare an optimisation model, formulate a set of equations, and subsequently use a library of numerical optimisation procedures to calculate the solution. There are standard numerical libraries (Conn *et al.* 19 (Drud, 1985) for continuous and discrete problems and researchers are now developing libraries for dynamic optimisation. Thus, the art of solving a problem is in preparing an optimisation model, i.e. transferring the problem from a conceptual form into a set of equations. Preparing a model usually involves the following steps (Fishwick, 1995):

- Prepare conceptual model in plain language.
- Identify major simplifying assumptions.
- Translate conceptual model into language of equations.

Separation of modelling from execution (Figure 2,) is a very useful concept that results in more powerful and flexible software.

Optimal control and design problems include a list of requirements that can be used to define a constraint set allowing many possible decisions. A search procedure chooses one that satisfies some beneficial and/or economic criteria. Typical hydraulic analysis problems that can benefit from the optimisation approach are optimal scheduling, model calibration and component sizing.

Optimal scheduling:

Minimise {*pumping cost+treatment cost*}

subject to

network equations; (3)

operational constraints;

where decision variables are operational schedules for control elements such as *pump schedules, valve schedules, and water production schedules at treatment works.*

Model calibration

Minimise {*error between measurements and model*}

subject to

network equations; (4)

where decision variables are parameters of the model such as *pipe roughness and nodal demand.*

Pipeline design

Minimise {*capital cost + future operational cost*}

subject to

network equations; (5)

where decision variables are *pipe diameters*.

Consider the properties of the above tasks. Decisions in the optimal scheduling problem are time functions (pump and valve schedules) and some of them are discrete (pump on/off controls). The dynamic problem can easily be transferred into a static one using time discretisation. Furthermore, the discrete scheduling problem can be relaxed to a continuous one as is argued in the next section (continuity conjecture). Consequently, the scheduling problem can be reduced to a continuous mathematical programming problem. The model calibration problem is already a continuous mathematical programming problem, as dictated by the conceptual problem formulation. In the pipe-sizing problem, the decisions are represented by a vector of discrete variables because pipes are produced in discrete sizes. However, the continuous solution is normally a good approximation to the optimal discrete solution.

4. Optimisation algorithm

The mathematical model will be formulated for the optimal scheduling task. Other models can be formulated in a similar fashion.

Continuity conjecture

For optimal scheduling of most practical water systems, the optimal continuous solution is close to the optimal discrete solution.

Using this conjecture the optimal scheduling problem can be relaxed to a continuous one by assuming that all pump controls are continuous variables. This assumption means that the number of pumps switched on can vary continuously and, for example, 3.57 is a possible value for this variable. For practical application the continuous schedule, in the form of flow and head increase values versus time, must be translated into a valid pump control schedule. If a given operating point is not reachable instantaneously it can be achieved as an average over a time period. For instance, a sequence of 3 and 4 pumps would satisfy the above example. This procedure can be automated or it can be competently controlled by human system operators.

The continuity conjecture is not formally proven in this chapter but is confirmed in practice and in solved cases as illustrated in Table 1. One can attempt to find a contradiction or even try to prove this conjecture formally. However, the results are obviously going to be system dependent.

Optimal scheduling problem

The conceptual formulation (3) will be converted into a set of equations. Not all details can be included here so an explanation will only be given for some essential aspects. Network equations are given by Kirchhoff's Laws I and II together with the element laws. The mixed model is used here (Brdys and Ulanicki, 1994) which implies one equation for each reservoir, each element and each node.

Assuming that the model has been discretised in time and that there are K time steps covering the control horizon. This gives an indexing of $k=0,1...K-1$, where k corresponds to Δt.

For each reservoir:

$$h_r(k+1) = h_r(k) - (S^{-1}\Delta t)q_r(k) \quad \textit{for } k=0,1,...,K-1 \tag{6}$$

where h_r is the reservoir head, q_r is the net reservoir outflow, S is the reservoir cross-sectional area and Δt is the discretisation time step. Reservoirs are the only dynamic elements in the water network. Constraints (6) are linked in time from one step to the next.

For each element, except pump stations, the following equation is satisfied:

$$h_{orig}(k) - h_{dest}(k) = f\ (q(k)) \quad for\ k=1,2,...,K\text{-}1 \tag{7}$$

where h_{orig} and h_{dest} are heads at the origin and destination nodes, and q is the flow through the element. For a pipe, for example, the equation is:

$$h_{orig}(k) - h_{dest}(k) = R\ q(k)\,|q(k)|^{0.852} \tag{8}$$

where, for Hazen-Williams formulation, the pipe resistance R is dependent on length l, diameter d, and roughness c.

The pump model is created by invoking the continuity conjecture. Either of the two following approaches are possible. In the first, hydraulic equations of pumps can be written assuming that the pump control variables are continuous and explicitly present in the problem formulation (Ulanicki and Kennedy, 1994). Alternatively, a pump station can be represented by an operating point $(q, \Delta h)$ and its internal structure hidden (Coulbeck and Orr, 1984). The second approach has been adopted here.

By way of example, the model of a fixed-speed pump station, consisting of a number of identical fixed-speed pumps (FSP), is given by:

$$-(h_{orig}(k) - h_{dest}(k)) = \Delta h \geq 0; \quad q(k) \geq 0 \tag{9}$$

$$-(h_{orig}(k) - h_{dest}(k)) = \Delta h \leq \left[A\left(\frac{q(k)}{u_{\max}}\right)^2 + B\left(\frac{q(k)}{u_{\max}}\right) + C \right] \tag{10}$$

where A, B, C are coefficients of the pump hydraulic model, Δh is the pump head increase and u_{max} is the maximum number of pumps in the pump station. Inequality (9) ensures that each pump is a unidirectional element and equality (10) limits the operational area that can be reached if all pumps are used. Taken together, inequalities (9) and (10) represent a convex area in the head increase versus flow space.

The network also satisfies Kirchhoff's law I for flow balance at each node:

$$\lambda\ q(k) = -d(k) \tag{11}$$

where $q(k)$ is a vector of element flows, λ is a row vector from the node-element incidence matrix, and $d(k)$ is the node demand.

The operational constraints have the form of inequalities to maintain the feasible operating range. Typical examples are for reservoir levels, which must be kept inside minimum and maximum bounds, as indicated below:

$$h_{r,\min}(k) \leq h_r(k) \leq h_{r,\max}(k) \qquad k=1,2,...,K \tag{12}$$

The cost function may include pumping cost and treatment cost. However, the treatment cost is usually a simple linear function of the volume of treated water and can be included without difficulty. For each individual pump station, the pumping cost over a given time step obeys the following equation:

$$J_u(k) = \gamma(\text{k}) \times \frac{gq\Delta h}{\eta\,(q,w)} \times \Delta t \tag{13}$$

where $\gamma(k)$ is the electricity tariff, g is a constant, Δh is the pump head increase, q is the pump station flow, and Δt is the discretisation time step. For general pump stations, η is the pump station efficiency, which depends on flow q and an internal, pump control variable w. However, for FSP stations this can be derived as (Coulbeck and Orr, 1984):

$$\eta = \eta^* \left\{ 1 - \left(\frac{q}{q^* u} - 1 \right)^2 \right\} = \frac{\eta^*}{q^{*2}} \left(\frac{q}{u} \right) \left(2q^* - \frac{q}{u} \right) \tag{14}$$

where η^* is the peak efficiency for one pump, q^* is the corresponding peak efficiency flow and the general variable w has been replaced by u, the number of pumps in operation.

For the proposed method the pumping cost must be expressed as a function of the operating point $(q, \Delta h)$. In order to prepare such a function it is necessary to solve the simple auxiliary minimisation problem of:

$$J_u(q, \Delta h, k) = \min_{w \in \Xi} J_u(q, \Delta h, w, k) \tag{15}$$

where w is an internal control variable of the pump station, and Ξ is the constraint set implied by the hydraulic characteristics of the pumps. The evaluated function $J_u(q, \Delta h, k)$ will be the least expensive way of reaching the operating point $(q, \Delta h)$.

In the special case of an FSP station, w (equal to u) can be eliminated from equation (13) by use of equations (10) and (14). This gives an explicit expression for power consumption, in terms of $(q, \Delta h)$, as follows:

$$P = const \times \frac{q \times \Delta h}{(-B - \sqrt{B^2 - 4A(C - \Delta h)})(4q^* A + B + \sqrt{B^2 - 4A(C - \Delta h)})} \tag{16}$$

where P is the power consumption, q^* is the peak efficiency flow for a pump, and A, B, and C are the coefficients of the quadratic hydraulic characteristic. The graph of the function is shown in Figure 3. This indicates that, over the operating region, the function is convex, which can be confirmed by formal mathematical proof. For variable speed pumps (VSP) and other complex pump stations the power function must first be evaluated numerically, point by point, and then interpolated using some derived analytical expression (Ulanicka, 1997).

5. Modelling environment and case-studies

Water Software Systems at De Montfort University has developed a software environment for performing enhanced hydraulic modelling including simulation, optimal scheduling and other optimisation tasks. Figure 4 shows the architecture. There is a separate module, GINAS, for solving hydraulic simulation tasks (Coulbeck, *et al.* 1985). Solution of different optimisation tasks is based on the GAMS modelling language and the CONOPT solver. The modelling environment includes previously prepared templates for different types of tasks. In order to solve a specific network the templates are filled with data from the data store. The optimal scheduling problem can be solved for any network topology. Because there are plenty of existing network models, as GINAS input data files, the software is equipped with an auxiliary module to import existing models into the data store. If a model contains too many pipes a special network simplification module (Ulanicki, et al. 1996) can automatically simplify it.

Using the presented algorithm a number of optimal scheduling problems, taken from previous studies, were solved. Table 1 contains the statistics in terms of the network complexity, the time discretisation, and the calculation time on a Pentium 75Mhz PC.

Name	No of nodes	No of elements	No of reservoirs	No of time stages	Compilation + execution time
GIPOS network	9	9	1	24	4 sec
Kilham	9	9	1	8	1 sec
Yorkshire Grid	13	16	4	8	8 sec
South Staff.	24	28	3	8	12 sec
SCP	82	84 1 open canal	7	12	2.5 minutes

Table 1. Statistics of the case studies

6. Application to the Yorkshire Grid

The Yorkshire Grid network is shown in Figure 5. It includes 4 fixed-speed pump stations, 4 reservoirs, 2 treatment works, 2 control valves and a number of pipes. Because of certain design aspects two significant scheduling difficulties can occur for this system. The first of these concerns the treatment works outflow, each of which are constrained in their hourly rate of change. A second problem arises because the capacity of the reservoir at node 1 is very small. This makes it essential to balance the treatment works inflow and the pump station outflow so that the reservoir does not empty or overflow.

The network was solved for the demand conditions shown in Figure 6, which also gives the electricity tariff. The optimal continuous schedules are shown in Figure 7. As an illustration of constraint satisfaction, the treatment works schedules exhibit restricted hourly changes. Also for node 1, the reservoir level is maintained within its bounds because of the close correlation between the treatment works schedule and that of the pump station between nodes 1 and 5. As an illustration of economic operation, the pump stations power consumption show an increase during the cheap overnight period accompanied by a decrease in cost.

The Yorkshire Grid was modelled for 12 time steps giving 563 equations with 403 variables. GAMS/CONOPT required 257 iterations to converge to the results shown in Figure 7. Complete details of the study are given in (Ulanicki and Matz, 1995).

For practical application the continuous pump schedules would require conversion to integer schedules as discussed previously.

7. Conclusions

Current trends in evolution of computer aided water engineering software have been identified. In line with these aims, the work described in this chapter is a step towards intelligent computer analysis of water networks. An important aspect of the work concerns the use of software based on a domain specific language GAMS. This approach required development of a new generic optimisation algorithm that can solve many types of optimisation tasks. The algorithm is based on an explicit assumption - the continuity conjecture; this relaxation enables the standard network simulation model to be used directly for optimisation purposes. Separation of modelling and execution activities makes the software more generic and provides increased functionality. With the GAMS modelling language it was possible to define equations for new elements and new constraints rapidly and efficiently. A number of case studies have been solved using the software package developed. The summary results demonstrate the versatility of the new approach in comparison with some earlier methods. Detailed results using actual Yorkshire Grid data have been presented.

8. References

[1] Brdys, M. and Ulanicki, B., 1994. Operational Control of Water Systems: Structures, Algorithms and Applications, Prentice Hall, New York, London, Toronto.

[2] Brooke, A., Kendrick, D. and Meeraus, A, 1992. GAMS A User's Guide, Release 2.25, Boyd & Fraser Publishing Company, The Scientific Press Series

[3] Conn, A.R., Gould, N.I.M., and Toint Ph.L. 1992. LANCELOT, A Fortran Package for Large-Scale Non-linear Optimisation, Springer Verlag, Springer Series in Computational Mathematics, Berlin, Heidelberg, New York.

[4] Coulbeck, B. and Orr, C. H., 1984. Optimised Pumping in Water Supply Systems. Proc. 9th IFAC World Congress, Budapest, Hungary, Vol. 6, pp. 3175-3180.

[5] Coulbeck, B., Orr, C. H. and Cunningham, A. E., 1985. Computer Control of Water Supply: GINAS 5 Reference Manual, Research Report No. 56, School of Electronic and Electrical Engineering, Leicester Polytechnic, UK.

[6] Drud Arne, 1985. CONOPT: A GRG Code for Large Sparse Dynamic Non-linear Optimization Problems, Mathematical Programming, Vol. 31, pp. 153-191.

[7] Fishwick, P.A., 1995. Simulation Model Design Execution, Prentice Hall, New Jersey.

[8] Russel, S.J. and Norvig, P., 1995. Artificial Intelligence, A Modern Approach, Prentice Hall, New Jersey.

[9] Ulanicka, K. 1997. Mathematical Models of Water Networks for Hydraulic Modelling, Research Report, Water Software Systems, De Montfort University, Leicester, UK (in preparation).

[10]Ulanicki, B., Zehnpfund, A. and Martinez, F., 1996. Simplification of Water Network Models, Proceedings of the Hydroinformarics 96 International Conference, International Association for Hydraulic Research, ETH Zurich, September 9-13.

[11]Ulanicki, B., Rance, J.P., Davis, D., and Chen, S., 1993. Computer Aided Pump Selection for Water Distribution Networks, Journal of Water Resources Planning and Management, American Society of Civil Engineers, September.

[12]Ulanicki, B. and Kennedy, P., 1994. An Optimization Technique for Water Network Operation and Design, Proceedings of the 33rd IEEE Conference on Decision and Control, Buena Vista, Florida USA, December 14-16.

[13]Ulanicki, B. and Matz, H.,1995. Non-linear Programming and Mixed-integer Approach for Optimal Scheduling and Optimal Design of Water Networks, Research Report No. 16, Water Software Systems, De Montfort University, Leicester, UK.

[14]Yu, G. and Powell, R.S., 1994. Optimised Pump Scheduling in Water Distribution Systems, Journal Optimization Theory and Applications, Vol. 83, No.3.

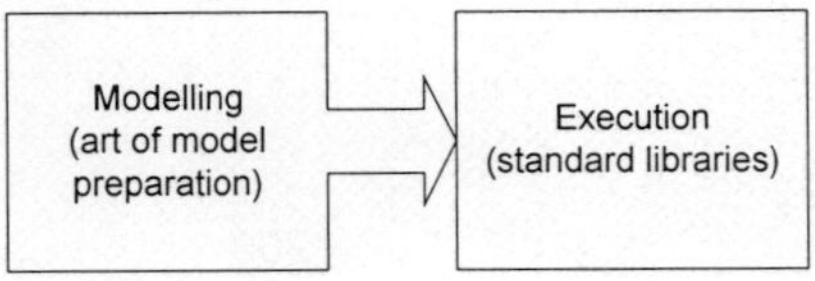

Figure 1. Separation of modelling and execution.

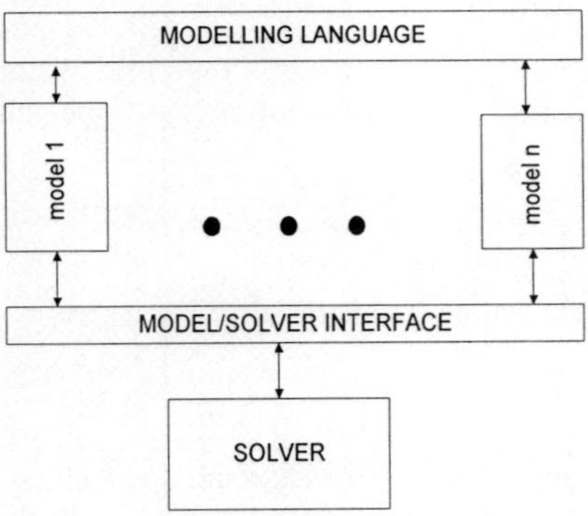

Figure 2. Concept of a software environment based on a modelling language

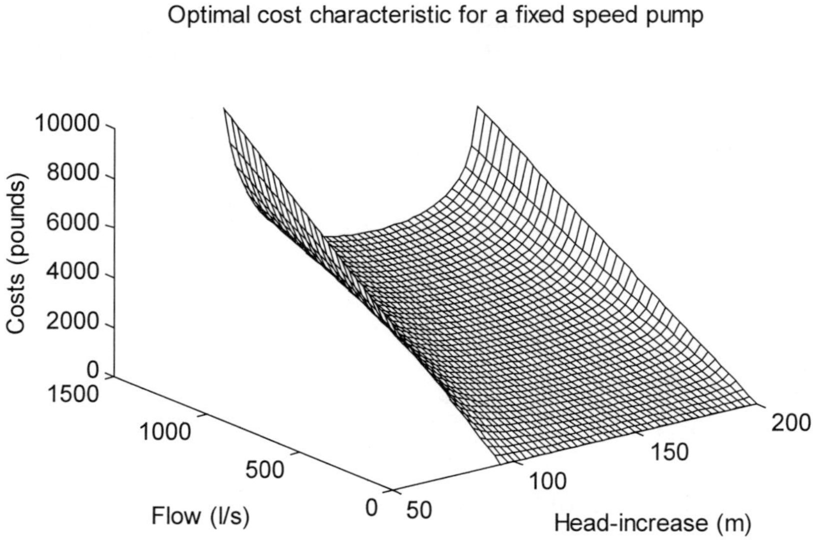

Figure 3. Cost function for a fixed-speed pump; A=-.001521, B=-0.005513, C=203.53 q*=140 l/s

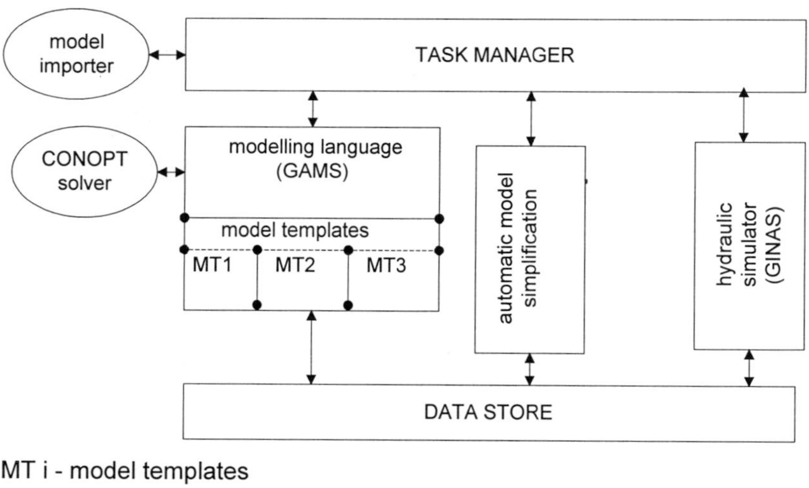

Figure 4. Hydraulic analysis environment

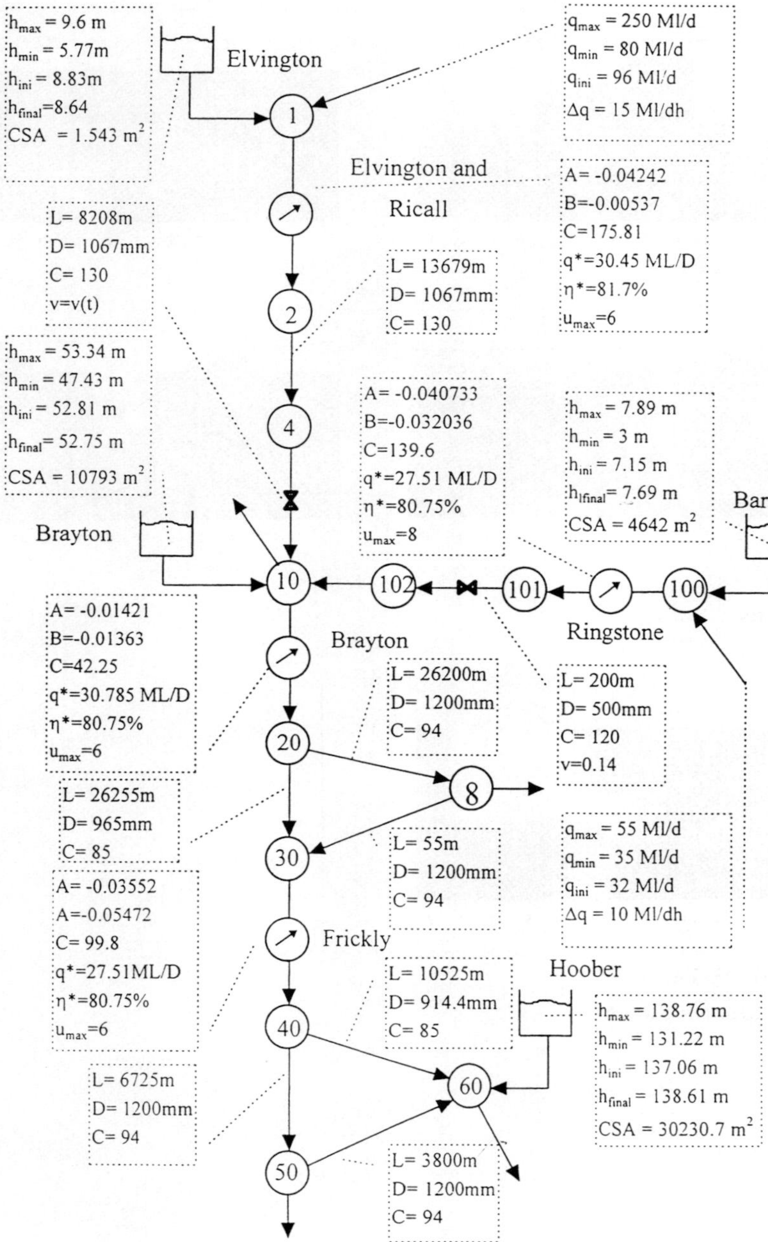

$v(t)=(0.4, 0.47, 0.55, 0.45, 0.43, 0.4, 0.4, 0.4, 0.4, 0.6, 0.55, 0.5)$

Figure 5. The Yorkshire Grid Network

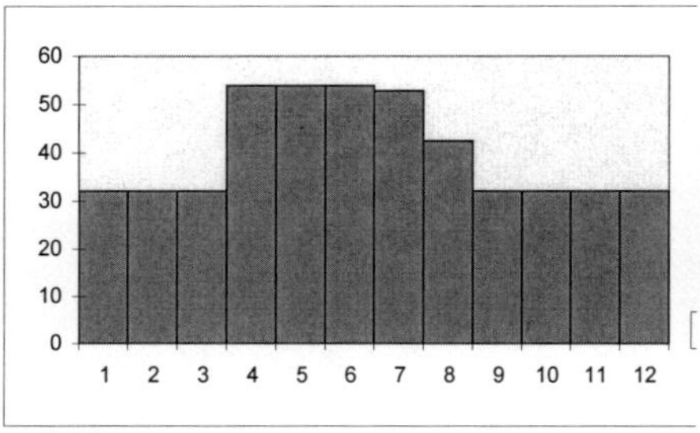

node10

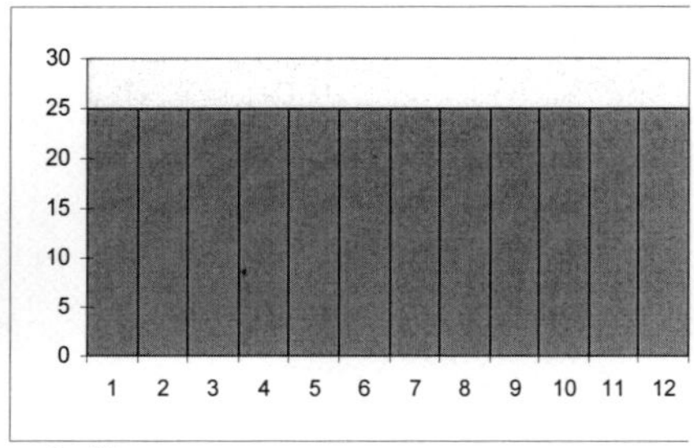

node 31

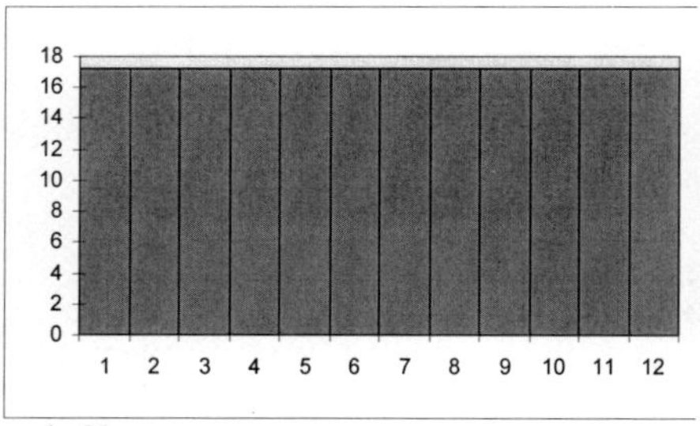

node 50

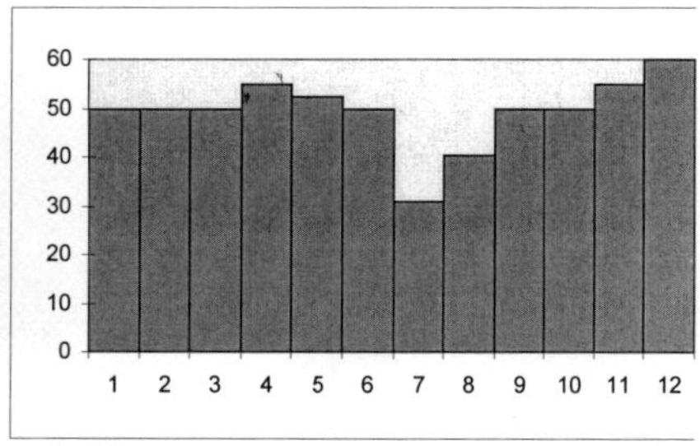

node 60

DEMANDS

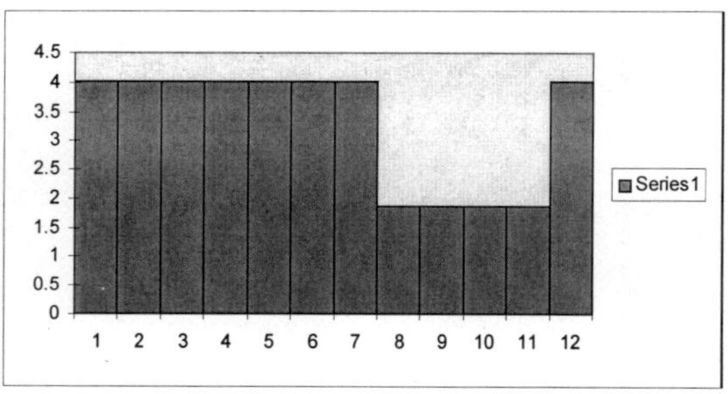

ELECTRICAL TARIFF

Figure 6. Demands and tariff.

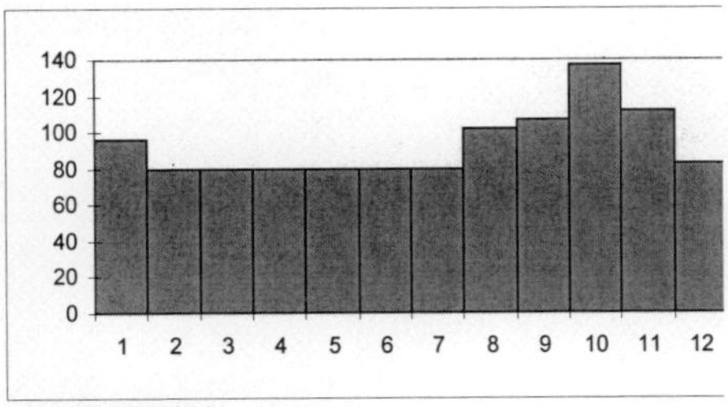

ELVINGTON

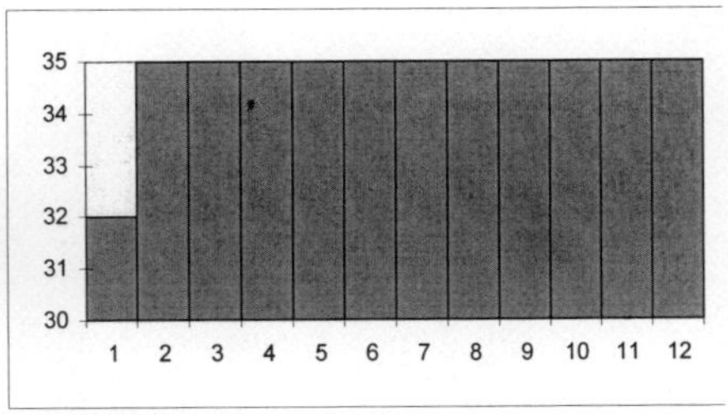

BARMBY

TREATMENT WORKS FLOW

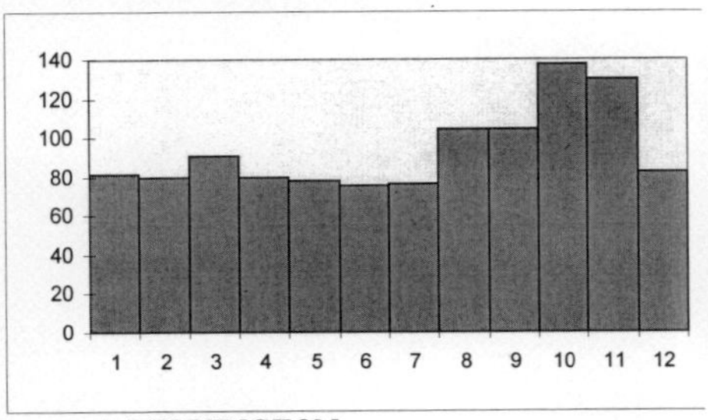

pump 1-2 ELVINGTON

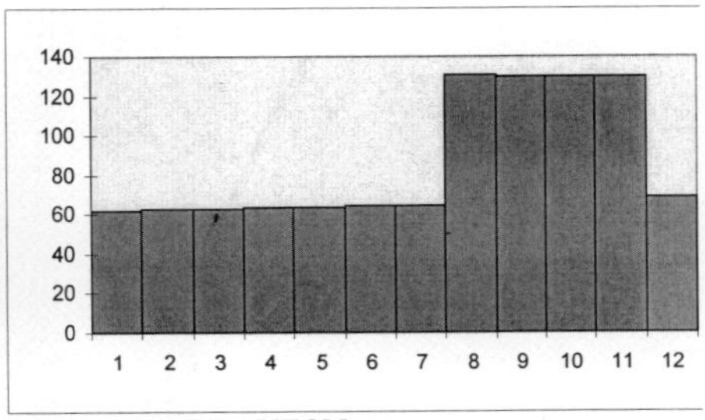

pump 10-20 BRAYTON

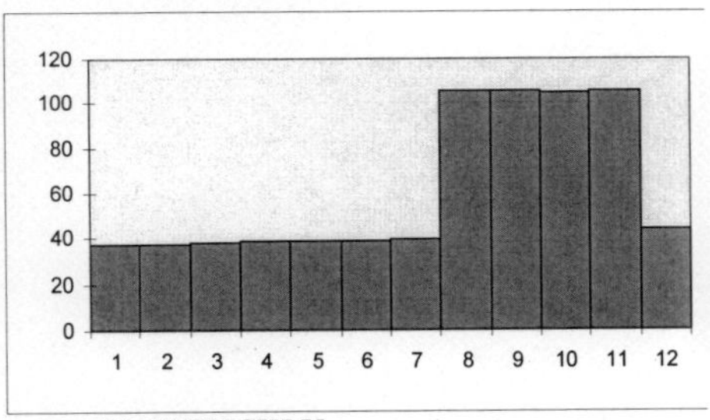

pump 30-40 FRICKLY

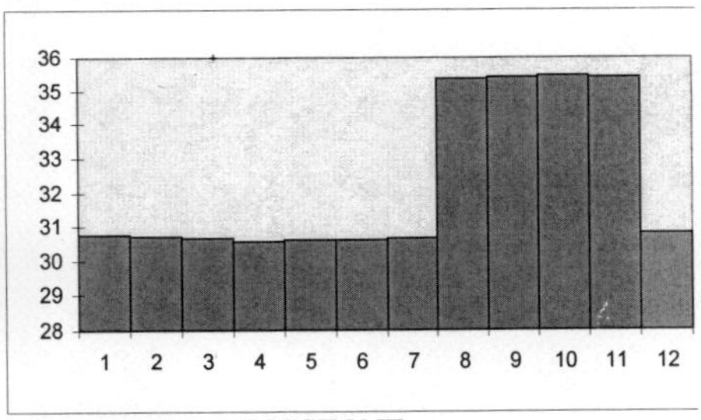

pump 100-101 RINGSTONE

PUMP FLOWS

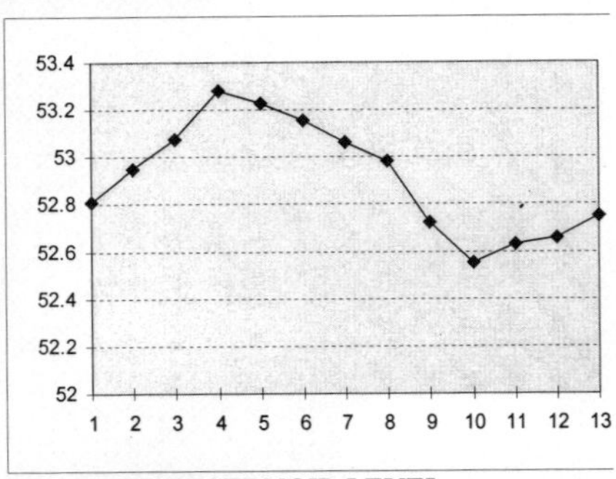

BRAYTON RESERVOIR LEVEL

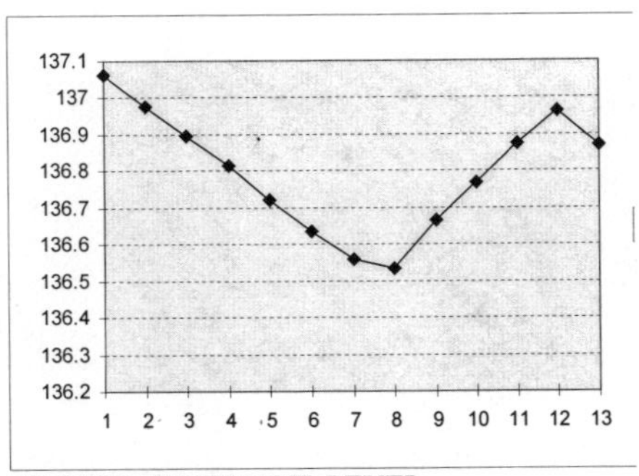

HOOBER RESERVOIR LEVEL

Figure 7. Calculated schedules

CHAPTER 13

A Pump Optimisation Suite for Large Scale Water Distribution Systems

R.S.Powell, M.J.H.Sterling, J.H.Andersen *and* A.Burgess

Abstract

This chapter describes the structure of a pump optimisation system undergoing trials by South West Water Services Ltd. It also addresses some of the problems of data integration from the point of view of large-scale optimisation.

Abbreviations

WASMACS	Water Systems Monitoring And Control Software
PDF	Problem Definition File
SWS	Stoner Workstation System (Stoner Associates, Solihull)

Introduction

Pump optimisation and resource optimisation generally refer to optimisation problems over a 24-hour horizon and up to a 12-month horizon, respectively. These types of problems have been the focus of research spanning more than four decades and can be traced back almost to the birth of computers. Many papers have been written on pump optimisation, e.g., [2, 3, 10], and many software packages have been designed. Only a few water companies have ever tried these in earnest and still fewer have been genuinely successful over a long period of time.

Water distribution networks are very large interconnected systems comprising many elements which themselves are characterised by a mixture of non-linear, non-smooth, continuous, discrete and multi-valued functions. The associated operational cost functions are almost certainly always non-convex. Water networks, unlike power distribution networks, are dominated by storage. Whilst this makes sound engineering practice, it makes the task of determining optimal operational strategies all the more difficult. In fact, the task of finding optimal operational strategies for anything but a trivial distribution system is probably one of the most demanding optimisation problems that exist.

However, as the regulatory authority continues to apply pressure for evidence of best practice and the price/performance index of modern computers continues its fall, the requirement for large-scale operational control using optimisation techniques will naturally increase.

The advances in information technology in recent years have permitted the integration of software applications with SCADA, asset databases and geographical information systems (GIS). With so much information available, the challenge now facing application designers is to find the means to exploit the information in a seamless way. This challenge is not just a matter of using technologies such as SQL, OLE, ODBC and CORBA etc., it lies in the way the data can be used with or without simplification. Much work has been done recently on the integration of network solvers (analysis) with GIS systems and their databases. However, the challenge of integrating an optimisation system with un-simplified asset data is a somewhat greater problem as the requirements for the underlying model are stricter than those for network analysis.

In this chapter a complete system for large-scale pump optimisation is described. The system is currently undergoing trials with South West Water Services Ltd.

Objectives

One might categorise the overall design objectives of a pump optimisation package as:

1. Optimality.
2. Feasibility (i.e. practicality of schedule).
3. Computational speed.

The first objective is often the one that stimulates academic research. Given the high degree of non-linearity and the mixed integer nature of the problem it is almost certainly the case that local optima abound. This often motivates choosing a method that will hopefully avoid the embarrassment of finding only a local rather than a global optimum. Techniques such as genetic algorithms, dynamic programming are sometimes chosen when a global optimum is to be found [6, 7]. However, these techniques are often computationally slow for anything but very small-scale systems. Network simplification is a way around this and has been shown to be very effective [8]. Nevertheless, diurnal network changes, such as changes in topology, would require a new simplification run. However, run-time topological changes must be catered for during the search for an optimum point because the optimiser might alter flow directions and thus change the state of one-way valves.

The quest for feasibility (practicality) is sometimes thought of as secondary, after optimality. However, if network constraints are to be considered they must be known to the optimiser at each stage of the computations and any method which fails to take account of a constraint might produce a schedule that would be impossible to implement. Therefore feasibility is actually more important than optimality.

Expectations from modern computers today are high and many consider that it will no longer be acceptable to leave a package for operational use 'running overnight'. What if the model parameters were wrong? Or the plant changes state during a run? Then the whole process would need to be started over again and its usefulness would have diminished in the meantime. Therefore the need for speed in on-line operational scheduling is paramount. Moreover, if real-time usage is envisioned then speed is a prerequisite.

It is the authors' contention that,provided a good local minimum can be found, the marginal cost benefit in continuing the search for the global minimum would be small. One can easily observe, from the utilisation of various tariffs, whether a sensible solution has been determined. This will show up in many different ways, for instance:

1. Has the operating cost been significantly reduced?
2. Are the reservoir profiles sensible? (If they are on the discharge side of a pump, do they fill during the cheap tariffs and vice versa if they are on the suction side.)
3. Are the pump schedules sensible? (Do the pumps make use of the cheap tariffs as opposed to the more expensive tariffs? Are the pumps utilised near their maximum efficiency point? Do they turn on or off infrequently?)

We conclude then that the most important consideration is feasibility, then speed, then optimality. This allows design of optimisers for large-scale systems with control room implementation in mind. With a fast optimiser that produces feasible schedules, the operator can learn to interact with the optimiser as a tool, trying out different constraints in order to get the best from the supply system.

Description of the WASMACS Pump Optimisation System

Water Systems Monitoring and Control Software (WASMACS), developed by WASMACS Ltd., comprises a suite of packages that address a range of applications for the needs of the water industry. The part of this suite known as the 'Pump Optimisation System' comprises a pump scheduler, a demand forecaster, a database system and some additional database support packages.

The architecture of the Pump Optimisation System is shown in Fig. 1. Basically, it comprises two packages: the pump optimiser itself, 'Pump_X', and the Demand Forecaster. These are connected via a database interface library (DBILIB) to a relational database. The network can be displayed in geographical form using a program known as Water~PACS, which has been licensed from OCEPS Ltd.

The database can be instantiated automatically using a package called 'STINT' (Stoner[1] Interface) which reads an SWS[1] problem definition file and uses the database interface layer to write the model into the WASMACS database. STINT was developed by Cambridge Control Hydromantis Ltd. in collaboration with WASMACS Ltd. WASMACS Ltd. also developed a package to convert an SWS graphics file into a Water~PACS file. The result of the two conversions is that the user can see a full network diagram in Water~PACS with all relational database links automatically set up.

SCADA data interchange is provided by a package called 'SCINT' (SCADA Interface) also designed by Cambridge Control Hydromantis Ltd. SCINT reads the latest reservoir levels and updates the WASMACS database accordingly.

---

[1] 'Stoner' and 'SWS' are registered trade marks of Stoner Associates

Functionality of the WASMACS system

The whole system is integrated so that the user can create, backup, restore and delete databases and run each of the modules from a single pull down menu.

The relational database acts as a common data repository for the two principal WASMACS application packages, namely: Pump_X and the Demand Forecaster. DBILIB provides open interconnection to the database and support applications written in either the C language or in DEC FORTRAN. This open philosophy enables third party packages such as Water~PACS, STINT and SCINT to use the same relational database as the WASMACS applications.

Pump_X

Pump optimisation is a dynamic problem that must take account of system storage, time-varying electricity tariff structure and operational (hydraulic) constraints in order to minimise the overall operational cost for a particular control period. The problem must be solved so that, given the forecasted demands for the optimisation period, the initial and desired final reservoir levels, the unit and maximum electricity charges and the set of hydraulic network constraints, an optimised programme of pump activity is found.

In Pump_X, the optimisation algorithm employs the projected gradient method and a non-linear sensitivity analysis for the basic scheduling problem. There is no need for the user to specify which pumps control which reservoirs — this is achieved by utilising full 24-hour dynamic simulations at every optimisation step.

The algorithm has been designed so that iterations always produce feasible schedules (in terms of the network hydraulic constraints) and thus will find better and better optimised solutions. The program was originally designed for the situation where variable speed pumps are used but has since been modified to deal with both variable and fixed speed pumps. Further details of the method can be found in [1, 9].

The program has a comprehensive Motif interface which permits tariff selection, pump availability control, the setting of minimum off or on times, reservoir initial and final levels etc. as well as graphical displays of reservoir levels, pump speeds, power consumptions etc. The results (time varying flows, pressures, etc.) can also be written into the relational database and displayed on the network diagram using Water~PACS. The schedule itself is available in three forms: an instruction sheet (ASCII file), as a table in the database, or as a graph. The intention is that a package such as SCINT should read the schedule directly from the database and implement it via the SCADA system (subject to operator overrides etc.). In the meantime, however, the operator can implement the schedule manually using the instruction sheet.

It is appropriate in this section to mention that Pump_X has been applied successfully to a system containing 42 pumps and 40 reservoirs (an 1800 node, 2000 link model). Systems of a higher dimensionality could be handled but it is not time-efficient to attempt to optimise super-large systems unless they are heavily meshed and it is impossible to split them into smaller sub-systems. The time it would take to solve a given system is dependent on a number of parameters. Unlike network analysis packages, the time taken by a pump optimiser is affected primarily by:

1. The number of pump stations.

2. The number of pumps and reservoirs.
3. The number of constraints.
4. The number of sub-time steps required by the simulator.

Sub-time step iterations are automatically generated when an event occurs (e.g., reservoir reaches full, a PRV closes, etc.) during the 24-hour simulations. Therefore a large number of small reservoirs (tanks) can have a marked impact on the speed of the system. The important conclusion from this is that a network with a large number of nodes could actually be quicker to optimise than a much smaller network containing more discrete elements.

In the system reported in [2], there are 22 pumps, 15 reservoirs, 13 float-valves, 19 PRVs, 3 one-way valves, 587 nodes, 648 links. For this system the optimiser takes less than three minutes on a low-end DEC Alpha computer (166 MHz). Early indications suggest that it would be significantly faster on a high-end Intel Pentium-Pro computer.

Hence we claim that Pump_X is very fast (even though it carries out thousands of individual network analyses) and it should be capable of synchronising with most SCADA systems in an on-line, real-time mode. This would allow the schedule to be re-computed many times during the day to keep up with the changes in the system state and any discrepancies between the predicted and the actual demand. It would also provide a useful tool in dealing with emergencies as it would provide rapid decision support.

Demand Forecaster

The objective of water distribution control is to satisfy, at minimum cost, the consumer demands wherever and whenever they occur. Knowledge of the variation of water consumption makes it possible for the operator to take appropriate control actions. In the case of computer assisted control, short-term predictions provide the necessary information upon which optimisation depends; the more accurate and reliable the demand forecast, the more effective the optimisation.

The Demand Forecaster employs an artificial neural network technique that has been tested extensively against an earlier system that used the ARIMA algorithm [4]. The motivation for the neural method was to solve the problem of weather effects without attempting to write down deterministic laws of how changes in the weather affect demand. The neural technique almost always produces an identical forecast to the ARIMA algorithm when weather data are unavailable but it is significantly better when provided with the type of weather for the prediction day. The recorded weather data are used in a classifier to determine the day type and the demand behaviour is 'learnt' by the algorithm for that day type.

The interface uses GKS and is fully colour graphic with mouse operation providing the control over the program. The user can display forecasts over a week or per day and can step forward or backward a day at a time to investigate either new forecasts or examine the prediction error when actual demand data have been received.

When the operator is satisfied that the demand forecast is appropriate, the data are loaded into the database. Every time the optimiser retrieves the plant data from the database the demand allocation is recomputed on a pro-rata basis such that the total demand for the system at each half-hour equals the value given by the forecaster. (If for some reason there is no forecast in the database, the original analysis model demand allocations are used.)

Functionality of the support software

Introduction

The two main WASMACS packages (Pump_X and the Demand Forecaster) are supported by a suite of other software that includes the database, the database interface, the network display system and a graph-plotting package. In keeping with the main software packages, all the support software complies with international standards in their use of SQL and Motif.

WASMACS uses four GUIs: Water~PACS is a Motif based network display system capable of geographical and/or schematic network representations; Graph_X is a Motif based results plotting utility; Pump_X (front-end) is the interface to the optimiser and is also written in Motif; and finally, the front end to the demand forecaster is written using GKS.

Water~PACS

Water~PACS was developed jointly by Sterling Associates and OCEPS Ltd. and is licensed in the current project from OCEPS Ltd. It uses OSF/Motif standards to provide pull down menus, dialogue boxes and mouse functions. Water~PACS displays the water distribution system geographically allowing the user to pan and zoom rapidly from area to area. Perhaps the key feature of this system is the direct interface it offers to the relational database. Water~PACS diagrams can be produced automatically by SGC (see below) which places pre-drawn symbols, each with database entity associations, according to the X-Y information provided by SWS.

Multi-window and/or multi-database operation is permitted. In this way, the user can enter data into the database and display that data in Water~PACS.

Database and database utilities

DEC's relational database product 'RDB' (now called ORACLE RDB) was chosen for this project. The relational database schema has been designed to act essentially as an asset database. It holds asset data in its simplest form and it is hoped that it mirrors the way similar asset databases have been designed in the water industry. The topology information held in the database is produced automatically as the data is loaded. This enables mathematical models to be derived automatically from the data in the database [5].

The data are accessed by means of libraries comprising C, FORTRAN and SQL modules. For each plant type there are normally five procedures: get all, get singleton, insert, update and delete. The update functions are further broken down into update all attributes, update status, update pressure, update flow, etc.

Utility programs are also provided for WASMACS database creation, backup, restore and deletion. These can all be run from pull down menus.

Interface to Stoner Workstation System: Stoner Interface (STINT)

STINT (designed by Cambridge Control Hydromantis Ltd.) allows the user to instantiate the WASMACS database from an SWS PDF so that, provided the model makes operational sense, the WASMACS programs can be used without further operator intervention. STINT also supports a WASMACS to Stoner conversion so that the user can export a network back into a PDF. For instance, the pump schedule can be written into the database and the entire plant data can be converted into a PDF so that the schedule can be checked using SWS.

Interface to Stoner Workstation System: Stoner Graphics Conversion (SGC)

SGC reads a Stoner .XY file and relates each graphical component described therein to the WASMACS database items that originated from STINT. It then automatically creates a Water~PACS diagram that is geographically identical to the original by copying pre-drawn library symbols from the Water~PACS library into the X-Y locations specified in the SWS file. Each symbol is associated with the correct entity in the database as it is copied into place. The graphical symbols can include the dynamic conditions as well as the database references and can be tree-structured composite objects containing many sub-objects.

SGC includes a host of subroutine libraries that handle the data conversion and data-database-graphics cross-referencing. Both STINT and SGC require the database and the WASMACS database interface routines.

Intended Usage

Overview

The anticipated use for the Pump Optimisation System is on a day-to-day basis in an operational control room. This section explains how the operator would interact with the system.

Off-line operational pump scheduling

The applications provided in the main pull down menu can be categorised into data management tasks and operational tasks. Data management tasks include:

1. Database creation, backup, restoration and deletion (using the four utilities provided).
2. Database instantiation (using STINT).
3. Water~PACS file creation (using SGC).
4. SCADA data transfer (using SCINT).

The only data management task that the operator would be concerned with is the last one: SCINT should be used to update the database with the latest reservoir levels etc.

The operational tasks include the Demand Forecaster, Pump_X and Water~PACS. The sequence of events for the operator, once a fully instantiated relational database has been created, is:

1. Update the database with the latest reservoir data using SCINT.

2. Run the Demand Forecaster and load the results into the database.
3. Run Water~PACS and enter (or change) as necessary any pressure constraints at nodes.
4. Select Pump_X from the menu and choose the tariff file and the optimiser start and stop times. Enter additional constraints (pump outages, reservoir levels etc.). Adjust the demand forecast if necessary. Start the optimiser, noting any informational messages it produces.
5. Plot the results using Graph_X. Observe the network flows and pressures (at the Snapshot Time) using Water~PACS.
6. If satisfied with the result, select the 'Save Schedule to File' option in the Results Menu of Pump_X.
7. Print out the Instruction Sheet and implement the schedule.

The operators should, by virtue of the fact that they are using data created by network analysts, feel more closely in contact with that side of the company's business. This will enable network analysts to gain a greater working knowledge of the network models and operators to feedback modifications and/or updates to the working database.

On-line operational pump scheduling

Before considering an on-line mode of operation one must consider the degrees by which the loop can be closed. Consider the following three modes:

a) Manual - The operator closes the loop. This is the situation described above but with the additional tasks of transferring data into the WASMACS database from SCADA via SCINT, prior to running the optimiser, and then, when the optimisation results are available, back into SCADA from the database.

The system would be run as and when the operator requires but not on an automatic cycle or tied to events such as reservoir level violations or deviations from predicted trajectories.

b) Reactive - System variables updated automatically but operator initiates commands. In a reactive mode of operation, the optimiser would be triggered on the basis of a comparison between the forecast demand and the actual demand or, alternatively, by comparing the predicted reservoir trajectories against the actual. As a result of a discrepancy a new schedule could automatically be created. Responsibility for final implementation of the new schedule would still rest with the operator.

c) Automatic - System variables updated automatically and system initiates commands. A fully automatic mode of operation could be implemented whereby the system monitored the progress of demand for water through the day and re-implemented the scheduler to make up any deficit or reduce any surplus in the reservoirs. Manual overrides could be designed into the data communication layer between WASMACS and SCADA so that the operator could take full control at any instant. (Of course, the optimiser can be shut down at any time simply by pressing the QUIT button with the mouse.)

Tariff Negotiation

An important benefit of a fast optimiser is that it can be used to assess the impact and true cost of different electrical tariffs. This can be achieved in the Pump Optimiser System by creating tariff data files, testing each one and noting the total operational cost that results. Because some tariffs will favour pumping at different times from others, the only way to fully assess their true cost is to test them in this way.

Flexible 'what-if' studies for analysis and design

Because the optimiser is reasonably fast, the system can also be run as an intelligent simulator. One can determine the operational cost of different network configurations, plant maintenance etc. using the optimiser. The optimiser will always try to find the best way of scheduling the pumps given the targets set by the user and the available plant. A network analysis package in which the user is required to specify the pumping schedules a priori cannot do this.

If an operator has to, for example, shut down a pump for maintenance, it would be advisable to assess the effect of this using the optimiser and check which time of day would be best in terms of operational cost savings. (It is this type of what-if study that can help the operator get the best out of the optimiser.)

Data

In order to obviate data duplication there is a need to unify optimisation models with network analysis models, asset databases, GIS data and SCADA. The benefits (and certain disadvantages) are obvious. If operations staff, network analysts and asset management staff all work and communicate with the same data (albeit using different views of that data) the database would become more refined and anomalies would be more rapidly identified. Moving toward this goal requires a paradigm shift in data and personnel management since it would be necessary for each discipline to communicate with the others for the benefit of data refinement, even though this may not seem to be a direct or measurable objective.

In this work, a system has been devised which uses 'asset data' in a relational database, provides links to GIS data and supports pump optimisation. Details of this system are described later. The main problems of optimising systems from asset databases are twofold:

1. The basic model must be operationally complete.
2. The optimiser must be able to cope with a model of a very high dimensionality.

The second of the goals is met with good software design, large arrays and a fast computer. However, the first goal is generally outside the scope of the optimiser. Although one could argue that an automatic method could attempt to convert a model into one that makes operational sense, such a method, as can be seen from the following section, would have to have an ability to 'see outside' the data in the database.

Network models and their use in operational scheduling

It is important to recognise that the process of network data collection, modelling and analysis is actually a process of data conversion which can, and usually does, include data addition, modification and deletion. The goal of a network analyst is to achieve a 'balanced' network. A network is said to be 'balanced' when two things simultaneously occur:

1. The software package converges to a solution – 'numerical convergence'.
2. The solution matches the observations during the field tests with an acceptable level of accuracy.

A balanced network model is a necessary but not sufficient requirement for a successful optimisation run. There are at least two reasons why a good analysis model is not necessarily a good operational model:

1. Model extents (boundaries) might be inappropriately chosen.
2. So called 'balanced' network models often contain unacceptably high degrees of approximation.

Since an optimiser is ultimately to be used in controlling the physical plant, its data requirements are stricter than for network analysis. It is relatively easy for a user of a network analysis package to achieve a 'balanced' network model. The real questions concern the points above. For instance, are all the pumps that the operator knows about actually in the model? Are all the infusions from other systems modelled correctly? In other words, is the model genuinely realistic?

Whilst the WASMACS pump optimiser (no doubt like any other system) is very robust and can accept just about any model built and balanced using a network analysis package, the main reason an optimiser will fail to produce useful results is if it is optimising something which is not representative of the reality. There is therefore a new responsibility on the network analyst to produce operationally correct models. This may expose, amongst the personnel using analysis packages, the difference between know-how in producing 'balanced' network models and understanding how water distribution systems actually work.

A number of typical and frequently encountered approximations, that could give rise to misleading solutions, have been listed below:

Important model/plant discrepancies:

1. Topology errors (e.g. placing a fictitious bypass pipe or valve around a pump).
2. Modelling errors (e.g. modelling a one-way valve back-to-front).
3. Additional plant items (e.g. the use of PRVs to help balance the model).
4. Missing plant items (e.g. the omission of pumps which could, and should, have been used by the optimiser).
5. The use of false parameters to model observed network resistances (e.g. part-closing a valve at certain times of the day to account for an unexpected head loss).

6. Poor choice of model extents (e.g. the inclusion of a reservoir which fills from a pump station omitted from the model such that the reservoir fills or empties uncontrollably).
7. False loading (e.g. using fictitious demands or supplies to balance the network).

Minor effects (depending on severity):

Some approximations are inevitable and normally have little adverse effect on the solution. Nevertheless, approximations might indicate that the modelling phase has not been carried out with sufficient rigour. Examples are:

1. The use of extra demands to model leakage. This is generally OK since it is difficult to differentiate between the two. However, leakage flow is sensitive to pressure in a manner that is different from consumer demand. Any pressure reduction will give rise to reduced leakage flows and an optimiser will have marginally less water to despatch.
2. The incorrect setting of plant parameters (e.g. modelling pipe roughness using infeasible values).
3. Boundary nodes. Boundary nodes (e.g. 'fixed-head' nodes or 'fixed-flow' nodes) do not physically exist. The term 'boundary node' is a hand-me-down from the parlance of mathematical programming. Boundary nodes are used in network analysis programs because they provide a convenient way of representing certain inflow devices (or sometimes outflow devices). Boundary nodes are sometimes created where there exists a reservoir, a pump or a PRV on a network boundary. From the point of view of the optimiser, the use of a boundary node in place of the correct plant item could lead to a significantly inappropriate result since boundary nodes promise infinite flows at constant heads (or vice versa) and thus could conceivably be used as infinite pumps. Moreover, if the boundary node was a reservoir, it would be impossible to add level constraints; if it was a PRV there would be no way of checking whether the flow and pressure drops for the valve were feasible, etc.

Further examples:

In some network models, valves are given time-varying profiles, i.e. the valve setting changes throughout the day, every day. If these are motorised valves with a controller operating a pre-specified schedule then this may be the correct representation. However, in reality, the settings of these valves probably do not change every day and the profile is just a way of balancing the model.

During a field trial of WASMACS using a recently imported model, the operations personnel pointed out that some pumps known to exist in the system were actually missing from the model. If there are more pumps in the physical system than in the model, the optimiser might not even be able to schedule the pumps it knows about effectively, let alone incorporate the missing pumps.

One model appeared to be constructed so that water was pumped into the top of a reservoir, the discharge of which ended up, by a circuitous route, back at the suction side of the pump. In another model a pump was found to be pumping into a 'leaf node' with no other links. Unfortunately, the demand profile on this node was such that the pump was expected to provide a bi-directional flow!

In many models, pumps have been found discharging into closed, or nearly closed, valves. It is unlikely that an operator would allow this to happen. Optimisers can of course schedule valves and pumps together but for very large-scale systems the additional decision variables are unwelcome in terms of speed and the convexity of the problem. More importantly, there is no point in scheduling valves unless they can be actively controlled by a SCADA system.

Correctness of data is of course the user's responsibility. It is crucial to understand that an optimiser cannot know what approximations or simplifications have been made to the network model; it will simply use the data as is. The most important conclusion is simply this:

If the model is incorrect then the results of the optimisation are unlikely to be appropriate for the actual plant.

Final usage methodologies

As this chapter has emphasised, the effectiveness of the optimiser, in terms of the cost savings from the implementation of its schedules, lies, to a large extent, in the accuracy of the data it uses. Since plant data change with time, a procedure or mechanism is required which will ensure that the models used by the optimiser are kept up to date. This is not as bad as it may seem because if the models are being used by the operator on a regular basis any anomalies in the models should show up and can be checked with the analysts responsible.

This procedure might also benefit the company by providing a means of creating a feedback loop between operations and the network analysis staff, thus encouraging the sharing of operational knowledge as well as data.

Strategic integration

In a project such as this, where accurate and up-to-date data is so vitally important and where the software package is part of the company's core business of operating its water supply systems, it is clear that data integration is highly desirable.

Large-scale data integration is non-trivial and the complexity is often underestimated. A number of problems have to be solved:

1. Ensuring that the data have a common key referencing convention. This means that the reference to each plant item, whether from GIS or SCADA, must share a common identifier or key. For example, the tag number of a SCADA point should be recognisable as belonging to a particular plant referenced by, for example, GIS.
2. Managing data changes. In the past, a data description such as an asset database was often thought of as a static repository of data. Now, however, it is realised that data are dynamic, and this is particularly so in large engineering system databases. Managing these changes requires care if data consistency and referential integrity are to be maintained.

3. Vertical structure. While there are very great benefits from having a unified data repository, one obviously needs to draw the line somewhere in order to get the maximum from such a system. As a somewhat simplistic example, if a SCADA system constantly had a certain table open for write operations, it might be impossible for any other application to open that table for a read operation!
4. Horizontal structure. Dividing up corporate data into various locations on a distributed database clearly has attractions from the point of view of managing wide area network traffic. A well designed horizontal system could also give benefits from the security point of view but this must be weighed against optimising transaction processing.
5. Security. One needs to consider how to manage the risk of all operational and asset data being held (or at least managed) by one system. No company would permit a situation to arise where their entire water distribution operations depend solely on the reliability of a computer network and computer system. An integrated data management system used for operational control must fail safe, permitting a bumpless transfer to local control in the event of any contingency.

Conclusions

In the field of Operations Research (OR), it is recognised that the pump scheduling problem is one of the hardest to solve. It has one of the most severe combinations of non-linearity, non-convexity, and high dimensionality; the behaviour is described by a mixture of discrete, continuous and multi-valued functions. A great many methods have been tried including network simplification, linearisation of the cost function or restricting applications to very small systems. Often, an optimiser is specifically designed for a particular system and is not general. Occasionally, optimisers are designed to be sophisticated enough to deal with non-linear hydraulic constraints but take hours to run, even on quite small systems.

The design of Pump_X was very ambitious. The objectives were to solve the full, non-simplified problem for any system (subject to the model making operational sense), in a short enough time to be integrated with an on-line control system. Pump_X had to be capable of using any tariff (provided that it was expressible over the optimisation period), a non-linear cost function, non-linear hydraulic constraints, fixed or variable speed pumps and be capable of dealing with data created by another package. The system has met these aims.

As the emphasis shifts from using network models for analysis to using them for operations, problems will arise where the models turn out to be inappropriate. Nevertheless, water companies should not shy away from these problems and they should appreciate the benefits that true corporate data unification could bring. Not just in terms of operational cost savings but also in terms of better vision and management of their assets.

Acknowledgements

This work was supported, in the first instance, by the Engineering and Physical Sciences Research Council. More recently, the Pump Optimisation Suite has been developed by WASMACS Ltd. with support from South West Water Services Ltd.

References

[1] Andersen, J. H., Powell, R. S., 1997. 'An efficient loop-based algorithm for the analysis of water networks containing controlling elements', submitted to *Jour. of Water Resources Planning and Management*, ASCE.

[2] Brion, L. M., Mays, L. W. 1990. 'Methodology for optimal operation of pumping stations in water distribution systems', *Jour. of Hydraulic Engineering,* ASCE, Vol. 117, No. 11, pp 1551 - 1569.

[3] Carpentier, P., Cohen, G. 1992. 'Applied mathematics in water supply network management', IFAC

[4] Hartley, J. A. 1995. 'A neural network and rule based system application in water demand forecasting', Ph.D. Thesis, Brunel University, 1995.

[5] Powell, R. S. 1993. 'A proposal for full closed loop control of a water distribution system', in 'Integrated Computer Applications in Water Supply, Vol.1', (Ed. B. Coulbeck), Research Studies Press, pp 273 - 291.

[6] Savic, D. A., Walters, G. A., Schwab, M. 1997. 'Multi-objective genetic algorithms for pump scheduling in water supply', presented at Evolutionary Computing Workshop, AISB '97, Manchester, 7 - 8 April.

[7] Sterling, M. J. H., Coulbeck, B., 1975. 'A dynamic programming solution to optimization of pumping costs', *Proc. Instn. Civil Engrs.*, Part 2, Vol. 59, pp. 813 - 888.

[8] Ulanicki, B., Zehnpfund, A., Martinez, F. 1995. 'Water network simplification' *Jour. of Civil Engineering Systems*, March. 95

[9] Yu, G., Powell, R. S., Sterling, M. J. H., 1994. 'Optimised pump scheduling in water distribution systems', *Jour. Optimization Theory and Applications*, Vol 83, No. 3 pp 463 - 488.

[10] Zessler, U., Shamir, U. 1989. 'Optimal operation of water distribution systems', *Jour. of Water Resources Planning and Management*, ASCE, Vol. 115, No. 6, pp 735 - 751.

CHAPTER 14

Optimal Operation of a Water Reservoir System for Different Operational and Hydrological Situations Using an SQP-Type Optimisation Method

P.Fritsch, S.Hopfgarten *and* H.Puta

1 Introduction

In the past a lot of investigations were carried out concerning the modelling of water reservoir management and operation, [20]. According to the latest findings of climate and environment researchers slight climate changes are likely to come during next decades, [9], [18] . Without doubt these changes will have effects on precipitation and thus on the hydrological situation, [4], [3], [17], [13], [12], [16]. Even the behaviour of consumers can be influenced, e.g. irrigation due to longer periods of dryness. Other factors, e.g., the ground water recharge, also influence the water balance in a region. At present not all effects of long-term ground water exploitation are foreseeable. All these reasons are responsible for attaching more importance to water resources systems planning and management under different hydrological and operating conditions. This influence is investigated within the framework of the European 'CHEWS' project.

The aim of the investigations described in this chapter is to develop a computer-aided decision-support method for planning and management of water reservoir systems. When applying this method, different scenarios can be investigated concerning changed hydrological conditions and the expected behaviour of water consumers due to climate changes. Also one is able to analyse different operating regimes.

2 Influences of Climate Changes on Hydrological Conditions

Due to the activities of mankind climate changes will be expected in the next decades. The problem of assessing the influence of climate changes on hydrological conditions is tackled by several hydrological institutions, e.g. by one of our 'CHEWS' partners, the Institute of Hydrology, Wallingford, U.K. Also water consumers can change their behaviour under different climatic conditions (e.g. irrigation). Furthermore, the recharge of ground water could be influenced, and the usage of ground water may be restricted due to water quality issues. The effects of climate changes on water resources are taken into account in models which are used to simulate different flows into water reservoirs. These changed natural (external) influences cause new water reservoir management plans or operation rules to be calculated.

3 Water Supply Situation in Thuringia

The water supply in the Free State of Thuringia, Germany, is controlled by several authorities, institutions and companies. The Thuringian State Institution for the Environment in connection with the State Environment Offices is responsible for the elaboration of reservoir management plans, especially for those reservoirs (dams) which deliver raw water to the drinking water treatment plants. The planning, construction, maintenance and operation of dams are Thuringian Reservoir Administration's responsibility. This administration applies the reservoir management plans within its bounds in normal situations. In extraordinary situations, e.g. flood, the operation is carried out by the State Environment Office.

The raw water from dams is treated and transported over large distances (up to 100 km) by three Long Distance Water Supply Federations to local federations and municipal services, which finally distribute the water to the consumer. The reservoir system containing three dams (Ohra, Schmalwasser, and Tambach-Dietharz) including the transition tunnels between them and the coupling to the North Thuringian Long Distance Water Supply Federation, which delivers drinking water to about 500,000 inhabitants, serves as a pilot system for the purposes of investigation, see Fig. 1. A reservoir management plan was worked out for this system on behalf of the Thuringian State Institution for the Environment containing the operation scheme, [11], [15]. This reservoir management plan will be used for purposes of comparison.

In the first part of the investigation the main emphasis is put on the usage of surface water because the Reservoir Administration and the Long Distance Water Supply Federations only use that kind of water for drinking water supply purposes. The ground water effect can be taken into account at a later stage, but then one must consider the problem of water distribution up to the local federations or municipal services, which are responsible for ground water resources.

In Thuringia, which belongs to the east part of Germany, water consumption dropped after the German reunification because of a step-wise introduction of water meters in nearly every household, company, etc. and the introduction of water and waste water charges according to these measurements (about 5-15 DM/cu. m.). Other reasons for the decrease of water consumption are the changes in industry and agriculture. An increase in water consumption is now expected because of the development of new industrial areas and modernisation in households, from 80-100 up to 120-130 litres per person per day. Furthermore, the possible reduction in the exploitation of ground water stocks can lead to an increased demand concerning surface water.

4 Tasks

4.1 Planning problem

The long-term planning problem consists of investigating the water supply in decades to come under different hydrological scenarios caused by climate changes. Details on the changes in the hydrological situation, i.e. different monthly factors concerning precipitation/inflow to the reservoirs, are received from hydrologists. On the basis of measurement of inflows into the reservoirs from 1931-1992 historical time series are available. These historical data served as fundamentals for generation of a synthetic 2,000 years inflow time series of 5 rivers with nearly the same statistical properties (e.g. mean, standard deviation, etc.) as the historical ones. After formulating and calculating the solution of an optimisation problem, described in section 5, the results (releases from reservoirs and transition flows between the reservoirs) are evaluated in comparison with the results of the existing water management plan elaborated using a Monte-Carlo simulation [14]. Using these synthetic time series the long-term behaviour of the system can be investigated and the results can be evaluated with respect to statistical statements such as the level of service (probability of safe water supply), the frequency and amount of demand shortfall, the low water level frequency and the probability of overflow at reservoirs. Using the computer-aided decision tool planners can gain valuable information, which can be applied if the water reservoir system must be extended or if a change is needed to the long-term operation policy.

4.2 Control problem

The mid- and short-term operational control problem regards operation of the reservoir system in shorter time horizons with the need for information about the reservoir contents and better predictions of inflows and/or demands. The reservoir contents can be measured. During winter time statements about the snow heights and a forecast about snow melting is obtained from the meteorological service. This information and further forecasts about precipitation can be utilised to improve the forecasts of inflows into the reservoirs using rainfall-runoff models. The optimisation problem (see next section) is solved taking into account the water levels of reservoirs and the improved forecasts.

As another control problem one may consider management of a reservoir system in extraordinary situations. One example is the reconstruction (sealing) of the Ohra dam from September 1997 until December 1998. At the beginning of this time period the content of the Ohra dam must be at a minimum level. During reconstruction the reservoir is empty, and the other two reservoirs, in particular the Schmalwasser dam, must work according to a different operating plan. After reconstruction the Ohra dam will step by step go into operation.

The authors prefer to follow a concept of repetitive optimisation, i.e., firstly, solving an optimisation problem for system behaviour over the time horizon of one year using the mean values of inflows and demands in every month. Secondly, taking these results as reference trajectory for the reservoir contents and we will follow it gradually by calculating optimal releases in dependence of actual reservoir contents and better prediction of external disturbances such as inflows and/or demand. This control problem is solved repeatedly, e.g. month by month. The whole synthetic time series can also be compared to the existing water reservoir management plan.

5 Optimisation Problem and Solution

With respect to system dynamics, originally the well-known dynamic time-discrete difference equations were chosen as a model for describing system behaviour concerning mass balances over K time intervals. In view of the optimisation procedure to be applied, this model is transformed to the following equivalent large scale non-linear optimisation problem with control parameterisation, [1], [2], [7]. The vector y of optimisation variables, the vectors of equality and inequality constraints (h and g, respectively) read as follows:

$$y = \begin{pmatrix} x^0 & u^0 & \dots & x^{K-1} & u^{K-1} & x^K \end{pmatrix}^T \tag{1}$$

$$h(y) = \begin{pmatrix} f^0 - x^1 & \dots & f^{K-1} - x^K & h^0 & \dots & h^K \end{pmatrix}^T = 0 \tag{2}$$

$$g(y) = \begin{pmatrix} c^0 - {c_l}^0 & \dots & c^K - {c_l}^K & c_u - c^0 & \dots & {c_u}^K \end{pmatrix}^T \leq 0 \tag{3}$$

with the following meaning

x^k	–	*discrete-time state at discrete-time* k, $k = 0, 1, \dots, K-1$
u^k	–	*discrete-time control in interval* $[t^k, t^{k+1})$, $k = 0, 1, \dots, K-1$
f^k	–	*right-hand side of discrete-time state equation,* $k = 0, 1, \dots, K-1$
h^k	–	*possible additional equality constraints, e.g. fixed initial and/or final states*
${c_l}^k, {c_u}^k$	–	*lower and upper bounds, resp., at discrete-time* k, $k = 0, 1, \dots, K$
c^k	=	$c^k(x^k, u^k)$ – *value of constraint function*

Both the tasks of planning and management of the reservoir system can be formulated as an optimisation problem with optimisation criterion, equality and inequality constraints. Aspects of operating the system under consideration are:

- Discharge at least a minimum flow which is necessary for the environment downstream the dam (compensation release).
- Deliver the necessary amount of raw water for water supply purposes with a certain level of service.

- Prevent flooding.
- Reach special targets concerning the stock in the dams.
- Generate electrical energy by hydropower.

These verbally formulated aims are reflected in the performance index $J(y)$ of the nonlinear optimisation problem (NLOP) with several parts each weighted according to its importance related to reference values. Thus the NLOP becomes

$$\min_y\{J(y) \;=\; \frac{1}{2}\tilde{y}^T Q \tilde{y} - c^T P_{el} \mid h(y) = 0 \;,\; g(y) \leq 0\} \tag{4}$$

$$\begin{aligned} \tilde{y} &= y - y_{ref} \\ y_{ref} &- \textit{vector of reference values} \\ Q &- \textit{diagonal weighting matrix} \\ c &- \textit{vector of weighting and units factors} \\ P_{el} &- \textit{generated electrical energy by hydro power} \end{aligned}$$

The solution of this constrained NLOP is calculated using the HQP optimisation tool [5],[6] which includes an iterative Sequential Quadratic Programming (SQP) algorithm with an interior point method for solving the quadratic convex sub-problems. The resulting non-linear equation system is solved numerically by an iterative Newton procedure. The sparsity pattern of the coefficient matrix is used in connection with an ordering algorithm for effective computations. Algorithms are partly taken from the Meschach library for matrix computations [19], and from the ADOL-C package for automatic differentiation [8].

6 Results

Firstly, the results of the Ohra dam reconstruction scenario are presented because it is a very recent scenario. In accordance with the first recommendation of the State Environment Office the investigations were carried out assuming a dry weather situation occurred, corresponding to its probability, every 50 years. The main result was that the water demand could only be met with a demand shortfall of about 6 % during the reconstruction period. Testing cases where dry weather situations occur more often allow the demand shortfall to be reduced to less than 0.1 %. Representatively, the optimal reservoir contents and drinking water releases for a 26 yearly dry weather situation are shown in Fig. 2. In this case the demand shortfall amounts to 0.03 % during the reconstruction period.

The contents of the small Tambach-Dietharz reservoir ranges between its lower and upper bound, 0.55 and 0.78 million cu. m, respectively. The optimisation horizon amounts to 4 years in all cases. The solid and dashed reservoir content lines represent the 26 yearly dry weather situations with 3 and 2 year dryness periods, respectively. The dotted lines show from bottom to top the minimum, desired, and maximum reservoir contents, respectively. The drinking water releases are the same in both cases.

Secondly, the following results were obtained concerning the system behaviour when applying different hydrological scenarios. In a first stage, the existing reservoir management plan was compared with the results of the proposed SQP-type algorithm concerning statistical measures. To obtain statistical statements, a 2,000 year artificial inflow time series was applied to the system, and a simulation was performed, i.e. given initial states were taken, the optimum releases were computed using the SQP-type algorithm, the system behaviour was simulated during the next month applying the optimal controls and the inflows from the artificial time series. Thus, new final states were obtained for the end of the simulated month which were used as the new initial states at the beginning of the next month. Then the whole procedure was repeated month by month over the whole 2,000 year time horizon.

In a second stage, the influence of a changed hydrological situation due to climate change on the planning and management of the pilot system was investigated. Climate change software modules are offered within the 'CHEWS' project by the Institute of Hydrology, Wallingford, U.K. [10]. The climate data of the years 1961–90 serve as baseline data. No full climate data set was available for the pilot system but inflow time series data were available from 1931. Two of the climate change models integrated into the climate change software modules deliver runoff factors in addition to changed climate data (e.g. temperature, precipitation, evaporation). One of them, the CCC model developed by the Canadian Climate Centre, delivers, in the case of the pilot system under consideration, raised inflows in some months and yearly means. Therefore these inflow data were not used. The second model, the HadCM1 model developed by the UK Meteorological Office (Hadley Centre) computed the following values as listed in Table 1 for Ohra inflow. The inflows to the other reservoirs are similar to the values depicted in Table 1.

The control strategy was slightly modified because the system contains two large reservoirs (Ohra and Schmalwasser, 17.5 million cu. m. and 20.54 million cu. m., respectively) and a very small one (Tambach-Dietharz, 0.78 million cu. m.) immediately ahead of one of the water works. As there are relatively large natural inflows and transitions into the Tambach-Dietharz reservoir, the minimum and maximum values are reached frequently using a time discretisation of 1 month. In addition, only 0.23 million cu. m. can be used during operation due to technical restrictions in connection with the water works and because of water quality in this reservoir. The modifications consist of retaining water in the Schmalwasser reservoir if the maximum level is reached and delivering water from the Schmalwasser reservoir if the level is at the minimum, to avoid overflow and demand shortfall, respectively. If we take a shorter time discretisation, especially for a mid- or short-term operation interval, these problems do not occur.

The results of optimisation are shown in Table 2. The results documented in the

Table 1. Inflow and flow change factors

month	measured[a]	f[b]	calculated[c]
Jan	0.918	1.202	1.103
Feb	0.879	0.741	0.651
Mar	1.045	0.961	1.005
Apr	1.804	0.893	1.612
May	1.073	0.841	0.902
Jun	0.787	0.877	0.690
Jul	0.574	0.944	0.542
Aug	0.486	0.763	0.371
Sep	0.424	0.727	0.308
Oct	0.529	0.843	0.446
Nov	0.706	1.035	0.731
Dec	1.129	1.092	1.233
yearly mean:	0.863	—	0.800

[a] measured monthly mean inflow 1961-92 $[\frac{m^3}{s}]$

[b] flow change factor according to HadCM1 model and the year 2025

[c] calculated flows according to HadCM1 model and the year 2050 $[\frac{m^3}{s}]$

Reservoir Management Plan (RMP) serve as a basis for comparison. In this RMP only a few statistical measures are given. They are listed in Table 2 in the first column. In the second column comparable results can be seen when applying the proposed SQP-type algorithm using the same data (S). Columns 3 and 4 (S2025 and S2050, respectively) contain the results of the application of optimal control proposals computed by the SQP-algorithm under changed inflow data for the years 2025 and 2050, respectively.

If we compare S with RMP, the slightly higher reliability of supply can be seen in both frequency p_f and duration p_d. The low-water frequencies are also lower at both main reservoirs. Other figures for comparison with the RMP were not available.

The main results of the investigation of the hydrological scenarios (S versus S2025 and S2050) are the decreasing reliability of supply (p_f, p_d, p_a) with decreasing inflows, the slightly increasing demand shortfalls (the difference between 100 and the corresponding reliabilities of Table 2), the reduced water surplus, the reduced frequencies of spillage and the slightly growing low-water frequencies for reduced inflow. The assumed overall drinking water demand of 140,000 m^3/d was chosen to be the same as in the RMP, in order to compare all variants. But, because the RMP was designed some years ago, the assumption was made that the demand will be higher. In a normal operating situation about 88,600 m^3/d are consumed due to developments described above, i.e., at present the demand reaches only 63.28 %

Table 2. Statistical data

variable	RMP[a]	S[b]	S2025[c]	S2050[d]
p_f	97.80 %	99.42 %	96.24 %	91.19 %
p_d	99.40 %	98.81 %	98.59 %	95.68 %
p_a	no spec.	99.97 %	99.77 %	99.29 %
$l_{f,O}$	0.20 %	0.09 %	0.20 %	0.28 %
$l_{f,S}$	0.10 %	0.02 %	0.93 %	2.46 %

[a] Reservoir management plan at present
[b] SQP-type algorithm at present
[c] SQP-type algorithm in year 2025
[d] SQP-type algorithm in year 2050
with

$$\begin{aligned} p_f &= \text{reliability according to frequency in } \% \\ &= \frac{n_{ycds}}{n_s} \cdot 100 \\ p_d &= \text{reliability according to duration in } \% \\ &= \frac{n_{mcds}}{n_s} \cdot 100 \\ p_a &= \text{reliability according to amount in } \% \\ &= \frac{r_c}{d} \cdot 100 \\ l_{f,x} &= \text{low-water frequency at reservoir x in } \% \\ &= \frac{n_{mrm}}{n_s} \cdot 100 \end{aligned}$$

and

n_{ycds} - number of years with complete demand satisfaction,
n_s - number of years of simulation time horizon,
n_{mcds} - number of months with complete demand satisfaction,
r_c - controlled released water amount for drinking water supply,
d - overall demand in simulation time horizon,
n_{mrm} - number of months, when reservoir is at minimum,
$x \in \{O, S\}$, O = Ohra, S = Schmalwasser,
no spec. - no specification was made.

of the demand used in investigations. Therefore, the influence of climate changes on hydrological situation and the corresponding effect on water supply processes is small, however, we have to keep in mind that the demand could rise to the value used during investigations.

In the investigations given in this chapter, the energy generation, which is mentioned above as a possible part of the performance index, has been neglected. Originally it was intended to take into account the use of water for energy generation via turbines, but by the end of this work the data of the turbine to be installed was still unknown. Further investigations that take into account the possibility of electrical energy generation will be carried out by the authors when these data become known.

7 Conclusion

The approach presented shows that it is possible to formulate the planning and management problems of a water resources system as an optimisation problem and to solve it efficiently using an SQP-type algorithm. The results obtained by simulation can serve as decision support for further planning and management in normal and extraordinary situations.

Acknowledgments

The authors are grateful to the EC for funding the 'CHEWS' project (ENV4-CT95-0138) in the Fourth Framework of ESPRIT programme - Environment and Climate subdivision.

References

[1] E. Arnold and H. Puta. An SQP-type solution method for constrained discrete-time optimal control problems. In R. Bulirsch and D. Kraft, editors, *Computational optimal control*, volume 115 of International Series of Numerical Mathematics, pages 127–136. Birkhäuser, Basel, 1994.

[2] E. Arnold, P. Tatjewski, and P. Wołochowicz. Two Methods for Large-Scale Nonlinear Optimization and Their Comparison on a Case Study of Hydropower Optimization. *JOTA*, 81(2):221–248, May 1994.

[3] G. Balint, I. Dobi, and J. Mika. Runoff simulation assuming global warming scenarios. XVIIIth Conference of the Danube Countries on Hydrological Forecasting and Hydrological Bases of Water Management. Schriftenreihe zur Wasserwirtschaft, vol. 19/1, pages A-131 - A-136, Technical University Graz, Austria, 1996.

[4] T. Brandsma. *Hydrological Impact of Climate Change - A Sensitivity Study for the Netherlands*. PhD thesis, Delft University of Technology, 1995.

[5] R. Franke. HQP - a solver for sparse nonlinear optimization, version 0.91. Technical report, Technical University of Ilmenau, Germany, 1995.

[6] R. Franke. Internet enabled HQP optimization service - software demonstration. Computer-Intensive Methods in Control and Signal Processing, 2nd European IEEE Workshop, Prague, pages 245-246, 1996.

[7] R. Franke and E. Arnold. Applying new numerical algorithms to the solution of discrete-time optimal control problems. Computer-Intensive Methods in Control and Signal Processing, 2nd European IEEE Workshop, Prague, pages 67-72, 1996.

[8] A. Griewank, D. Juedes, and J. Utke. ADOL-C: A Package for the Automatic Differentiation of Algorithms Written in C/C++. *ACM Transactions on Mathematical Software*, 22(2):131–167, 1996.

[9] J.T. Houghton, B.A. Callander, and S.K. Varney (Eds.). *Climate Change 1992. The Supplementary Report to the IPCC Scientific Assessment.* Cambridge University Press, Cambridge, 1992.

[10] IoH. Notes on the use of the Institute of Hydrology's Climate Change software. Institute of Hydrology. Wallingford, U.K, 1997.

[11] Krippendorf. Talsperrensystem Ohra/Schmalwasser/ Tambach-Dietharz - Wasserwirtschaftsplan. Thüringer Landesanstalt für Umwelt, Jena, 1995 (in German).

[12] H. Lang, A. Baltensweiler, J. Gurtz, and J. Schulla. Die Auswirkungen von Klimaänderungen auf die Komponenten des Wasserkreislaufs. In W. Bechteler, F.W. Günthert, H.-B. Kleeberg (Hrsg.). Klimaänderung und Wasserwirtschaft. Int. Symp. München, Tagungsband, Teil a, S. 73-88, 1995 (in German).

[13] C.-D. Schönwiese. Problematik der Klimaänderungen: Ursachen und Beobachtungen. In W. Bechteler, F.W. Günthert, H.-B. Kleeberg (Hrsg.). Klimaänderung und Wasserwirtschaft. Int. Symp. München, Tagungsband, Teil a, S. 16-32, 1995 (in German).

[14] M. Schramm. Zur mathematischen Darstellung und Simulation des natürlichen Durchflussprozesses. *Acta hydrophysica*, XIX(2/3):77–191, 1975 (in German).

[15] M. Schramm and U. Dietzsch. Das GRM Ohra/Schmalwasser. WASY - Gesellschaft für wasserwirtschaftliche Planung und Systemforschung mbH, Dresden, 1993 (in German).

[16] A. Schumann. Veränderungen des Wasserhaushaltes durch Klimaänderungen. In W. Bechteler, F.W. Günthert, H.-B. Kleeberg (Hrsg.). Klimaänderung und Wasserwirtschaft. Int. Symp., München, Tagungsband, Teil a, S. 89-99, 1995 (in German).

[17] P. Serban and C. Corbus. Impact of climatic changes an the water balance of a basin. XVIIIth Conference of the Danube Countries on Hydrological Forecasting and Hydrological Bases of Water Management. Schriftenreihe zur Wasserwirtschaft, vol. 19/1, pages A-143 - A-148, Technical University Graz, Austria, 1996.

[18] N. Sreenath. *Systems Representation of Global Climate Change Models*, volume 186 of *Lecture Notes in Control and Information Sciences.* Springer, 1993.

[19] D.E. Stewart and Z. Leyk. Meschach: Matrix Computations in C. Vol. 32 of The Centre for Mathematics and its Applications, The Australian National University, 1994.

[20] W.W.-G. Yeh. Reservoir Management and Operation Models: A State-of-the-Art Review. *Water Resources Research*, 21(12):1797–1818, 1985.

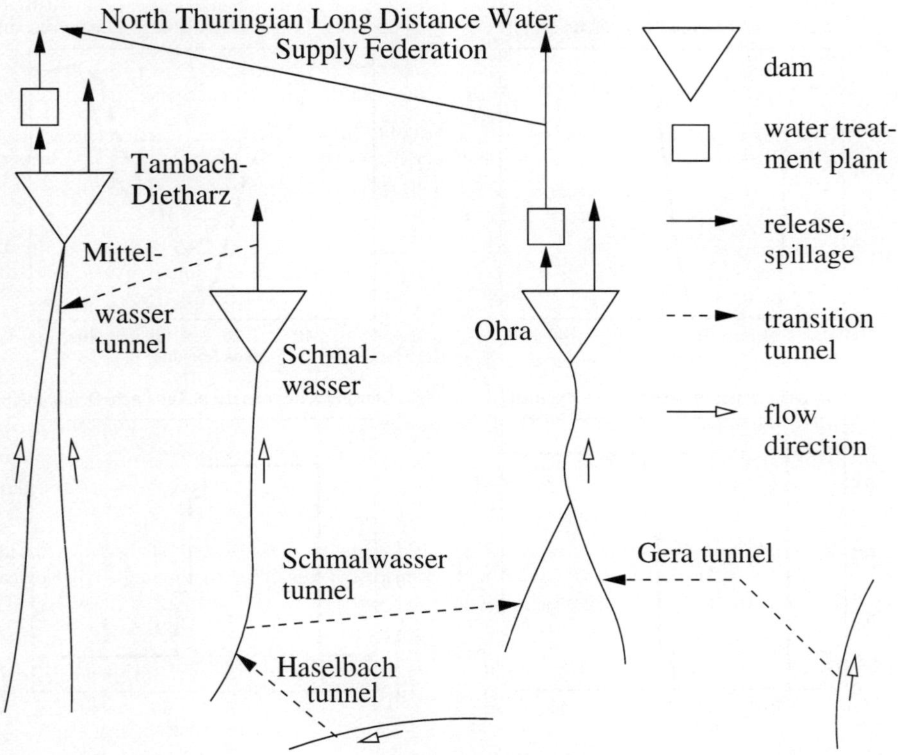

Figure 1. Ohra/Schmalwasser/Tambach-Dietharz dams system

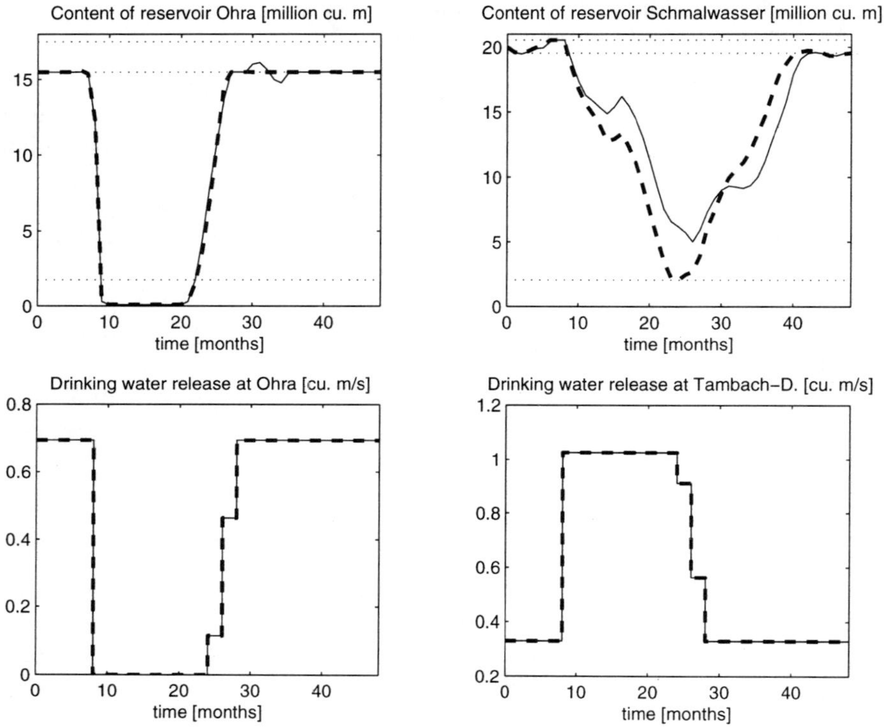

Figure 2. Reservoir contents and drinking water releases

Section 3

Information Technology and Systems Integration

CHAPTER 15

Integrated Operational Systems - Breaking the Paradigm!

G.D.Morris

1. Introduction

Whilst all water companies are spending considerable sums of money on the introduction of new technology into the distribution side of their businesses, the results of this investment are unlikely to be the Integrated Operational Systems that they all desire. Most approaches seek to build upon operational experience and technological capability to meet the demands of management for integrated systems. This ignores, or places too little emphasis, on the one factor that is essential for long term success.

This chapter will argue that not only is there a missing ingredient but furthermore few organisations have recognised what it is they are actually trying to develop. If there is no real understanding of what is needed, it is obviously going to be very unlikely that the desired results will be produced. There is a need for a new approach. Companies must consider

"Breaking the Paradigm"

if they want to develop truly *Integrated Operational Systems*.

2. Evolution of the Industry: how it used to work!

Management of a water distribution system by utility companies is probably one of the most difficult business problems to solve. It is amazing that water utilities have, since the last century, managed to supply their customers with ever increasing levels of efficiency and reliability. Service failures involving breaks in supply (e.g. water restrictions), faults (e.g. major pipe bursts) or inadequate quality (e.g. cryptosperidium) are sufficiently rare to warrant headlines in the daily press. These relate to the practical issues of taking the raw product through a manufacturing process and then delivering it to the customer, albeit the spatial aspect of this exercise can extend over many miles of pipelines. Much of this success has, in the past, been achieved by use of considerable manpower, with well co-ordinated gangs undertaking, manually, the tasks in the supply chain. Until recently there was no alternative. Technological assistance was limited to the transport necessary to ferry the operational staff to their workplace and a few telephones for communicating between head office staff.

Knowledge of the extensive under and above ground infrastructure was to a considerable extent vested in staff with many years of experience, many of whom kept their own notes on pipe layouts so that they could remember valve and switch settings when responding to incidents several years later. Draughtsmen were employed to painstakingly draw the networks over Ordnance Survey maps, either directly onto the maps themselves or onto transparent overlays. However, maintaining these plans was difficult because the single master could not be easily copied and made available to the outside staff.

The question that arises is "How did all this work when there was so little information or technology available to the operators?". There are probably three main reasons:

Low wages - the relatively low wages for manual staff meant that large numbers of labourers could be employed.

Size - the water undertakings themselves were much smaller and had responsibility for a much smaller geographical area which meant that communications and efficient transport were less important.

Lack of mobility - allied with the local nature of the businesses was the fact that the staff were, themselves, not mobile and had often worked with the utility "man and boy". Absence of detailed plans was not therefore such a major problem as it would have been if operation supervisors had been new to the area when they were appointed.

The amalgamations and mergers of these small utility organisations have now resulted in companies that are probably some of the largest of their type in the world today. They serve large populations dispersed across a considerable area. The scale of the present undertakings, the new requirement for profitable returns to investors and the penalties inflicted by increasingly stringent regulatory controls mean that the old ways are no longer appropriate. A new way must be found.

3. The Problem

In the past operational decisions were often made in the field using a combination of local knowledge and experience of the system. The high staff turnovers in modern utility companies mean that this inherent understanding of the system is no longer there and fewer staff must operate in a far greater geographical area.

The problem facing present day water companies is how to manage their distribution networks whilst not only minimising their staff costs, but also using staff who in many cases are new to the area within which they operate.

4. The Solution

Tantalisingly, the solution is obvious. If water companies cannot afford to employ large numbers of staff who know their area, and they want to control activities without staff in attendance, they must make use of technology in order to:

Store Information about their networks.

Monitor Activity on their key processes.

Activate Equipment whenever this is necessary.

If the answer is clear, the question remains "How do they do it?"

The first step is to study the systems that are currently in use in order to understand their deficiencies.

5. Existing Water Distribution Systems

Over the last twenty years there has been a steady increase both in the number and sophistication of the Information Systems (IS) that are available to help run the operations side of the water industry. The principal systems used are:

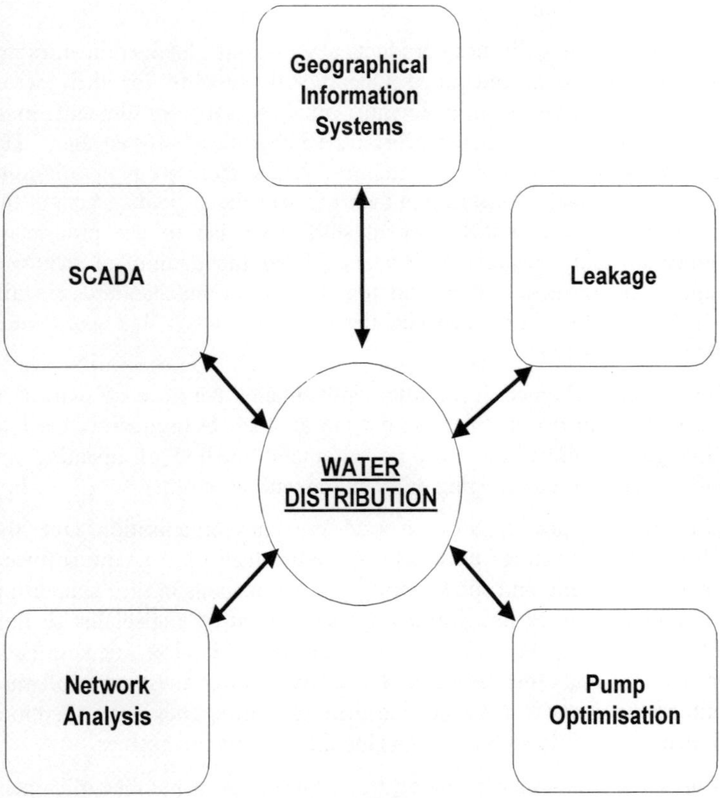

SCADA – Telemetry and remote control systems which form the basis of the systems used in control rooms to monitor activity over the distribution network.

Geographical Information Systems (GIS) – Mapping systems that enable companies to record the precise position of their underground assets (e.g. pipes, valves etc) and above ground assets on a backdrop of Ordnance Survey maps. Data can be linked to graphical representations, so that when users point to them the relevant data is displayed.

Network Analysis – The early versions of these systems used simplified networks to produce their models. Increases in computer power have enabled the latest packages to generate a model from detail network information. Some companies have therefore experimented with network information downloaded from their GIS.

Leakage Control – Systems are designed to identify losses on the network using a number of different tests.

Pump Optimisation – One of the largest water company costs arises from the use of electricity for pumping water. This is a particular concern for companies operating in hilly parts of the country. New systems try to make optimal use of pumps commensurate with satisfying demand. Demand prediction and modern half-hourly electricity tariffs mean that complex algorithms are needed to provide the best results.

5.1. Issues Limiting Integration

The question that arises is "Why, if these products already exist, have companies not managed to develop their own Integrated Operational Systems for their water distribution networks?" The answer is that whilst all these software elements exist they are mainly free standing systems with very little integration between them. The market for operational software is still in its infancy. Whilst there are many different software developers, they are all pioneering in their own specialist fields. Much of the software is processor hungry and development staff have had to use proprietary techniques in order to gain adequate performance from the equipment that was available at the time. The newness of the technology has meant that standards are still evolving. This lack of commonality between the products means that worthwhile integration is difficult to achieve.

Where integration has been claimed, it has often only entailed the once-off extraction of data from one system for use as the base data in another. Subsequently the two systems have diverged as there has been no automatic method of updating the duplicated sets of data and thereby keeping them in line with each other.

This fragmented approach is also apparent in water company organisation. Over the last few years different departments have seen the advantage of the new software packages, have purchased them, and subsequently become responsible for supporting them. Often this embryonic work has resulted in the creation of a specialist section with staff dedicated to using the software. Information Technology departments, concentrating on financial and other textual systems, have viewed these new software packages as technical products that are outside their province. They have therefore allowed these pioneering users to select and develop the systems themselves.

Thus, there has arisen a situation where water companies use a number of largely proprietary systems for which responsibilities are fragmented. Furthermore, not only does no one person have overall responsibility for the systems, but also many small sections wish to retain their involvement in the software that they have introduced.

6. Developing a New Operational Management System

6.1. Adopting the Right Approach

Having commenced a project, we rarely restart it later. As a result decisions made at the outset will largely determine whether ultimate success is possible. It is therefore essential to spend sufficient time considering how to tackle the problem before commencing a project. This section explains the issues that are involved.

6.2. Building the Team

Designing water distribution systems is a practical activity in which one can measure one's success by checking whether adequate supplies of water emanate from the end of the pipes on the customers' premises. Failures can be corrected by the provision of additional components in the network or by increasing the quantity of water supplied into the system. Effective water mains systems have been in use for the last hundred years and their design and construction, whilst complex, is now well understood.

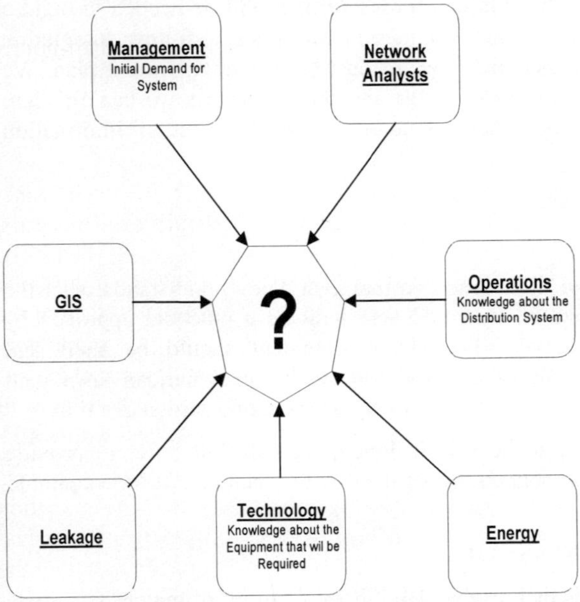

However, the present focus should not be on water distribution systems but on building an effective operational management system. The difference is significant and highlights what this paper contends is the missing ingredient for success. Confronted with the requirement to create an Integrated Operational System, the tendency is for the task to be entrusted to a team of interested parties. Unfortunately, whilst this team may well be capable of devising a water distribution system, it is ill equipped for its new brief. The missing ingredient referred to at the outset is not just an omitted party but a lynch pin upon which this group must depend if it is to be successful.

The essential missing ingredient shown holding the above group together is the **Systems Designer**. Whilst not involved in the past, he/she must now be introduced. Good information systems need to be engineered in the just the same way as roads, bridges or reservoirs. To ignore the systems designer's contribution is akin to appointing a team comprising a policeman, pedestrian, motorist and lorry driver to build a road. All are road users and can describe what they want to use the road for, but none is competent to know where or how to build a road.

6.3. Deciding Where to Start

Companies will not start a project unless they have recognised that they do not currently have the systems that they want. The temptation at this stage will be to try to build upon the existing systems because staff understand them. However, if this were the correct approach the systems would probably have been integrated already and they are not! The underlying incompatibilities between the software elements limit the scope for integration.

If integration cannot be achieved by developing current systems, an alternative approach is needed. Considerable innovation will be required to deliver the desired results where previous attempts have failed. Strong resolve will be needed to build a new system from scratch but this is what is required if success is to follow. Integration is not something that can be considered later. It must be part of the initial plan. We would not consider making the parts of a car and then seeing if we can fit them together but often this is the approach taken in the development of Information Systems.

6.4. Specifying the Requirement

6.4.1. The Vision

The first step should be to develop a vision so that everybody understands what the ultimate objective of the project is. It should also indicate a practical approach by which the vision can be achieved. The vision statement should be short and memorable. An excellent example of a vision was set by an American lawn seed company whose business vision was "To turn America green, one garden at a time."

An IT project vision may have to be a little longer than that in order to provide objectives for its individual components. Nevertheless, the memorable aspect should not be lost in the extra length.

6.4.2. Conceptualisation and Minimisation

The problem with big systems is that they are BIG! Specifications of major IT projects tend to run to several weighty tomes by the time all parties have added detailed statements of their requirements. The result is a document that human beings find difficult to assimilate. This leads to a breakdown in understanding between the IT staff charged with delivering the system and the users who are looking forward to using it.

When the system fails to materialise and the post-mortems are concluded, the usual verdict is that the project was specified in too little detail. In practice, the converse was true. There was so much detail that the development staff never understood the overall objectives of the project.

IT projects can be considered in two parts:

The System – this must be described conceptually as a series of discrete components, each of which performs a single business function. It is more important that everyone understands the overall concept than that every little operation is described in minute detail. The details can always be elicited as the development progresses but failure to understand the complete picture will result in a poorly structured system, which has to be progressively modified in order to achieve the original objectives. If the underlying structure is right, the system will be able to cope with all the detailed requirements.

The Information – This is another area where systems can try to do too much and thereby achieve very little. In this case, minimisation of the requirement is needed.

With Operation Management Systems this is particularly important because there is plenty of scope for collecting vast amounts of data either from detailed network information or real time telemetry data. The next section "Setting the Scope" expands upon this subject and explains how it is important to ensure accuracy and limit data gathering to essential data.

Ultimate success will depend upon everyone understanding the business requirement and ensuring that the data needs are initially limited to essential information. A well-designed system can always be expanded to provide more functions and to cater for more information after it has been proven in a basic environment.

6.4.3. Setting the Scope

Whilst the vision can be an ultimate dream of what one would like to do, the scope should temper desire with the realities of what can be successfully achieved. The system should place great emphasis on the accuracy of its results using on-line data wherever possible. There are distinct dangers in modelling at levels of detail that can neither be verified nor calibrated. If some data are inaccurate, they tend to degrade the value of the other valid information. Wherever possible the day-to-day control of the operational network should be based on accurate information. The intention is to actually supply water, as opposed to proving that it should have been delivered!

The requirements should be considered in the following areas. These equate to the operational needs:

Network Management and Control – The information needed to ensure that adequate water is available to meet demand and to monitor the transmission of water from source through to the customer. Wherever possible the system should use measurable information, which means that some simplification of the network must take place in order to limit scope to those portions that can be monitored. Achievable accuracy is essential if the intention is to move to a fully automated closed loop system.

Telemetry systems should be used to deliver information on the current state of the network at all key points, including controls and alarms.

Maintenance of Network – This area encompasses all the activities carried out by the operations department in maintaining the network. Ideally, detailed information is needed with plans showing network design and layout. However, whilst the best data possible are required, accurate data cannot always be obtained because much of the equipment is underground. Pipes thought to be on one side of the road are often found on the other. This inaccuracy is inconvenient but it is not critical when applied at a local level.

Where local modelling is needed, detailed models can be created with suitable calibration at strategic points on the network.

A few words should be stated about archiving data. More data means more cost in terms of the increased complexity of the systems needed to manage it, the space needed to store it, the time taken to collect it and the time taken to process it. Data should only be retained if it is being kept for a specific purpose (e.g. maintenance, leakage detection.). Even then, arrangements should be made to delete data after it has fulfilled its planned purpose.

6.4.4 Rationalising the Network

Considerable thought needs to be given to how the network used within the network management and control side of the system can be rationalised. Much of the planning will involve deciding which parts of the network are to be included and which parts excluded. From this it will be possible to determine the places at which measuring is required in order to provide the up to date information needed by the system. An iterative process may have to be carried out in order to adjust the system's boundaries to suitable measurement points.

In the past, there has been a tendency to insert telemetry devices wherever possible. This meant that some key places were excluded because it was difficult to arrange the necessary communications or power supply. It is important to start by deciding where you want the equipment to be fitted onto the network and then find ways of achieving it! Existing telemetry points that are not essential for the running of the system should be removed in order to limit data collection to the key data needed to manage the network.

Difficult decisions need to be made on how frequently data are collected, how data are used and what needs to be kept for use elsewhere.

6.5. Design Considerations

6.5.1. System Components

If the biggest stumbling block to real integration is the lack of standards and the proprietary nature of much of the current software, it is sensible to consider how these factors can be accommodated in the design of the replacement systems. The question is how to design an operational control system in order to achieve the maximum level of integration, both now and in the future.

The system should comprise five essential elements:

Data Collection – the part of the system that collects the data, much of it on-line.

Data Storage and Processing – the information that is collected and used by the system.

Graphics – the way in which the output from the system is displayed for the users.

Control Switching – the methods used to remotely trigger activity on the distribution system.

Note: ultimately the data collection and control switching components will enable the system to become fully automated with switching triggered as a direct result of data received.

Data Archiving - This has been kept separate from the data storage element in order to differentiate between the short and the longer term use of the data. The latter use is different (trends and regulatory reporting etc.) from the immediate control use and the degree of urgency is missing when processing archived data.

Total integration is not completely practical because different applications require different types of data. For example, a Geographical Information System (GIS) needs totally accurate records of the position and type of each pipe. A supervisor's schematics need some details to be shown accurately (e.g. key valves) but the rest of the network to be rationalised to enable the supervisor to quickly ascertain the way in which the water distribution system works. Thus some nodes will exist on both networks but others may not even exist on the schematic. The mains may consist of fifty separate pipe sections and cross the road several times on a GIS. On the schematic, it may be shown as a single line running down the centre of the road.

Nevertheless, if a system is to have any chance of achieving real integration it will have to be achieved in the database. In fact, the system must be "database driven" with a single database, which will be used to provide the information for all the graphical functions.

6.5.2. The Platform

An Operational Management System will comprise a number of complex components ranging from SCADA equipment through to graphics display systems (e.g. Geographical Information Systems; SCADA displays; Network Analysis; Schematics). Obviously it would not be sensible to reinvent all of these systems and so a new system must seek to use the latest "best of breed" with the proviso that it provide opportunities for the type of integration that is desired. The following is a list of issues that should be decided before real design work commences. They are not listed in any particular order of priority:

Open Products – The system must be developed using as few proprietary products as possible. Software should be able to interface with other market leading products, which might be required elsewhere within the system.

Basic Framework – The following should be used throughout the system and will form the glue upon which all the component products must run:

- **Operating System**– A standard operating system should be used and all products would have to run on it (e.g. Microsoft Windows NT).
- **Database**-A single database must be used (e.g. Oracle).
- **Communications Protocol**–All the products must be able to "talk" to each other easily using the same protocols wherever possible (e.g. TCP/IP which would also provide Internet/Intranet compatibility).
- **Workstation**– The products must be capable of running and displaying their results on the same workstations (e.g. Pentium PCs).

Many hardware and interfacing problems can be avoided by carefully choosing this uniform base before selecting application software.

Object-Oriented (OO) – Theoretically, these types of systems demand object oriented software. Unfortunately OO systems are not easy to develop and the individual developer should decide whether he wishes to use this approach.

Object Linking and Embedding (OLE) – Undoubtedly systems should make extensive use of this type of function, which enables a process in one product to be invoked from another.

Graphics Software – It has already been stated that any system will need to display a number of different graphical screens (e.g. network analysis, SCADA, GIS, schematics, and even photos and live video). Whilst different graphics software packages could be used for each display type, a product that can support several of these displays would be preferable.

Sound selection in the above areas will greatly improve the ease with which the system can be developed

6.6. Other Issues

Finally it is worth mentioning that any development should attempt to give its users a “quick win”, in other words something that the user can usefully use whilst the rest of the system is being developed.

7. Conclusion

Integrated Operational Systems are probably the most complex systems used by Water Companies in the United Kingdom today. Still in their infancy, they currently comprise a number of complex pieces of software, much of it proprietary. Whilst some attempts have been made to integrate the different products, these do not provide the full integration that water companies desire. This chapter has described the background to the existing systems and then explained why an entirely new approach is needed if fully integrated systems are to be developed. Finally, it has stressed the importance of the systems designer’s role and discussed many of the issues that will need to be resolved when designing the ultimate **Integrated Operational System**. The only question that remains is:

“Who is going to break the Paradigm?”

CHAPTER 16

SCADA-Network Analysis Systems Linking from Plan to Integration

R.W.Cameron, R.J.Barrett, P.A.Jarrige, L.Tocqueville *and* N.Cazottes

Synopsis

Modern water production and distribution utilities require more systematic handling of system complexities providing more efficient guidelines for overall operations. Such an objective is achieved with a Geographic Information System (GIS), SCADA system and Network Analysis System (NAS).

Systems integration has emerged as the key to successful computer systems. The days are gone when systems can be viewed as standalone entities. Such new thinking towards Information Technology is at the heart of United Water Idaho's (UWID) computer systems master plan. UWID has already linked their GIS and NAS packages. The company is now looking to connect the supervisory system with the network model in order to enhance the design and real time analysis of the water distribution system.

SCADA and Network Analysis System linking provides a full understanding of hydraulics throughout the system and validates pumping strategies regarding pressure and water quality. The objective is to allow operators to have a complete overview of their network and to investigate the consequences of different operating actions before actually selecting an action.

For ease of use, the linking package has the same look-and-feel as the SCADA interface. For process speed, the data exchange between applications is not file-based but uses the latest data transfer technology. Multitasking allows simultaneous simulation of real time and prospective scenarios.

United Water IDAHO and SAFEGE have been working on the project for three years. The chapter will present aspects of the project from application functional analysis to the first operational results in BOISE.

Information Technology, an answer to operator's needs

In their quest for premium-quality potable water services and cost-effective operations, water companies gain from the evolution of Information Technology aimed at finding an answer to management constraints, planning, design, operation and maintenance.

Today, in every operation of a potable water supply network, there is a need for a systematic approach to solve problems as well as a need for better control of complex systems and/or use of relevant tools to meet water distribution needs. Information Technology (IT) provides several solutions:

- Geographic Information Systems (GIS) manage the asset database and graphic display.
- Telecontrol and supervisory systems (SCADA) receive data from local stations and concentrate vital information for permanent control.
- Network Analysis Systems (NAS) deal with water capacity and quality questions leading to improved decision-making by planning engineers designing infrastructure development.

Current factors, such as the lack of water resources or the expensive price of energy, have obliged the water industry to implement telecontrol and supervisory systems. Similarly, engineers are using network modelling tools.

Most of the time, the implementation of such computer tools is problematic because of a lack of homogeneity in equipment or communication fields.

Therefore, it is very difficult indeed to get a steady link between supervisory systems, recording tools and network modelling. Such a link was still considered utopia by most of the operators.

However, if the supervisory and network analysis systems were linked, the network model would become « alive » and the operator would have the appropriate tool to help him in managing the distribution network from the production sites right up to the customer's tap.

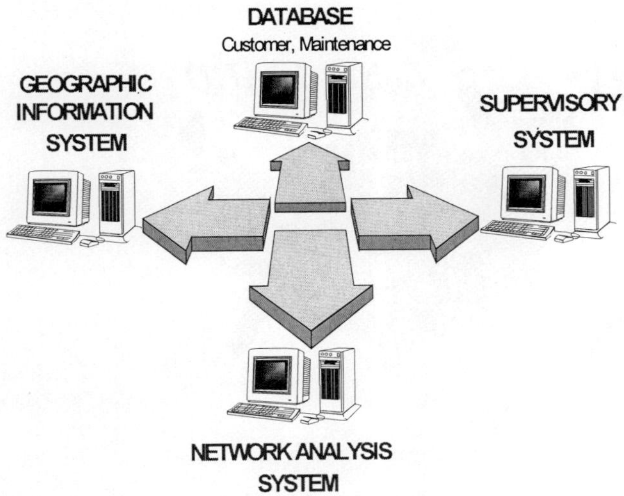

Figure 1. Information System Integration

In September 1994, United Water Idaho, operator of Boise's water distribution network, clearly targeted the link between SCADA and NAS: « *Linking SCADA with simulation will provide for a better understanding of the hydraulic and water quality behaviour...The operators will investigate the consequences of different operating actions before actually selecting an action...* ».

Interested by this approach, Suez-Lyonnaise des Eaux joined United Water Idaho and Safege to develop this project whose implementation took the following steps:

- Functional analysis, which specifies the tool, design.
- Information program development.
- Integration of the SCADA-NAS bridge on site in Boise.

The water company, United Water Idaho (Boise - U.S.A.)

Rooted in the foothills of the Rockies, Boise, capital of Idaho (USA), is characterised by the contrast of its geology and climate. The Owyhee desert plateau stretches to the South and the West. Towering up to the North are the mountainous and wooded massifs of the Rockies where the Snake River meanders its way as it follows the contours of the valleys.

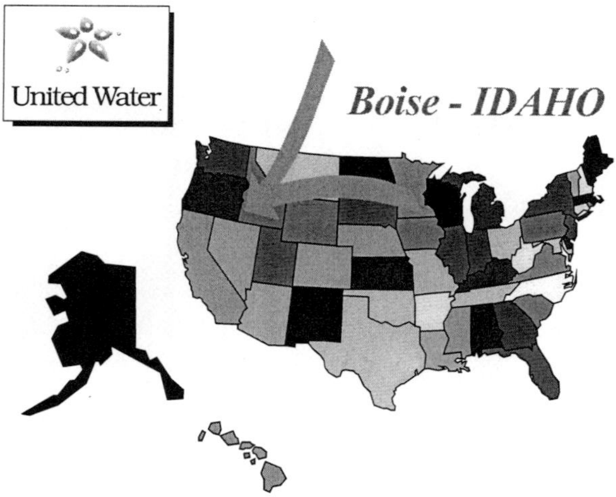

Figure 2. Boise Location Map

United Water Idaho supplies water to 56 000 customers with a total of 51 000 Ml pumped during 1996. 70 bore wells with the ranney collector at Marden Street treatment plant, produced 300 Ml/d during the peak day. This demand comes down to an average of 140 Ml/d.

The wells directly feed the 1250 km pipe system. The management of such a system is often a complex affair. It is difficult to comprehend the hydraulic interactions between 37 pumping stations, 29 reservoirs and 7 service levels, and even more difficult to assess the impact of a well's operation on the water quality.

UWID uses different information tools for handling its system complexity and for provision of efficient guidelines covering overall operations.

The Geographic Information System, Arc/Info, manages the pipe system data, the facility location and characteristics, and considerable maintenance and operations data. The system benefits as well from using an asset database under Oracle.

The Network Analysis System, Piccolo, is frequently used by the Engineering Department for pipe and utility sizing. A system masterplan is on going with specific attention paid to water quality improvment using the NAS.

UWID's SCADA system consists of dual DEC Station 5000/125's. The supervision software, Valmet's OaSYS, controls communication of the 90 RTU's through 9 leased wire lines and 1 radio channel. The poll processes allow interrogation of all sites in less than a minute. The data are organized in a CMX proprietary database for real-time information and then archived in an Oracle relational database.

A second SCADA system, Intellution's Fix, deals with control of the treatment plant. UWID developed a link between this second SCADA system and the Oracle archive database.

UWID's information system is based upon system integration. The systems are viewed as communicating entities that share data.

UWID has already linked the Geographic Information System and the Network Analysis package. This link follows a pre-scheduled procedure to update the network model for system simulation. Integration of network analysis with real-time data from a SCADA system will enhance the model maintenance and will offer wider services to the company's personnel.

The on-line simulation, Piccolo Real Time

An economical and technical study based on a sample of 110 operators located in different European and American countries, has enabled the synthesis of expected product functions. Although there were some expectation gaps from one country to another, results can be described as follows:

- Firstly, the importance of a perfect « friendliness » of the software's user-end and its need to be completely integrated within the operator's environment, that is to say the supervisory system.
- Secondly, the need for the software to be introduced as a real time analysis of the network behaviour and the validation of network management strategies regarding hydraulic parameters and water quality. Four ways had been emphasised in developing the software :
    - ♦ the *automatic super sensor*, to provide the operator with an instant view of the network in terms of pressure, flow and quality;
    - ♦ the *training tool* for management of the network, capable of carrying out simulations using real-time data to validate the pumping strategy and the various valve operations;
    - ♦ the *super-automation* for overall management of the operation, to predict the behaviour of the network using short term extended-period simulations;
    - ♦ the *crisis assistant* to help with managing critical situations, capable of detecting hydraulic malfunctions and of warning the user in the event of deviations from the ideal curves of reservoir levels or pressures.

This was both an ambitious and a realistic project because each step of the development referred to works that the developers had already experienced.

Currently, the first two ways are running as PICCOLO Real Time on BOISE's network.

This first stage objective is to run on-line snapshot simulation. The development is oriented toward three modules: the processor for data management, the calculation kernel, and the processor for analysis of results.

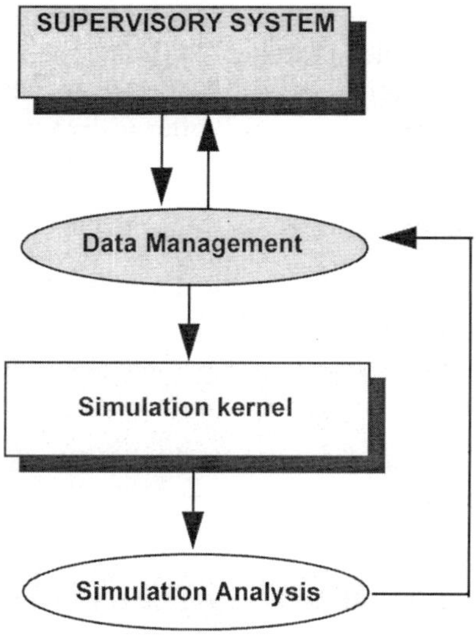

Figure 3. Piccolo Real Time Software Structure

Processor for data management

This processor enables the operators to gather simulation data, filter this information and monitor current water demands.

Globally, the network analysis system uses a set of subdivided structural and operational data. The structural data are adapted to the network structure, its equipment and the geographical distribution of its customers. This is the basis on which come operational data that in fact configure the model in order to cope with the current system status.

Structural data

Structural data are subdivided into *branches* (characteristics of the pipes, non return valves, valves, pressure controllers and pumps), *nodes* (that can be a specific point where consumption is aggregated, a junction between two branches, a source of supply or a reservoir), and *reservoir* characteristics.

For effective operational reasons and model integrity, structural data can only be modified by somebody in charge of the network modelling.

Operational data : real data and virtual data

Operational data deals with network status (reservoir current level, etc.) and facilities operations (pump switch, etc.), and are issued from the supervisory system.

However, the operator has the ability to modify the state of the devices in order to simulate a command that he wishes to be applied, i.e. « what if » simulation. To avoid any conflict, we have developed two simulation modes: automatic for real data, and manual for the data modified by the operator, so called «virtual ».

Data exchange with the supervisory system

The communication interface with the supervisory tool currently runs through a DDE link, and will soon be able to evolve towards OLE. These choices are standard links within the Windows environment, and therefore offer an opportunity towards the use of supervisory tools under this operating system.

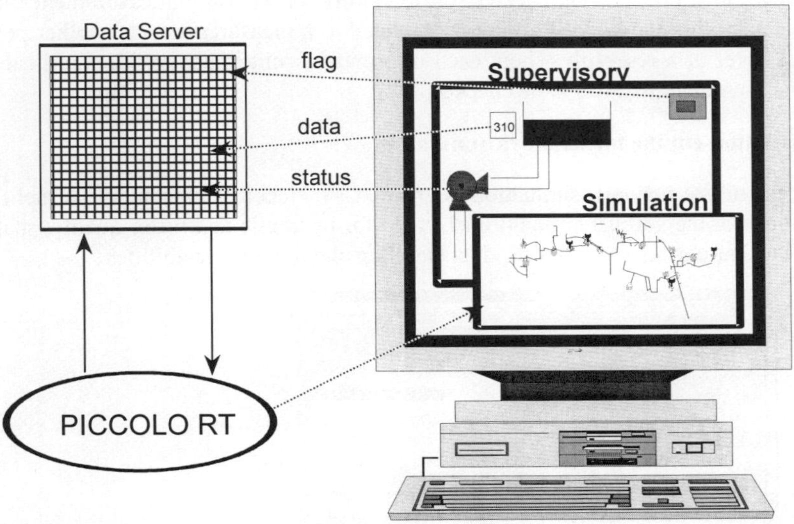

Figure 4. Data link between SCADA and Network Analysis System

Specificity of water demand

From the information on the network hydraulic state (levels of reservoirs, flow rate throughout the system, number of working pumps, etc.), it is necessary to estimate water demands by type or demand area. This task is compulsory in order to be able to run a real time simulation.

To solve this problem, we have aggregated demands by area. This method relies on the measurement of output in mains supplying an area and on the storage variation of reservoirs linked to it. For instance, if one takes into account an area supplied by three main pipes with two reservoirs, it is possible to estimate the total consumption as follows:

$Q_{\text{Pipe 1}} + Q_{\text{Pipe 2}} + Q_{\text{Pipe 3}} =$ Variation of reservoirs storage + Demands

To adjust the consumption in the model, we have assumed that consumption distribution is always the same and that the adjusting factor is equal to the estimated demand divided by the nominal demand (yearly average).

The necessity to filter input data

Inaccurate information can, even with a correct algorithm, lead to some impracticable or mistaken calculations. Automatic diagnosis points out and proposes a corrected value for each data-gathering mistake that can occur.

These security constraints deal with all conflict risks or lack of data by the edition of priority rules or default information. They are handled with a parametered module for each information and site. The module is written in Visual Basic. It is run using an OLE compliant server, providing filtering capabilities to the main application (acting here as an OLE client).

Through this process, the degree of reliability of pressure measurement can be associated with the work of a pump, or related to a measurement on another point or to the level of a reservoir. Then, each information contributes to the significance of the measurement that has to be checked.

Calculation engine for network simulation

Success of the network simulation is ensured by Piccolo's calculation kernel. Inner functions of the software remain unchanged for hydraulic and water quality, snapshot or extended-period, calculations, data handling and graphic capabilities.

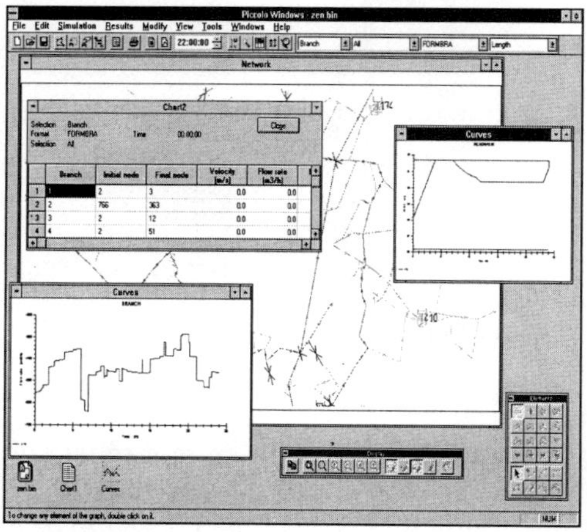

Figure 5. Piccolo (off-line) Network Analysis System

Response time and multi-tasks simulations

A real time simulation tool imposes handling times compatible with the distribution network operating context. The Piccolo* calculation engine therefore enables some extremely fast calculation times (15 seconds are needed with a Pentium 120 MHz, for the simulation of a 20000 branches network).

This speed is due to the use of a global iterative resolution method, the « hybrid » algorithm from Hamam and Brameller. Although some other methods use a calculation time that increases exponentially with respect to the number of branches, the simulation needs to grow linearly with this algorithm and, therefore, enable real time simulations to be efficient and accurate for highly detailed models.

* Piccolo software is developed by Safege Consulting Engineers. It performs hydraulic and water quality modelling. The simulation can be run in steady state or extended period mode. The package also includes other modules such as operational cost analysis, and sediment transport calculation.

Piccolo Real Time software has been implemented in a Windows NT environment. Windows NT has been chosen because it constitutes a reliable operating system that is adopted for industrial software application. It offers both the wealth of a 32-bit multi-task system and the man-machine Interface of Windows. Moreover, a broad range of supervisory software is available within this environment.

Processor for simulation results analysis

The evaluation processor for simulation results is in charge of displaying results. In addition to this function it brings results back to the supervisor and generates alarms from calculation results.

For example, these alarms can detect problems related to a group of nodes where pressure is too low (i.e. inferior to a given limit at service level), to some speeds which may be too fast in pipes, or to some discrepancies between results and measurements given by a sensor. These alarms are also transferred to the supervisor and can be managed later in a similar manner to other SCADA alarms or warnings.

Man-Machine Interface

Specific attention has been paid to user-software interface development which had to be displayed in the same « look and feel » as the supervisory screens themselves.

For this purpose Piccolo Real Time operators use a computer with a dual video monitor system.

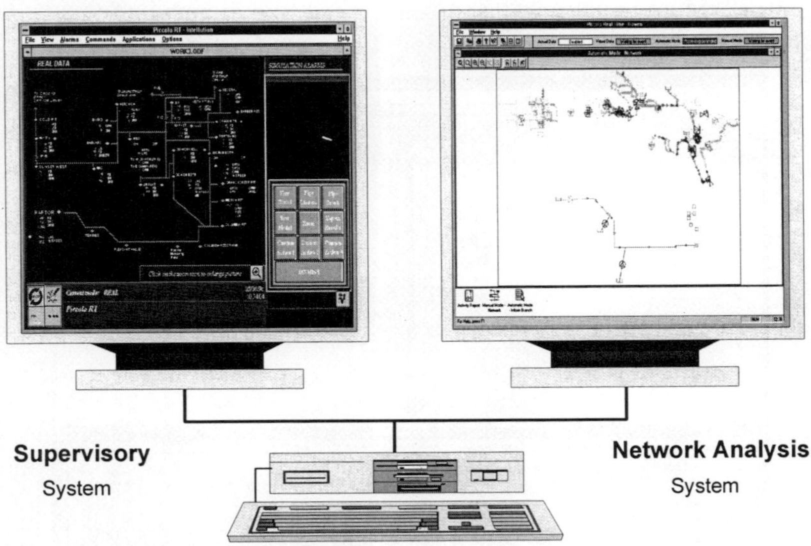

Figure 6. Piccolo Real Time double-screen

On the first screen, the operator views the supervision from which he can display real time data, change system states in order to run « what if » simulations and analyse simulation results.

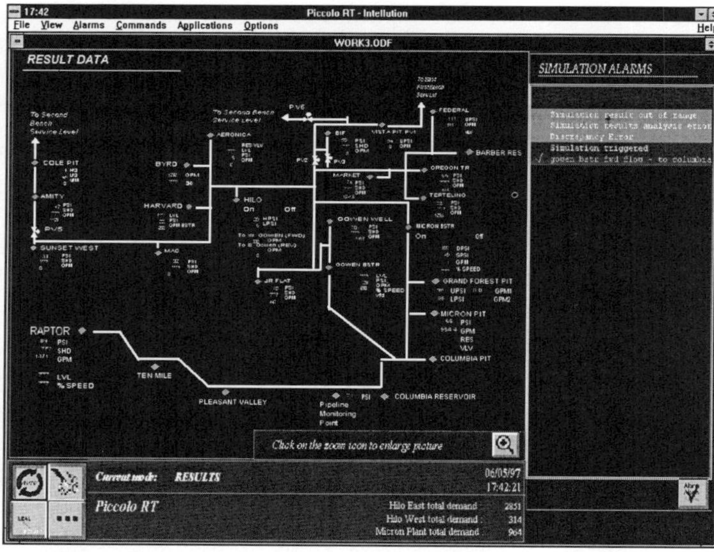

Figure 7. Supervisory screen linked to Network Analysis System

On the second screen, the operator disposes of the simulation software graphic interface to analyse results with all the precision he wishes. He can then display simultaneously « what if » and real time simulation views. Finally, an activity window presents all the events (alarms) that may affect real time data processing, calculation engine and results analysis.

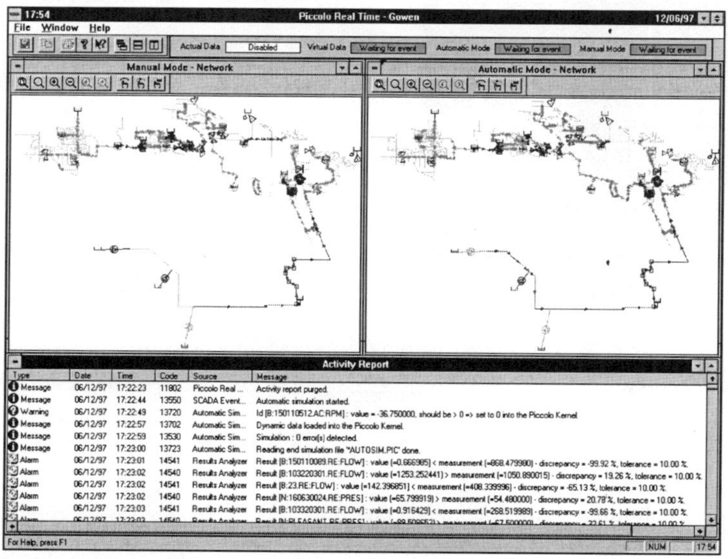

Figure 8. Network Analysis screen linked to SCADA

Implementing the SCADA to NAS linking

Several actions must be performed to run Piccolo Real Time within potable water operating system:

Telecontrol the system

It is necessary to have a real time telecontrol system linking each installation to a control centre through permanent links such as specialised/private lines, or a radio network. For example, to be effective, a control centre should be informed of changes of state at an installation (pump stop, level of reservoir, output flow).

Assess network structure.

To facilitate the implementation of the model in Boise, we linked the GIS to the simulation software through a bridge that converts each GIS information into network modelling structural data. In parallel, we used a function to simplify the network and set minimum diameters in order to eliminate pipes considered as non-representative of network flow.

Calibrate the model

The parameters, such as pipe roughness and demand allocation, have been initiated by the model generation process. A series of changes in the network has enabled a lean calibration of the detailed model. Field testing has been implemented through the use of equipment dedicated to measurement, i.e. characterised by a very reduced tolerance. This detail is quite important, because calibration leaning is determined by telecontrol. Calibration is then validated by comparing network model results to supervision data.

Parameterize supervision software

Piccolo Real Time implementation does not affect, or minimally affects, supervisory system parametering. However, it is necessary to create some real data, virtual data and results tables. Parametering of the graphic interface is then completed with the datapoint address setting.

Interface the supervisory to the network model

The information interface needs the creation and parametering of a cross-reference table, indicating supervisory and network model element names.

Moreover, one has to define water balance related to the establishment of customer demands and to set results analysis.

Integrate data filter

Parametering of the data filter may sometimes be limited to the definition of tests relevant to filter operations. Greater effort may be necessary by implementing an algorithm for data checking in the filter module written in Visual Basic.

System performance analysis

The SCADA-NAS bridge has been tested on a sub-system of Boise's network. This sub-system represents two distribution service levels.

The Gowen and Columbia service levels were used for the test because their facilities are well instrumented and they present all the network configurations met in Boise's whole supply system.

The main characteristics of Gowen and Columbia service level are:

Average demand (Ml/d)	10
Total pipe length (km)	150
Pipe diameter range (mm)	50 to 600
Number of deep wells	25
Number of boosters	1
Number of pressure-reducing valves	14
Number of storage tanks	4
Total storage capacity (Ml)	20

The Gowen and Columbia service level mathematical model is made of 2166 branches, 2043 nodes and 21 reservoirs or grade nodes.

The model snapshot simulation takes 2 seconds on a Pentium 133 MHz with 64 Mb of RAM in UWID's control room.

Both Intellution's Fix SCADA and Piccolo Real Time programs share the same processor. The Fix program uses the Windows ODBC link to poll data from the Oracle archive database (2 minutes delay). The SCADA and NAS programs communicate together using the Windows DDE link in both ways, i.e. *advise* and *poke* processes. Piccolo Real Time populates and reads its own database via the ODBC link as well.

Each communication process updates about 500 datapoints, which then bring the overall information exchange up to 1500 asynchronous data flow.

When the Piccolo Real Time operator triggers a simulation, the program gets input data, runs a simulation, stores and analyses results, and sends information back to the SCADA system in 12 to 25 seconds.

The limiting factor is not the network simulation but the communication load. As the program modules run in a multi-thread mode, the system receives information from the SCADA system while a simulation is triggered. A peak of data inflow will reduce the system performance.

The Gowen and Columbia network model has been carefully calibrated before using it with Piccolo Real Time. Some changes need to be done to validate the model for operational real time usage. The divergence between the calculation results and SCADA measurements lies below or is equal to 10%.

The compliance of the simulation results with the SCADA data was of primary importance to make the operators confident with the on-line simulation tool.

Awaiting Piccolo Real Time extended-period simulation

The first phase of the development of the SCADA-NAS linking, Piccolo Real Time, was completed in December 1996. The system has run **on-line snapshot simulations** for ten months in Boise.

It provides the operator with snapshot simulation capabilities allowing him to know the instantaneous flow and head throughout the network at any particular instant in time and evaluate changes in the facilities operation. Alarms are generated to highlight discrepancies or events.

The next phase of the development will implement **on-line extended-period simulation** capabilities. The controllers will then be able to evaluate different time-scheduled operations and investigate reservoir storage variations. The managers will forecast the consequences of different command actions, schedule efficient system controls, and train to face emergency situations.

Zen and the Art of Network Modelling (reference 7)

This software is puzzling because bringing monitoring and modelling together into one central terminal turns perceived ideas upside down!

Piccolo Real Time has gained its pugnacity from the Dog, the year when it was conceived (1994); and from the Rat, the year in which it was born (1996), it has acquired flair and vivacity. We hope that the concept brought by linking SCADA with Network Analysis System frees the operators from heavy and complex tasks for the benefit of the customer of the water company.

« All evolution in thought must at first appear as heresy and misconduct »
George Bernard Shaw

Acknowledgements

The work discussed in this chapter has been carried out with the support of United Water Idaho, Suez-Lyonnaise des Eaux and Safege. Problems have been investigated by a number of our colleagues that we wish to thank. A very special reference is due to Georgette Pez, Robert Walker, Olivier Tridon, Pascal Jussac and Pascal Petit.

References

1. "An applications review of modelling and control of water supply and distribution systems", B.COULBECK, C.H.ORR, Research Studies Press Ltd. (Computer Applications in water supply, Vol.2, 1993).

2. "Integration of a network simulator into the On-line control system for London's Water Networks", J.P.RANCE, P.L.M.BOUNDS, S.T.TENNANT, B.ULANICKI, Research Studies Press Ltd.(Computer Applications in water supply, Vol.1, 1993).

3. "Hybrid method for the solution of piping networks", Y. M. HAMAM and B. BRAMELLER, (PROC IEE, Vol.118, No. 11, 1971).

4. "Instrumentation and Computer Integration of Water Utility Operations", AWWA and JWWA, (American Water Works Association Research Foundation, 1993-1994, 476p.).

5. "Real time supervision and simulation of the water distribution network in the city of Malmö - Sweden", P. Stahre, L. Andersson, S. Strunge (VBB VIAK - Fifth IAWPRC workshop on ICA, July 1993 , 9 p.).

6. "Using optimisation for integrated water network management", P.A.JARRIGE, T.HARDING, D.KNIGHT, D.HOWES, (Civ. Engng Syst. 1991, vol.8, 5 p.).

7. "Zen and the Art of Motorcycle Maintenance", R.M. PIRSIG, (1974, 351p.)

CHAPTER 17

Object-Oriented Modelling for the Operational Control of Water Distribution Systems

C.Wang *and* R.S.Powell

1. Abstract

This chapter describes the design of an object-oriented model for use in operational control and analysis of large-scale water distribution systems. The chapter aims to show that object-oriented programming provides advantages over the traditional programming paradigm. Based on a thorough analysis of water distribution systems and some current software packages, a comprehensive object model has been designed and implemented using an object-oriented programming language and an object-oriented database management system. This chapter focuses on the object model and the philosophy in this object-oriented modelling process.

2. Introduction

The design and development of software packages for operational control and analysis of large-scale water distribution systems is a major software engineering exercise. Object-oriented programming is recognised as a revolutionary paradigm in software development. This process is founded on the design of an appropriate object model. Therefore, object-oriented modelling is the first step in the development of such software.

Water distribution systems consist of a variety of pipes, reservoirs, pumps, valves and meters, etc. [4]. Software packages are often designed around a particular data model and application model of a water distribution system [1]. Data models contain the physical data, hydraulic data, quality data and management data of both the system and components. Application models include the mathematical model for hydraulic analysis and quality analysis, optimisation models for pump scheduling and valve switching, etc. Using the object-oriented paradigm, the data models and application models are integrated into a suite of object models. Object models define attributes for the data items and methods describing their behaviour; they also define a consistent interface for interaction with other objects. Objects can be classified and arranged into a hierarchy, which facilitates a means by which common attributes and behaviour can be inherited from their parent objects. A consistent interface is also retained by this strategy.

This chapter describes our work on the object-oriented modelling of water distribution systems, which is a part of our work in the design and implementation of an object-oriented framework [11] for the development of computer software applications for operational control and analysis of large scale water distribution systems. The models are classified into three categories: water networks and components; graphical modelling and editing of water networks; computing algorithms supporting simulation, optimisation, etc. A functional model that describes the relationship between the control and analysis applications is also given.

3. Abstraction

The elements of water distribution systems can be modelled as objects, which in this chapter, we call components. These objects encapsulate the data related to both the physical attributes such as the descriptions of location, manufacturer, diameter, length, etc. and dynamic (operational) parameters such as flow, pressure, and so on. They also encapsulate the operations on the data, such as the interpretation of command objects, calculation of head loss, flow rate, flow sensitivity, etc. *Components* are the main objects used for application programming. The *command* objects convey control messages from the user to the components. For instance, a command can be dedicated to getting application-specific data from components. We define the *view* objects as those that are also associated with components and are used to produce a graphical view and functional view of a water distribution system. The functional views are expressed as mathematical models of elements, or as profile data that represent a relationship between some attributes of an object. Network analysis and simulation will based on the components.

Therefore, a software system for analysing, on-line monitoring and control of water distribution systems can be abstracted as the integration of a set of components, a set of commands and a set of graphical views. Figure 1 shows the relationship between these sets.

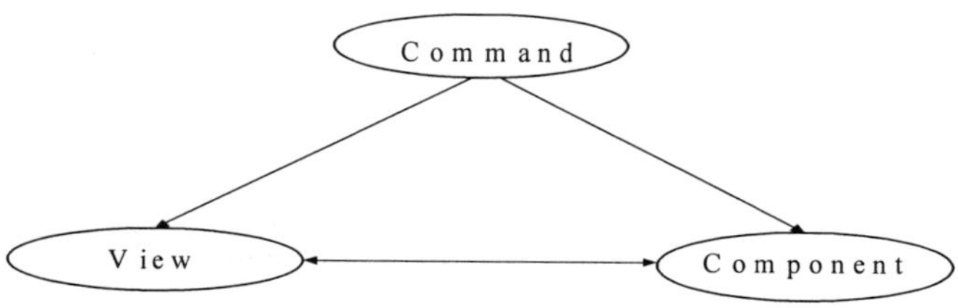

Figure 1. Abstraction of the objects in water system

3.1. Component and View

A strategy adopted in the design of the framework is the separation of components and their views. A component object may have more than one view. The graphical views of a system contain the graphic data necessary for display. The reason for this separation is to provide more flexibility and to support multiple views of the system. In the implementation of the design strategy, each view object retains pointers to its component. For example, a method designed to get data from a component object is the get-*component()* operation. It is implemented in each view object corresponding to a component object. A graphical editor can be built based on the view objects to display and edit the water system models.

4. Object Model of Water Distribution Systems

An object model for water distribution systems can be designed from the application viewpoint so as to meet the programming requirements for the development of analysis and operational management software. In order to facilitate the application development, the object model must be consistent with a topological network model. As such, the component objects are further classified as port and element, respectively, corresponding to the node and link of a network. The object model is shown in Figure 2, which is drawn in OMT [9] notation. Note that not all objects are drawn in the figure since there are over 50 object classes defined in the full framework. The objects can be categorised into two basic categories: primitive and composite objects. Primitive objects are objects that model the basic components of water systems, such as port, pipe, valve, pump, tank, bore hole, consumer, flow meter, etc. Composite objects are those that define a container that integrates a group of objects into one object by using a defined mechanism to manage them, such as plant and pump station objects.

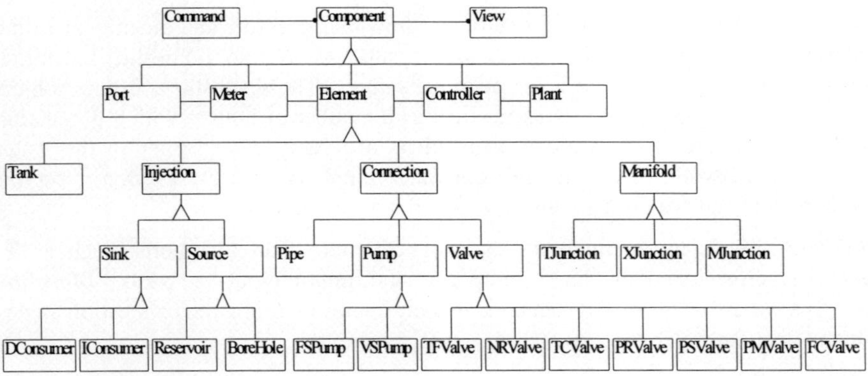

Figure 2. Object model for water distribution systems

4.1. Port

Port models a type of component that can connect two or more elements without a head loss across the connection, such as pipe junctions and some other points of interest in water systems.

4.2. Element

Element models the hydraulic components in water systems which connect more than one port.

Pipe is a simple element object used to connect two ports. The pipe object encapsulates attributes and equations used for calculating the performance of a physical pipe, e.g. the diameter, resistance, head loss and flow rate equations, etc.

Valve objects model water flow control components. A valve object connects two ports, but the water pressure at the input may be different from that at the output. Based on the physical valve types, there is a family of valve objects defined and implemented by sub-classing the general valve class. The tank fill valve object is always associated with a tank object. The *TCValve* models a variety of valves, such as throttle valve, sluice valve, plug valve, butterfly valve, streamline valve, screw down plug valve, etc. The position of the valves' stem can be adjusted through a controller object. Other models are for non-return valves, flow control valves, pressure regulation valves, pressure sustaining valves, pressure modulated (demand sensing) valves.

Tank models water storage components (i.e. service reservoirs) with the water level changing dynamically, according to the water inflows and outflows. It connects an input and an output port. The tank object contains the data related to the water storage volume, elevation and the water pressure at its output port. It may also be associated with valves and meters. A tank object may have more than one tank-fill valve and inlet pipe, and also may have more than one outlet connection.

The *Pump* object is defined for any type of physical pump in general. It connects two ports with different water pressure and a consistent water flow. According to operational features, specific pumps are defined as subclasses of the general pump object class, e.g. for fixed speed pumps and variable speed pumps.

Sink models the demand of water in terms of flow rate, pressure and quantity at a time point or over a period. The sink class is sub-classed into domestic, industrial, commercial, recreational and emergency consumers. The domestic consumer object models a set of domestic water users, such as a number of houses with a population attribute in an area, which are considered as one lumped consumer in the water distribution network. *Source* models the water suppliers such as infusion, reservoir and bore hole and provides a volume of water at a certain head.

Manifold models the components that connect more than two ports, such as T-junctions, cross-junctions, and multiple-in and multiple-out elements. *TJunction* models a variety of three-port junctions with attributes to define the connection angles which affect the water head loss through such junctions.

4.3. Plant

Plant models the integration of a group of components as one component. This composite object can represent a pumping station, a distribution zone, or even a large scale water distribution system hierarchically. It provides the hierarchical concentration mechanism by representing the plant as a component together with a list of interface ports.

A plant object for a water distribution system can contain all elements, all meters and the connectivity of the system. For a large-scale water distribution system, the distribution zones can be modelled as plant objects, which are contained in the plant object at the system level. In this way, the plant object can model any size of water distribution system. Sub-plants can be derived from the plant object and, provided the sub-plant can be delineated with boundary components (e.g. reservoirs, demand nodes etc.), the simulator will be able to solve the sub-plants individually.

A pumping station is a multi-port object comprising a set of pumps, valves, pipes and meters; it is modelled as a sub-class of plant, called *PumpingStation*. The sum of the inflows at any time into a pumping station object is equal to the sum of the outflows. An electricity tariff object is associated with each pumping station object.

4.4. Controllers

Controllers are used to control network components, that is, they change the component state variables according to the requirements and current conditions. *Controllers* implement the control functionality for classified control tasks. For example, the valve status of a pressure-modulated valve depends on its down-stream pressure and the pressure at the specified demand point.

4.5. Meters

Meters in water distribution systems are used to measure water flow and pressure, water quality, or water level in reservoirs. They are not hydraulic components, but they provide data about hydraulic variables. The *Meter* object classes can be further defined for level, flow, quality, and pressure meters.

Meter objects are associated with *Port* or *Element* objects. For example, a flow meter is attached to an element such as a pipe object, and a pressure meter is attached to a port object. *Meter* objects contain system dynamic data at a definite time. From another viewpoint, they record the actual system status, which can be used to support the implementation of applications for operational decision-making.

4.6. Operational Control Data

4.6.1. Measurements

In the control and management of water distribution systems, applications need a time based series of measurement data in order to analyse the system and provide operational decision-making support. The *Measurement* object is defined to meet this requirement. It contains a component reference and flow, pressure or level data together with their respective sample times.

A composite object, called *PlantStatus*, is designed to contain and manage the pump status, valve positions and the measurements of reservoirs level, water head and flow in the system.

4.6.2. Functions

Component functions can be represented by formula, look-up table, and text objects according to the representation format of the functions concerned.

The representation of the dynamic features of components, operational data and so on are 'data extensive function' objects. These data reflect a relationship between two or more variables, but some of the relationships are impossible or very difficult to implement using an explicit formula. It is also impossible to provide all the data needed. Therefore, the functional relationships are modelled as *FunctionData* objects, which sample a finite number of points of the function (relationship), and use some approximate methods to interpolate the data between the known data sets. According to the approximate methods, the *FunctionData* objects are further classified into ramp function-data, step function-data, smooth function-data, etc. The ramp function-data object uses a linear interpolation between points. The most common data relationships used in water distribution systems are ramp and step relations.

4.6.3. Commands

Command models operational data for system control and management. A command object defines time and scheduled actions that a component should execute at a specified time. These objects are used to carry messages to components.

Command objects are designed for the objects that need specific operations, such as switch valves, pressure regulation valves, pumps with variable speed, etc. Command objects are interpreted by components which change the current operational status through their controllers.

A composite object, called *PlantOperations*, is designed to contain the water demands at junctions and the commands for the scheduling of pumping, valve switching and valve setting.

4.6.4. Mathematical Objects

Applications such as hydraulic and quality simulation, pumping optimisation, leakage detection, pressure regulation, and demand prediction, etc. use mathematical data structures and algorithms such as sparse matrices, linear and non-linear equation solving algorithms, etc. Therefore, mathematical objects are also provided in the framework. The sparse-matrix object defines the storage and operations of sparse matrices, and it is further sub-classed into the four commonly used storage strategies, namely, row-oriented linked list, column-oriented linked list, compressed column array, and compressed row array. The linear equation solver object defines the operations for managing equation data and solving methods. It is sub-classed according to the algorithms, such as Gauss, Crout and QR for factorisation methods [5], Gauss-Seidel and Conjugate Gradient for iterative methods [6].

5. Graphical View of Water Systems

Graphical views of objects include symbolic views and functional views at special viewpoints. A view object contains a pointer to its corresponding component object, from which the component object can be reached. Note that view objects are not derived from the corresponding component objects. This design gives more flexibility to application developers than would be the case if view object classes were derived from component classes. They also define the attributes and operations to support graphical views, editing, and for displaying objects.

The symbolic view objects are designed to be associated with the corresponding component objects. The concept is based on the *GEMS* (Graphical Editing and Modelling System) package, the previous work by Wang [2,3]. *GEMS* is a framework for developing graphical editing and modelling tools. It includes a cluster of classes, such as *GmComponent*, *GmLabel*, and *GmEdit* classes. For example, *GmLine* class defines the common link object, which has two connectors and uses polyline as its graphic appearance. GEMS could theoretically be used with the current object model. The combination of the two designs is shown in Figure 3. *PipeView*, for example, is defined as a sub-class of the *GmLine* class with an additional reference to a *Pipe* object and a text label object to display its diameter, length and flow rate, etc. Symbolic view objects for *Meter* objects have also been designed.

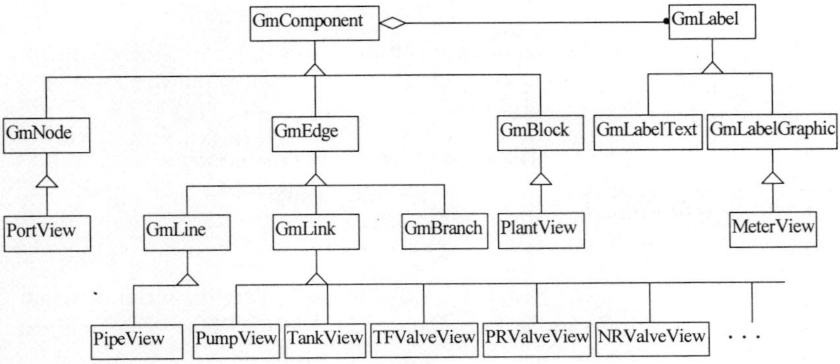

Figure 3. Component view class hierarchy

The functional view objects can use the format of formula, data table, data plot, etc. Therefore, the *FunctionView* object is further defined as *Formula*, *DataTable* and *DataPlot* view classes. Each functional view object could use a pop-up window to display symbolic formula, table, or data plot.

6. Implementation

The object models described in this chapter have been implemented as a cluster of object class hierarchies, called DAWN (Data structures and Algorithms for Water Networks), using the C++ programming language with an object-oriented database management system called ObjectStore [7]. The classes not only define the data attributes for particular object models but they also define the relationships between models to allow the database management system to ensure data consistency. For example, if a reservoir has one or more tank fill valves and that reservoir is deleted, then a triggered deletion of the connected tank fill valves will occur. This can be avoided, to allow flexible editing, by breaking the associations between the tank fill valves and their reservoir. However, the network would not be ready for analysis until another reservoir was connected.

The classes also define and implement methods designed for the object models. For example, the *float headloss(float flow)* method is defined in the *Connection* class and all of its sub-classes, but the implementation of this method is different among the *Pipe*, *Pump* and *Valve* classes. In *Pipe* class, for instance, three mathematical equations, namely, Hazen-Williams, Darcy-Weisbach and Manning equations, are currently implemented for this method. Users can chose any one of these three by calling the *set_use_model(UseModel)* method.

7. Applications

The application programs can be built around the object database of water distribution systems using the object model described above. Figure 4 shows the proposed applications based on the object model. The solid lines in the figure indicate that the applications have been implemented using the object model.

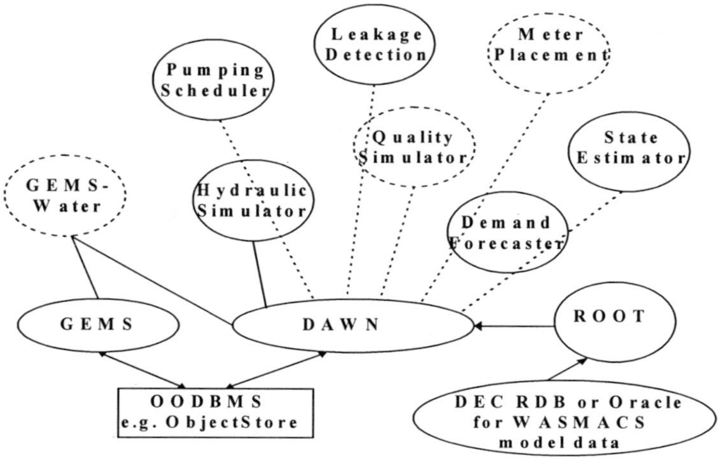

Figure 4. Applications supported by the object model

A graphical editing and modelling tool, to be called GEMS-Water, which will serve as the main user interface to all of the applications, is envisaged. It will be designed to edit the object data in a database and will be used to define water distribution systems including their operational settings. The simulator currently exists and is based on the object model with access to the object database. The other applications could be brought into this framework quite easily.

7.1. Build Object Models

A data transfer tool, called *ROOT* (Relational to Object-Oriented data Transfer), has been implemented to transfer water distribution system data stored in a relational database (such as the WASMACS RDBMS [10]) into the object-oriented database. Six water distribution system models have been built for testing. Three of them are practical water distribution systems, the largest one having 741 junctions and 819 hydraulic elements. All of them have been used successfully by the hydraulic simulator. This confirms that the object model definition is sufficient to be used as a foundation model for the operational control and analysis software packages of water distribution systems.

7.2. Hydraulic Simulator

An object-oriented simulator has been implemented using the object model. The simulator is designed as an object class, which performs dynamic simulation of a water distribution system over a given time period. It uses the plant name, initial plant status, plant operations, time step and period data supplied by the user to start the simulation process. The simulator uses the plant name to find the *Plant* object in the database, and then it finds the given *PlantStatus* object and *PlantOperations* object. It first uses the *PlantStatus* object to initialise the *Plant* object. The simulator starts by calling the *snapshot()* method, which is provided in the *Plant* object, to get the current plant status; i.e., the simulation process is static. Then the simulator moves to the next time step. It uses the *PlantOperations* object to update the demands at junctions and the status of valves and pumps by calling the *update-operations()* method, and calls the *update-status()* method to change the reservoirs level, tank fill valve status, etc. The static simulation process is repeated for the new time step.

In comparison with the applications using a relational database or files, the simulator saves time on assembling application data, e.g. building node and link data structures and allocating water demands. This is because the application model has already been built from the objects. Another benefit is using the *headloss(flow)* and *head-sensitivity(flow)* methods, which are provided by all *Element* objects, to build system equations (the simulator uses the so-called Linear Theory Method [12] to obtain a balanced flow-head state). The *head-sensitivity(flow)* methods are currently implemented using the first order derivatives of the non-linear head-flow equations, which are specific to particular *Element* objects.

The coding of the simulator should take less time since the methods provided by objects can be directly used in the simulation program. The simulator object itself can also be reused when coding another similar simulator. Actually, this is one of the benefits of using object-oriented programming.

8. Conclusions

Software developed for operational control and analysis of large scale water distribution systems can be based on a variety of models, such as network models, mathematical models, hydraulic models, etc. Applying the object-oriented paradigm to the modelling of water distribution systems gives a uniform model for both data management and software development. Based on our experience of modelling such large systems, object-oriented models appear to be more natural from both the conceptual and practical viewpoints than other models.

9. Reference

[1] Brdys, M. A. and Ulanicki, B., Operational Control of Water Systems, Structures, Algorithms and Applications. Prentice-Hall, 1994.

[2] Chen, M., Townsend, P. and Wang, C., A Development Environment for Constructing Graph-based Editing Tools, Computer Graphics Forum, the International Journal of Eurographics Association, Vol.11, No.3, pp.C345--355.

[3] Chen, M., Townsend, P. and Wang, C., Automated Construction of Application-Specific Graph Editors in an Object-Oriented Paradigm, in G. Salvendy and M. J. Simith, editors, Human-Computer Interaction: Software and Hardware Interfaces, Vol.19B, Advances in Human Factors/Ergonomics, pp415 -- 420. Elsevier, 1993.

[4] Golub, G. H. and Van Loan, C. F., Matrix Computations, North Oxford Academic Publishers Ltd, London, 1986.

[5] Hackbusch, W., Iterative Solution of Large Scale Sparse Systems of Equations, Springer-Verlag, Berlin, 1994.

[6] McGhee, T. J., Water Supply and Sewerage. McGraw-Hill, New York, 1991.

[7] Object Design, Inc. ObjectStore, Release 3.0, Reference Manual. Burlington, MA, USA.

[8] Powell, R. S., On-line Monitoring for Operational Control of Water Distribution Systems. Ph.D. Thesis, University of Durham, May 1992.

[9] Rumbaugh, J., Blaha, M., Premerlani, W., Eddy, F. and Lorensen, W., Object-Oriented Modeling and Design, Prentice-Hall, Englewood Cliffs, New Jersey, 1991.

[10]Stoner Associates, Inc., Stoner Workstation Service, Liquid Time-Varying Network Analysis Module, SWSL 1.5, Reference Manual, 1994.

[11]Wang, C., An Object-Oriented Framework for Building Analysis and Operational Control Software for Water Distribution Systems, Internal Report, Department of Manufacturing and Engineering Systems, Brunel University, March, 1996.

[12]Wood, D. J., Hydraulic Network Analysis Using Linear Theory, Journal of the Hydraulics Division, ASCE. Vol.98, No.HY7, July 1972, pp. 1157–1170.

CHAPTER 18

A Systematic Approach to Information Integration in a Water Company

B.Ulanicki, J.P.Rance *and* P.L.M.Bounds

1. Introduction

Water companies are often large organisations with many employees organised into different departments and management levels. The companies have objectives which are translated into working activities performed by the staff and contractors. Ideally, all of the activities would be perfectly co-ordinated and directed towards the achievement of the objectives. However, this is not possible in practice, owing to the complexities of managing large organisations, and the fact that there are changing external factors which affect companies. Nevertheless, it is possible to improve efficiency by applying systematic approaches to organising and integrating water company activities.

This chapter primarily considers the integration of information in water companies. Section 2 defines what is meant by information integration and the typical levels of integration found in water companies. Section 3 introduces the idea of modelling human organisations. Subsequently, a systematic approach to modelling and planning information integration is presented in section 4, and section 5 contains an example software integration platform.

2. Information Integration

Information is distributed across a water company in different departments and geographical locations. It is also distributed vertically according to management level. This distribution and the use of different computer and paper-based information systems, causes difficulties when ensuring that shared information is up to date, correct and consistent.

Employees spend much of their time gathering and checking information, which is time consuming and costly. Easy access to information improves the efficiency of a company. Difficult access or incomplete and inaccurate information leads to inefficiency and erroneous decisions.

The general objective of information integration is to provide timely, reliable and relevant information to perform activities and make decisions. This usually involves the use of digital computer systems, which is the dominant technology for information storage, retrieval and processing. However, the efficient exploitation of this technology requires the use of systematic analytical and planning methods. The main problems in achieving information integration arise from organisational complexity, organisational change, and in managing the introduction of new technology and existing systems.

In practice, information integration often occurs piecemeal by evolution under the pressure of different forces. Competition and regulatory pressures drive water companies to address particular aspects of the business such as asset management, leakage reduction, and customer service. Computer technology develops rapidly and offers new tools for companies to improve efficiency. There are different levels of integration and different interpretations of integration, for example:

1. Separate databases and applications implemented to support specific aspects of the business such as asset management, operational control, and customer service. Examples include Geographical Information Systems (GIS), Supervisory Control and Data Acquisition (SCADA) systems, asset maintenance databases, and customer billing systems. Many companies implement such databases as the primary sources of information for these aspects of the business. The philosophy is to collate all relevant information about a particular aspect in one database, and thereafter to maintain and use this database as the primary source of information.

2. Interconnected databases and applications are required by some activities. For example, the management of leakage requires information that is typically stored in the asset and operational control databases. Some companies have developed specialised software interfaces to extract and process the required information, and to exchange it across computer networks. Such interfaces are specialised to the requirements of a particular activity. There are standards and products that facilitate the development of such interfaces.

3. The company-wide integration of information systems requires a systematic analytical approach and planning method. Information integration proceeds through the theoretical analysis of the operation of a company and the development of a migration plan that takes into account the investment in existing systems and the improvement opportunities within the company. Such an approach can lead to improvement in the operation of the company as a whole. It may involve changing some working practices.

Most companies have achieved successes at levels 1 and 2. Although, coherent plans and policies towards fully integrated information systems are uncommon in the water industry at present, many companies are now considering the issue.

The WaterCIME Methodology is an example of such an approach, which generates a design of the target system and a migration plan from the AS-IS information system to a new TO-BE system. The implementation of such a system in practice requires a software platform that is flexible enough to allow for the implementation of the integration concepts. An example of such a platform is presented in this chapter in the form of a two layer architecture (WaterCIME, 1995).

3. Enterprise Modelling

Methods of modelling human organisations are developing in a relatively new branch of engineering called enterprise modelling. They are described, for example, in Vernadat (1996), and Bernus and Nemes (1995). The notion of *activity* is fundamental to enterprise modelling. It embodies the process of doing something. Different methodologies use various specialised definitions of an activity. Below is a full definition of activity which covers all aspects of enterprise modelling - function, information, resource and organisation. The definition is based on results given in Uschold et al., 1996, ISO, 1990, and AMICE, 1993:

♦ An activity has *pre-conditions*, which must be satisfied for it to occur, e.g. the availability of information from other activities.

♦ An activity has *effects*, which describe the state of affairs that exist after the activity.

♦ An activity is performed by a *doer*.

♦ An activity uses and consumes *resources* (e.g. staff-time, computers, materials etc.).

♦ An activity has a *measurable efficiency*.

♦ An activity has some duration that is defined by *begin time* and *end time*.

♦ Activities are organised into some management structure defined *by management links*. Management links determine the relationships between actors.

This is an informal description of a formal definition, but it should be apparent that it can be formalised and implemented as software, as in the TOVEsim software for enterprise modelling (Chionglo, 1995). The description contains the four aspects of enterprise modelling: function, information, resources, and organisation.

There is a number of developed enterprise-modelling techniques and software tools. However, few, if any, cover all four aspects comprehensively. The design of integrated information systems mainly concerns the function and information aspects of activities, which are viewed as consumers and producers of information, and which can be represented in a data flow diagram (e.g. figure 1).

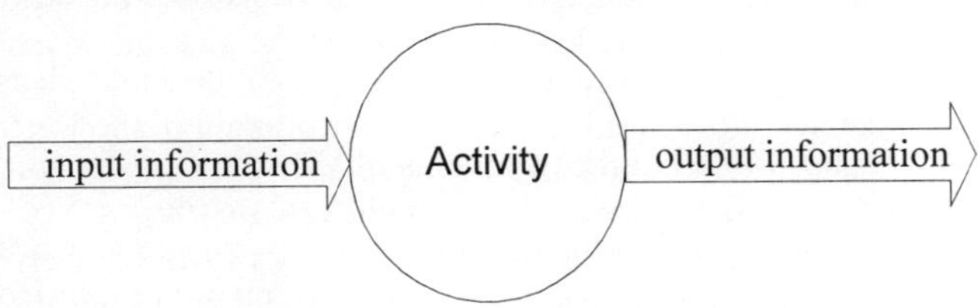

Figure 1. Representation of an activity

The pre-condition of carrying out an activity is the availability of input information, and the result of an activity is output information that will be available for other activities.

4. WaterCIME Methodology

The WaterCIME Methodology was developed to address the problem of information integration in water "production management systems" - a term which is used to cover the activities required to run a water system (Rance, Ulanicki, Bounds, 1996).

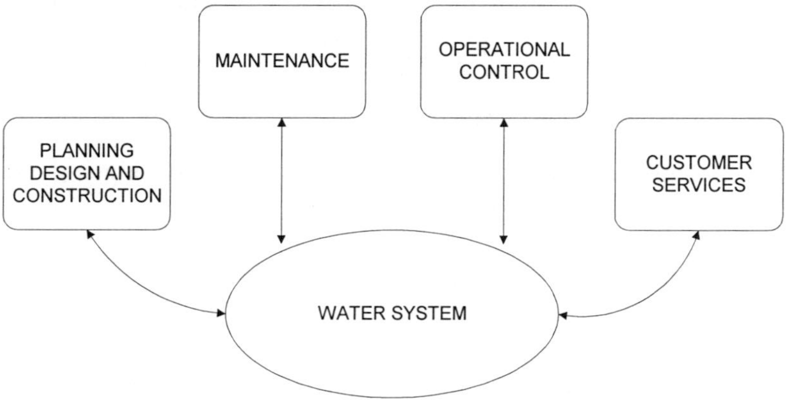

Figure 2: Production management system

Four groups of activities are identified in the production management system: operational control, maintenance, planning design and construction, and customer services (figure 2). These activities contain functions specific to water systems, whereas other groups of activities, such as Personnel Management, Finance, etc. are common to every economic organisation and other workers have already extended enterprise modelling into these common activities.

The groups of activities shown in figure 2 include tasks, which are automated and/or performed by people. The methodology treats activities as information producers and consumers. Hierarchical models of the production management system are built, starting with the corporate objectives which are mapped on to corresponding decision processes. Then the associated information requirements are identified. Information objects and flows are then mapped onto the existing information system. The modelling enables the rational identification of improvement opportunities. The decision processes may be reorganised to facilitate achieving the corporate objectives, and the management information system is tailored to the required decision processes. The outputs of the methodology include models of the existing and improved company, and a migration plan and cost/benefit analysis.

The methodology contains a procedure to build two models of the water production management system (figure 3). One model describes the existing system, (the "AS-IS" model). The model building process reveals potential improvements to the system. These, and other acquired knowledge, are used to construct a model capturing the improvement opportunities (the "TO-BE" model). The experiences of a number of water utilities have been generalised to form a Reference model, which is a starting point for building the AS-IS and TO-BE models of a specific company.

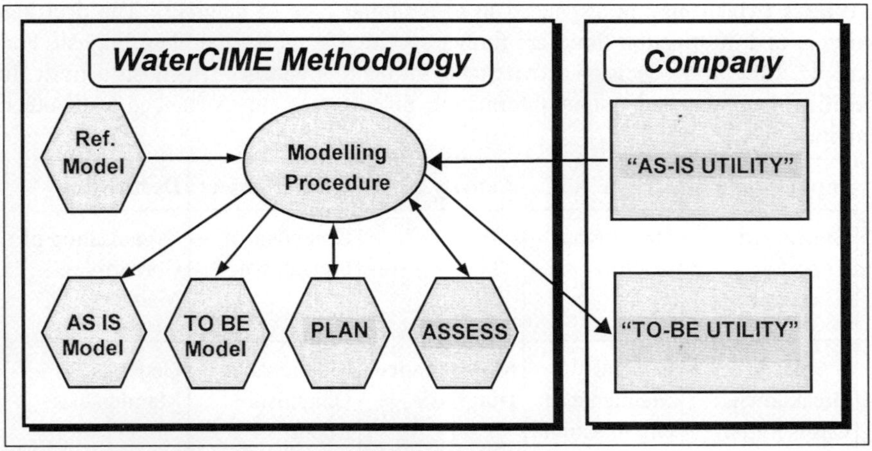

Figure 3: Overview of the WaterCIME Methodology

A migration plan is developed by comparing the differences between the AS-IS and TO-BE models, and a cost benefit analysis is performed. In the light of this assessment, the TO-BE model and migration plan may be modified and re-assessed.

Each model is composed of sub-models providing successive layers of abstraction and different views of the organisation. The sub-models include:

- Corporate Objectives and Constraints.
- Functional Decision Model.
- Information System.
- Outline Computer System.
- Outline Evaluation & Transition Planning Methods.

Different modelling techniques are appropriate for each of the sub-models. The Corporate Objectives and Constraints sub-model is a hierarchical list of the enterprise's objectives written in plain English. The Functional Decision Model is a data flow diagram using the Yourdon method (e.g. figure 4). The decision activities are also analysed and allocated to different categories and levels in the decision hierarchy using the GRAI enterprise modelling method (Doumeingts et al, 1992).

The Information Model is developed using an object-oriented data modelling technique. The Information System and Computer System are developed using text and computer architecture diagrams. The Migration Plan and Evaluation Method are based on project planning and financial models, respectively. It is possible to apply different modelling techniques to the sub-models, for example, different migration planning and evaluation methods may suit different enterprises.

Figure 4 shows part of a decision activity sub-model covering maintenance activities (WaterCIME, 1995). The decision activities are represented by the circular nodes, and the information flows by links. The square nodes represent the other major decision categories (which may be expanded in to a similar type of diagram). The decision activities and information flows are further specified in tables and plain English. For example, Table 1 is a decision activity table for the Maintenance Diagnosis activity. It specifies the input and output information objects that are exchanged with other activities.

Input object	**Origin**	**Activity**	**Output object**	**Destination**
Breakdown Report	Operational Control	**Maintenance Diagnosis**	Diagnosis of breakdown	Organisation of Corrective Maintenance
Similar Breakdown Cases Report	General Maintenance Organisation		Maintenance Diagnosis Report	General Maintenance Organisation

Table 1. Maintenance Decision Activity Model from the WaterCIME Methodology.

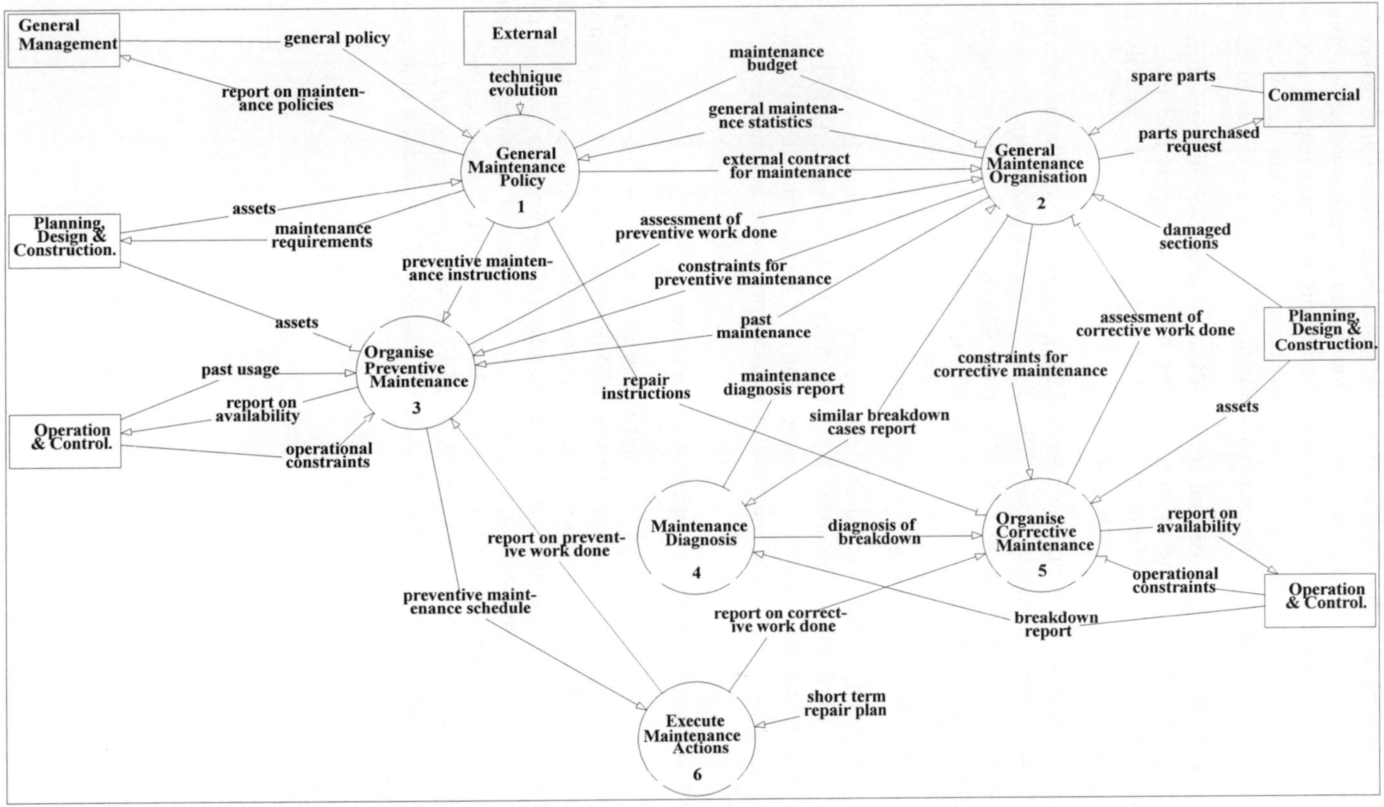

Figure 4. Maintenance Diagnosis activity from the WaterCIME Methodology

The objective of the activity is to produce a diagnosis report of the possible causes of a breakdown, which will be sent to an activity that organises corrective maintenance. The activity is event driven. The pre-condition is that a breakdown report from the Operational Control category is received. The activity will then request a report of similar breakdown cases from the General Maintenance Organisation activity and will compile a report of the possible causes of the fault. These links are shown in figure 4.

The activity also produces general reports about all diagnoses performed during a certain period of time. The existence of the breakdown report and maintenance diagnosis report are the effects of the activity. The doer of the activity is an appropriate maintenance diagnosis unit.

The final product of the WaterCIME methodology is a plan to migrate the information system to a more integrated one. Therefore, it mainly addresses function and information aspects by identifying objectives, corresponding activities, and their information requirements. It partially addresses organisation aspects by allocating activities to levels in the decision hierarchy, and to categories of related activities. It does not address resource aspects at present.

The methodology is based on existing practice and common sense. It is one outcome of the WaterCIME project involving 8 partners from 5 EU countries (ESPRIT project no. 8399). Computer Integrated Manufacturing and Engineering (CIME) concepts, originally developed for the manufacturing industries, were adapted to the water domain.

5. An Example Software Integration Platform

The WaterCIME methodology does not pre-suppose any particular technology for information integration. However, the WaterCIME consortium developed a software integration platform which is used for the implementation of information integration. The term "software integration platform" encapsulates the architecture, software tools, and communication protocols of a product used to implement information systems. The platform is composed of two layers as shown in Figure 5 and described in the subsequent sections. The lower layer (CIMVIEW) provides monitoring and control of the physical water system and the upper layer (CIMWORK) provides a management information system.

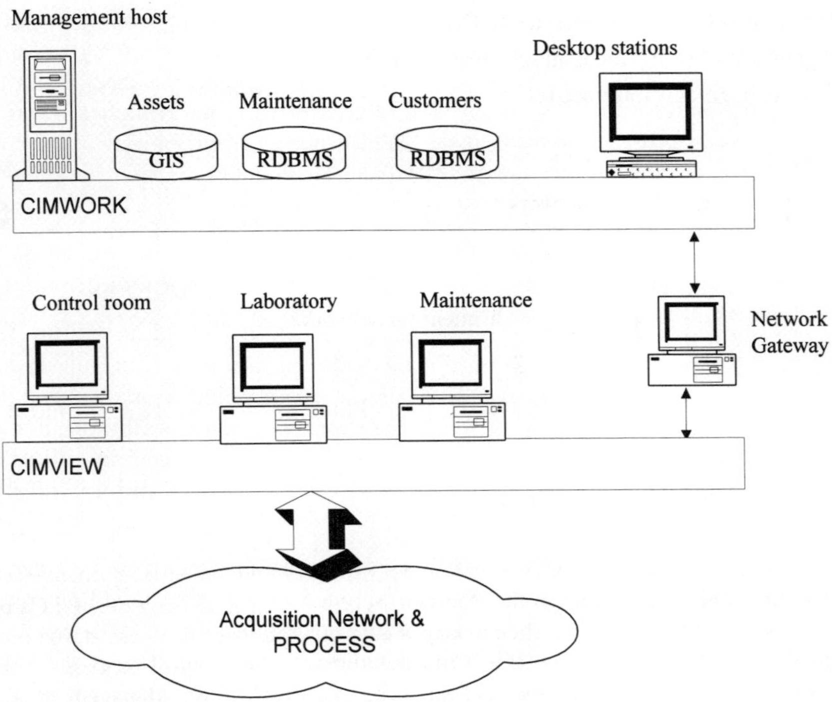

Figure 5. Two level architecture for information integration in a water company

5.1 CIMVIEW

CIMVIEW is an established product of the Belgium company CIMTECH, which enables the connection of many types of PLCs and control computers into a complex supervisory control system. The basic data structure of CIMVIEW is a variable together with all its attributes. CIMVIEW is distributed across PCs running multi-tasking operating systems, which are located to gather data and control devices. The PCs communicate by a network. CIMVIEW has many configurations and uses many different communication protocols. Other data acquisition networks can be connected to a CIMVIEW network as shown in Figure 6.

The primary objective of CIMVIEW is to enable communication between the physical process and an operator and/or control applications. Distribution of the control and data acquisition is provided by the kernel concept. Each PC in the CIMVIEW network has a kernel module that is responsible for one or more of the process variables and contains complete information about the entire network and can communicate with other nodes using a message passing mechanism. Kernels are responsible for receiving, transmitting and distributing real time values of the process variables.

The overall software architecture is based on the following five modules (see also figure 6):

1. Kernel.
2. Data Bank (DB).

3. Distributed Controller Interface (DCI).
4. Application Management and Supervision (AMS).
5. Graphic Operator Interface (GOI)

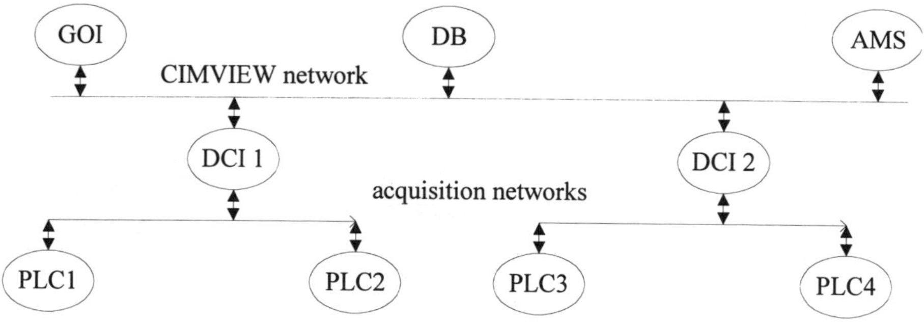

Figure 6. Architecture of CIMVIEW

The Kernel is present at each CIMVIEW node (i.e. PC) in the network. It operates on the real time data set residing in the Random Access Memory (RAM) of the PCs on the network. The Data Bank module manages data in a reference database stored on a PC hard disk. This database contains a full description of the control process for the purposes of system configuration and start-up. The Application Management and Supervision module provides facilities to interface applications with the CIMVIEW network including:

1. Automatic applications for alarms, data logging, event management, etc.

2. Interfaces to programming languages such as REXX, C, ADA, Basic and FORTRAN.

3. Interfaces to external application packages: such as Excel, Lotus123/G, etc.

4. Archiving of data on the disk.

The Graphical Operator Interface module enables graphical representation of the physical process. The CIMVIEW system is scaleable in the sense that it can be extended at low cost with little disruption by adding new PCs and kernels to provide additional data acquisition nodes.

5.2 CIMWORK

CIMWORK provides a mechanism to integrate different relational and object-oriented databases and software applications. The data structure is based on the concept of folders which provide a flexible way of grouping and structuring information. Folders are used to define the addresses of the information and are implemented on a single reference database known as the CIMWORK database. Other databases and software applications communicate with the CIMWORK database using an application programming interface (API) which is based on a client server model. Folders are identified by names and can be accessed from different computers.

An example of the concept is shown in figure 7. The information relating to a single physical object such as a pump, is often distributed across a number of databases in a company. For example, the location and physical description of the pump is stored in a technical database (or GIS), the current operating condition is stored in a real-time database, the operational measurements are stored in an archive, and the maintenance records are stored in a fourth database. It is possible to create a folder that defines all the information relating to the pump and the associated information addresses. An operator or software application can send a request for the folder to the CIMWORK database server. The CIMWORK server would then provide the most recently saved data for the pump, and/or issue requests to the other databases to provide such information. The information is collated by the CIMWORK server and sent to the requester.

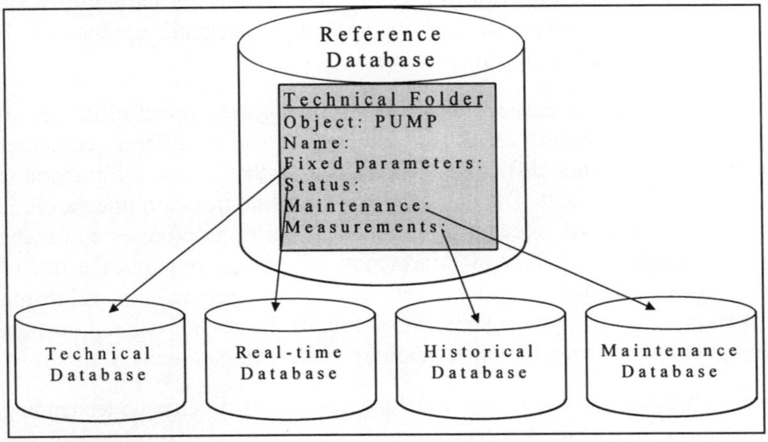

Figure 7. Concept of CIMWORK Distributed Information Storage

CIMWORK simplifies the structure of the information system by providing a central reference of information and associated addresses. The architecture reduces the potential number of specialised links which would be required to integrate the various databases and applications in the information system on an ad hoc basis. However, a communication module must be developed for each connected database or application. This is facilitated using the API which is a library of functions to perform operations on folders such as open, read, write, close etc.

Folders can also be updated by CIMVIEW variables thus providing a mechanism to integrate the two layers. The two levels provide horizontal and vertical integration. Horizontal integration is provided by CIMVIEW on the supervisory control level and by CIMWORK on the management level. The vertical communication is provided by a network gateway that runs both CIMVIEW and CIMWORK on a separate computer. This gateway enables CIMVIEW to read and write CIMWORK folders. The information in folders can be updated from CIMVIEW using real time information (the current state of the physical process) or it can be updated by values calculated by management applications such as optimal set points.

The CIMVIEW layer is designed to meet the requirements of continuous real-time monitoring and control. The CIMWORK layer is customised to meet the requirements of management applications. Usually, the variables in the CIMVIEW network are updated in real-time, so that a view of the most recently measured state of the physical process is available.

The internal mechanisms of CIMVIEW and CIMWORK for exchanging data are provided by product specific software. However, standards are emerging for common access mechanisms such as ODBC (Open Database Connectivity) (Geiger, 1995) which could be adopted in the architecture.

6. Conclusions

♦ Water companies are often large organisations with many employees organised into different departments and management levels. There are changing external factors which affect water companies. Consequently it is difficult to manage and improve the global efficiency of water companies without applying systematic approaches to analysing and integrating water company activities.

♦ Information integration is a decisive factor in improving operational efficiency in water companies. The distribution of information and the use of different computer and paper-based systems causes difficulties when ensuring that shared information is up to date, correct and consistent. The general objective of information integration is to provide timely, reliable and relevant information to perform activities and make decisions. The efficient exploitation of information technology requires the use of systematic analytical and planning methods. The main problems in achieving information integration arise from organisational complexity, organisational change, and in managing the introduction of new technology and existing systems.

♦ The emerging discipline of enterprise modelling can lead to a better understanding and uniform representation of an enterprise. It can help in the planning and management of organisational change, and can provide a model used to control and monitor enterprise operations. Motivations for using enterprise modelling for information integration, apart from introducing an efficient information system, are: managing complexity, better management of all types of processes, capitalisation of enterprise knowledge and know-how, business process re-engineering and enterprise reorganisation.

♦ Most water companies have approached information integration by developing systems for specific aspects of the business in isolation, such as asset management (e.g. GIS) and operational control (e.g. SCADA) etc. Some are developing specific interfaces between such systems to support activities that require information from different sources. However, coherent plans and policies towards fully integrated information systems are uncommon in the water industry at present, although many companies are now considering the issue.

♦ The WaterCIME Methodology presented in this chapter is an example of an approach towards company-wide information integration. It generates a design of the target system and a migration plan from the AS-IS information system to a new TO-BE system. The methodology is a modelling and planning procedure. It is based on common sense and established modelling techniques that are organised into an overall procedure and supported by reference models. It is independent of any particular computer technology. The methodology is for design only; the implementation can be performed using other integration platforms not described in this chapter.

♦ The implementation of widespread information integration requires a software integration platform. An example of such a platform is presented in this chapter in the form of a two-layer architecture based on the products known as CIMVIEW and CIMWORK. The CIMVIEW layer is designed to meet the requirements of continuous real-time monitoring and control. The CIMWORK layer is customised to meet the requirements of management applications.

♦ There are many potential applications of enterprise modelling. The WaterCIME Methodology provides an example in the area of information systems planning and integration. Some typical problems were identified by water companies at a recent European workshop. Three are briefly described as examples of where enterprise modelling could be beneficial:

1. The management of technical documents is a major problem in water companies. Engineers spend a lot of time retrieving, processing and storing information. The same information resides in different places in different forms, and the same activity is repeated unnecessarily many times. Enterprise modelling could be used to analyse information sources and flows, and to improve the process of managing the information.

2. In some companies, different budgets and teams are set up to focus on specific problems, such as mains rehabilitation for water quality improvement, leakage detection, and general pipeline maintenance. Each of these business processes is a complex problem but they all relate to the same physical pipe-network. Enterprise modelling would allow an overview of the processes and their co-ordination and integration.

3. Water utilities are increasingly considering customer service and some are introducing computerised customer complaints systems. Procedures for investigating and responding to complaints are costly. In some cases the cause of the problem is already known somewhere else in the company but not by the Customer Services Department. Relaying this information requires co-ordination of activities and access to information that is stored in many different places in the company. Enterprise modelling could model the customer complaints process and identify beneficial links with other activities.

There is a clearly a benefit in using systematic approaches to modelling, designing and planning information integration across a company.

ACKNOWLEDGEMENTS

The authors wish to acknowledge that the WaterCIME Methodology was developed with funding support of the European Commission under the ESPRIT 8399 programme.

REFERENCES

[1] AMICE, 1993. Open System Architecture for CIM, 2nd extended and revised version, Springer-Verlag, Berlin.

[2] Bernus, P. and Nemes, L. (Eds.) 1995. Modelling and Methodologies for Enterprise Integration, Chapman & Hall, London.

[3] Chionglo J.F. & Beck C. 1995. TOVEsim: A Simulation Executive for TOVE, Enterprise Integration Laboratory, University of Toronto, Canada.

[4] Doumeingts, G. et al, 1992. GIM, GRAI Integrated Methodology: A Methodology for Designing CIM Systems, Version 1.0, University of Bordeaux, France.

[5] Geiger K. 1995. Inside ODBC, Microsoft Press, Washington, USA.

[6] ISO, 1990. Reference Model for Shop Floor Production Standard. Technical Report 10314, Part 1. ISO TC 184/SC5/WG1 N126.

[7] Rance, J. P. Ulanicki, B. and Bounds, P.L.M. 1996. Modelling and Integration of Production Management system in Water Utilities, Proceedings of the Hydroinformatics 96 International Conference, Muller (Ed) pp. 861-868, Balkema, Rotterdam.

[8] Uschold, M. King M. Moralee, S. and Zorgios, Y, 1996. The Enterprise Ontology, Research Report of the Enterprise Project, AIAI, The University of Edinburgh, UK.

[9] Vernadat, Francois B. 1996. Enterprise Modelling and Integration, Principles and Applications, Chapman & Hall. Boundary Row, London. SE1 8HN

[10] WaterCIME consortium 1995. WaterCIME Methodology Guide (Use of CIME Concepts for the Development of Open Water Management Systems), Deliverable D1, WaterCIME ESPRIT Project 8399, WaterCIME Consortium.

CHAPTER 19

A Generalised Data Format (GDF) for Water Supply and Distribution Systems

C.Wang *and* R.S.Powell

1. Abstract

This chapter describes the design of a generalised data format for storing the data of water supply and distribution systems. It uses the network model to describe the system topology and the connectivity of components. Data are stored based on an Entity-Relationship model and using a customisable format.

2. Introduction

More and more computer software packages have been developed for the analysis and control of water systems. Most software packages do not communicate with any other package, especially one developed by another vendor, and almost every package has its own specific data storage format. Consequently, they do not exchange or share data and so the users cannot share the services of other packages. This leads to difficulties when users need to exchange data between software packages or need services from other packages. Hence, a consistent data format for water supply and distribution systems is essential when different computer software packages are to be used within a company and when data exchange is required.

However, it is impossible to design a uniform data format suitable for all of the existing software packages. This is because the design of existing software packages is based on their own models and for specific applications for water supply and distribution systems. They are programmed to read and write data files or databases using their own data storage format. A practical solution is to design a generalised data format that can be easily converted to the data storage format used by each particular model.

In addition to providing users with a medium for converting different data files, the generalised data format should provide a set of favourable features for prospective uses. The objectives of the design of a generalised data format are:

- To be compatible with frequently used data models, such as those in EPANET [5], GINAS [3], WATNET [8], SWS [6] and WASMACS [4], etc.
- To provide support for relational constructs (where necessary) and consistent data storage, such as those in hydraulic analysis, quality analysis, pumping and valve scheduling, demand prediction, and graphics, etc.

- To provide an extendible format so that both new data entities and new attributes can be added in an existing data file without affecting the compatibility of existing software packages.
- To be text based and human readable so that the files can be edited easily.

This chapter describes the design of such a generalised data format aimed to meet the above objectives.

3. Problems

Although most of the water system models are based on network topology, there are no standard conventions for water network models. There are differences in the modelling of system components and their connectivity, and also in the mathematical models used to describe the system components. For example, service reservoirs are modelled as a storage node, a two-port tank, or a tank element incorporating valves depending on the package. Some packages model valves together with connected pipes as a pipe component plus a minor loss coefficient; while other packages separate valves into two or more components.

The data models used in most of the packages under investigation are entity-relationship based [1, 2], even though their designers might not have been using the Entity-Relationship model on purpose. Most classify the system components into two basic categories, i.e. node and link, and the system operational data are also categorised as entities, such as control data (e.g. pump schedules, valve schedules), demand data, tariff, meter readings, etc. Each entity in its category has a unique identifier and is referenced by other entities through the entity type and identifier. However, the differences are extended into the data model, both for the entities and their relations. For example, some packages use a formula to calculate reservoir volume and some use a look-up table of volume versus water level. Even the water demand at nodes is classified into different types and different attributes are used.

Data format is another major difference among these existing packages. It is not only in the number of attributes used in a similar entity, but also in the names of the attributes, their definitions, and the order in which they are stored.

These problems lead to the conclusion that the data conversion between different software packages is not simply a matter of converting the data items and entities, but it must also include the conversion of system models and data models. Hence, the generalised data format must adopt a comprehensive system model, a neutral data model, and an extendible data format.

4. System Model

Water supply and distribution systems consist of a large number of pipes, valves, meters, pump stations and reservoirs. To operate such a system, operators are concerned with water flow rate, head, quality, pumping efficiency, electricity tariff, and system security, etc. Therefore, the data stored must meet the requirements of software packages designed for a variety of operational control and analysis tasks. The data requirements are:

- The network model of the physical components and its topology.
- Operational characteristics of the physical components, such as pump efficiency curves.

- Geographical data of the system.
- Time series data, such as demands and schedules.

The system model here is designed as a network based model by classifying all the physical components as link elements and the connection points as node elements. A sub-network can be treated as a multiple-branch link element. For example, a service reservoir is modelled as a link connecting two nodes with a storage capacity and where the inflow and outflow are decoupled. Valves, pumps and pipes are modelled as links with unique flow rates. Time series data are associated with their corresponding physical components.

5. Data Model

Existing software packages use ASCII files, relational databases, or object-oriented databases to store and manage the water system data. Considering this requirement, an entity-relationship model is a good choice of representation, because it is compatible with the existing data storage, and can easily be converted into the models used in the three data management systems.

The entities identified here are based on the physical components and the operational control and analysis data requirements. There are two categories of entities, namely plant data and operational data. Plant data constitute the backbone of the water system data and operational data is associated with the plant data. The properties of the entities are defined as attributes. The operational data entities are defined as an association with the corresponding physical components. Figure 1 shows part of the data model.

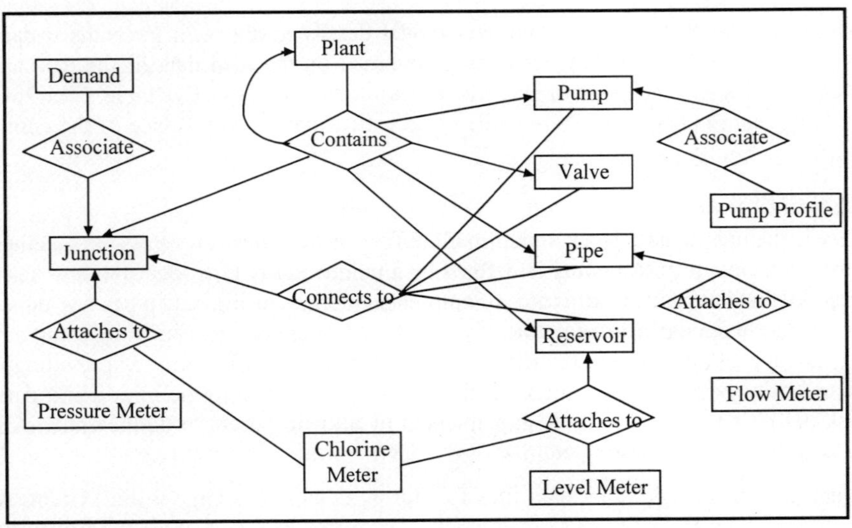

Figure 1. Entity-Relationship model of data objects in water systems

The plant data entities are categorised into *Junctions* and *Elements*, the latter being further classified into fixed speed pumps, variable speed pumps, reservoirs, pipes, tank-fill valves, pressure reducing valves, pressure modulating valves, etc. The connection information of water system (network) components is stored in *Element* entities. Each element stores the connected *Junctions*. All meters are designed as entities, which are attached to *Junctions* or *Elements*. Profiles for reservoirs and pumps, and tariffs for pumping stations are defined as attributes of the corresponding entities.

All operational data entities are designed to be associated with the corresponding physical component entities. This is implemented by storing a reference to the corresponding physical component entities. Time series data are stored in a dynamic data structure, i.e. discrete meter readings for 24 hours and demands during a week.

As the attributes of entities are not always simple data types, some specific data types have to be defined to ease both data storage and access. The basic data types identified are integer, real and string. Defining the function versus one variable as a data type, called function-data, may help to define and store profiles, curves, patterns, and time series data. To be more flexible in describing the characteristics of systems and components, both function-data and formulae are defined as data entities. A formula can also be formed using data at some points on a given curve. For example, demands, reservoir volumes and pump characteristics are defined using function-data. A quadratic equation for a pump operating in a specific range, for example, can be formed using data at three or more points from the pump characteristic's curve.

6. Generalised Data Format (GDF)

Considering the system model and data model described above, a generalised data format has been designed [7]. This design is based on the idea that all the data are stored in tables and each type of entity is represented by its respective table. Each row in a table represents one attribute value of an entity, that is, an instance of the entity type.

6.1. Syntax

Entity is the unique data block stored in GDF files and entities can be nested together to form a meta entity. An entity is defined by a unique entity type identifier and a set of user defined attributes. Attributes of entities are defined using data types and units, and the data types can also be defined by the users. Comments, bracketed by comment tags, can appear anywhere in the file. Users can define a specific entity by providing a unique entity type identifier. Figure 2 shows the syntax of entity definition and data block definition. Extendibility is implemented by allowing users to define entities or add new attributes to existing entities.

A data file can include other data files for storing details of a large water system. A data file consists of data blocks. Each block is bracketed by a pair of block identifiers, and contains information about the block, i.e. the number of instances in the block. An instance of entity can be stored in one line by ending with a new-line character or in more than one line by using a pair of the entity instance tags. The separator between attribute values is one or more spaces.

Entity Definition Format :

<ET> entity-type-identifier

{<EA>attribute-name (data-type, unit-name) </EA> separator | <EA>attribute-name (data-type, unit-name); | attribute-name (data-type, unit-name) </EA>}

</ET>

Data Block Format :

<entity-type-identifier> optional-information

{[new-line] attributes-values | <EI> attributes-values </EI>}

</entity-type-identifier>

Built-in Definitions:

<IN> {file-name | , filename } </IN>

<DT> data-type-identifier (data-type, size) </DT>

<! comments /!> or <CM>comment lines</CM>

data-type ∈{ integer, real, char, string, function-data, formula, user defined data-type-identifiers}

unit-name ∈{ mm, m, m3, m3/s, g, kg, ft, ft3, ft3/s, l, ml, Ml, l/s}

optional-information := {information-key-word=string | ; informatin-key-word=string}

Figure 2. GDF Syntax

In contrast to the existing data formats that are used in most software packages, the syntax defined achieved both extendibility and flexibility. For instance, the entity definition facilities allow programmers to define their data formats and programs to process the data format with their preferred methods. Using <EI> and </EI> tags solves the problem of storing an instance of an entity in multiple lines. Using data block tags facilitates data access and process programming, and guarantees the data integrity.

6.2. GDF Definitions

GDF is defined using the above syntax and definition tags, and is based on the system model and the data model described above. The entities defined in the GDF format are listed in Figure 3. The general data types are function-data (e.g. function of one variable) and formula (e.g. quadratic with three constants).

The plant data entities:

Junction, Tank, Reservoir, Bore hole, Pipe, Fixed speed pump, Variable speed pump, Throttle control valve, Non-return valve, Tank fill valve, Pressure breaker valve, Pressure regulation valve, Pressure modulating valve, Pressure sustaining valve, Flow control valve, Flow meter, Pressure meter, Level meter, Chlorine meter.

***Composite entities**: Plant, Pumping station.*

The operational data entities:

Control, Demand, Tariff, Quality, Head, Flow rate, Level, Measurements.

***Composite entities**: Plant status, Plant operations.*

The Plant View entities:

Junction-location, Pipe-path

Figure 3. Entities defined in the GDF format

For example, the pipe entity definition is defined before the pipe data block and is shown below. The pipe data block in Figure 4 is just used to show the format.

<ET> pipes <EA>id; from_junction; to_junction; diameter (real, mm); length (real, m); roughness </EA></ET>

<pipes> num=2 <! Two pipes in this data block /!>

1 1 2 100.0 100.0 0.01 <! Pipe 1 connects junction 1 and 2/!>

2 2 3 150.0 1000.0 0.01

</pipes>

Figure 4. A GDF definition and data example

The existing data formats deal with the dynamic data, i.e. time related data, in different ways. GDF uses a function-data and a formula entity to unify data storage. For example, the demands at junctions can be stored using a formula or function-data entity. Figure 5 gives the definition of junction entity and demand entity. The demand attribute can be a real number for a fixed demand or supply, or a pointer to a function-data entity. Figure 6 shows the definition of a function-data entity. In this way, any format of demands can be expressed uniformly and flexibly.

<ET> junction <EA> identifier (integer); name (string); type (string); elevation (real, m); demand (pointer); quality (pointer) </EA> </ET>

<ET> demand <EA> identifier, junction (pointer), demand-bias, demand-factor, function-data (pointer) </EA> </ET>

Figure 5. The definition of junction entity and demand entity

<ET>function-data <EA> identifier; type (1); variable initial; step; function initial; step </EA> </ET>

<ET>function-data <EA> identifier; type (2); variable initial; step; function { ; function } </EA> </ET>

<ET>function-data <EA> identifier; type (3); variable , function { ; variable , function } </EA> </ET>

Figure 6. The definition of function-data entity

6.3. File Organisation

Water supply and distribution system data in GDF files are organised as blocks that can be stored in more than one file. No specific order is required for storing data blocks in a file. However, we suggest that each type of data is arranged in one section and the plant data block is stored first to speed up the data input process by software packages.

7. Implementation

7.1. ASCII File

The generalised data format is designed to be easily edited and stored in ASCII files. This means that users can use any text editor to create and edit the data items of a water supply and distribution system.

7.2. ODBC Definition

Using database systems to store data is more advantages than using a plain text file from the point of view data management. ODBC from Microsoft provides a versatile means by which the application developer can be shielded from the data storage format. It is envisaged that, in due course, an ODBC driver for GDF will be written to permit the data to be managed as if it were in a relational database.

7.3. Utilities

It is proposed, if time permits, to set up data conversion tools on the World Wide Web. These tools are to be implemented in such a way that any existing data format can be bi-directionally converted to and from the GDF format.

8. Conclusions

The generalised data format can serve as a medium for water system data exchange between existing software packages. Users of existing water software packages will hopefully benefit from the data format converting tools.

9. References

[1] Chen, P. P., The Entity Relationship Model – towards a unified view of data, ACM Transaction of Database System, vol.1, No.1, pp9—36. March 1976.

[2] Bounds, P. L. M., Rance, J. P. and Ulanicki, B., Relational Data Model for Decision Support Systems for Control of Large Scale Water Supply Networks. Department of Electronic and Electrical Engineering, De Montfort University, UK. WSS Research Report, 1993.

[3] Coulbeck, B., Orr, C. H. and Cunningham, A. E., GINAS 5 Reference Manual, Department of Electronics and Electrical Engineering, De Montfort University, Leicester, UK. 1995.

[4] Powell, R. S., On-line Monitoring for Operational Control of Water Distribution Systems. Ph.D. Thesis, University of Durham, May 1992.

[5] Rossman, L. A., EPANET Users Manual, Drinking Water Research Division, Risk Reduction Engineering Laboratory, Cincinnati, Ohio, USA. January 1994.

[6] Stoner Associates, Inc. Stoner Workstation Service, Liquid Time-Varying Network Analysis Module, SWSL 1.5, Data Reference, P.O.Box 86, Carlisle, USA. 1994.

[7] Wang, C., A Generalised Data Format for Water Networks, Reference Manual, Water Operational Research Centre, Brunel University, Uxbridge, UK. June 1997.

[8] Water Research Centre, Analysis and Simulation of Water Networks and a Guide to the WATNET3 Computer Program, Swindon, UK. September 1987.

Section 4

Water Treatment and Water Quality Modelling

CHAPTER 20

Control System Simulations for Water Treatment Works

E.P.Evans, A.P.E.Green *and* T.M.Hoggart

1 Introduction

In recent years major changes have been taking place at water treatment works in the UK to meet changes in quality standards and to improve efficiency of operation, e.g.,

- Addition of new Process Units such as DAF plants, Ozonation, GAC filters.
- Installation of extensive monitoring, automation and control systems.

Usually the new units have been installed to tight deadlines and into existing plants that have to be kept operational. In particular, the time available for commissioning has been limited.

For three of Thames Water's (TWUL) large water treatment works that supply London, Halcrow has carried out studies of the hydraulics and control systems, including development of detailed simulation models. Hampton WTW is the largest works. It has an output of 790Mld and extensions there are currently under construction. Ashford Common WTW has a design capacity of 690Mld; work there is complete and it has been operated typically up to 760Mld. The third smaller works is Kempton WTW, which has an output of 205Mld, still large by national standards. Construction work at Kempton is complete.

The purpose of this chapter is to describe some key features of the developments, the simulation models used and to outline some findings of studies and experience of implementation and works operations.

2 Key Features of the Works

Ashford Common WTW

Ashford Common WTW was constructed in the 1950s by the Metropolitan Water Board to give an output of 410 million litres per day(Mld). Treatment processes included aeration (not used in later years), microstrainers, slow sand filtration, low lift pumping to chlorine contact tanks and high lift pumping to supply. Inflow through the works was by gravity from the nearby stored water reservoir via a dedicated tunnel.

The control and monitoring of the system were largely manual and operators would cycle out onto the works to adjust valves or pump speed as required. Flows at key positions could be monitored by Venturi flow meters.

The uprating of Ashford Common was a major exercise that transformed the works into a much more complex modern plant that is automatically demand driven from the inlet to new connections to the Thames Water Ring Main. New pre and post ozonation process units, rapid gravity filters, a new contact tank, and stored water and low lift pumping stations were installed, along with extensive pipe work and tunnel modifications, valve actuation and control and SCADA systems.

In the summer of 1995, when work had just been completed, the works played a valuable role in meeting high demands and produced significantly above its uprated design output of 690Mld.

Kempton Park WTW

Kempton Park WTW is an older works that has used rapid gravity filters, slow sand filtration and chlorination since the 1920s. An old beam pumping station and the site of older filter beds bear witness to an even longer history of use and changes at the site. Before the recent work, TWUL had installed a SCADA control system and automation of the primary filters allowed operators to set the required flow rate. Actuation of the original sluice valve on the slow sand filters had also been attempted but was not reliable enough to allow operators to adjust valves by remote control.

The work comprising Phase One of the uprating of the works was less extensive than at Ashford Common. It included construction of a new low lift pumping station and main ozonation tank, connecting pipe work and provision of new actuated valves to control inflows to the slow sand filters.

Hampton WTW

Hampton WTW is the largest works in the country (790 Mld output) and has a long history dating from the first uses of slow sand filtration. The site is large, and has a complex maze of pipe work dating from different periods, laid by many different water utilities that predated the Metropolitan Water Board. For these reasons the hydraulics of the works is particularly complex.

The Phase One uprating work included construction of tunnelled connections to a low lift pumping station and the main ozonation plant, with return feed to the existing slow sand filter pipe work. Slow sand filter valves are being replaced and monitoring equipment such as flow meters and level sensors are being updated as needed. One key concern of TWUL was that the control system for the new works should be robust and reliable, and that the uprated works is operational in time for statutory undertakings concerning water quality improvement to be met. Partial shutdowns of the works for making connections have to be carefully planned and scheduled, and can only be of very limited duration due to the key role of the works in London's water supply.

3 Simulation Models

Given that the uprating of works must be carried out in the most efficient manner, without a long commissioning time, TWUL commissioned models from Halcrow for detailed simulation of the hydraulics and control systems at Ashford Common. Later work on Kempton and Hampton has been carried out directly for the civils contractor, under design and build type contracts.

The hydraulics of large water treatment works differs significantly to that of water distribution systems, and standard network models are not very well suited to analysis of treatment works. Key differences come from the importance of losses at fittings and variable losses at junctions that depend on flow splits. Also important are the changes in velocity heads and the hydraulics of flow over weirs and in open sections of conduit. The program developed and used by Halcrow for analysis of treatment works (HYDRAN) includes all the above features. Models of the existing works are built and verified against field data. HYDRAN uses a sparse matrix solver and is a combination of earlier developments in pipe modelling and river/open channel models.

The HYDRA Control Module was then developed to work alongside HYDRAN. This permits the comprehensive simulation of hydraulic control systems that involve elements such as sensors, PID and logic controllers, control valves, automatically controlled variable speed pumps etc. The control code runs at the same time as the hydraulic code, changing valves and pumps as would occur in the real system. The advantages of having a full and computationally efficient hydraulic simulator coupled to a powerful control simulator has been established in studies of the water treatment works described here. It is also becoming more widely used for other applications such as canal control studies, and for automation of structures such as flood control gates.

4 Control System Philosophies

Traditionally, water treatment works have been designed to be self-managing to a certain extent. Good hydraulic design using regulating structures such as weirs and sluice gates would ensure that levels and flows remained within acceptable bands under normal operating conditions. Local, manual control of valves and pumps would then be used to achieve particular short-term operational objectives, such as achieving the target total works output. However, this approach meant that the design of works had to be somewhat conservative, with structures such as tanks and valves deliberately oversized to guarantee safe operation and to minimise spillage.

The uprating of the Hampton, Kempton and Ashford Common treatment works involved significant civil works to increase their output. Improvements were also made to the treatment process itself; for example, ozonation plants have been introduced into the primary treatment phase at all three works. As the plants are all within densely populated urban sites, severe physical constraints on the size of the new structures exist. This made it more important to ensure tight control of the flows and levels at various points within the works. In addition, a fully-automatic control system would improve the overall efficiency of the various treatment processes, reduce loss of water through spillage, and allow the works to be operated more cost-effectively.

The control systems adopted at the works allowed the maintenance of levels and flows without excessive complexity, or over dependence on long communication links crossing the sites. This essentially meant that processes are controlled locally, using simple downstream PID controllers, usually used in conjunction with a small deadband around a set point. The final control elements are control valves or variable speed pumps. Sometimes double, or even triple cascade loops were employed where some measure of control at two or three points of the works was needed, using only one final control element. Such a simple approach to the control philosophy had the great advantages of being robust and of having the confidence of the operational staff. The latter factor is particularly important, as it has often been found in the past that control systems had been turned off when operational problems had been encountered, particularly if they were thought to be overly complicated. Operators often prefer to rely on manual control rather than trust in a control system that does not have their complete confidence.

At all three works the main control point is the set point for a flow control valve at the downstream end of the works. This is also just upstream of the point where each works discharges into the Thames Water Ring Main (TWRM), and the works output is set here via the central SCADA controller. It was an important operating principle that the output to the TWRM should be tightly regulated. Changes in the works set point would gradually feed back through the other control points by hydraulic effects only. A schematic representation of the main treatment processes at Ashford Common, which is typical of the three works, is shown in the attached figure.

The works output set point was not fed back directly to the front of the works. This would have undoubtedly speeded up the response time of the stored water pumps upstream of the blending tanks, for example, so that the flow at the front of the works would closely match that at the back. The disadvantage of this approach, however, is that flow disturbances at the works' outlet would be fed into the control loops further upstream. By sticking to the principle of local control, disturbances in one control loop would not be introduced into other loops. Instead, the hydraulics of the system would act to dissipate any disturbance propagating between neighbouring control systems. This was particularly true of the large volume slow sand filters which are found in all three works. Because of their large storage and balancing capacities, these can almost be said to isolate the upstream and downstream parts of the works, preventing disturbances from crossing from one half to the other.

The resultant control schemes are very simple to maintain and operate. Once correctly tuned to optimise performance, and to reduce any potential crosstalk between neighbouring controllers, they are also robust in operation. In addition, the traditional principles of hydraulic control have not been totally abandoned even in the uprated works. Thus, each works is reasonably robust in operation even in the face of a catastrophic control system failure.

5 Lessons Learnt

A great deal has been learnt from using the simulation models, from examining shortcomings of the existing control systems and from experience in operations. Several key issues have emerged that should receive a high priority at the start of any future studies:

- What is an appropriate level of control system complexity for the future operators of the system and can some flexibility be allowed for adjustments by operators?
- What is the behaviour of the system following a power failure; are appropriate overflows and bypasses allowed for?
- Do existing control 'islands' work as intended and can they be reliably integrated into an overall system?
- Can existing valves be reliably actuated to give the level of control desired or do they need to be replaced by more suitable units?
- How often will valves move and are appropriate actuators used? Can actuation rates be decreased to improve life of the units?
- What are the details of the controllers to be used? It was found at Ashford Common, for example, that the type of deadband used on the level controllers had a significant impact on the optimum controller tuning, and on the effectiveness of making use of the storage available.

6 Benefits Realised

The use of simulation models allowed the testing of a range of options for control of the works, and permitted the evaluation of its performance under different conditions. The benefits or otherwise of increased complexity could therefore be quickly shown, and preferred options chosen. The combination of simulations using detailed hydraulics and control gives much more confidence in the solutions derived.

The task of commissioning many individual controllers was greatly helped by having initial tuning parameters from the modelling that would fit together to give a system that functioned as an integrated unit.

Simulation models are particularly useful for developing and testing procedures for abnormal situations. For example, at Hampton procedures are being developed for the starting up or the shutting down of the new part of the works without disrupting output. More normal occurrences such as the backwashing of filters, the switching on or off of backwash pumps, etc., can all be tested before commissioning. These tests might then reveal that these events form the most severe tests for the control system.

7 Future Developments

The use of linked hydraulic and control simulations has been found to have a significant benefit in the planning and implementation of uprating works. Future use of the technique is likely for similar situations as the need for more efficient operation increases. At Ashford Common the model was used in conjunction with output from a three-dimensional flow model, as well as a process model developed to design a control system for the chlorination process. The latter control strategy was based on hyperchlorous acid concentration and very much closer control. More effective disinfection has been achieved using this method than has traditionally been the case.

Further development of procedures for dealing with abnormal situations and training of operators is a possible future area of use. Other uses of the models are also being considered. These could include linking to models of process efficiency and operating costs for optimisation of the operation of treatment works.

8 Conclusions

Detailed simulation models incorporating hydraulics and control systems have been shown to have significant benefits in the uprating of large water treatment works. Building upon existing techniques, a whole new area encompassing both hydraulic engineering and control engineering has been developed overcoming traditional boundaries between these disciplines. This approach also permits time and money to be saved on the commissioning phase, and allows engineers to design cheaper and more effective treatment works, secure in the knowledge that their control system will not fail them.

CHAPTER 21

Investigating Reservoir Water Quality Using Computer Modelling

J.Creasey

1. Background And Approach

It is important that the quality of potable water meets the required standards and regulations for health and aesthetic quality. Storage in a service reservoir directly influences the quality of the water delivered to the customer. Thus, the effects of reservoir design and operation on the quality of water need to be understood in order to cost effectively achieve the required standards..

Surprisingly, there has been no consensus on the best design and operation to maintain good quality. Indeed, there have been papers that have put forward conflicting views. The work described in this chapter had the objective of settling some of these arguments by answering such questions as: "Is there a best shape?"; "Can quality be improved by changing inlet conditions?"; "What is the effect of various operating regimes?".

A particular area of disagreement concerns the value of baffle walls. Some designers believe that they are beneficial because they induce "plug flow". Plug flow is a regime in which all the fluid progresses from inlet to outlet at the same rate and all arrives at the outlet having the same age. Others argue that, from a water quality standpoint, it is preferable to have a well-mixed regime and therefore baffles should not be used.

The approach was based on a computer modelling technique called Computational Fluid Dynamics (CFD). It was considered important to validate the use of CFD in this context by checking simulated results against field measurements. With the confidence given by this validation, models were created to investigate the effect of design changes and operating regimes on quality throughout the body of stored water.

The results of the investigation were used to produce design and operating guidelines.

2. Computational Fluid Dynamics

CFD is a computer modelling technique in which the fundamental equations of hydrodynamics are solved numerically. The fluid volume (in this case the water in the reservoir) is divided into a number of cells. The differential equations are solved using a numerical approximation within each cell. This produces a value of flow, pressure and other variables of interest for each cell.

CFD is therefore tailor-made for investigating the effect of reservoir design on the flow patterns within the reservoir. The model dimensions can be changed or the inlet moved to a number of different positions and then the flow patterns examined to see the nature and importance of the effects.

The issue of interest in this work was water quality and so one or more parameters were needed to measure water quality changes. There are a number of candidates but it was decided that the best general indicator of quality is chlorine concentration. It was modelled using a first order reaction:

$$dC/dt = -kC$$

where C is chlorine concentration

k is the rate constant

This addition to the CFD allows chlorine concentration to be calculated throughout the water volume, given the value at the inlet.

CFD is a tried and tested technique. The software used in this project has been applied to a wide range of problems over many years. It is perhaps surprising that, at the start of this work, we could find no report of the use of CFD in the investigation of service reservoir behaviour. In view of this, it was considered important to validate the use of these models against measurements on reservoirs.

3. Fieldwork

It soon became clear that there are practical difficulties that militate against making measurements or taking samples at selected points within a reservoir. In addition, none of the reservoir operators involved in the research was willing to allow any sampling within the reservoir. Therefore, validation had to be based on measurements at inlet and outlet only.

It is clear that a demonstration of software capability to predict outlet values is not so convincing as a demonstration involving values at interior points. In normal operation, the values of quality parameters at outlet do not vary much. It was necessary to produce a more convincing test; something that would put greater demands on the predictive capability.

It was decided to inject a safe, inert substance into the inlet flow for a few hours and to sample the water at the outlet. The ability of the software to reproduce this outlet profile would be a more stringent test of its capability to model flows and therefore to model quality variation within the reservoir. Similar techniques have been used extensively in the investigation of the performance of process plant.

Lithium chloride is the only widely accepted tracer substance in potable water applications and this was used in all the fieldwork. Other parameters were recorded throughout the day. These included: inflow, outflow, water level and chlorine concentrations.

It was necessary to include a model for the behaviour of an inert substance within the CFD software. This enables the prediction of lithium throughout the reservoir from the profile of lithium against time at the inlet. In particular, a lithium profile at the outlet is produced and may be compared with the measured values.

4. Model Validation

Fieldwork was carried out at three reservoirs: one with a circular plan and two rectangular. One of the rectangular reservoirs had a single baffle wall and the other had four baffle walls. Of the three sites, two had a submerged inlet and the third a free discharge above the water level. It was felt that (as far as is possible with three cases) these covered the important variations in design.

Computer models were built for each of the reservoirs where field measurements took place. Model building required the input of the reservoir geometry and a description of operating conditions on the day of the fieldwork (e.g. the inflow and outflow variation). The measured trace of lithium concentration in the outlet flow was compared with the computed values. These comparisons were used to improve the modelling.

A number of important decisions needed to be made about the modelling approach. These included:

- The number of cells into which the water volume is divided.
- The extent to which detail is needed in the modelling of features such as the inlet.
- How to model the effect of a free inlet on the main body of water.
- The way in which turbulence is modelled.

These decisions can be modified and validated by comparing the predicted profile with the measured one. For example, a number of turbulence models were used in turn and the effect on the results was investigated. This activity gave the confidence necessary to move on to the central part of the work, which was to investigate the effect of design and operation on water quality.

All three sets of reservoir results were valuable for this process. As an example, Figure 1 shows a comparison of the measured and modelled tracer outlet concentrations for the circular reservoir. The agreement between the two values is very good in this case.

5. Design Investigations

Three dimensional computer models were used to investigate the effect of reservoir design features on water quality. These features included dimensions, inlet and outlet positions, inflow rate and baffle wall arrangement. The investigation started from two "base models": one with a rectangular plan and one with a circular plan. The features were varied from the base model values and the water quality results examined to determine the effect of these variations.

Plots of velocity vectors can give insight into the behaviour of water within the reservoir. For example, Figure 2 shows velocities in a horizontal plane, near the surface of a rectangular reservoir with no baffles. The submerged inlet is at the bottom left of the figure and the outlet is in the floor near the top right of the figure. The length of the arrow is proportional to the velocity.

High velocity activity is clearly visible near the inlet. Flow away from the outlet and towards the inlet can be seen in a number of areas. There is considerable mixing and recirculation. Results from other planes show that there is a three-dimensional pattern with interchange between this and other levels. This mixing gives good water quality throughout.

One design factor investigated was the effect of reservoir depth. Figure 3 shows the effect of reducing the depth whilst keeping the volume and inflow conditions constant. This plot shows the velocity vectors at half water depth. In this case a more regular circulatory pattern can be seen at this and other depths. Mixing is much less widespread and a semi-stagnant area is obvious at the centre. Thus, the work on this aspect suggests that shallow water be avoided.

As previously discussed, chlorine concentration was used as a more direct way of considering water quality. Clearly the value at outlet is important. However, the distribution of chlorine across the reservoir is of equal interest. Some designs produced low concentrations in some areas. (An example of this has been seen above for the shallow reservoir case.) It is argued that these are sites where microbiological growth could occur and that, therefore, this is indicative of a poor design.

By comparing the results from a range of simulations, it was possible to develop design guidelines with the objective of preserving good water quality in reservoirs.

6. Investigating Operations

Further computer simulations were carried out to discover the effects on water quality of reservoir operating styles. The results of constant inflow were compared with those from other pumping patterns, including pump schedules that might be used to minimise power costs.

One of the interesting results concerns the variability of chlorine at reservoir outlet with and without baffles. Figure 4 shows chlorine concentration for a reservoir without baffles when inflow pumping is for 12 hours a day followed by 12 hours without pumping.

Average concentration in the reservoir is shown as well as chlorine at the outlet. The two values are very similar, which indicates the continued high level of mixing even when the pump has stopped. The range of concentration at outlet over the day is large and could be a source of customer complaint. The equivalent result for a reservoir with baffles is quite different (Figure 5). In such a case, the concentration at outlet varies very little over the 24-hour period in spite of the pumping pattern.

7. Summary

The work has demonstrated that Computational Fluid Dynamics can be used to model water quality in service reservoirs. Encouraging results were obtained when comparing predictions with field measurements. By varying parameter values it was possible to investigate the effect of design and operation on water quality. Guidelines were produced for the use of the organisations that supported this research. They included recommendations on:

- The ratio of length to breadth.
- Reservoir depth.
- Inlet velocities.
- The use of baffles.

Acknowledgements

The work reported in this chapter was funded by Bournemouth and West Hampshire Water, East of Scotland Water, North of Scotland Water Authority, Portsmouth Water Plc, Severn Trent Water Limited and West of Scotland Water.

The modelling software used was Phoenics from CHAM UK and initial investigations were performed by Dr David Glynn at Flowsolve Ltd.

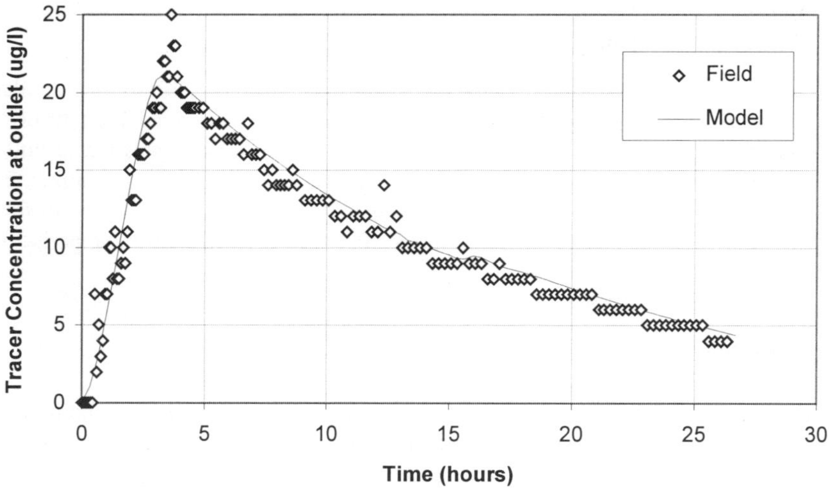

Figure 1. Circular reservoir: tracer concentration at outlet (measured and modelled)

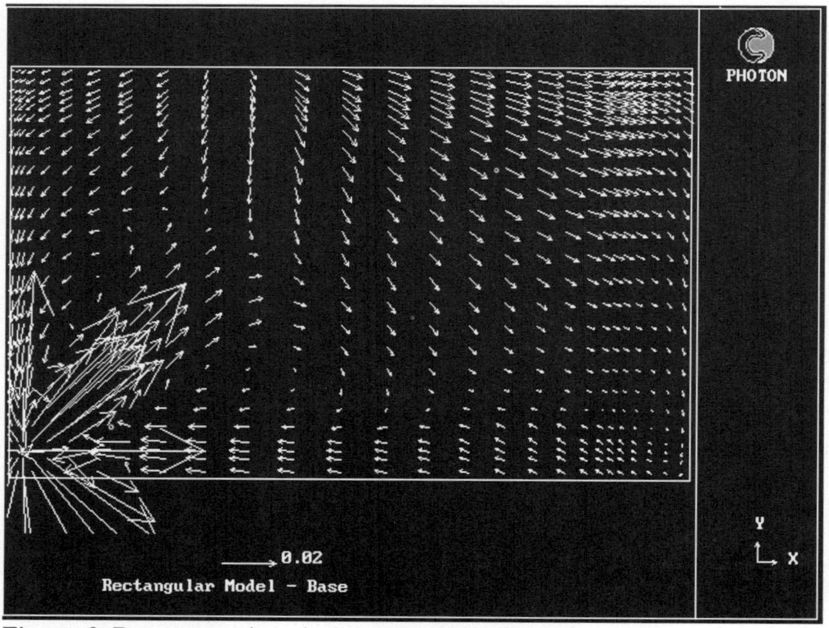

Figure 2. Deep reservoir: velocity vectors near the surface

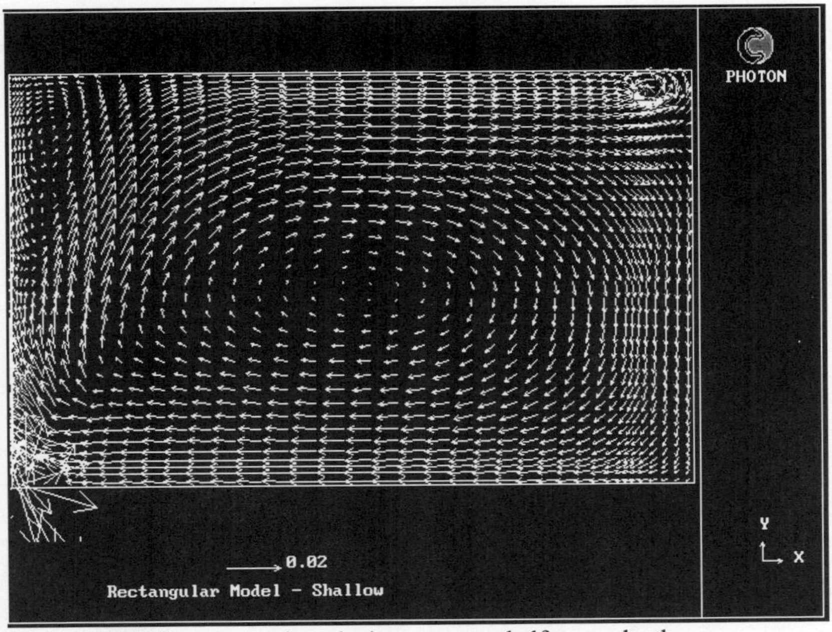

Figure 3. Shallow reservoir: velocity vectors at half water depth

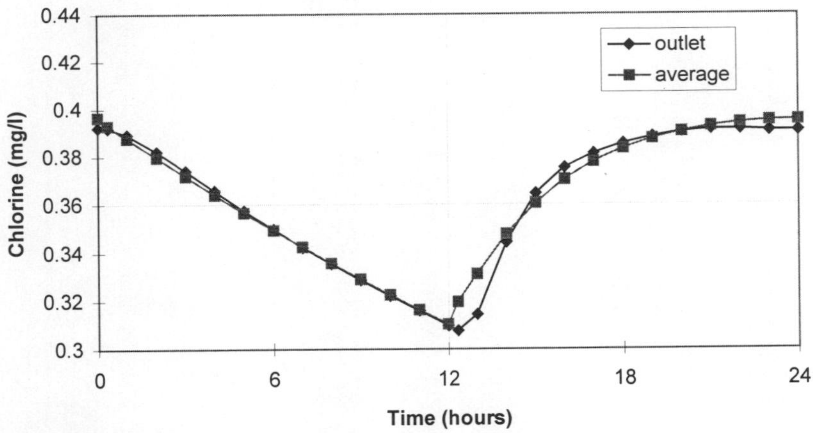

Figure 4. Chlorine concentration in reservoir without baffles: pumps 12 hours off, 12 hours on

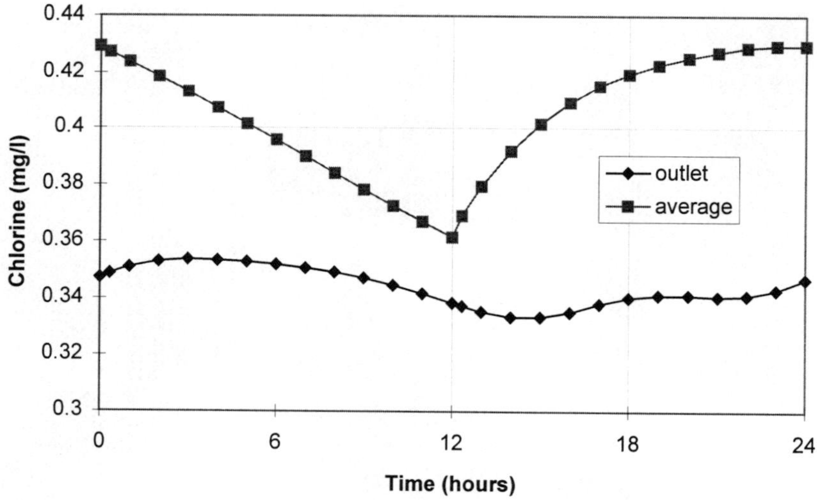

Figure 5. Chlorine concentration in reservoir with baffles: pumps 12 hours off, 12 hours on

CHAPTER 22

Optimising the Choice of Sampling Points in a Drinking Water Supply Network

A.Nace, F.Fotoohi, Y.Levi *and* P.Villon

1. Introduction

Water quality monitoring and surveying are important for drinking water production and distribution managers. According to the European and national standards, the potable water is continuously inspected. Unfortunately, satisfying quality standards at the outlet of the treatment plants is not always sufficient to prevent quality problems in consumption areas. The water quality tends to degrade inside the distribution mains and its final state depends on multiple parameters, such as pH, temperature, state of the pipes and their materials, the retention time of water in the pipes etc.

Thus, it is necessary to perform regular samplings and analyses on representative points of the network. On the other hand, new sensor technology provides the possibility of real time monitoring of water quality on the distribution network. In this context, choosing the sampling points (or location of the sensors) on the network is an important task.

To select monitoring stations or sampling points in a rational manner, it is important to know (for a given consumption pattern) the flows in the distribution system. The use of a hydraulic model is therefore necessary. Based on these hydraulic simulations, an interesting approach is proposed by Lee and Deininger [ref 1]. Their objective is to find the best feasible coverage of the consumption points using a limited number of sampling points (or sensors). Intuitively, if a node is sampled, the water quality of the closest upstream nodes can be assessed under certain assumptions. The terms of coverage are defined to denote the possibility of inferring the quality of water at one node based on measurements made at some other points. The authors assume that the node i covers node j if i receives sufficient water coming from j. In this way they define a covering matrix giving the relationship of all nodes in the network. This matrix is used frequently in the optimisation process.

However, in a drinking water supply network, the growth rate of bacteria or residual chlorine depends also on the retention time in pipes. Thus, it is important to cover the nodes where retention is likely to pose quality problems. Furthermore, the coverage term defined must take into account pollution propagation times from one node to another in order to detect and prevent problems rapidly.

In the sections 2.1 & 2.2, we will briefly describe the method proposed by Lee and Deininger. Then, in section 2.3, we will concentrate on the necessary adaptations concerning the retention time. The results of the method are discussed through a case study on the drinking water distribution network of Cholet.

2. Definition and resolution of the problem

We will suppose throughout this chapter, that there is a hydrodynamic model able to determine the flows and the pressures in a water distribution network according to a given consumption pattern.

2.1 The covering matrix

The method researches the sampling points among nodes receiving the greatest water quantity. A water fraction matrix $[W(i,j)]$ with $(i,j) \in \{1,\ldots,n\}^2$ is introduced. Each term of this matrix represents the flow contribution of node *j* to the node *i* according to all pathways going from *j* to *i*. For example, W(i,j) =0.36 means that 36% of water sampled at node *i* came through node *j*.

Information on the water flow in a network is collected by the water fraction matrix W(i,j). A knowledge-carrying matrix is derived from the water-fraction matrix W, based on the fraction of water in which it is acceptable to call a node covered. So a threshold (or water fraction criteria) « c » is introduced:

if $W(i,j) < c$: we pose $Wc(i,j) = 0$

if $W(i,j) \geq c$: we pose $Wc(i,j) = 1$.

If W(i,j)>c, then we say that the node j is covered by node i.

In this way the covering matrix Wc (i,j) is constructed and used for the resolution of the optimisation problem.

2.2 Formulation of problem

The optimisation program is formulated as follows

$$\text{Maximise} \sum_i \mathbf{D_i * y_i} \qquad (1)$$

subject to :

$$\sum_{i=1}^{n} x_i \leq NS \qquad (2)$$

The constraint (2) imposes on the network's nodes a maximum number of sampling points that should not be exceeded.

$$\sum_{i=1}^{n} W_c^T(i,j)x_i - y_j \geq 0 \qquad (3)$$

We impose constraint (3) on the entire nodes of the network. According to that constraint, *if node j is covered at least by one sampling point i, then consumption in j is sufficiently covered (controlled), where:*

Di - the consumption at node i ,

n - the number of nodes,

xi, yi = 0 or 1.

The sampling points obtained by this method often lie at the ends of antenna, which have high retention times. Obviously, these points do not permit correct inference regarding the water quality of upstream nodes nor prevent quality problems in time.

2.3 The retention time

Firstly, we wish to reconsider the definition of the retention time. When the network has only one source, the retention time is rather simple to define. It becomes difficult when the network contains several sources. The retention time is regarded as an average of the retention time of water flows from different nodes, according to the percentage of re-entered flows. Therefore, if 10% of the water arrives at node *i* from the node *j1*... 20% from the node *j2* etc, then the retention time of node *i* will be an average of 10% of the retention time of the water from node *j1*, 20 % of the retention time of the water coming from *j2* and so on.

According to the type of monitoring (chlorine residual rate, rate of bacteria etc), the intervals of the most significant retention times do not remain constant.

The experiment of monitoring drinking water supply networks and the studies undertaken showed that the bacteria growth rate increases after moment T1 to stabilise after moment T2. It will thus be especially necessary to supervise the network in the interval of the time [T1 T2]. This interval is different according to the type of bacteria.

In the following, we propose two solutions that take into account the retention time:

1. Instead of computing the water faction matrix W(i,j), we introduce a matrix Wt (i,j) which will simultaneously take into account the water fraction matrix W and the matrix of time Ψ|(i,j) taken in each arc of the network. We have already noted that the matrix W contained information on the flows. Let us suppose the time taken for water to travel through each arc of the network Ψ|(j,i) is known. Intuitively, the greater the time Ψ|(i,j) taken by water, the less node j can cover node i. If Ψ|(i,j) is much more than a number of hours (to be defined), it will be impossible to prevent the problem in time. We thus define a new matrix Wt(i,j). Each term of Wt matrix is expressed by W(i,j) and Ψ|(j,i).

In order to determine if a node is covered by another one, we will simultaneously use two thresholds:

- The water-fraction criterion C.
- A criterion Ct depending on the retention time.

The definition of the water-fraction criterion C is not an easy problem. The definition of the Ct criterion is even more complicated. The results obtained largely depend on choosing these criteria well, which is not an easy task.

2. Distribution of the sampling points according to retention time. We firstly consider only the zones where the retention time is lower than a threshold, above which the quality of water degrades (because of the reduction of the chlorine rate or other reasons). In the same way, we then consider only the zones where the retention time is higher than a threshold, below which quality is very good.

According to the type of problem that we want to solve, we define an interval of securities of retention time $[T_1..T_2..T_3.....T_k...T_n]$. We impose that at most n_1 sampling points be chosen in the nodes with an average retention time in the interval $[T_1..T_2]$, n_2 sampling points in the interval $[T_2..T_3]$, n_k sampling points in the interval $[T_k..T_{k+1}]$ and so on. The number of sampling points chosen in an interval depends on the priority given to the interval. This priority expresses the possibility that important changes concerning the water quality may happen in this retention time interval. So, if we have many more sampling points in the high priority intervals than in the others, we are likely to have a sampled node not far from the origin of failure.

The results obtained in this case depend quite simply on the intervals and the number of sampling points that we set for each interval.

In both cases the problem maximises the coverage of consumption of all the network's nodes by taking into account:

- The information over the retention time contained in the matrix (method 1).
- The number of sampling points according to various zones (method 2).

The cases treated above correspond to only one hydraulic scenario. The demand, the flow and the retention time change every hour and every day. A scenario consists of data such as demand, flow and retention time during a period of one or more hours. When we take into account several scenarios, we consider the retention time as the average of the retention times of the various scenarios, or as a weighted average according to the importance of each scenario.

2.4 The consumption areas

Depending on the type of objects within an area, we can distinguish important areas such as hospital areas, residential areas etc. and much less important areas. A coefficient representing the importance of each area of supply is assigned in relation to the consumption of each area. The consumption of each area is thus modulated by these coefficients, i.e., the very important areas are treated as if consumption were too high, while other areas are treated as if consumption were relatively low. The result of the programming obviously depends on these coefficients.

3. Application and results

We developed a working tool integrating these methods. For this, we have used a hydrodynamic model (provided by PICCOLO software). This model analyses and determines flow rates and times taken in each arc of the network and consumption in each node of the water distribution network. After reading these data, the tool carries out the resolution of the linear programming. We tested this tool on some real networks such as Cholet (a 2000-nodes network). During these tests, we observed that considering the retention time allows a better distribution of the sampling points.

3.1 The functional diagram of the optimisation tool

Several types of information are essential to our optimisation tool, such as:

- Scenarios (flow and consumption on the entire network in each hour).
- Type of consumption (residential area, industrial park, etc).

The objective of optimisation relates to the maximisation of consumption coverage through the network.

Depending on the objectives, this tool provides us with the sampling points, the covered consumption nodes and finally the total value of covered consumption.

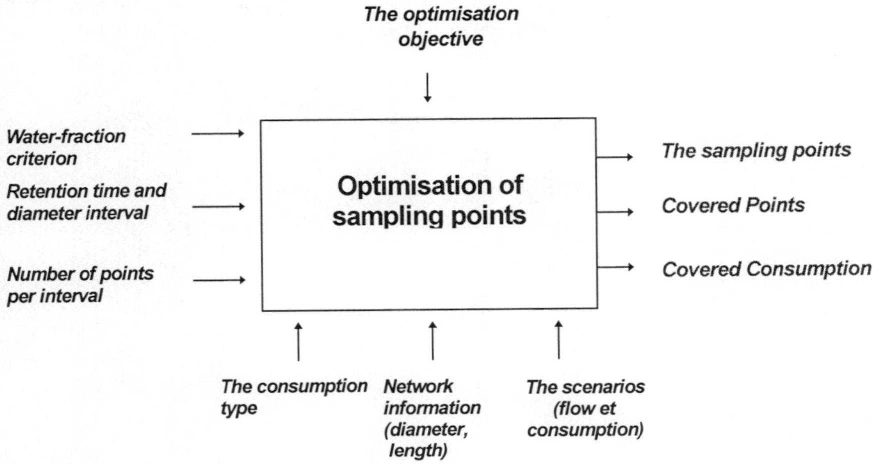

Figure 1. Functional diagram of the optimising tool

3.2 Description of the Cholet network

In the absence of any large streams or significant aquifers, the main water resource in the region around Cholet (population 60000) consists of the water from the reservoirs of Moulin de Ribou and Verdon. The Moulin de Ribou plant produces most of the drinking water consumed in Cholet ; its production capacity is around 30000 m^3/day.

The network consists of pipes, t-pieces, joints etc. To improve its operation, other apparatus can be used such as valves; boosters; governors, volumetric or pressure; break-charge and so on.

Water is distributed to the subscribers via more than 250km of conduits; 182.68km of the conduits were modelled. It was considered sufficient to model the pipes of diameter greater than 100 mm. This is why not all the lines were considered. However, in certain essential grids for correct operation of the network, the pipes with a diameter of 60 mm were modelled.

The distribution of the retention time for the Cholet network is given by the following graph :

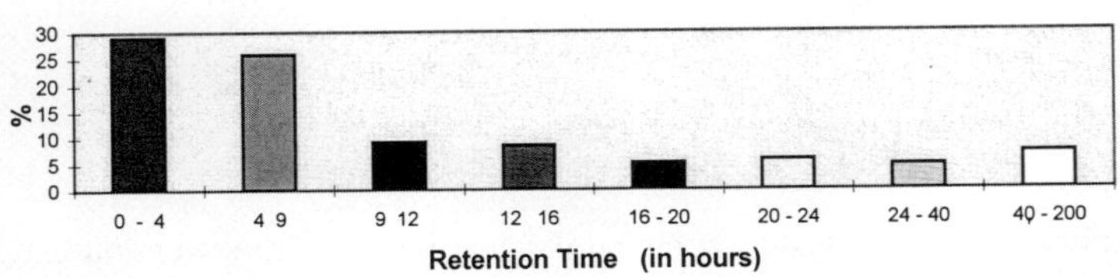

Figure 2. Distribution of the retention time (Cholet Network)

The application of the Lee and Deininger algorithm to the entire Cholet network (25 sampling points) gave the following results:

Figure 3. Sampling points obtained without taking account of the retention time

We see that some of the sampling points were placed on the ends of antenna. In addition, no sampling points were placed at the centre of the city (which is at the top left of the figure). We have a poor representation of the global quality evolution.

We then carried out optimisation with the following distribution of the sampling points: 2 sampling points in the interval 1-4 hours, 7 sampling points in the interval 4-9 hours, 11 sampling points in the interval 9 - 12 hours, 2 sampling points in the interval 12-16 hours, 2 sampling points in the interval 16-24 and finally 1 sampling point in the interval 24-48 hours.

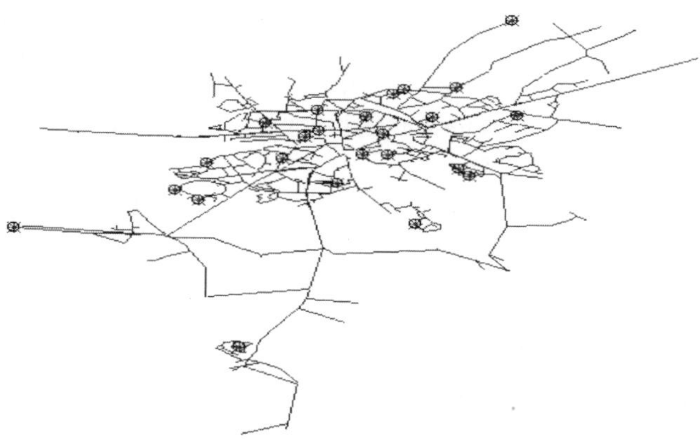

Figure 4. Sampling points obtained by applying the distribution of the retention times

We note in the second case that sampling points were placed at the town centre, and that the number of sampling points on the ends of antenna decreases. The results obtained enable us to place the sampling points according to the importance attached to the respective interval of each retention time. But at the same time these sampling points ensure the best coverage of the consumption in the intervals that we emphasised. Notice that the intervals of retention time intrinsically depend on the network type.

4. Conclusion

It is difficult to establish an evaluation indicator to express the efficiency of a set of sampling point locations. Therefore, the comparison between several solutions remains a difficult task.

However, we believe that optimising the sampling point locations should take into account the relationship of all nodes of the drinking water network, both in terms of flows and retention times. The second parameter is specially important if one needs to know in real time the state of a drinking water network and to prevent any kind of quality degradation which may occur.

5. References

[1] Byoung Ho Lee and Rolf A. Deininger(1992), Optimal locations of monitoring stations in water distribution system, Journal of Environmental Engineering.

[2] Lee Byoung HO (1990), Locating monitoring stations in water distribution network, PhD thesis presented to University Of Michigan.

CHAPTER 23

PICCOBIO: Modelling Bacterial Regrowth in Drinking Water Distribution Systems

P.Piriou, S.Dukan *and* Y.Levi

Abstract

Mathematical modelling is necessary in view of the complexity of the different phenomena involved in the evolution of water quality during distribution. A determinist type of modelling called PICCOBIO was developed to predict bacterial variations (viable and total bacteria) during distribution. The fixed biomass has been modelled as a layer uniformly distributed over the pipe surface, expressed as an equivalent thickness of carbon, which enables us to distinguish between phenomena depending on their locations (two dimensional model). To model the action of chlorine, the metabolism of bacteria has been associated with that of an enzyme and the inhibiting action of chlorine is expressed in accordance with a Kcat type enzymatic model. To model the action of chlorine on the fixed biomass with its stronger resistance compared to the free biomass, the diffusion of the chlorine through the boundary layer and the biofilm has been taken into account. It enables the identification of two layers into the biofilm: a chlorinated layer and a layer not reached by the chlorine which provides a material indication of the better resistance of the fixed biomass. As detachment is a key phenomenon in the modelling of bacterial dynamics in distribution systems, the influence of different formulas of detachment kinetics on the model results were determined by literal calculations. The model has been interfaced with PICCOLO software, the SAFEGE hydraulic calculation model. It is constructed by using hydraulic results previously generated by PICCOLO and a numerical scheme to predict bacterial count at each node and on each link of a network. The first model validation was done using data from a pipe loop pilot under various operating conditions. The model has been also used to simulate a variety of real distribution systems of different sizes and levels of detail and a validation of the model has been carried out by means of measurement campaigns on different distribution systems. Animating and visualising variations in bacteria counts in distribution systems is an unique approach for studying the changes in water quality. This tool is helpful when proposing strategies for the management of distribution systems and treatment plants and defining the different zones of bacterial regrowth problems in relation to hydraulic conditions.

Introduction

Water quality degradation in distribution systems due to biological phenomena is undoubtedly the subject of numerous studies and is very closely monitored because of short-term public health risks (Payment *et al.* 1991). In view of the complexity of bacteria dynamics, mathematical modelling is necessary in order to describe and control bacterial water quality degradation in full-scale networks.

This chapter describes the characteristics of a model, called PICCOBIO®, developed by the CIRSEE (Suez-Lyonnaise des Eaux Company Research Centre) to predict bacterial regrowth in full-scale distribution systems.

Model description

Main characteristics

A determinist type of modelling was developed to predict bacterial variations (viable and total bacteria) during distribution (Dukan *et al.* 1996).

The model takes into account (Figure 1):

- The fate of available nutrients consumed for the growth of suspended and fixed bacteria. These available nutrients are determined by the Biodegradable Dissolved Organic Carbon method (Levi & Joret 1990), assuming that only the carbon fraction limits the growth of bacteria.
- The influence of temperature on bacterial dynamics.
- The natural mortality of bacteria by senescence and grazing.
- The mortality of bacteria resulting from the presence of chlorine disinfectant, with a differentiation between the action on free and fixed bacteria. The mortality rate takes into account the different forms of chlorine in water ($HClO/ClO^-$) which depend on pH.
- The deposition of suspended bacteria and the detachment of fixed bacteria.
- The chlorine decay kinetics under the influence temperature, hydraulics and pipe materials (Kiene *et al.* 1993).

The fixed biomass is modelled as a layer uniformly distributed over the pipe surface, expressed as an equivalent thickness of carbon. In this way, a differentiation between the mathematical expression of the free and the fixed biomass can be made in the model. This means it is possible to distinguish between phenomena depending on their respective locations: reactions in solution, reaction at the water/biofilm surface interface and within the biofilm.

Modelling of chlorine bactericidal action

Modelling Principles: At the disinfectant concentrations generally observed in distribution networks, the bactericidal action of the free chlorine seems to result in numerous alterations of various cellular functions, such as the inhibition of the transport of electrons (Barette *et al.* 1987), the transport of various compounds such as succinate, glucose and numerous amino acids (Thomas 1979) and/or the inhibition of cellular division (McKenna & Davis 1988).

To model the action of chlorine, the metabolism of bacteria has been associated with that of an enzyme. The inhibiting action of chlorine is expressed in accordance with a Kcat type enzymatic model (suicide inhibitor). The mechanism leads, via an activated complex, to the inhibition of the enzyme, that is the inactivation of the bacterium. Its expression is as follows:

$$\textbf{Enzyme} + \mathbf{Cl_2} \leftrightarrow [\text{Enzyme - Cl}_2] \rightarrow \textbf{Blocked Enzyme.}$$

For the chlorine concentrations used in networks, the bactericidal effect of the hypochlorous acid may be considered to be instantaneous (Albrichh & Hurst 1982). This gives an expression of the mortality rate due to chlorine for suspended bacteria as follows:

$$K_{mort}([Cl_2]) = Ao \,.\, (1 - \exp(-(\frac{B.[Cl_2]}{1 + A.[Cl_2]}))) \text{ until } [Cl_2] \geq [Cl_2]_{lim}$$

with: $K_{mort}([Cl_2])$ = mortality rate for suspended bacteria, Ao, A, B = constants, $[Cl_2]$ = chlorine concentration, $[Cl_2]_{lim}$ = chlorine limiting concentration for bactericidal action.

Figure 2 shows the results of two experiments performed in a jar with free viable bacteria (HPC - R2A media) in finished water. A good agreement between simulation and measurement is obtained that confirms the accuracy of the chlorine bactericidal model.

Modelling of chlorine action on fixed bacteria: to model the action of chlorine on the fixed biomass and its stronger resistance compared with that of the free biomass, the diffusion of the chlorine through the boundary layer and the biofilm has been taken into account. This calculation of the average penetration depth of the chlorine front into the biofilm enables the identification of two layers: a chlorinated layer and a layer not reached by the chlorine, which provides a material indication of the better resistance of the fixed biomass (Figure 3). This modelling approach is in accordance with experiments reported by De Beer *et al.* (1994), which indicate that the limited penetration of chlorine into the biofilm is likely to be an important factor influencing the reduced efficiency of this biocide against fixed bacteria as compared with its action against planktonic cells.

Detachment modelling

As detachment is a key phenomenon in the modelling of bacterial dynamics in distribution systems, the influence of different formulations of detachment kinetics on the model results were determined by literal calculations in steady state conditions. Three different modelling approaches were tested:

- M1: detachment rate is a constant (Characklis & Marshall 1989)

detachment = $K_{det}.E.Z$

- M2: detachment occurs only at the biofilm / fluid interface or at a fixed distance from the biofilm surface (Stewart 1993)

$$\text{detachment} = K_{det}.V_{max}.\frac{S_b}{S_b + K_s}.E.Z$$

- M3: local detachment frequency is assumed to be constant throughout the biofilm and is purely growth associated (Stewart 1993)

$$\text{detachment} = K_{det}.V_{max}.\frac{S_b}{S_b + K_s}.E^2.Z$$

where Kdet: detachment rate coefficient, Sb: nutrient concentration in biofilm, E: biofilm thickness, Z: mass cell density in biofilm, Vmax: maximum consumption rate, Ks: Monod half-saturation coefficient.

Table 1 illustrates the influence of M1, M2, M3 formulations on the expression of the percentage of viable fixed bacteria (biofilm activity), assuming that:

1. The deposition of free bacteria has little influence in relation to biofilm detachment.
2. The release of BDOC from dead bacteria has little influence in relation to BDOC supplied in the liquid.
3. The consumption of BDOC by free bacteria has little influence in relation to that of fixed bacteria.
4. The growth of free bacteria has little influence in relation to fixed bacteria growth and detachment.

For the layer not reached by chlorine, only M3 gives an expression of the percentage of viable fixed bacteria as a function of substrate concentration. For the chlorinated layer, only M1 leads to an expression of the percentage of viable bacteria as an inverse proportion of chlorine concentration. As a result, detachment modelling in the chlorinated layer is expressed by M1, and by M3 in the layer not reached by chlorine.

Coupling with a hydraulic computer model

The model has been interfaced with PICCOLO software, the SAFEGE hydraulic calculation model (Bos & Jarrige 1989). It is constructed by using hydraulic results previously generated by PICCOLO and a numerical scheme to predict the bacterial count at each node and on each link of a network (Figure 4). Installed on a PC computer, the model uses the graphic interface of PICCOLO and provides an effective and easy way to visualise on a computer screen water quality variations in the network, using a colour code for bacterial count, nutrient concentration and chlorine residual (Piriou *et al.* 1996).

Model validation

Model validation using a pipe loop system

To validate this model, we first used experiments performed in the pipe loop system, under steady state conditions (Figure 5) under various operating conditions. Each loop of the pilot is modelled as a perfectly mixed reactor (Piriou & Levi 1994). The staging of residence time is obtained by placing several loops in series. During the experiments, the pilot facility consisted of three loops in series and the contact time in each loop was 6 hours. Most of the model constants are taken from typical values in the literature. A first fitting was performed with a set of data to adjust model parameters. To validate the calibration, simulations were performed with another set of data obtained for different operating conditions.

Figure 6 shows the evolution of free total and viable bacteria versus residence time, for an experiment without chlorine. Total bacteria counts were determined using epifluorescence microscopy after DAPI staining, and viable bacteria counts by pour plate with R2A media (Reasonner *et al.* 1985). Figure 7 shows, for the same water quality, the evolution of the viable and total bacteria versus residence time and also the fate of the BDOC. For each parameter, the comparison between simulations and measurements indicates a good agreement between these two data values.

Figure 8 shows the evolution of free viable bacteria, for an initial chlorine concentration of 0.7 $mgCl_2/l$. We also notice that the model fits well with the measurement data which confirms the accuracy of the model PICCOBIO®.

Full-scale network model validation

Validation of the model in full-scale distribution systems of different sizes and levels of detail has also been performed. For example, the model has been validated on part of the distribution system of the city of Marseille (South of FRANCE). The treatment plant production flow rate is 1 m^3/s, which represents one fifth of the total consumption of the city of Marseille. The distribution system is composed of 910 links, 40 nodes and 7 reservoirs. Model validation has been carried out by means of measurement campaigns. 5 campaigns have been done during one year on 15 sampling sites (Figure 9). Sampling was done using fire hydrants. Bacteria concentrations were determined using epifluorescence microscopy after DAPI staining for total bacteria counts and CTC staining for viable bacteria counts (Rodriguez *et al.* 1992).

The initial chlorine concentration at the outlet of the treatment was around 0.1ppm Cl_2 and chlorine disappeared very rapidly in the distribution system of the city of Marseille. Figure 10 illustrates results obtained for two different measurement campaigns and shows the good relationship between simulated and measured active bacteria counts (r^2=0.795, n=15).

Simulations on a straight pipe and in full-scale networks

To determine the impact of different water quality parameters such as temperature, BDOC or chlorine on bacterial regrowth, simulations were carried out in a straight pipe of a 4-inch diameter for a 72hour residence time.

The influence of temperature can be represented by plotting the maximum value of bacteria counts obtained during the 72hour residence time simulation in relation to the different temperatures tested (figure 11). The maximum value of bacteria counts is a way of expressing the bacterial regrowth potential in the different operating conditions. According to this representation, bacterial counts significantly increase for temperatures higher than 15°C. As a result, a temperature around 15°C can be proposed for biological stability in the network. The BDOC concentration for each simulation is 0.5mg/l, which is a relatively high value to ensure that the amount of available nutrient is not a limiting factor.

Using the same representation, the maximum value of bacteria counts is plotted according to the different BDOC concentrations tested (figure 11). Nothing occurs for BDOC values lower than 0.2mg/l. As a result, a BDOC of 0.2mg/l can be proposed for biological stability in the network. The temperature for each simulation is 25°C to enhance all the kinetic phenomena.

To determine the level of chlorine that needs to be maintained to avoid bacterial regrowth, simulations were carried out in the straight pipe of a 4 inch diameter for a 72h residence time and the chlorine residual was maintained at the same level in the whole pipe. Using the previous representation, the maximum value of bacteria counts is plotted according to the different chlorine concentrations tested (figure 12). As a result, a chlorine residual level of 0.1mg HClO/l can be proposed for biological stability in the network, because the main effect of chlorine is noticed between 0 and 0.1 mg/l of hypochlorous acid. The BDOC concentration for each simulation is 0.5mg/l and the temperature is 25°C, which are relatively high values to ensure that chlorine is the only influencing factor.

Using the PICCOBIO® model, we can also evaluate the impact of different operating conditions on full-scale distribution systems. For example, the city of Cholet, in the west of France (60,000 inhabitants), has a network of around 2000 nodes and links, for which we have simulated the improvement of bacteria water quality due to booster chlorination application (Figure 13). Figure 14 shows the comparison between bacterial count distribution for 0.8mg/l Cl_2 only applied at the treatment plant and 0.6 mg/l Cl_2 at the treatment plant + 0.4 mg/l Cl_2 at the booster chlorine site. We notice that booster chlorination significantly improves water quality (reduction of 10% of the higher bacteria counts).

On the same network, we have also investigated the impact of a 2 times reduction of BDOC at the inlet of the network, due to an improvement in the treatment processes (figure 15). We notice that BDOC reduction significantly improves water quality (reduction of 35% of the higher bacteria counts) and its impact is higher than booster chlorination for this network where the spreading of chlorine is difficult.

Conclusion

The bacterial regrowth model PICCOBIO® is an unique tool for the study, diagnosis and management of water quality in distribution networks. Through its possibilities for simulating and visualising bacteria counts on the scale of real networks, it enables an evaluation of the impact of changes in water quality or in the operation of the network.

The tool can be used:

- To propose network management strategies and determine of booster chlorination sites.

- To propose treatment plant management strategies by enabling an evaluation of the impact on the network of the choices made for treatment process modification.
- To define a sampling strategy to ensure a more rational monitoring of the network.

This bacterial growth model already exists in steady state conditions and in non steady state conditions, on the scale of a straight pipe. The incorporation of the non steady state bacterial regrowth module in PICCOLO will form the subject of forthcoming work concerning the enrichment of this tool.

REFERENCES

1. Albrich, J.K. Hurst. 1982. Oxidative inactivation of *Escherichia coli* by hypochlorous acid. *F.E.M.S. Lett.*, **144**, 157-161.
2. Barrette, J.M. Albrich, J.K. Hurst. 1987. Hypochlorous acid promoted loss of metabolic energy in *Escherichia coli*. *Infect. Immun.*, **55**, 2518-2525.
3. Bos, P.A. Jarrige. 1989. Mathematical modelling of water distribution networks under steady state conditions - recent development future projects. *Aqua*, **38**, 352.
4. G. Characklis, K.C. Marshall. 1989. *Biofilms. Ed. John Wiley and Sons*, New york. ISBN 0-471-82663-4.
5. DeBeer, R. Srinivasan, P.S. Stewart. 1994. Direct measurement of chlorine penetration into biofilms during disinfection. *J.Appl.Env.Microbiol.*, 60, **12**, 4339.
6. Dukan, Y. Levi, P. Piriou, F. Guyon, P. Villon. 1996. Dynamic modelling of bacterial growth in a drinking water network. *Wat.Res.*, 30, **9**, 1991.
7. Kiene, W. Lu, Y. Levi. 1993. Parameters governing the rate of chlorine decay throughout a distribution system, *Proc. AWWA WQTC*, San Antonio, 503.
8. Levi, J.C. Joret. 1990. Importance of bioeliminable dissolved organic carbon (BDOC) control in strategies for maintaining the quality of drinking water during distribution. *Proc. AWWA WQTC*, San Diego, 1267.
9. Mckenna, K.J.A. DAVIES. 1988. The inhibition of bacterial growth by hypochlorous acid. *J. Biochem.*, **254**, 685-692.
10. Payment, L. Richardson, M.J. Ewardes., E. Franco. 1991. A randomized trial to estimate the risk of gastro intestinal disease due to the consumption of water meeting current microbiological standards. *Am. J. Public Health*, 81, **6**, 703.
11. Piriou, Y. Levi. 1994. A new tool for the study of the evolution of water quality in drinking water distribution systems: design of a network pilot. *Proc. AWWA Ann. Conf.*, New York, 543.
12. Piriou, S. Dukan, Y. Levi, F. Guyon, P. Villon. 1996. Modelling free and fixed bacterial biomass behavior in drinking water distribution systems. *Rev. Sci. Eau*, 1996, **3**, 381.
13. J. Reasoner, E. E. Geldreich. 1985. A new medium for the enumeration and subculture of bacteria from potable water. *Appl. Env. Microbiol.*, **1**, 1-7.
14. G. Rodriguez, D. Phipps, K. Ishiguro, H. F. Ridgway. 1992. Use of fluorescent redox probe for direct visualization of actively respiring bacteria. *Appl. Env. Microbiol.*, **6**, 1801-1808.

15. Thomas. 1979. Myeloperoxydase hydrogen peroxide chloride antimicrobial system: Effect of exogenous amines on antibacterial action against E. coli. *Infect.Immun.*, **25**, 110-116.

16. Thomas. 1979. Myeloperoxydase hydrogen peroxide chloride antimicrobial system: Nitrogen-chlorine derivatives of bacterial components in bacterial cation against E. coli. *Infect.Immun.*, **23**, 522-531.

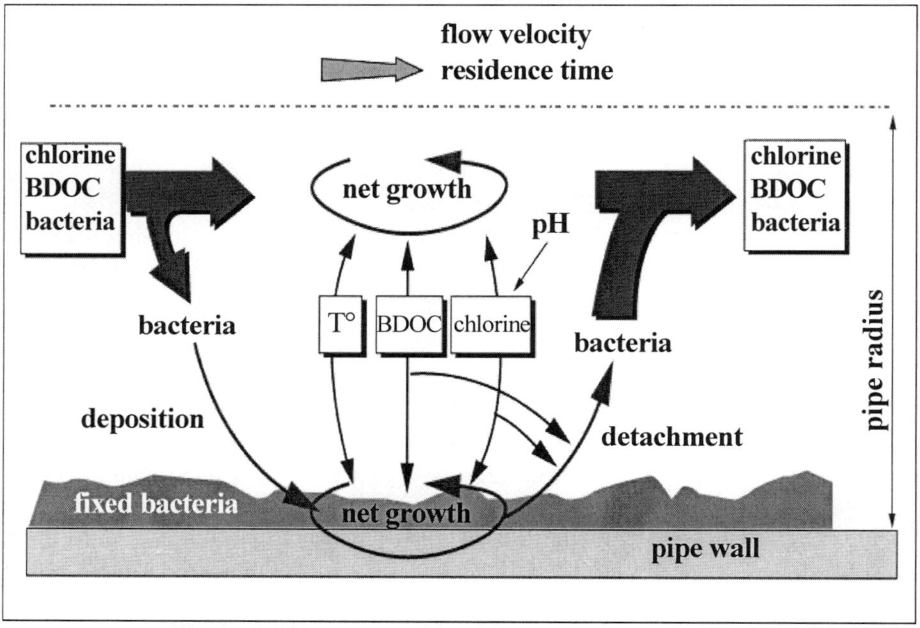

Figure 1. *Phenomena taken into account by the model*

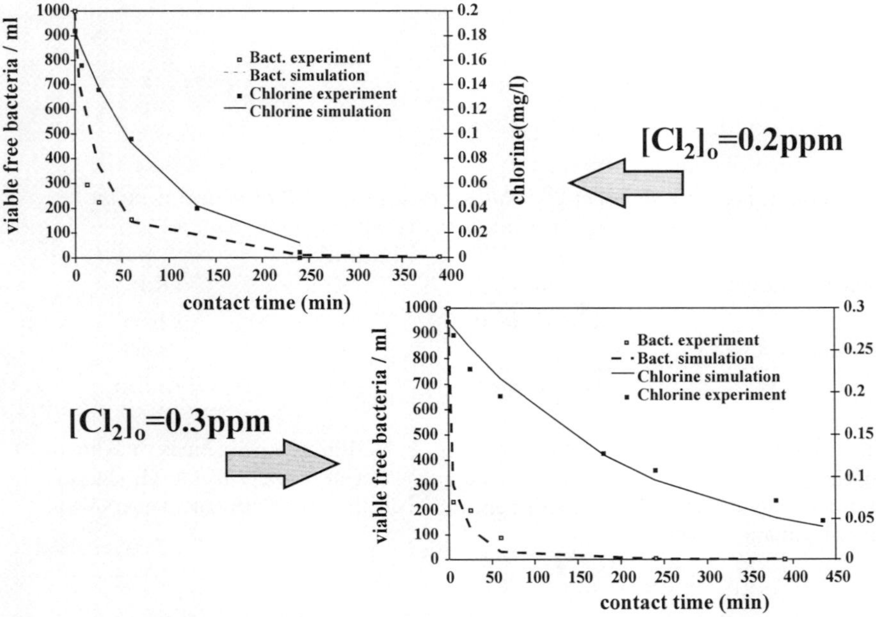

***Figure 2**. Impact of chlorine on suspended bacteria: comparison between measurements and simulation for viable free bacteria (HPC-R2A, finished water, T°=20°C*

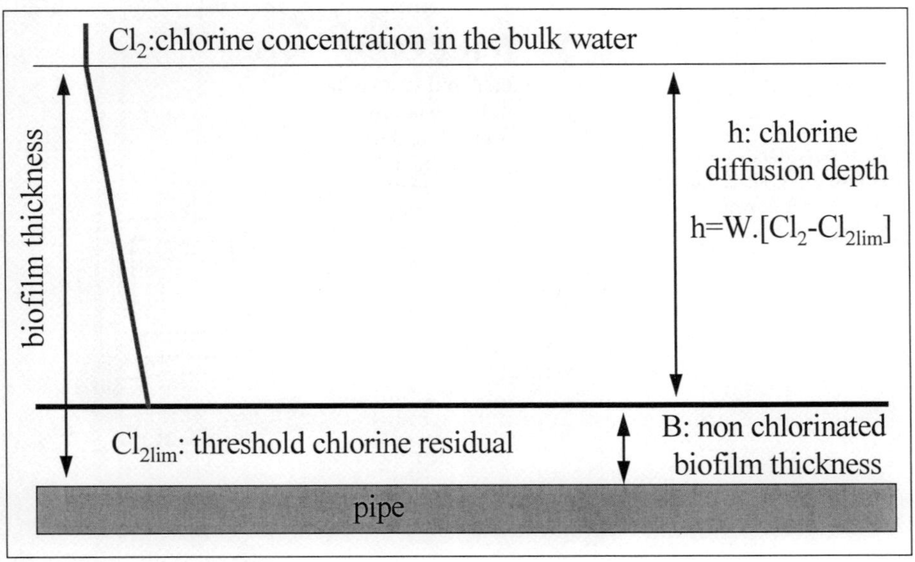

***Figure 3**. Chlorine bactericidal action modelling on fixed biomas*

Table 1. *Impact of different formulations of detachment rate modelling on the expression of the percentage of active bacteria in the biofilm*

	Model 1	*Model 2*	*Model 3*
non chlorinated layer	$\frac{Kdet}{Kdet + Kmort}$	$\frac{Kdet}{r.\,bmax}$	$\frac{Kdet}{r.\,bmax}.\,E(y)$
chlorinated layer	$\frac{Kdet}{Kdet + Kmort + G(y)}$	$\frac{Kdet}{r.\,bmax}$	$\frac{Kdet}{r.\,bmax}.\,h(y)$

Sb: average concentration of BDOC in biofilm, E: biofilm thickness, bmax: maximum consumption rate, Ks: Monod half saturation coefficient, r: yield factor, G: chlorine mortality rate for biofilm, h: chlorine penetration depth, Kdet: detachment coefficient, Kmort: natural mortality rate.

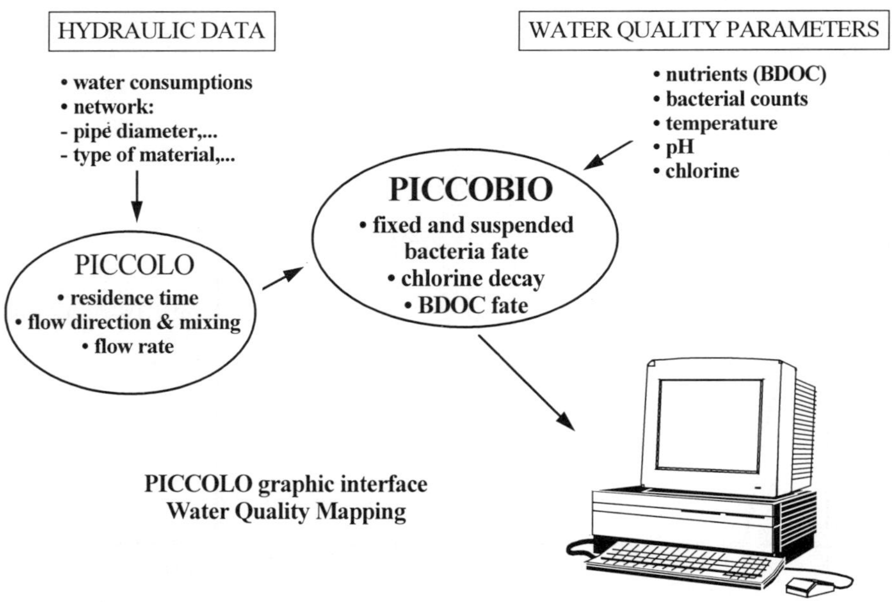

Figure 4. *Coupling of the model with an hydraulic calculation software: PICCOLO*

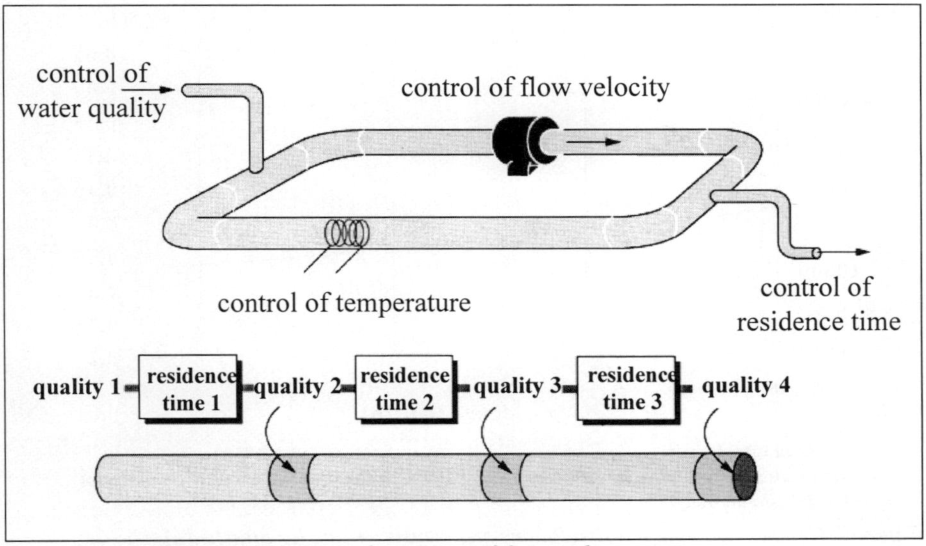

Figure 5. Schematic description of the pipe loop system

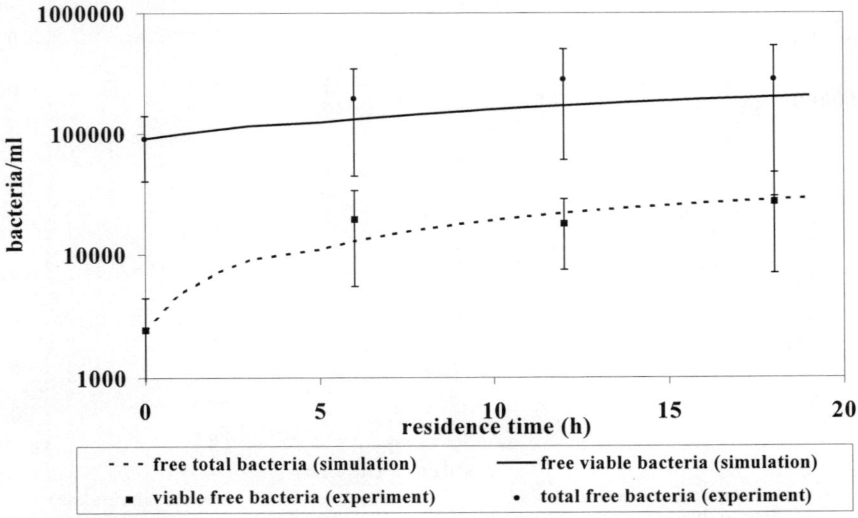

Figure 6. Comparison between simulations and measurements for free viable (HPC-R2A) and total bacteria (DAPI) versus residence time (T=20°C - BDOC=0.4mg/l - Cl_2=0)

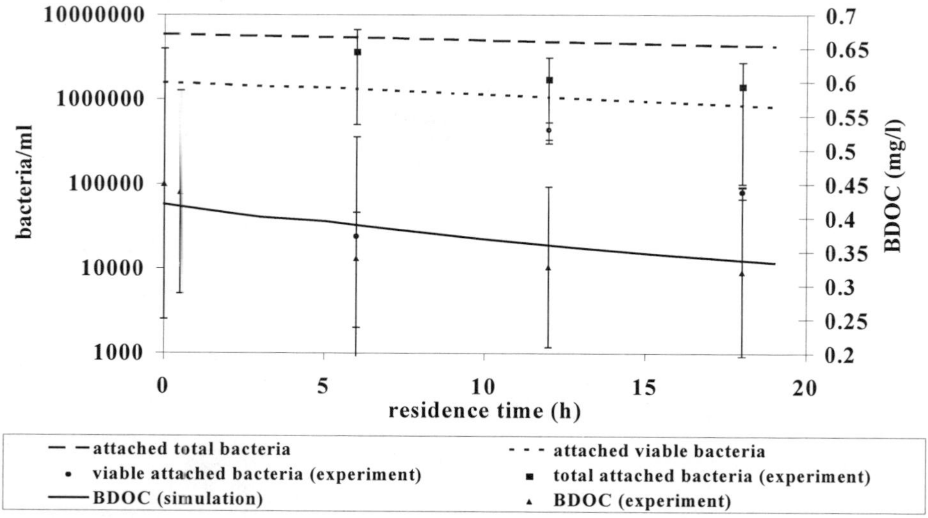

Figure 7. *Comparison between simulations and measurements for attached viable (HPC-R2A) and total bacteria (DAPI) versus residence time (T=20°C - BDOC=0.4mg/l - Cl_2=0)*

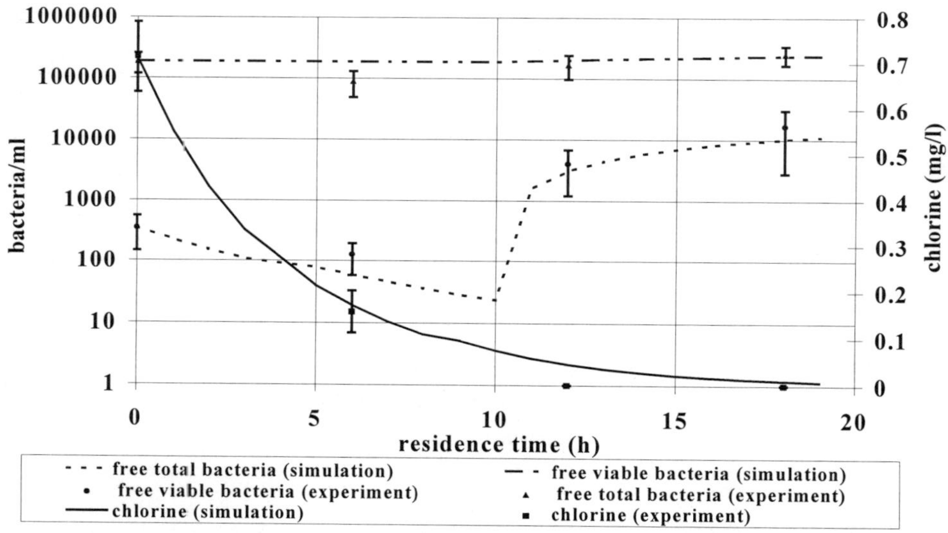

Figure 8. *Comparison between simulations and measurements for free viable (HPC-R2A) and total bacteria (DAPI) versus residence time (T=20°C - BDOC=0.45mg/l - Cl_2=0.7mg/l)*

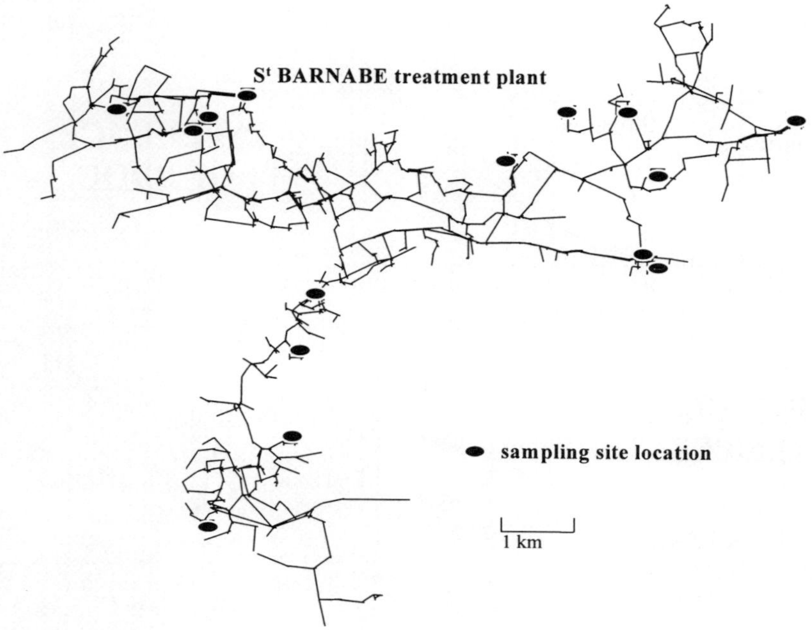

Figure 9. Network of the city of Marseille: location of the sampling sites

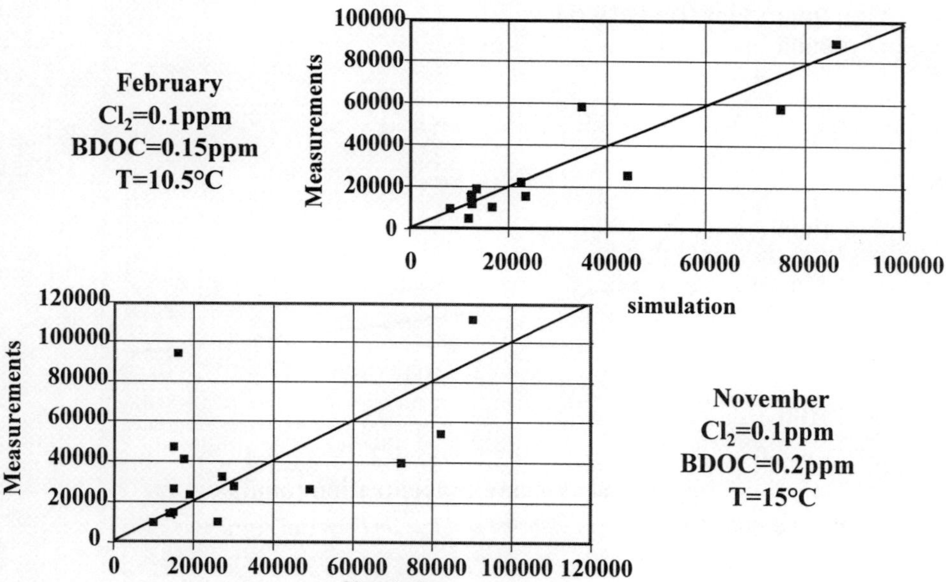

Figure 10. Marseille distribution system: comparison between measurement results and simulation of free viable bacteria (CTC) for two sampling campaigns

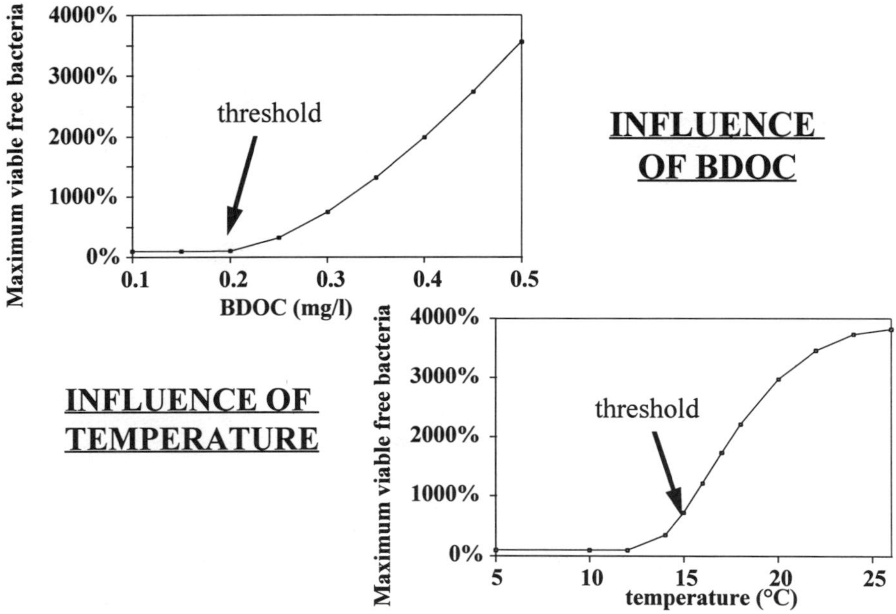

Figure 11. *Influence of temperature and BDOC on bacterial regrowth*

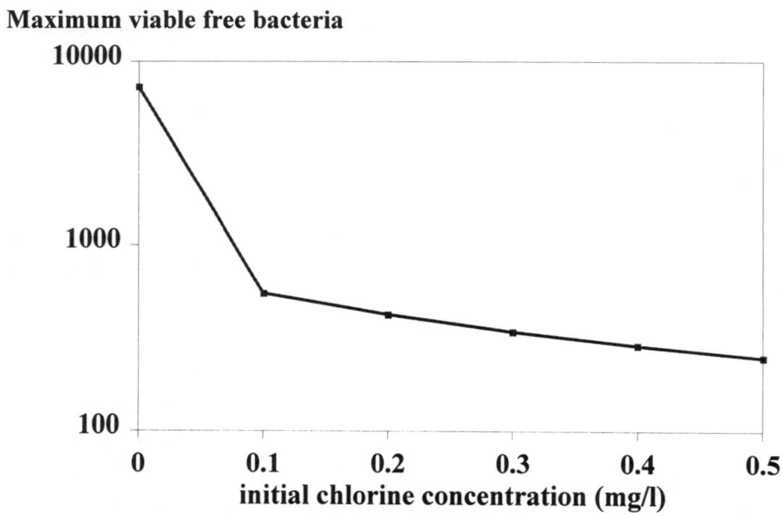

***Figure 12**. Influence of chlorine residual on bacterial regrowth*

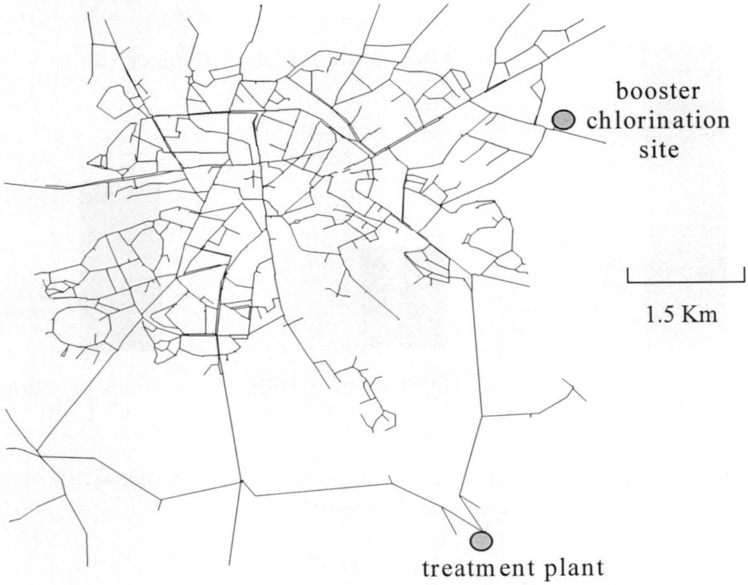

Figure13. *Network of the city of Cholet: location of the chlorination site*

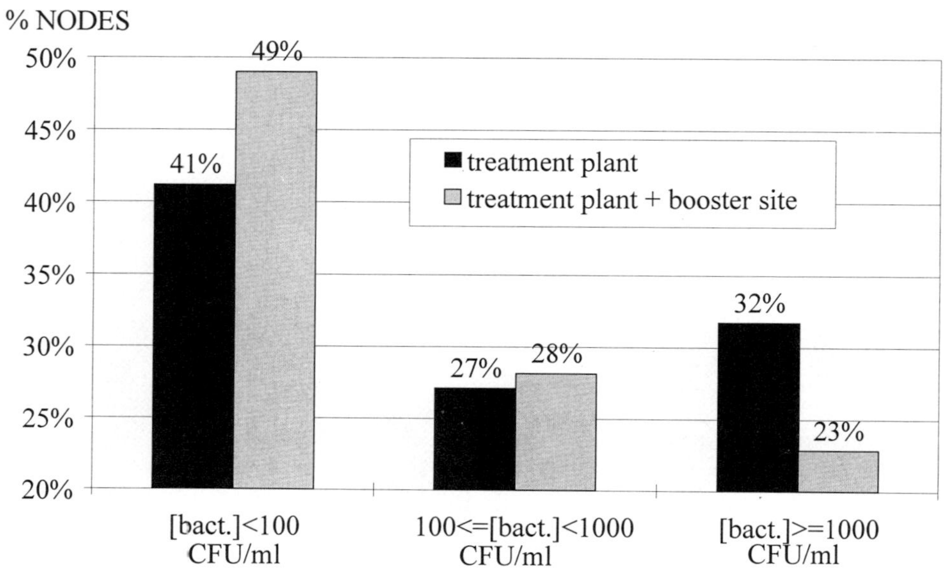

***Figure 14**. Simulation of the impact of chlorine booster on the distribution of bacteria counts in the network*

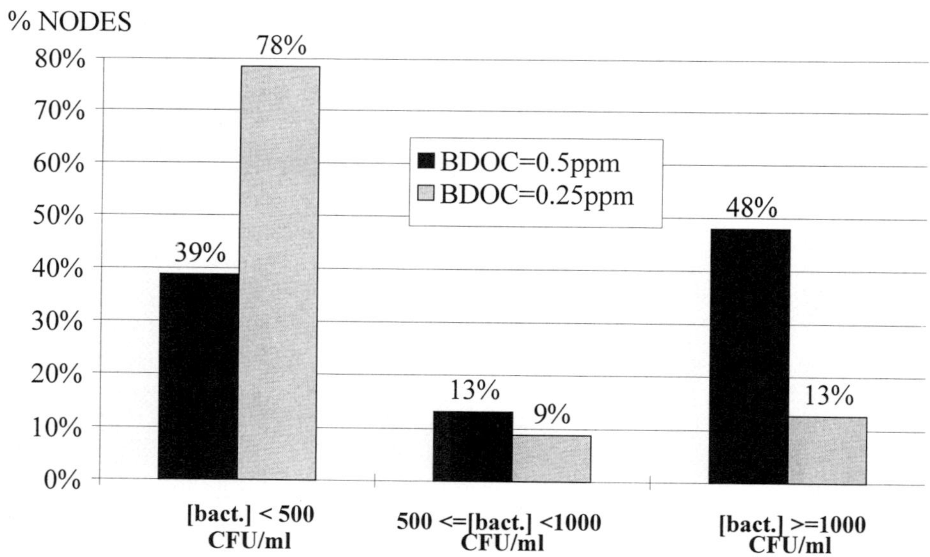

***Figure 15**. Simulation of the impact of BDOC reduction on the distribution of bacteria counts in the network*

CHAPTER 24

Behaviour of Monochloramine in a Pipe Test Rig

S.H.Maier, R.S.Powell *and* C.A.Woodward

1 Introduction

In recent years there has been an increasing awareness of the importance of maintaining water quality in water distribution systems [4, 3]. This has given rise to the need to utilise computer models to simulate changes in water quality in order to predict and control water quality throughout distribution networks [8].

The definition of water quality is by no means straightforward. Generally it is perceived to be a collection of upper or lower limits on selected possible contaminants of water [22, 2]. Thus a wide range of substances and physical parameters could be considered; however, the models presented in the literature frequently concentrate on water age, the propagation of conservative substances (e.g. particulate matter) or reactive chemical substances, such as disinfectants, as in [8, 17, 25] among others.

A number of results concerning suspended biomass and nutrient content, e.g. [11, 1], or effects of biofilms, for instance [5, 24, 23], have been published, but, to the authors' knowledge, no mathematical models of the processes in water pipes incorporating bacteria have been published until recently [6].

Despite the central role played by microbiological aspects, there is still a case for detailed investigations into disinfectant (i.e. free chlorine or monochloramine) behaviour within a distribution network. Free chlorine or total chlorine is a practical indicator of water quality since it is readily measured by online meters and the effectiveness of this type of disinfectant against bacteria is widely acknowledged, see, e.g., [12, 26].

The experiments described in this work focus on both microbiological (i.e. suspended bacteria and biofilm) and chemical (i.e. disinfectant residual) water quality. This chapter concentrates on disinfectant (monochloramine) decay characteristics while initial results concerning microbiological water quality are presented in [14, 15].

2 Monochloramine Kinetics

Most work on disinfection kinetics is concerned with free chlorine (Cl_2 or $HOCl^-$). It was originally assumed that free chlorine decays according to first order reaction kinetics, which implies a decrease in the concentration of free chlorine $c(t)$ according to

$$c(t_2) = c(t_1) \cdot \mathrm{e}^{-k(t_2-t_1)} \tag{1}$$

where t, t_1, t_2 represent travel time; thus the decay of free chlorine is characterised by just one (constant) decay coefficient k.

In recent years, however, more evidence has been published that shows simple first order kinetics do not fully match the behaviour of free chlorine in a distribution system. Lungwitz et al. [13] investigated booster (impulse) chlorination and found that they had to postulate several decay coefficients depending on the chlorine gradient. Schneider et al. [20] concluded that the decay coefficient (and possibly other parameters) are flow dependent. Woodward et al. [27] found experimentally that the monochloramine decay coefficient changes with flow rate. Heraud et al. [9] used different decay coefficients depending on pipe materials and diameter to fit their model to the data.

Simulation packages reflect these findings to some extent. EPANET [17, 18] includes a wall demand and a flow dependent mass transfer coefficient. Thus it replaces the constant decay coefficient k with

$$k = k_b + \frac{k_f k_w}{R_H(k_f + k_w)} \tag{2}$$

where k_f is a flow dependent mass transfer coefficient, k_b, k_w are constant, representing bulk and wall demand, respectively, and R_H is the hydraulic radius. In PICCOLO [19] it is possible to use a chlorine decay coefficient, K_{H20}, which depends on total organic carbon and temperature, or to use diameter dependent decay coefficients within the distribution system.

Monochloramine (NH_2Cl) is generally believed to behave in the same fashion as free chlorine, except that it reacts more slowly than free chlorine [26], although it was suggested that monochloramine is more efficient against biofilms than free chlorine [24]. In the present study monochloramine is investigated since it is used in the London distribution system; it also finds application in other water networks worldwide, e.g. [21].

It is generally impossible to directly measure monochloramine online. Thus total chlorine, which includes free chlorine, monochloramine, and organic chloramines, is measured using online meters. When ammonia is added in the correct ratio to free chlorine residuals, there will be no free chlorine left. However, organic chloramines, in addition to monochloramine, are generally still present in the water. These organic chloramines are relatively stable and have very low bacterial action [7] and thus are considered as a constant fraction of total chlorine in this work.

Thus first order kinetics, as in fig. 1, are obtained, which can be described as

$$c(t_2) = (c(t_1) - c_\infty) \cdot \mathrm{e}^{-k(t_2 - t_1)} + c_\infty. \tag{3}$$

As elaborated earlier, it may, however, be more realistic to replace the constant coefficient k by a function depending on flow, pipe materials, and possibly other variables. In this work the dependencies on flow and inlet chlorine concentration are investigated.

3 Experimental Work

3.1 Experimental Set-Up and Measurement Methods

The pipe-rig owned by Thames Water at Kempton Park was used as a flow controlled, large-scale, experimental drinking water distribution system.

This pipe rig is the only once-through, large-scale pilot facility in the world. It consists of a 1.3 km, 110 mm inside diameter pipe distribution system built of approved construction materials. It is divided into three sections of approximate length 500 m, 400 m and 400 m, respectively, which are buried 0.5-1.0 m underground. After each buried section, the water passes through a 24 m experimental testing station with facilities for on-line monitoring, water sampling and for studying the performance of pipe materials. In addition there is a sampling station with on-line meters at the pipe rig inlet. Measurements were taken at the inlet of the pipe-rig (i.e. at the balancing tank or shortly thereafter) and at three sampling points along the rig. Both grab samples and on-line meters were employed. The design and construction of this test distribution system are described in [10].

Measurements and instrumentation were as follows.

- Heterotrophic plate counts (R_2A agar, 7 days, 22^0C).
- Epifluorescence microscopy counts using acridine orange.
- Particle counters ("Versacount" from Hiac/Royco).
- Total chlorine meters ("Medway" from Portacel) and bench titrations using diethyl-p-phenylene diamine (DPD).
- Electromagnetic flow meter (Krohne).
- pH and temperature meters ("Meredian" from Leeds & Northrup).

This work concentrates on the total chlorine meters and titrations. Sample bottles of inlet water were also taken to facilitate a comparison between the chlorine decay in the pipe rig and the pure bulk decay.

3.2 Experiment

The experiment took about five months of preparation and seven months of actual data gathering. It consisted of 12 sharp flow increases lasting from 12 hours to three days and subsequent decreases to previous flow values (step flow trials). Furthermore there were four step chlorine trials. It was intended to investigate both microbiological and chemical water quality, thus chlorine was present only in the last four months of the experiment. The experimental schedule is depicted in fig. 2.

4 Meter Error Characteristics

The chlorine meters used during these experiments measure total chlorine by passing water through an electrolytic cell containing a gold and a copper electrode. The current produced by the electrolytic action is proportional to the concentration of chlorine in the water. The manufacturer implies the accuracy of the meters as ± 0.05 mg/l at a Full Scale Deflection of 2 mg/l. Analysis of our data suggests that this performance is easily obtained in the short term but that the instruments were subject to some long term drift. The chlorine residual measured in the considered system is generally in the range 0.05 and 0.4 mg/l i.e. fairly close to the limit of the meter range.

Potential errors associated with meter drift can be quite significant with respect to the measured signal. Therefore it is important to correct this as far as possible before attempting to calculate the decay coefficient(s). This was done by comparing the meter readings against those from titrations, a bench analysis which yields values for free chlorine, monochloramine and dichloramine. The sum of these measurements is called total chlorine. Although there are errors associated with titrations, it is generally assumed that they are not systematic and may be considered to give the 'true' chlorine concentrations of the system. To minimise errors as much as possible replicate titrations were performed (i.e. 3 to 5 titrations of the same water sample). After discarding outliers, the averages of the remaining titration values are used in the meter data correction procedure as detailed in the following.

It has been assumed that the (averaged) titration values give the 'true' total chlorine concentrations, whereas the meters are incorrect. It is further assumed that the error in the meter readings is due to a relatively slow meter drift. The aim is to find this error signal by using titration results, then adjust the meter reading values as appropriate. Since a titration is a bench analysis, titration values are unequally spaced and relatively rare (between one to five values a day, no values on weekends). However, if the error signal varies only slowly, the Nyquist theorem is still satisfied (i.e. there are at least two samples per period of the error signal). This assumption is reasonable, as indicated by the Fourier spectrum of a typical meter error function as depicted in fig. 3. The absolute value of the Fourier transforms decreased in that case at a frequency of 0.3 1/day to 2 % of its maximum value at zero frequency. One possible procedure to preprocess the data to correct these errors is outlined below.

The multiplicative error function $\epsilon_M(t_i)$ is calculated as the ratio between the titration data $x_b(t_i)$ and the chlorine meter data $x_m(t)$. It is

$$\epsilon_M(t_i) = \frac{x_b(t_i)}{x_m(t = t_i)}, \tag{4}$$

where t_i denotes the unequally spaced time instants of the titrations, t represents, for brevity, the equally and closely spaced time instants of the meter readings.

To reconstruct the error function between the time instants t_i, $\epsilon_M(t_i)$ is at first interpolated within recalibration windows:

$$\epsilon_M^{IW}(t) = \sum_{i=1}^{m} \epsilon_M(t_i) \cdot \ell_i(t), \tag{5}$$

where $\ell_i(t)$ denotes a linear interpolation function for time instant t_i. The superscript I indicates that $\epsilon_M^{IW}(t)$ is an interpolated signal; the superscript W refers to recalibration time windowing, i.e. the total error signal is split up into a set of functions limited by two recalibration times. This is necessary since recalibrations introduce sharp changes in chlorine readings which have to be preserved in the following filtering stage.

Finally the error function $\epsilon_M^{IW}(t)$ is filtered, in accordance with the assumption of slow varying error, to remove any high frequency noise and to smooth the signal. Thus we obtain

$$\epsilon_M^{IWF}(t) = \epsilon_M^{IW}(t) * b_5(t), \tag{6}$$

where $*$ denotes the convolution sum of the discrete Fourier transform and $b_5(t)$ is the impulse response of a fifth order Butterworth filter. In this case, a zero-phase distortion Butterworth filter (no time shift between filtered and unfiltered signals) was chosen with a fairly arbitrary (cf. fig. 3) cut-off frequency of 0.3 1/day.

Since the sampling frequency of the meters is adjustable, another interpolation step might be necessary at this point.

A typical example of the correction obtained with this procedure is given in fig. 4. In the time period investigated in this work the maximal absolute error is reduced from 0.21 mg/l to 0.098 mg/l, and the maximal mean square error from 0.086 mg/l to 0.035 mg/l.

Other correction procedures are also possible. For instance, one may consider additive errors, or reverse the calibrations and then use different windows or no windows. These possibilities were investigated but generally gave the same or worse results. In all cases each method did not perform satisfactorily at some point within the data.

Other approaches, like using the unequally spaced data without interpolation or other types of interpolating functions are possible topics of further research.

5 Determination of Decay Coefficients

Two possible descriptions of monochloramine decay as in eq. (3) were studied.

1) $k_1 = k = \text{const.}$

2) $k_2 = k_b + \frac{k_f k_w}{R_H(k_f + k_w)}$, as in EPANET.

To calibrate both models the unknown parameters k and c_∞ (case 1) or k_b, k_w and c_∞ (case 2) have to be found such that the data fits a model according to eq. (3).

If only free chlorine and a single decay coefficient as in case 1 are considered, it is possible to reduce this problem to a linear regression by taking the natural logarithm on both sides of eq. (1) and estimating $\ln c(t_1)$ and k. A weighted least-squares algorithm should be used to remove the bias introduced by taking the logarithm.

However, if one attempts to estimate c_∞ as well, or if a decay coefficient as in case 2 is considered (i.e. including an unknown k_w), this approach is no longer feasible; instead, a nonlinear optimisation problem has to be solved.

In the case of a single decay coefficient it has the following form. Find the minimum over k and c_∞ of

$$J_1 = \sqrt{\sum_i (y_i - g_1(t = t_i))^2}, \tag{7}$$

with

$$g_1(t = t_i) = (y_{0,i} - c_\infty) \exp(-k t_i) + c_\infty, \tag{8}$$

where y_i is the ith chlorine meter reading, t_i the travel time of the considered aliquot of water from the pipe rig inlet, and $y_{0,i}$ the respective reading of the inlet chlorine meter for the time when this aliquot started its travel.

In case 2 flow and diameter dependent terms k_f and R_H are included. It is invalid to use a decay coefficient as in eq. (2) in eq. (3) unless there is no change in flow while the travel time $t_2 - t_1$ is covered. Since the travel times in our case are determined by the fixed location of the meters, and therefore the flow rate cannot be chosen to be arbitrarily small, a step in flow will invalidate the model in the vicinity of the change. Therefore an accumulation of small time steps Δt in which the flow is constant is considered. Thus eq. (3) becomes

$$c(t_i) = (c(t_0) - c_\infty) \exp\left(-k_b t_i - \sum_{j=0}^{n_i} \frac{k_f(j) k_w}{R_H(j)(k_f(j) + k_w)} \Delta t(j)\right) + c_\infty, \qquad (9)$$

where n_i is defined through the travel time t_i,

$$t_i = \sum_{j=0}^{n_i} \Delta t(j). \qquad (10)$$

Note that in the pipe rig the hydraulic radius does not change, thus $R_H(j) = R_H = \text{const}$.

The resulting optimization problem is to find a minimum over all k_b, k_w and c_∞ of

$$J_2 = \sqrt{\sum_i (y_i - g_2(t = t_i))^2}, \qquad (11)$$

with

$$g_2(t = t_i) = (y_{0,i} - c_\infty) \exp\left(-k_b t_i - \sum_{j=0}^{n_i} \frac{k_f(j) k_w}{R_H(k_f(j) + k_w)} \Delta t(j)\right) + c_\infty, \qquad (12)$$

and

$$t_i = \sum_{j=0}^{n_i} \Delta t(j). \qquad (13)$$

where y_i, t_i, and $y_{0,i}$ are defined as above.

Minimizing these cost functions concerning c_∞ and k_w poses some generic problems. Estimation of c_∞ is very difficult if data points are only available in the initial portion of the exponential decay, as shown in fig. (1). The sensitivity of the estimate of c_∞ on errors in these data points is very high. This leads, in the case of our data, to spurious results, which include physically impossible solutions like large negative values of c_∞. Generally it appears that it is futile to attempt to estimate c_∞ unless the chlorine reading for the largest travel time is close to c_∞.

Hence we must investigate the problem of obtaining c_∞ from a different source. It is possible to get a fairly reliable estimate of the fraction of organic chloramines from a full chlorine speciation. In particular, before ammonia dosing, there is generally assumed to be only free chlorine present besides organic chloramines. In the following, c_∞ is set to the average result of these titrations.

Estimation of k_w poses a different problem. It is only possible if

$$\sum_{j=0}^{n_i} \frac{k_f(j) k_w}{R_H(j)(k_f(j) + k_w)} \Delta t(j) \neq K \cdot t_i, \qquad (14)$$

where K is an arbitrary constant. In other words, either $k_f(j)$ or $R_H(j)$ needs to change within the travel time t_i. Otherwise there remains the problem of estimating

$$J = \sqrt{\sum_i (y_i - (y_{0,i} - c_\infty)\exp(-k_b t_i - K t_i) + c_\infty)^2}. \tag{15}$$

It is not possible to obtain an estimate for both k_b and K from J, only the sum of both can be identified.

Therefore in the following we will attempt to estimate the EPANET decay coefficient (as in case 2) only around flow changes.

To minimize the cost functions J_1 or J_2, a Nelder-Mead type simplex algorithm for nonlinear systems as implemented in MATLAB is employed [16]. It is among the most popular and successful direct search methods which do not require the gradient of the cost function. Roughly speaking the minimum is found by repetitive 'casting of a net'. In more detail, a simplex of order $n+1$ is constructed among the initial values of the n parameters to be estimated. The initial value is iteratively improved by contracting or expanding the simplex and shifting the corner with the highest cost function toward the minimum, for instance, by reflecting the worst corner through an appropriately chosen centroid.

6 Initial Results

Only step flow trials to 0.6 l/s or less were considered for calculation of the decay coefficient, since at higher flows (e.g. 0.9 l/s) all chlorine readings throughout the rig are approximately the same.

Single decay coefficients (k), as in case 1, were calculated within 17 time periods at different flow and chlorine conditions, avoiding outliers in the data where possible. The flow rates investigated were 0.08 l/s, 0.3 l/s, 0.45 l/s, and 0.6 l/s; the inlet chlorine concentrations were approximately 0.4 mg/l and 0.65 mg/l of total chlorine. In every case the chlorine readings were preprocessed as described earlier and each estimate of the decay coefficient was based on five time instants or 15 data points. The final value c_∞ is assumed to be 0.08 mg/l. Two examples of monochloramine decay coefficients are depicted in fig. 5; the means of all 17 decay coefficients together with other relevant data are given in table 1.

As can be seen from table 1 the inlet chlorine concentration has hardly any effect on the decay coefficient. Furthermore there appears to be little or no variation in mean value for the flow rates below 0.6 l/s. At 0.6 l/s we see an increase in decay coefficient by roughly 50 %-100 %, however, the variance of these data increases markedly as well (cf. fig. 5b). It can be seen, from fig. 5, that the values of decay coefficients at low flow (here 0.08 l/s, fig. 5a) are well within the range of the decay coefficients at high flow (0.6 l/s, fig. 5b).

The decay coefficients of case 2 were also investigated. If the variation of the decay coefficient followed this model, the fit of that model would be better than that of a single decay coefficient model. For a flow change from 0.08 l/s to 0.3 l/s, both sets of decay coefficients were calculated, again assuming c_∞=0.08 mg/l. A sample of 1728 data points was used for each estimation.

The results were compared by taking the root mean square error between the data points y_j and the corresponding model output $\bar{y}$

$$E = \sqrt{\frac{1}{N}\sum_{j=1}^{N}(y_j - \bar{y})^2}. \tag{16}$$

The obtained decay coefficients were $k = 0.0393\ \mathrm{h}^{-1}$ (case 1) and $k_b = 0.0380\ \mathrm{h}^{-1}$ and $k_w = 5.55 \cdot 10^{-7}$m/s (case 2). The root mean square errors were $E_1 =$ 0.01253 mg/l and $E_2 =$ 0.01245 mg/l, an improvement of only 0.6 %. From this result it appears that there is hardly any benefit in using a decay coefficient as in case 2 in the investigated circumstances.

Although we see a relatively large variability of the simple first order decay coefficient, this does not appear to be related to flow or chlorine changes. Thus, it appears that the simple decay coefficient describes the monochloramine decay adequately. In particular, there is in this case no need to use a more complicated coefficient as in case 2. It is, however, noted that the investigated step flow trials were undertaken after a series of prior trials. Thus if an increase of decay coefficient were due to an increase in entrained particulate matter or sloughed off biofilm, the previous step flow trials will have decreased that effect. Further research is currently being undertaken to investigate this possibility.

7 Conclusions

In this chapter the issue of meter accuracy and the possible need to correct the meter data before it can be used for model calibration were discussed. A procedure for preprocessing the data was suggested.

The important task of model calibration was subsequently addressed. It appeared that the final value c_∞ can normally not be estimated and that the wall demand of the decay coefficient as used in EPANET is impossible to estimate unless flow or diameter changes take place.

Finally some values of monochloramine decay coefficients were presented. The results considered to date indicate that a single decay constant is sufficient to model the decay in the pipe rig under the investigated circumstances. However, the past history of step flow trials may have changed the conditions in the pipe rig in such a way as to have a decisive impact on this conclusion. Further research is required to establish the statistical significance and error levels and to clarify the range of conditions under which this result is valid.

Acknowledgements

Special thanks go to Jane Buntin, who did a large amount of work, especially concerning the titrations and other sampling. Many thanks also to all the members of the pipe rig team at Thames Water, Anaïck Delanoue, Sarah McMath and David Holt, who were all heavily involved in the experimental work. Furthermore, one of the authors (S.M.) is very grateful to Johannes Andersen for the many helpful discussions.

References

[1] J. C. Block, F. Bois, D. J. Reasoner, M. Dutang, L. Mathieu, J. L. Paquin, and J. Maillard. Disinfection of drinking water distribution systems. *Water Supply*, 13(2):1–11, 1995.

[2] R. M. Clark, D. J. Ehreth, and J. J. Convery. Water legislation in the U.S.: an overview of the Safe Drinking Water Act. *Toxicology and Industrial Health: An International Journal*, 7(516):43–52, 1991.

[3] R. M. Clark, J. A. Goodrich, and L. J. Wymer. Effect of the distribution system on drinking-water quality. *Journal Water Supply Research and Technology – Aqua*, 42(1):30–38, 1993.

[4] R. M. Clark, W. M. Grayman, R. M. Males, and J. D. Coyle. Predicting water quality in distribution systems. Technical Report EPA/600/D-86/230, Drinking Water Research Division, U.S. Environmental Protection Agency, Cincinnati, Ohio, Sept. 1986.

[5] R. M. Clark, B. W. Lykins, J. C. Block, L. J. Wymer, and D. J. Reasoner. Water quality changes in a simulated distribution system. *Journal Water Supply Research and Technology – Aqua*, 43(6):263–277, 1994.

[6] S. Dukan, Y. Levi, P. Piriou, F. Guyon, and P. Villon. Dynamic modelling of bacterial growth in drinking water networks. *Water Research*, 30(9):1991–2002, 1996.

[7] T. H. Feng. Behaviour of organic chloramines in disinfection. *J. Water Pollut. Control Fed.*, 38(4):614–627, 1966.

[8] W. M. Grayman and R. M. Clark. An overview of water quality modeling in a distribution system. In *The 1990 Annual Conference Proceedings*, pages 81–92, Cincinnati, Ohio, 1990. American Water Works Association.

[9] J. Heraud, L. Kiéné, M. Detay, and Y. Levi. Optimised modelling of chlorine residuals in a drinking water distribution system with a combination of on-line sensors. *Journal Water Supply Research and Technology – Aqua*, 46(2):59–70, 1997.

[10] D. M. Holt, C. A. Woodward, T. Rachwal, A. Delanaoue, and J. S. Colbourne. A pipe based experimental system to study factors influencing bacterial growth in London's water mains. In *Proceedings of the Water Quality Technical Conference*, San Francisco, 6–10th November 1994. American Water Works Association, Denver.

[11] P. M. Huck. Measurement of biodegradable organic matter and bacterial growth potential in drinking water. *Journal of the American Water Works Association*, 82:78–86, July 1990.

[12] M. W. LeChevallier, C. D. Lowry, and R. G. Lee. Disinfection of biofilms in a model distribution system. In M. W. LeChevallier, B. H. Olson, and G. A. McFeters, editors, *Assessing and Controlling Bacterial Regrowth in Distribution Systems*, chapter 1, pages 1–47. American Water Works Association Research Foundation, 1990.

[13] M. Lungwitz, S. Hopfgarten, K. Chen, M. Brdys, and H. Puta. Modelling and simulation of chlorine concentration in water supply systems for control purposes. In *Proceedings of the 39th International Scientific Colloquium*, Ilmenau, Germany, Sept. 1994.

[14] S. H. Maier, C. A. Woodward, A. Delanoue, D. M. Holt, S. M. McMath, and R. S. Powell. Relationships between total chlorine, particle counts and biofilm detachment in a drinking water distribution system. In C. W. Keevil, editor, *Proceedings of the International Conference on Biofilms in Aquatic Systems*, Coventry, April 13–16 1997. Royal Society of Chemistry.

[15] S. M. McMath, A. Delanoue, D. M. Holt, S. H. Maier, and C. A. Woodward. Importance of "clumps" shed from biofilms in a water distribution system. In C. W. Keevil, editor, *Proceedings of the International Conference on Biofilms in Aquatic Systems*, Coventry, April 13–16 1997. Royal Society of Chemistry.

[16] J. A. Nelder and R. Mead. A simplex method for function minimization. *Comput. J.*, 7:308–313, 1965.

[17] L. A. Rossman. The EPANET water quality model. In B. Coulbeck, editor, *Integrated Computer Applications in Water Supply. Volume 2 – Applications and Implementations for Systems Operation and Management*, pages 79–93. Research Studies Press Ltd., Taunton, England, 1993.

[18] L. A. Rossman. *EPANET User's Manual.* Risk Reduction Engineering Laboratory, U.S. Environmental Protection Agency, Cincinnati, Ohio, Jan. 1994. Version 1.1.

[19] SAFEGE, Consulting Engineers. *Piccolo 3.10 Reference Manual*, November/December 1992.

[20] S. Schneider, M. A. Brdys, H. Puta, and S. Hopfgarten. Modelling of chlorine concentration in water systems directed to integrated operational control. In B. Coulbeck, editor, *Integrated Computer Applications in Water Supply*, pages 143–159, 1993.

[21] P. M. Thomas. Chloramination of water supplies. Progress report no.1, Urban Water Research Association, State Water Laboratory, Engineering and Water Supply Department, S.A., Australia, Jan. 1988.

[22] R. E. Train. *Quality Criteria for Water.* Castle House Pub., London, 1979.

[23] D. van der Kooij and H. R. Veenendaal. Biofilm development on surfaces in drinking water distribution systems. *Water Supply*, 12(1/2):SS1–1 – SS1–7, 1994. Special subject: Biological activity in distribution systems.

[24] E. van der Wende and W. G. Characklis. Biofilms in potable water distribution systems. In A. McFeters, editor, *Drinking Water Microbiology*, chapter 12, pages 249–268. Springer-Verlag, 1990.

[25] O. Wable, N. Dumoutier, J. P. Duguet, P. A. Jarrige, G. Gelas, and J. F. Depierre. Modelling chlorine concentrations in a network and applications to Paris distribution system. In *Water Quality Modeling in Distribution Systems*, pages 77–87, Cincinnati, Ohio, Feb. 1991. American Water Works Association.

[26] G. C. White. *Handbook of Chlorination.* Van Nostrand Reinhold, London, 1972.

[27] C. A. Woodward, C. T. Ta, D. M. Holt, and J. Colbourne. Relationship between observed monochloramine decay rates and other physical and chemical parameters. In *Proceedings of the Water Quality Technology Conference*, New Orleans, 12–16th November 1995. American Water Works Association.

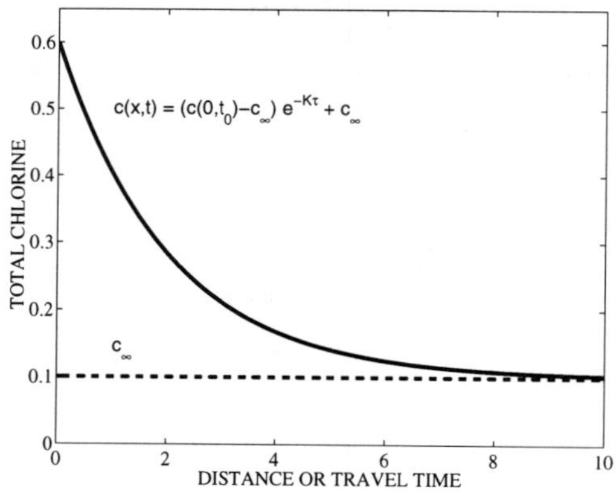

Figure 1. Simple first order decay of total chlorine

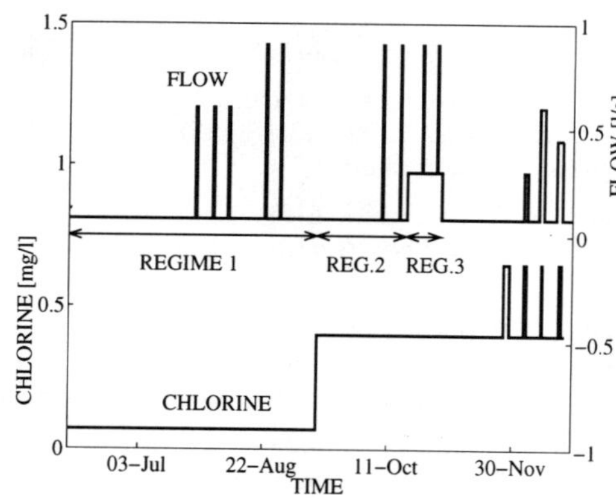

Figure 2. Experimental Schedule showing flow and total chlorine at the pipe rig inlet, three baseline regimes are indicated

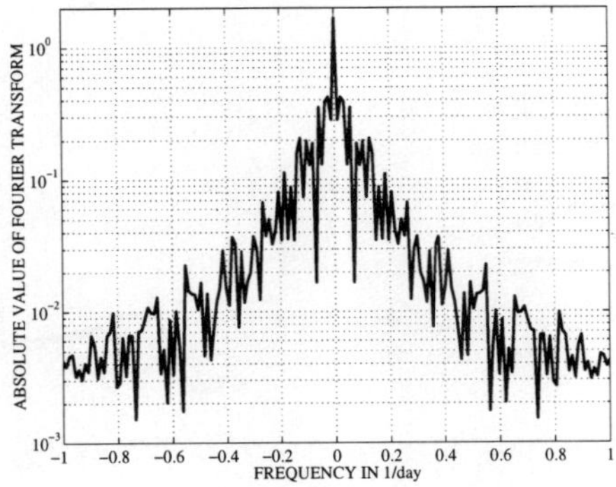

Figure 3. Discrete Fourier Transform of the complete multiplicative error function $\epsilon_M^{IW}(t)$ of sample point three before preprocessing

Table 1. Monochloramine decay coefficient data

	Mean 1/h	Variance 10^{-3} 1/h^2	Period days	Flow l/s	Inlet Chlorine mg/l	Sample Size
1	0.0535	0.0218	5	0.08	0.4	288
2	0.0391	0.0044	1.75	0.08	0.4	101
3	0.0416	0.0884	5.15	0.3	0.4	297
4	0.0448	0.0459	3.25	0.3	0.4	248
5	0.0353	0.0121	2.63	0.08	0.4	152
6	0.0304	0.0048	0.68	0.08	0.4	40
7	0.0204	0.0159	2.2	0.08	0.65	127
8	0.0454	0.4824	2	0.08	0.4	116
9	0.0451	0.0174	1.35	0.08	0.4	78
10	0.0483	0.1371	0.88	0.3	0.65	127
11	0.0470	0.2511	3	0.08	0.4	393
12	0.0814	0.8977	0.55	0.6	0.4	80
13	0.0909	0.5801	0.28	0.6	0.4	41
14	0.0638	0.2934	0.38	0.6	0.65	55
15	0.0332	0.0071	3	0.08	0.4	173
16	0.0521	0.1577	1	0.45	0.4	144
17	0.0650	0.1219	0.97	0.45	0.65	140

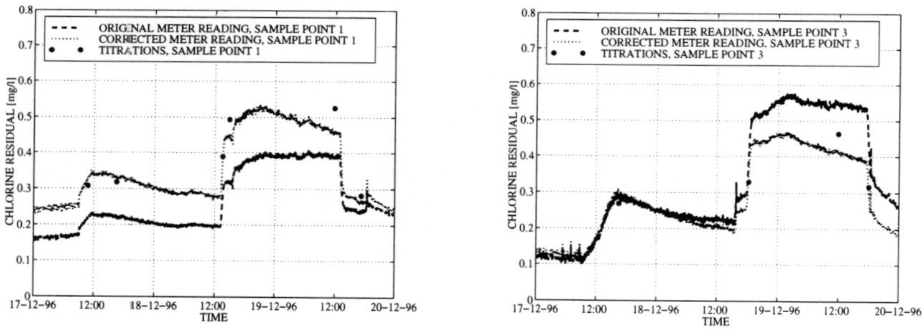

(a) Corrected and uncorrected chlorine data of sample point 1

(b) Corrected and uncorrected chlorine data of sample point 3

Figure 4. Typical example of the correction attained by preprocessing

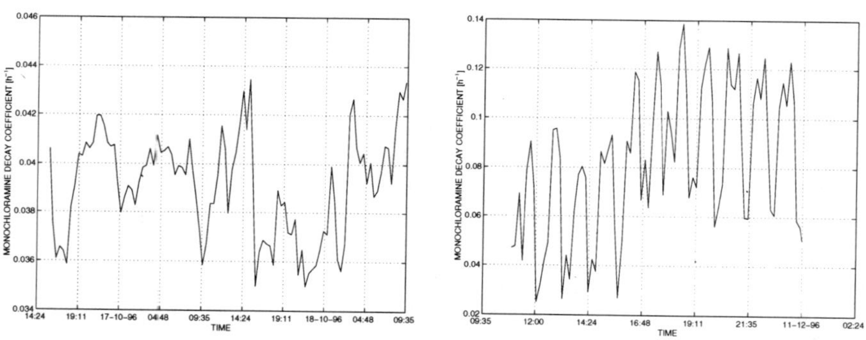

(a) Decay Coefficient in period 2, low variance

(b) Decay Coefficient in period 12, high variance

Figure 5. Examples of estimated single monochloramine decay coefficients

Section 5

Genetic Algorithms and Artificial Neural Networks

CHAPTER 25

Use of Artificial Neural Networks for River Water Quality Simulation

C.G.Wang, D.G.Jamieson *and* A.F.Tagg

Abstract

Traditionally, mechanistic models have been used for river water-quality planning in which the physical system is represented by a series of linked, internal sub-processes. However, such models are inefficient computationally and ill-suited to the introduction of optimisation techniques. Nevertheless, they can be used to evaluate different combinations of effluent discharges on which an artificial neural network can be trained. Thereafter, the artificial neural network would be used in preference to the mechanistic model, for determining, say, the optimal combination of effluent discharge standards within a given river basin. To that end, this chapter describes the formulation of a three-layer artificial neural network and outlines its application to part of the River Thames system.

Key words: River water-quality simulation, Artificial neural networks.

1. Introduction

Simulation is a practical way to delineate present and future river-water quality conditions and has played an important role in effective water-quality management. Conventionally, there are two broad approaches for creating water-quality models, namely mechanistic models in which all processes are physically represented in mathematical terms and empirical models (sometimes called black-box models) which do not attempt to postulate any physical reality.

The mechanistic models are designed to approximate the general internal sub-processes which, when combined, can physically relate water-quality parameters to the environment. Normally, a river water-quality simulation model includes three components, viz. hydrologic, biochemical and thermal sub-models. Many researchers have simplified formulating such models owing to the complexity of interactions between these sub-models see, for example, Streeter and Phelps (1925), Dobbins (1964), and Thomann (1972). In order to avoid poor performance caused by gross simplifications, appropriate biochemical and ecological routines can be incorporated within the water-quality model itself (Chen and Orlob, 1975, and Roesner et al. 1973). Subsequent developments in river water-quality models have included stochastic behaviour for compliance prediction and alternatives to the convective-diffusion equation for representing in-stream mixing. Although the mechanistic models are generally reported to be reliable in predicting river water-quality, even simplified models require numerous reaction coefficients to be determined. These coefficients include the decay rate, the diffusion coefficient, the re-aeration coefficient, etc. If more sub-processes are incorporated to improve the prediction-capability, more reaction coefficients need to be involved. Moreover, these models encounter difficulties when applied to river water-quality management, for example, the optimisation of waste-load allocation. The problems are mainly caused by the sheer computational effort required in the optimisation scheme with which the water-quality simulations, usually the time-consuming components, are coupled as subroutines.

In order to avoid the computational burden imposed by complex, mechanistic models, environmentalists frequently resort to empirical models such as polynomial, power and time-series models to identify a direct mapping between the inputs and outputs, without the need for detailed consideration of the internal structure relating to the physical processes. Such models do not always perform particularly well due to gross simplification, inadequate calibration, system noise etc. However, during the past few years, significant progress in the realm of non-linear pattern recognition has been made possible through advances in a branch of empirical modelling called artificial neural networks (ANNs). ANNs are non-linear mathematical structures that are capable of representing arbitrarily complex non-linear processes that relate the inputs and outputs of any system. ANN models have been used successfully to model complex non-linear input-output time-series relationships in a wide variety of fields, including water resources, as for example, in forecasting water consumption (Canu et al., 1990, Daniell, 1993), determining the optimal sequence of waste-treatment processes (Krovvidy and Wee, 1990) and predicting salinity (DeSilets et al. 1992). Additionally, Smith and Eli (1995) and Kang et al. (1993) developed a neural-network model for the rainfall-runoff process. Tryba (1996) employed a neural network for supervision of water quality. The success with which ANNs have been used to model dynamic systems suggests that the approach may prove to be an effective and efficient way to simulate the complex river water-quality process in situations where explicit knowledge of internal sub-process is not required.

The aim of this study was to investigate the potential use of ANNs to represent the variation of river water-quality due to different pollution sources, in combination with a complex stochastic model such as TOMCAT (Bowden and Brown, 1988), with a view to improving the latter's computational efficiency, particularly where optimisation is involved. The case study presented here is based on the River Thames and involves some six effluent discharge points along the river, together with three monitoring stations. The ANN's performance has been evaluated using comparative plots of outputs and computing the root-mean-square (RMS) error of the test sets.

2. River Water-quality Simulation

Water quality in streams and rivers is influenced by many factors, including the channel characteristics, river flow, water temperature, effluent discharge and so on. Generally, these characteristics can be separated into five recognisable categories: (1) hydrologic variables; (2) hydraulic parameters; (3) inputs of pollutant constituents; (4) background concentrations of pollutants in the river; (5) internal parameters including decay rate, re-aeration coefficient etc.

2.1 Hydrologic Variables

The two major hydrologic variables required as inputs to a river water-quality model are flow rate and temperature. The flow rate is very important in causing pollutant-dispersion, which is due to the random variations in the river velocity (turbulence). Additionally, temperature is normally a necessary variable for river water-quality simulations. Its importance is mainly due to the temperature dependence of many chemical and biological processes by means of which many indicators, such as oxygen levels or pollutant concentration, are determined. On the other hand, temperature has to be considered as a water-quality indicator in its own right since, amongst other things, it affects the type of fish found in the river.

2.2 Hydraulic parameters

Hydraulic parameters are supporting inputs related to the reaction rates, retention times and so on. The required hydraulic parameters include velocity, hydraulic radius and/or depth, gradient and channel roughness. In some cases, the velocity can be directly computed from a velocity equation, such as Mannings or Chezy, amongst others. For a given river with a certain flow, the above parameters are assumed to be constant.

2.3 Inputs of pollutant constituents

The variability of river water-quality is mainly the result of natural processes, discharging wastewater into the river or some combination of both. Whereas wastewater discharges usually come from municipal, industrial or agricultural activities, as point sources, natural processes take the form of distributed inputs. The physical and biochemical characteristics of point-source pollution are much more clearly understood and measurable than those of the distributed sources. The complex and often random time-variable nature of both point and non-point sources is often disregarded in many studies because of insufficient knowledge or modelling complexity, but effective and economical river water-quality management needs to consider their uncertainty.

2.4 Background concentration of pollutants in the river

Background river water-quality is a basic characteristic which should be measured rather than estimated since it depends on many factors, including climatic conditions, natural biota, erosion rate, etc. In most river basins, reaches exist in the headwaters which are representative of the undisturbed conditions. Information on the natural mineral contents of streams can be obtained by analysing the water quality in the upper reaches, before degradation by pollutants takes place along the watercourse and other factors cause background values to vary. As such, background water-quality should be considered as an input variable.

2.5 Internal parameters

All biological, chemical and physical reactions among constituents within the river system are considered as internal processes which are represented by the decay rate, de-oxygenation coefficient, re-aeration coefficient and so forth. Temperature and flow influence many coefficients, but empirical models do not need to consider their processes in detail.

3. Artificial Neural Networks

ANNs are based on a simplified mathematical representation of biological nervous systems. ANNs are massively parallel systems composed of many processing elements connected by links of variable weights. Of the many ANN paradigms, the feed-forward network is by far the most popular (Lippman 1987) and the back-propagation algorithm is widely used for adjusting weights during the training process. The methodology used here for adjusting weights is referred to as "momentum back-propagation" which is based on the "generalised delta rule", as presented by Rumelhart et al. (1986). The network comprises layers of parallel processing elements called neurons, with each layer being connected to the proceeding layer by various interconnection strengths, or weights. Figure 1 illustrates a three-layer neural network consisting of input, hidden and output layers, with the interconnection weights W_{ij} and W_{jk} between the layers of neurons. Initial estimated weight values are progressively corrected during a training process that compares predicted outputs with target outputs and back-propagates any errors (from right to left in Figure 1) to determine the appropriate weights while minimising the errors.

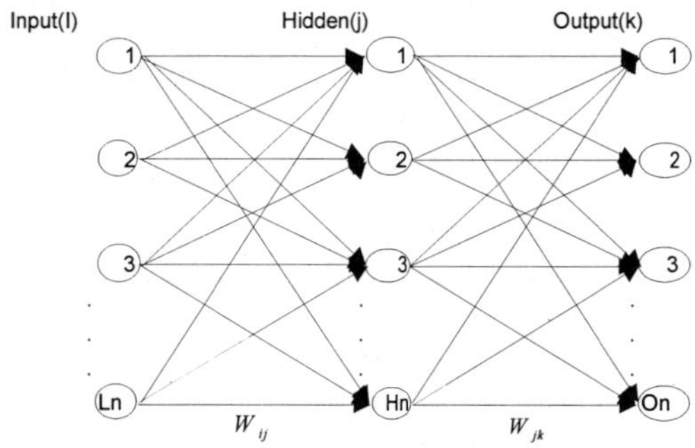

Figure 1. Configuration of a three-layer neural network

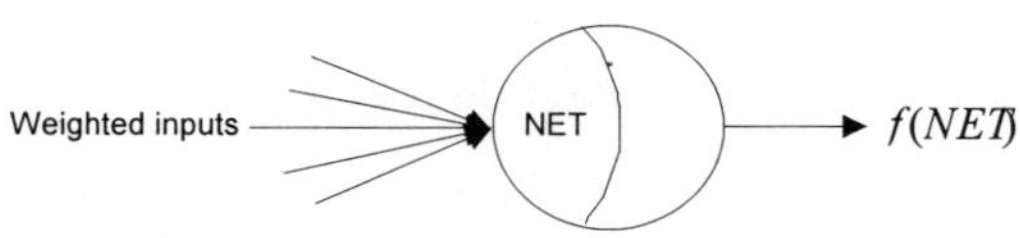

Figure 2. Output of each neuron in hidden and output layers

The input patterns vector I_p (pattern p, of dimension Ln) is presented to the input layer of neurons i, and is simply passed through unchanged as output O_p ($I_{pi} = O_{pi}$), to be distributed to the second layer of neurons j. Each neuron in the hidden and output layers (Figure 1) receives the weighted sum of outputs (*NET*) from the previous layer as input (Figure 2). As an example, *NET* for neuron j in the hidden layer is given by

$$NET_{pj} = \sum_{i}^{Ln} W_{ij} O_{pi} + \theta_j \tag{1}$$

where θ_j = a bias, or threshold value, for neuron j, that is trainable by treating it as a weight W_j in product with an output O_p set equal to 1. Each neuron in the hidden and output layers produces its output *f(NET)* by passing its value of *NET* through a non-linear activation function (sometimes called a transfer function or threshold function). A commonly used activation function is the sigmoid function, which is continuous and differentiable everywhere (Hecht-Nielson, 1990). The most popular form of sigmoid function used for ANNs is the logistic activation function:

$$f(NET) = \frac{1}{1+e^{-NET}} \quad (2)$$

It should be noted that $f\,(NET)$ has a minimum value of 0.0 and a maximum value of 1.0, and is equivalent to the output O_p of each neuron in the hidden layer and the output layer.

The main task of the learning procedure is to update the weights of the links connecting the nodes by minimising the system error between the known and the predicted outputs. Large numbers of input-output pattern pairs are presented to the network in a repetitive fashion designed to provide iterative corrections to the weights. Each iteration (called an 'epoch') is a single pass through all training pattern pairs. The process consists of presenting an input pattern p to the network, computing output O_{pk} and then comparing this output with target output T_{pk}. The total error E_p, based on the squared difference between O_{pk} and T_{pk} for pattern p, is defined as:

$$E_p = \sum_{k=1}^{N}(T_{pk} - O_{pk})^2 \quad (3)$$

To train an ANN system, an adequate number p of unique input-output pattern pairs is required. When coupled with a suitable methodology for iterative correction of interconnection weights, a final set of weights are identified that minimises the global error E, defined as:

$$E = \sum_{p=1}^{P} E_p \quad (4)$$

The first step in the learning process is a feed-forward operation that calculates the output of the nodes from the input layer through the hidden layer to the output layer using Equations (1) and (2). Then the error for each node is calculated and the average squared system error is computed using Equation (4). If the error is greater than a certain predefined value, further iterations will be required, which, in this case, were performed by back-propagation of the error.

In practice, there are several criteria that can be adopted to terminate the training process. One is called error threshold, which can be selected based on the magnitude of the global error E, or the individual pattern errors E_p. Alternatively, the termination may be determined by completion of an arbitrary number of epochs. Both methods were used in this study.

In order to reduce the system error, the weights and threshold value were adjusted. At the beginning of the training process, the weights W and the biases θ are assigned random values, so the predicted outputs of the network will differ from the target outputs and the pattern error E_p would be a non-zero value. Assuming that E_p is a function of the multidimensional weight space, the minimum of the pattern errors is sought by a method called 'gradient descent':

$$\Delta_p W_{YZ} = -\eta \frac{\partial E_p}{\partial W_{YZ}} \quad (5)$$

where $\Delta_p W_{YZ}$ is the change in interconnection weight between arbitrary layers Y and Z on pattern p; η is a proportionality constant and $\partial E_p/\partial W_{YZ}$ is the slope of the error surface. η is called the learning rate and controls the rate of gradient descent and must be held at relatively small values to avoid oscillations in weight corrections during training. Each weight, W_{YZ}, is then adjusted as follows:

$$W_{YZ} + \Delta_p W_{YZ} \quad (6)$$

Equation (5) can be expressed in a similar way to the expression for the delta rule as follows:

$$\Delta_p W_{YZ} = \eta \delta_{pZ} O_{pY} \quad (7)$$

where δ_{pz} is the error term associated with neuron Z for pattern p and O_{pY} is the output of the connecting neuron in the previous layer Y for pattern p. The error term δ_{pz} is calculated differently, depending on whether it is associated with a neuron in the output layer k, or with a neuron in the middle (hidden) layer j. Details of the derivation of these error terms can be found in Rumelhart et al. (1986). The final formulae for the three layer neural network are:

$$\delta_{pk} = (1 - O_{pk}) O_{pk} (T_{pk} - O_{pk}) \quad (8)$$

for neurons in the output layer k, and

$$\delta_{pj} = (1 - O_{pj}) O_{pj} \sum_k \delta_{pk} W_{pk} \quad (9)$$

for neurons in the hidden layer j.

As mentioned previously, the term η in (5) is the learning ratio. To permit more rapid learning rates, Rumeelhart et al. (1986) proposed adding a momentum term to the delta rule of Equation (7) in the following form:

$$(\Delta_p W_{YZ})_{n+1} = \eta \delta_{pZ} O_{pY} + \alpha (\Delta_p W_{YZ})_n \quad (10)$$

where α =momentum constant which makes the current weight change at iteration $n+1$ proportional to the previous weight change at iteration n.

4. Use of ANNs in River Water-quality Simulation

A model that simulates changes in water-quality can be formulated in a wide variety of ways, but it always involves the following stages: (1) analysis of the system, which may be theoretical, observational or experimental; (2) synthesis of a mathematical replica of the system.

The steps involved in the configuration of a model are: (1) selection of input-output data suitable for calibration and validation purposes; (2) identification of the model structure; and (3) calibration of the model by means of an iterative procedure.

4.1 ANN model identification and configuration

The ANN model structure is ideally suited for modelling highly non-linear input-output relationships. During the training procedure, the sigmoid function is used to pass the combined input (*NET*) and produce the output O_p. Since sigmoid functions are used in the

ANN model, all hydrologic and wastewater discharge data must be normalised within the range [0,1] before applying the ANN methodology.

As mentioned previously, the value of water-quality index C_j in a specific section of the river is assumed to be mainly related to the hydrologic variables (flow (Q), water temperature (WT)) of the river and discharge from wastewater source (C_{dn}, q_n, n=1,2,..., N). The adjustable weights reflect the interaction between the neurons (input variables and output variables) in the ANN model and the hydraulic parameters are assumed to be constants for a specific river. Therefore:

$$C_j = f(Q,WT,(q_1,q_2,...,q_n,...,q_N),(C_{d1},C_{d2},...,C_{dn},...,C_{dN}),C_b) + err \quad (11)$$

where, $f(\ )$ is the unknown non-linear mapping function, err is the unknown error (to be minimised), and C_{dn}, q_n are the effluent flow and the concentration of pollutant concerned from nth discharge, respectively. For the time-series problem, the water-quality output is assumed to be related to past inputs $X(t\text{-}k)$, and outputs $C_j(t\text{-}k)$:

$$C_j(t) = f(X(t-1),...,X(t-n_a),C_j(t-1),...,C_j(t-n_b)) + err\ (t) \quad (12)$$

where $X(t - n_a)$ is a vector of inputs including Q, WT, q_n, C_{dn} etc.; n_a, n_b are an unknown number of past inputs and outputs, respectively, contributing to the present output.

The network configuration comprises a series of layers with a number of neurons in each layer as depicted in Figure 1. The number of neurons used in the input and output layers depend on the system being modelled. The number of input variables determines the number of input neurons L_n, while the number of variables being predicted determines the number of output neurons O_n. However, for the hidden layer, determination of the number of neurons H_n is more difficult but normally is related to the numbers of input and output neurons.

After the network is trained with training sets, the results are evaluated using the test sets. The network's performance can be evaluated by comparing the target outputs with the predicted outputs and computing the root-mean-square (RMS) error of the test sets.

4.2 The application of ANNs to river water-quality simulation

The ANN model described in the previous section has been applied to a simplified but realistic situation. This was based on the River Thames between Farmoor and Day's Weir; modelling this section of the River Thames required 14 neurons in the input layer (L_n = 14) corresponding to the discharge volumes and Biochemical Oxygen Demand (BOD) concentrations at six discharge points and hydrologic variables (river flow and temperature), with three neurons in the output layer (O_n = 3) corresponding to the BOD concentrations at three monitoring stations. One of the drawbacks of using an ANN for river water-quality modeling is that it cannot cope with changes relating to the physical system (for example, the possible construction of a wastewater treatment plant) since there are no historic data sets which can be used for training purposes. However, this can be overcome by first using a mechanistic model such as TOMCAT, which was fitted to the observed river water-quality data provided by the Environment Agency. This complex stochastic model was then used to generate the training and testing sets, which include the effects of a different combination of effluent discharge standards. Some 200 sets of input and target output data were used for training the neural network, whilst 46 sets were used for testing.

The water-quality neural network was trained using the above method with a tolerance value of 0.05 for the system error (RMS). The test results are shown in Figure 3 and Figure 4. Figure 3 is a graphical comparison of the target and predicted values and Fig 4 shows the RMS values of the test results (values that exceed the tolerance value of 0.05 are indicated as negative). In this particular exercise, the RMS values for 91.3% of testing patterns were below the tolerance value of 0.05 and the average RMS was 0.03. Obviously, this value could be improved if more training sets were used, particularly if they had included extreme scenarios. Either way, the performance of a non-linear ANN model appears to provide a good representation of river water-quality, as defined by a complex stochastic model such as TOMCAT.

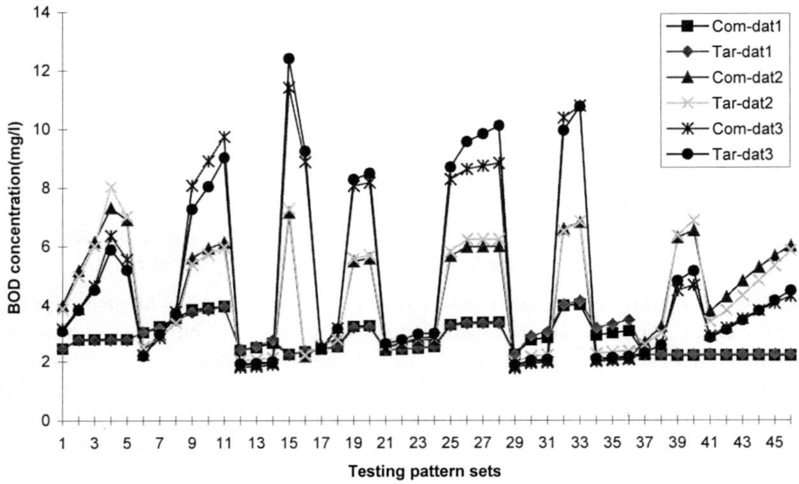

*** Com-dat =Computed value; Tar-dat = Target value; The index (1,2 or 3)=Monitoring station ***

Figure 3. The test results comparing the target values with those predicted by ANN

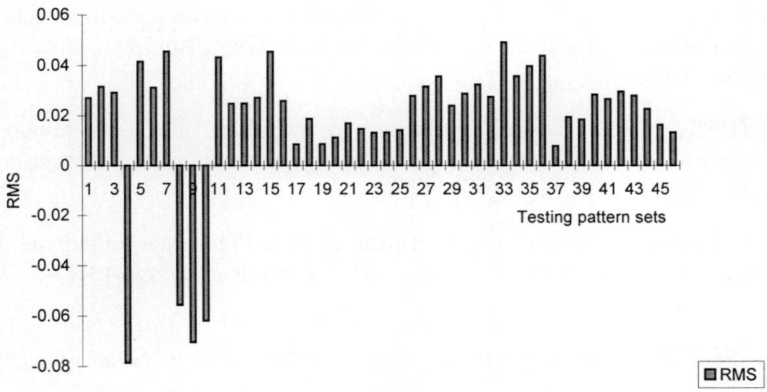

Figure 4.

Residual RMS value for each of the testing patterns (values that exceed the tolerance value of 0.05 are shown negative).

5. Conclusions

The benefit of replicating the performance of a complex mechanistic model by means of an ANN may not be immediately obvious to those who have not tried to optimise a simulation model. Simulation is essentially an evaluation procedure, which is generally dependent upon manual trial-and-error procedures to achieve the design objectives. Attempts to introduce optimisation techniques have at best, met with mixed success (for example, Smith, 1977). Moreover, the computational burden is enormous since each iteration normally requires re-running the simulation model. The advantage of using an ANN instead of the complex mechanistic model is that it is orders of magnitude more computationally efficient, thereby enabling the possibility of optimisation to be considered.

The eventual aim of this research programme is to develop a river water-quality planning process that is capable of optimising effluent discharge standards for an entire river basin, taking account of location, in-stream dilution, natural purification etc. The objective function would be to minimise the overall cost, both capital and operating, of achieving whatever river water-quality requirements are prescribed. Developing a means to rapidly evaluate different combinations of effluent discharge standards in terms of the resulting river water-quality is but the first step. Thereafter, it will be necessary to include an appropriate optimisation technique and cost function for wastewater treatment.

References

Bowden, K. and S. R. Brown (1988), Relating effluent control parameters to river quality objectives using a generalized catchment simulation model, *Water Science and Technology*, 16, 22-31.

Canu, S., R. Sorbal and R. Lengelle (1990), Formal neural network as an adaptive model for water demand, *International Neural Network Conference*, Paris, Vol. 1, 131-136.

Chen, C. H., ed. (1991), *Neural Networks in Pattern Recognition and Their Applications*, World Scientific, Singapore.

Chen, C. W. and G. T. Orlob (1975), Ecological simulation for aquatic environment, in Pattern, B. C. (ed.), *Systems Analysis and Simulation in Ecology*, Vol. 111, Chap. 12, Academic Press, New York.

Daniell, T. M. (1993), Neural network-applications in hydrology and water resources engineering, *Proceedings of the International Hydrology and Water Resources Symposium*, Perth, Australia, 797-802.

De Silets, L., B. Golden, Q. Wang and R. Kumar (1992), Predicting salinity in the Chesapeake Bay using backpropagation, *Computer and Operations Research*, 19(3/4), 277-285.

Dobbins, W. E. (1964), BOD and oxygen relationships in streams, *Journal Sanit. Eng. Div.*, ASCE, 90, 53-78.

Hecht-Nielsen, R. (1990), *Neurocomputing*, Addison-Wesley, Reading, Mass.

Hins, W. G., D. A. Rickert, S. W. Mckenize and J. P. Bennett (1975), *Formulation and Use of Practical Models for River-quality Assessment*, U. S. Geol. Surv. Circ. 715-B, Reston, Virginia.

Kang, K. W., C. Y. Park and J. H. Kim (1993), Neural network and its application to rainfall-runoff forecasting, *Korean J. Hydrosci.*, 4, 1-9.

Krovvidy, S. and W. G. Wee (1990), A knowledge based neural network approach for wastewater treatment system, *IJCNN International Joint Conference on Neural Network*, San Diego, California, 1327-1332.

Lippman, R. (1987), An introduction to computing with neural networks *IEEE ASSP Mag.*, 4, 4-22.

Roesner, L.A., J. R. Mouser and D. E. Evenson (1973), *Computer Programs Documentation for the Stream-Quality Model Qual-II*, EPA Cont. No. 68-01-0739, Water Research Engineering, Walnut Creek, California.

Rumelhart, D. E., G. E. Hinton and R. J. Williams (1986), Learning internal representation by error propagation, *Parallel Distributed Processing*, Vol. 1: Foundation, Rumelhart D. E. and J. L. McClelland (eds.), MIT Press, Cambridge, Mass.

Smith, D. K. (1977), *An approach to the optimisation of simulation models of water resources systems*, Ph. D. thesis, University of Lancaster, UK.

Smith, J. and R. N. Eli (1995), Neural network models of rainfall runoff process, *Journal of Water Resources Planning and Management*, ASCE, 11-12, 499-508.

Streeter, H. W. and E. B. Phelps (1925), *A Study of the Pollution and Natural Purification of the Ohio River*, U.S. Public Health Service, Publication Health Bulletin, No. 146.

Thomann, R. V. (1972), *System Analysis and Water Quality Management*, Environment Research and Application, Inc., New York.

Tryba, V. (1996), Neuro-ASIC for low supervision of water pollution, *Proceedings of International Workshop on Neural Networks for Identification, Control, Robotics, and Signal/Image Processing,* NICROSP, 111-116.

Zurada, J. M. (1992), *Introduction to Artificial Neural Systems*, West Publishing Co., St. Paul, Minn.

CHAPTER 26

The Application of Parallel Processing to GA-based optimisation of Water Supply Systems

R.W.F.Thurley, D.A.Savic *and* G.A.Walters

Abstract

Genetic Algorithms have proven to be very effective in the optimisation of Water Supply System designs. These systems are complex, non-linear and have a large parametric spread: optimum designs are buried within a huge space of possible designs. The search for optimum designs for typical systems, even when directed by a Genetic Algorithm, can take many tens of hours, and it is worthwhile exploring ways to speed up the procedure.

Distributing the computational effort across many processors (parallel processing) is an açcepted way of speeding up a computer program, where one can expect an increase in performance proportional to the number of addition processors, less an operating overhead. However, it has been reported that for some Genetic Algorithm (GA) searches there are methods of implementing parallelism that can give a greater than linear speed up.

The object of this study is to explore the benefit of a Distributed Genetic Algorithm (DGA) on the Water Supply Systems design problem. A specific well known design problem was tackled (New York Tunnels), and the best solutions found using a DGA and a standard GA approach were compared. No significant improvement was found, in terms of processing time taken to achieve a given solution, or in the quality of solution found, by using a DGA approach. The results of the experiments are presented and discussed.

1. Introduction

The pipe networks of our water and gas distribution infrastructure are large, very expensive and extremely important. Optimisation in their design, management and maintenance can make great capital savings, and has been the subject of many years of research at Exeter University's School of Engineering.

The design problems associated with distribution networks are complex and non-linear. The basis of optimising these systems has to be a *solution search.* Optimum designs are sorted out from the huge number of different ways a real system can be formed. Solutions are formulated, evaluated, compared and ranked to find the best in the required terms, which is a time consuming process. The search space is very large, especially in terms of its number of dimensions; it is too large for it to be completely enumerated. Because of its complexity many iterative methods of searching, like 'hill climbing', too easily find local optima.

At Exeter, Genetic Algorithms have been employed and proven to be very effective methods of 'directing' the search for optima in many of the design problems associated with pipe networks [1]. The work has led to the development of the computer model GANET [2]. It has been successfully used in a number of real optimisation problems and produced valuable results [3,4].

Genetic Algorithms (GA) are computing methods well suited to searching for optimal solutions in a massive 'solution space'. They are based on mimicking nature's own very successful optimisation process: the process of evolutionary development whereby a species adapts itself in the best possible way to its environment under the pressures of natural selection. The basic operation of a GA is conceptually simple:

a) maintain a population of solutions to a problem, b) select the better solutions for recombination with each other, and c) use their offspring to replace poorer solutions. The combination of selection pressure and innovation (through recombination and mutation) generally leads to improved solutions. The selection process requires that solutions be evaluated by modelling their performance and conducting a cost/benefit analysis.

GANET integrates a general-purpose set of Genetic Algorithm management functions and the Epanet Hydraulic Model [5] with a set of 'plug in' cost and evaluation routines that are specific to the design problem. These components are linked into a Windows 95 package. Figure 1 shows the basic structure.

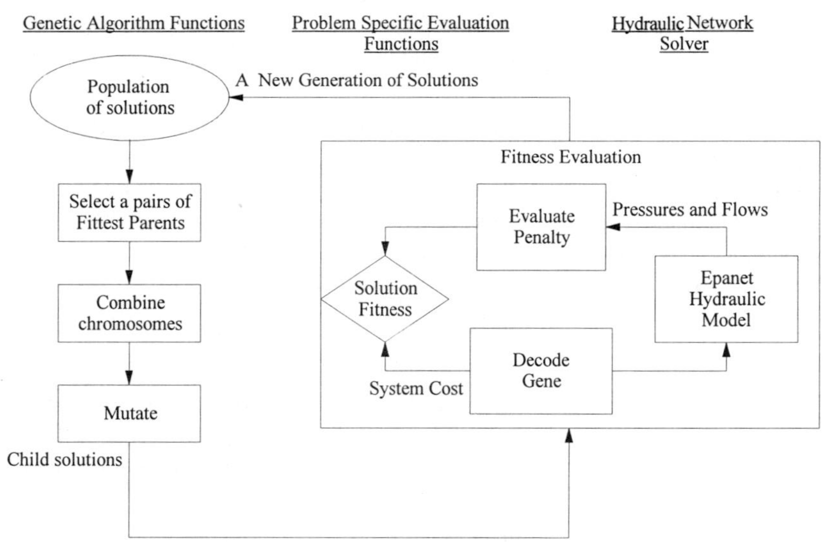

Figure 1. The Basic Structure of GANET

A problem of all searching techniques, including GA methods, is that of the time taken to converge on a good design solution. The execution time can often be many tens of hours even on a high performance PC. Speeding up the process is clearly worth doing, and this is one of the main reasons for investigating the use of parallel processing.

2. Parallel Processing

Parallel processing is a technique for increasing the computation speed for a task. The overall process is divided into several sub-processes and these are allocated to separate processors that are free to execute their respective tasks simultaneously. For specific types of problems it is possible to improve the performance almost linearly with the increase in the number of processor elements. However, it is accepted that for most applications computational speed-up does not increase linearly with the number of processes. There will always be some element of the overall algorithm that has to be executed sequentially and, as a result, the algorithm does not utilise all of the processors all of the time.

A basic GA is ideally suited to parallelism, offering many ways of being subdivided onto multiple processors, the most natural being to allocate a processing element for each member in the population of design solutions. Evaluation of the whole population's fitness would take as long as the evaluation of a single design. There would be a period of data exchange, evolution of new designs and their distribution to new *home* processors that would be the inevitable inefficient overhead, but it would be a straightforward implementation on a purpose built multiprocessor system.

Another model for distributing the genetic algorithm is to subdivide the global working population of designs into smaller sub-populations and distribute these onto separate processing elements. Here different strategies of managing interactions between populations can be formed with potentially very different results, for example:

1) Each sub-population could be allowed to evolve independently. With no communication between processors, this method has very little overhead and is very easy to implement: run the same program on each processor with a different initial population of designs; identify the fittest from each fully evolved population and choose the best. However, as the working populations would be relatively small, diversity within each would be hard to maintain and its designs would quickly converge.

2) Alternatively, each sub-population could be allowed to evolve semi-independently, with occasional interaction between populations in the form of migrating designs. The level of inter-process communication overhead depends on how regular and how extensive the migration phase is. The most productive balance is the lowest level of migration that allows populations to maintain their evolution rate and diversity.

These methods are variously known as the Distributed Genetic Algorithms (DGA), or Medium-Coarse Grained Parallel GAs. Both strategies were used by Tanese [6] in the optimisation of a class of Walsh polynomials. A 64-processor computer was used and a near linear computational speedup was achieved. The method did not degrade the optimisation process. Indeed the distributed methods generally found fitter individuals. Tanese varied the migration interval and migration rate. (The migration level is a product of the migration rate and migration interval, i.e. 1% of a sub-population migrating every generation is equivalent to 50% of a sub-population migrating every 50 generations, although the evolutionary outcome would be different.)

Tanese suggested that the success of the Distributed Genetic Algorithm relative to a single population GA may be connected with the theory in evolutionary biology that small, loosely connected island populations can evolve more rapidly than a single large population [7].

Other theories are reviewed by Belding [8]. Whatever the mechanism, this form of parallelism has an additional benefit of increasing the effectiveness of a solution evolution, on top of the near linear computational speedup obtained from using multiple processing elements.

Belding [8] has shown that the advantages of Distributed GA are dependent on the type of system to be optimised. The purpose of this work was to see if a significant improvement in speed and quality of search could be achieved with water distribution network problems. GANET was used as a basis for a distributed algorithm, and a number of networked PCs were used instead of a multiprocessor machine. Part of the reason for such a simple implementation was to keep the method in the realms of the small institution or commercial organisation.

3. Method of Implementing the Distributed Genetic Algorithm

Many instances of the standard single population program GANET were run simultaneously on many PC computers connected to a network. The processes interacted as follows:

1. Each instance of the program records its existence by writing a token file with a unique name to a directory on a shared file store.
2. The programs run as normal: evaluating populations of solutions, and using genetic operators to generate new populations, etc. The only difference is that after a given number of generations the best solution is copied to the shared file store. It is given a filename taken from the name of a randomly chosen instance of GANET that has been registered as simultaneously running.
3. The file contains a chromosome image of the solution, and is picked up by the named instance of GANET when it next checks the file store, (only checked periodically to save on disk access overheads).
4. The imported solution is re-evaluated and placed in the new population pool according to its rank.

These migrations occur asynchronously between any pair of sub-populations. Only one solution is moved in a migration.

Incidentally, the method also works identically, but with no speedup, on a single computer running Windows 95, a multitasking operating system. This is not true parallel processing, but each population is processed concurrently. The processes interact as before and, although it largely defeats the objective, it is a convenient method of testing the approach.

4. Multiple Population experiments with migration of solutions

The Distributed GA was tested on a well-known pipe network optimisation problem: the expansion of the New York water supply system [9]. The objective is to determine the most economic additions to the existing system of tunnels that will meet the projected demand without detrimental fall in pressure at key nodes. The method of expansion is to construct new tunnels alongside the existing tunnels, i.e. a parallel system. There are 21 existing tunnels in the system and each could be paired with a new tunnel from 15 available diameters (3 to 17 feet). Including the option of not pairing a link there are 16^{21} possible network designs $=1.93\text{x}10^{25}$. The most expensive solution, 21 new pipes of 17 feet diameter, cost $294,000,000 US. The cheapest design solution is to do nothing, but this is obviously not feasible.

A design solution is described by a chromosome that contains 21 sub-strings, one for each new tunnel. The sub-strings specify which of the 15 options is to be applied. When evaluating the design the chromosome is decoded and a hydraulic network model of the tunnel system is modified accordingly. The performance of the new network is simulated and evaluated. If the pressures at key points are not reached then a penalty is applied to the design, the level of penalty reflecting the severity of the pressure shortfall. The penalty is added to the cost of the network additions specified by the design to give an overall measure of the solution's fitness. A high fitness reflects a low cost and a low penalty.

A note on the penalty function: The Genetic Algorithm operates to evolve a population of design solutions that tend to become fitter generation after generation. A proportion of these supra-fit solutions will have a very low cost but a high penalty burden. These are deemed infeasible solutions, as they do not deliver the water demanded at the required pressure. However, they are an important part of a diverse population of solutions that will ultimately lead to the lowest cost solution that is feasible and does not have a penalty. It is important to select a penalty function that allows a proportion of good infeasible solutions to flourish.

Single population runs were conducted as controls for comparison. Here the population size was 300, the GA functional form was generational, selection of parents was by the roulette method, crossover of chromosomes was uniform, random mutation was performed, and child solutions simply replaced parents with no elitism.

For the first set of distributed GA trials three island populations were set up with different initial populations of 100 each, giving a total of 300. Each island population was subjected to identical cost and evaluation methods and the same GA form (detailed above). In a second trial, six island populations of 50 were used. Here the initial populations were identical, but the cost and evaluation function were different (a different penalty rate was applied). Again the GA functional form was kept the same.

5. Experimental Results

Results of running the New York tunnel trials are tabulated below. The number of evaluations that were processed before reaching the best solution is given as a measure of the rate of convergence. A trial is conducted in approximately the same amount of time whatever the circumstance. The relative quality of the best solution found is given by its cost. These are all feasible solutions, and incur no penalties. The control runs are given in Table 1, the first set of island runs in Table 2.

For the island runs the number of evaluations taken to find the best solution is given for each sub-population as well as a global number of evaluations. The best solution found is the best from all island populations.

Table 3 shows the equivalent results for the second series of parallel runs, where different penalty rates were used to grade a design's fitness. The varying penalty rates are given for information.

Run	Number of evaluations to find best solution	Best Solution found by GANET (US Million $)
single 1	229300	43.28
single 2	217508	43.28
single 3	203935	43.28

Table 1. Control Runs

Island	Number of evaluations to find best solution	Best Solution found by GANET (US Million $)
i1	333604	42.43
i2	1020059	46.49
i3	1150918	46.53
Combined	2504581	42.43

Table 2. First series of Test with distributed island sub-populations.

Island	penalty (US m$ per meter of low head)	Number of evaluations to find best solution	Best Solution found by GANET (US Million $)
a	0.5	390317	48.62
b	1.0	138070	43.28
d	5.0	332375	43.28
d	10.0	378308	43.28
e	50.0	31402	47.52
f	100.0	237847	44.84

Table 3. Distributed island populations with different penalty functions.

6. Discussion and Conclusions

From the worst case result of the single population control runs (Table 1) an optimum solution was rapidly converged on after 229300 evaluations, or 764 generations of the population of 300. From the first series of tests with migration between island sub-populations (Table 2) the number of evaluations required to reach the optimum was at best 333604, or 3336 generations of the population of 100, although a slightly better local optimum was achieved (by 2%), which is encouraging. The total number of evaluations required to arrive at that point, counting the processing of all three sub-populations would be more than 1,000,000. This limited test shows that the number of evaluations required to reach a particular level of solution, and therefore the overall processing time, is not reduced by employing a Distributed GA.

In the second series of tests of a distributed GA the same global population is distributed to more islands with smaller populations of 50. Also each island population is subject to a different penalty function. Here, the quality of the best solution found is no better than with the single population control runs. However, the number of evaluations required to find the solution was less in one of the sub-populations (138070), although the total number of evaluations conducted across all populations to reach this point is more than 800,000. So again there would appear to be no advantage in using a distributed GA.

These test are a 'first look' survey. GA based optimisation is a statistical method and large numbers of trials are required to improve the certainty of a result. It is likely that the outcome is very sensitive to the parameters and methods involved, including: migration rates and intervals, the selection of the migrant, the number of islands and sub-population sizes, the effect of different evaluation functions on the sub-population and global population diversity.

Better results (a solution with a cost of $37.13 million) were obtained by the original single population version of GANET for this problem [2]. This was achieved using a slightly different GA functional form that is not appropriate for the island model. The result suggests that the New York Tunnel optimisation problem may not lend itself to this type of parallel GA. It is likely that the nature of the solution space is important, and so other problems should be tested.

References

[1] Walters, G.A. and Savic, D. A., (1994), Optimal Design of Water Systems using Genetic Algorithms and Other Evolution Programs, Keynote paper in Hydraulic Engineering Software V Vol.1: Water Resources and Distribution, W.R. Blain and K.L. Ktsifarakis (eds.), Computational Mechanics Publications, pp.19-26.

[2] Savic, D.A. and G.A. Walters (1997a) "Genetic Algorithms for Least-Cost Design of Water Distribution Networks." Journal of Water Resources Planning and Management, Vol. 123, No.2, March/April, 1997. Pp. 67-77.

[3] Savic, D.A. and G.A. Walters, (1997b), Model Calibration Using Genetic Algorithms, South West Water Ltd. Seminar: A Leakage and Network Strategy for the Millenium, London, Feb. 1997.

[4] Walters, G.A. and D.A. Savic, (1997), Planning the Rehabilitation and Strengthening of Distribution Networks Using Genetic Algorithm Software, Proceedings of the 3rd International Conference on Water Pipeline Systems – Leakage Management, Network Optimization and Pipeline Rehabilitation Technology, BHR Group Conference Series, Publication No. 23, pp. 407-416.

[5] Rossman, L. A. (1993). EPANET, users manual. U.S. Environmental Protection Agency, Cincinnati, Ohio.

[6] Tanese, R. (1987). Parallel genetic Algorithms for a hypercube. In Grefenstette, J.J. (Ed.), Genetic Algorithms and their Applications: Proceding of the Second International Conference on Genetic Algorithms, pp. 177-183. Hillsdale, N.J: Lawrence Erlbaum.

[7] Wright, S (1932). The roles of mutation, inbreeding, crossbreeding and selection in evaluation. In Proceedings of the sixth International conference of Genetics, Vol.1, pp.356-366.

[8] Belding T. C., (1995). Proceedings of the sixth International Conference on Genetic Algorithms. Morgan Kaufmann, San Francisco, CA.

[9] Schaake, J., and Lai, D. (1969) "Linear programming and dynamic programming applications to water distribution network design." Rep. 116, Dept. Civil Engineering., Massachusetts Inst. Of Technology, Cambridge, Mass.

CHAPTER 27

Optimal Design of Water Systems Using Genetic Algorithms: some recent developments

G.A.Walters, D.A.Savic, R.W.F. Thurley, D.Halhal, Z.Kapelan *and* R.Atkinson

Abstract

This chapter describes recent applications of Genetic Algorithms to Water Systems Engineering. The principles are first outlined, drawing attention to the parallel with natural evolutionary development. The various numerical mechanisms by which a population of solutions in a computer evolves over a number of generations are described. There follows a discussion of the advantages and disadvantages of Genetic Algorithms for practical engineering design over more conventional optimisation techniques such as Linear Programming, Dynamic Programming and Gradient Based methods. The opportunities for applying Genetic Algorithms to optimisation problems within the water industry are then considered, with recent examples quoted from personal experience and published literature.

1. Introduction

The optimisation technique now known as Genetic Algorithms was first applied to the engineering of Water Systems in the mid 1970s. [1]. However, it was not until the mid 1980s that the method began to attract increasing attention among the academic community, corresponding to the increased availability of powerful personal computer facilities. In the last few years, Genetic Algorithms have gained acceptance among researchers as probably the best technique for optimisation of very large complex systems, these being typical of those found in the water industry. They are now starting to be applied by specialist consultants to a variety of water industry problems.

1.1 Genetic Algorithms

Genetic Algorithms and other Evolutionary Design approaches are numerical search techniques that are based on simple models of biological evolution, incorporating various mechanisms from nature. A set (*population*) of solutions to a problem develops (*evolves*) over a large number of iterations (*generations*) to meet in the best possible way the problem criteria and constraints (*environment*).

In the basic iteration, new populations of solutions replace old populations, simulating birth and death. To create a new population, the breeding process is simulated, with parent solutions selected preferentially from the old population according to their quality (*fitness*), thereby incorporating the *survival of the fittest* principle. Design information is handed down from parents to *offspring* using the principles of genetic coding. The parameters for a design are stored as a numerical data string, analogous to a *chromosome*, and an offspring inherits part of the data string from each of its parents, using a *crossover* procedure. The resulting solution (offspring) will therefore have some of the characteristics of each of its parent solutions. As parents were preferentially selected from the old generation, there is a very good chance that the new generation will be an overall improvement on the old generation. Finally, occasional mutation is added to the offspring to introduce new genetic material. Mutations usually die out, but can be the trigger for exploration of a new search area.

The reader is referred to other publications [2,3] for a fuller treatment of the ideas and details of the algorithms.

1.2 Why use Genetic Algorithms?

Prior to the development of Genetic Algorithms, engineering design optimisation tended to rely on Linear Programming (LP), Dynamic Programming (DP) and Hill Climbing techniques. LP has been widely used and will find the global optimum solution even with a large number of variables and constraints. However, LP is only strictly applicable to systems whose objective and constraints are linear with respect to the design variables, which must also be continuous. This severely limits its straightforward application, and considerable ingenuity has been exercised in developing approximate linearised system models to allow LP to be used for some non-linear problems. Inability to handle discrete or integer-valued variables is also a considerable drawback for engineering design work. Conversion of the optimal continuous solution to discrete values may be possible for problems involving only a small number of variables, but is very unlikely to identify the optimum for large systems.

DP has been successfully implemented for a narrow range of water engineering optimisation problems that can be treated as serial systems, such as sewer system design and reservoir operation. DP is a robust technique, which, like LP, will identify the global optimum solution, but is not suited to the majority of complex system problems that are present in the water industry.

Some Hill Climbing techniques have been used, generally based on evaluating a potential solution, and progressively altering the values of the design variables to improve the solution. Methods such as Hooke and Jeeves use only the function evaluations, which is much more practicable than calculus based methods using derivatives. In principle, a Hill Climbing technique can call a standard simulation package to evaluate a potential solution, with the minimal extra programming. Problems arise, however, in handling the large numbers of constraints that usually arise in engineering problems, as well as discrete variables, and the presence of multiple optima in most non-linear, constrained problems.

GAs can be viewed as a special kind of stochastic Hill Climbing technique in which an initially diverse population of solutions climbs lots of hills in parallel, and in which it is possible to jump from one hill to another when two diverse solutions are combined. The ability to converge on the global optimum is not guaranteed, but with sensible parameters (e.g. population size, crossover and mutation probabilities) near-optimal solutions are usually achieved. GAs also benefit from the presence of discrete values, effectively reducing the search space. Constraints are still a problem, but most can be handled by incorporation of penalty functions into the objective. However, the most useful feature of GAs is their ability to handle extremely large problems in a robust manner.

2. Water Industry Applications

Although various LP and other optimisation techniques have been applied to particular Water Systems problems in the past, the use of formal optimisation is still in its infancy, with the Industry showing reluctance to adopt the concept for routine design and systems planning. However, the ease with which GAs can handle the large, complex systems that are typical of water networks is leading to fresh interest, particularly in an economic climate that focuses attention on cost reduction, improved efficiency and meeting of performance targets. The following recent examples of the use of GAs are quoted from the personal experiences of the authors.

2.1 Water distribution network design

Although GAs can be used for the design of new water distribution systems, comprising looped networks of pipes, with pumps, reservoirs, valves etc., in practice most water distribution design work is on strengthening, expansion and rehabilitation of existing systems, with considerable interest in leakage reduction, pressure management and quality issues. The Water Systems Group at Exeter University has developed object-oriented software for applying GAs to a wide range of such problems [4], using the EPANET simulation package [5] for analysis of the distribution networks.

2.2 Metropolitan Toronto/York Region Network Strengthening

One major study, undertaken by *Optimal Solutions* (a collaborative venture between the Water Systems Group at Exeter and consultants Ewan Associates Ltd.) was on the proposed strengthening of the Metro-Toronto/York region water distribution system in Canada. The region of York is planning for a significant increase in population over the next 35 years. One option for meeting some of the extra demand for water is to increase the amount supplied from Lake Ontario, through the Metro Toronto and York region distribution systems. To accomplish this, major capital works are required to increase the network capacity. A previous study had proposed a scheme involving 9 new pipes placed parallel to existing lines, and 19 newly identified pipelines, together with new pumping stations and reservoirs, costing \$123.5M for the pipelines alone. No formal optimisation had been undertaken on this design, and analysis of the resulting network showed some quite major hydraulic deficiencies were still present for the proposed design loading.

The GA study was undertaken to determine whether substantial savings could be achieved on capital costs. An existing trunk main model of the network was converted to EPANET format, with all pumps, reservoirs and valve settings from the previous study retained, giving a network of 696 pipes with 19 reservoirs and 72 pumps. The only design variables considered were the locations and diameters of new pipes for the system. For each of the 696 existing pipe routes, a new pipe was considered, together with 25 previously identified potential new routes, giving 721 possible new pipes. There were 14 commercially available pipe diameters to choose from, plus the "do nothing" zero diameter option, giving 15 options for each pipe, or $15^{721} = 9.16x10^{847}$ possible network expansion schemes from which to choose the optimum.

Due to constraints on the system, it was not possible to find any solution that fully met all the hydraulic requirements. Changes to the pumps and/or valve settings would have been required, but these were outside the terms of this initial investigation. The GA came up with a range of solutions with varying costs and hydraulic penalties, demonstrating cost savings of at least 10% for schemes that were very much better hydraulically than that originally proposed. A typical solution involved placing 17 pipes parallel to existing ones, with 9 pipes along new routes. A follow-up study for the York region is currently being undertaken, involving pipe sizing, choice of layout, pump provision, sizing and location of reservoir storage and optimal operation.

2.3 Network Rehabilitation

A rather different example, but using essentially the same software, involved planning the rehabilitation of an old water distribution network. Due to leakage, corrosion and water quality problems, a water company wished to replace or reline 508 existing unlined cast iron pipes in a network of 1207 pipes. The remaining pipes had either been previously relined, or were made of other materials. The network had 1166 nodes and 38 valves and was supplied from a single source, there being no reservoirs or tanks in the system.

Seven rehabilitation options were specified, including relining with cement mortar or epoxy resin, slip-lining, pipe bursting and replacement using open trench excavation, unit costs being provided by the water company. Some techniques such as slip lining allow smaller pipes to be used. Other techniques such as relining allow no choice of diameter, whereas open excavation allows replacement in any diameter. Up to eight different combinations of rehabilitation technique and diameter were specified for each pipe length. The network was to be rehabilitated at minimum cost, subject to satisfactory nodal pressures under a specified 24-hour peak day demand profile. There were, in addition, constraints on the size of certain mains.

The GA was used to select one of up to 8 rehabilitation options for each of the 508 pipes in the network, so that the overall cost is minimised, while maintaining satisfactory hydraulic performance. As in the previous example, each trial solution was evaluated in terms of both its cost and its hydraulic performance. Routines were written to obtain the overall cost of the pipeline rehabilitation decisions, and the hydraulic performance was assessed using EPANET. For a successful GA run, network analysis is performed several hundred thousand times in the search for the optimal solution, and so it is important that the analysis routine and the interface between it and the GA software are as efficient as possible.

Solutions that fail to meet the hydraulic requirements incur a penalty cost that is based on the extent of the pressure violations. This is combined with the actual cost to give an overall fitness for the solution. Given a correct balance between cost and penalty, solutions with pressure violations tend to die out as the GA evolution proceeds, leaving only feasible solutions.

Unlike the previous example, there is no previously designed solution for comparison. However, limiting solutions were first obtained without using optimisation to give upper and lower bounds on the cost. The first solution was based on the most expensive rehabilitation option for each pipe. The second solution was based on the least expensive rehabilitation option for each pipe. The maximum possible cost was found to be £750,031 while the minimum cost was found to be £310,789. The minimum cost solution downsized all water mains to their smallest diameter, irrespective of hydraulic requirements, with hydraulic analysis showing that the minimum pressure was not provided at 42 nodes under design conditions.

The GA produced a design with a cost of £315,951, which fully satisfied the hydraulic pressure requirements at a cost only slightly higher than the cheapest possible, but hydraulically deficient, design. The solution involves downsizing to minimum diameter most of the network pipes, but with a few significant pipes chosen to be of larger size. There is a very significant saving over a policy of straightforward size-for-size replacement.

2.4 Model calibration

Design and operation of water distribution systems is critically dependent on the efficiency and accuracy of the models used to represent them. When building a computer model of an existing system, one necessary step is *calibration*, in which adjustments are made to unknown model parameters in order to match model output with the observed physical response of the system. Normally, it is the pipe roughnesses that are treated as unknown parameters in the model, but nodal demands and even pipe diameters can sometimes be assumed unknown. Usually, the calibration is attempted by a trial and error process, until an approximate agreement is obtained on pressures and pipe flows at a set of measurement points in the system for two or three diverse sets of recorded data. However, close agreement is notoriously difficult to achieve by this manual procedure.

Considerable interest has been expressed in the use of optimisation to speed up the laborious calibration process and to improve the quality of the results. By exploring the whole range of possibilities, an automatic process also helps to eliminate any preconceptions that an engineer might have in choosing pipe roughness values, thereby promoting consistency between model calibrations.

The GA is again well suited to this problem, which is mathematically difficult, as the objective (minimising the difference between modelled and observed values) contains many local minima. With only minor changes, the object-oriented software for network design and rehabilitation can be used for model calibration. New procedures for evaluating the objective are required, and a new set of design variables, the pipe roughnesses, needs to be defined. However, the same GA and network solver can be used.

A case study was undertaken by *Optimal Solutions* for South West Water in 1996, based on the Danes Castle network in the city of Exeter, U.K. Water is pumped from a riverside treatment works into two service reservoirs, and then flows by gravity into the distribution system. The network has 256 nodes with 284 pipes, 2 pumps and 15 valves. An existing model was modified to include recent changes to the system, and a 24 hour field test was undertaken in January 1996 to obtain flows at 19 locations and pressures at 10 locations, including reservoir levels.

A manual calibration was performed, based on snapshots representing peak demand, average demand and minimum (night) demand. These same loading conditions were used for the GA calibration, which was based on allocating roughness values (maximum 20mm) to all the 284 pipes in the system. The results of the GA simulation are given in a separate paper [6] and show a very much better calibration than was achieved manually. However, there were still some pressure mismatches of up to 3.5m, indicating that some throttling was occurring in the system that was not being adequately modelled.

2.5 Water resource development and scheduling

The choice and scheduling of capital developments presents considerable opportunities for the application of GA techniques. A study was undertaken in 1996 by *Optimal Solutions* of the 35-year development of water resources for the region of York, North of Toronto, Canada. Data for fourteen alternative supply links were provided by the client, with incremental costs and capacities, and a pattern of projected demands for the region over the period. The optimisation problem was to determine the best combination of resources to develop and the optimal timetable for their development, based on minimising the present value of capital and operational costs.

To ensure that water could be distributed where required, a seven-link network schematic was devised. The capacity of each of the seven links could be increased by up to 8 different increments in each of 31 years, giving approximately 8^{217} solutions to examine. The GA was used to identify a range of diverse solutions, from which the client was able to select a preferred option.

2.6 Pump Scheduling for minimisation of energy costs

On the operational side of water supply, minimising the cost of pumping water has been studied using optimisation techniques. Most supply systems are fed from one or more separate sources by a number of electrically driven pumps, which will deliver water to service reservoirs distributed throughout the system. Electricity is usually available at different prices during peak and off-peak periods. Demand for water varies throughout the day, with the service reservoirs providing storage to supply peak demands.

The problem of determining which pumps to operate at which times of day so that the predicted demand for water is met at minimum power cost can be handled quite effectively using a GA. The normal scheduling period is one day, split at most into 24 one-hour slots during which pump settings remain constant. After one day, the schedule is repeated, or a revised schedule may be implemented if the network has changed (e.g. for repair or maintenance or supply interruption) or if predicted demands have altered. Simple GA implementations were reported by Mackle et al [7] and by de Schaetzen [8]. Further work incorporating a multi-objective approach was carried out by Schwab et al.[9].

3. Genetic Algorithm Tool Kit

Although a Simple GA (SGA) can be used for all of the above applications, the authors have found it advantageous to implement special GA procedures to increase the efficiency for some of the applications. Some of these have been newly introduced, whilst others have been developed from previously published work. At present it is difficult to generalise on the comparative merits of the various techniques, as their efficiencies seem to be very much problem specific. For this reason, the object-oriented GA software developed includes many of the following as options.

3.1 Steady State population

SGAs use complete generational replacement, but all population members replaced simultaneously by a new generation. In a *Steady State Population*, a newly generated member replaces the worst in a population, one at a time, ensuring that the best members of a population have a very long lifetime. This seems to work well for very large water distribution problems.

3.2 Elitism

A generational replacement strategy is used, with the best one or more members from the old population are transferred to the next generation. This is found to increase the speed of convergence, but can lead to a local optimum.

3.3 Tournament Selection

SGAs use a probability based *Roulette Wheel* analogy as the mechanism for implementing a *survival of the fittest* strategy, the probability of selection of a member for breeding being proportional to its fitness. Tournament selection simply compares two randomly selected members, and selects the fitter (the tournament survivor) for breeding. This works well with the Steady State Population strategy, as it avoids continual recalculation of selection probabilities. It also strongly differentiates between solutions that have very similar fitnesses, which can be useful, but which can perhaps impede effective search in some circumstances.

3.4 Parallel Populations

Instead of using a single population, for some problems it is found that it is much more effective to run a number of separately developing populations, with a structured interaction among populations [10]. This is found to be very problem specific.

3.5 Real Number Representation

For most of the examples above, discrete or integer variables were used, which naturally map onto the binary strings of digits used to define designs in a SGA. However, for the calibration exercise, real number representation was used, with some modifications to the crossover and mutation mechanisms.

3.6 Multi-Objective Optimisation

Many engineering problems are best described as multi-objective, e.g. minimise cost and maximise benefit. GAs can be used very effectively to develop sets of non-inferior solutions, rather than a single best solution.

3.7 Structured Messy Genetic Algorithms (SMGA)

To handle very large systems in which most variables will take default values, a special technique has been developed [11]. By analogy with nature, which develops complex life forms from single cell organisms, the SMGA starts with small strings for active variable values, and gradually builds up larger strings, incorporating more variables as the process develops. This can be used to great advantage in, for example, rehabilitation or strengthening studies, where the number of pipes to be improved is possibly a small subset of the total number of pipes that need to be considered for improvement.

4. Conclusions

Genetic Algorithms provide a powerful tool for the optimal design of engineering systems within the water industry. Their use is still in its infancy, but case studies now demonstrate that considerable benefits can be obtained from their application to the design and operation of large distribution networks and other systems.

Acknowledgements

The co-operation of the following organisations is gratefully acknowledged: Consumer Utilities (Canada); South West Water plc; Optimal Solutions / Ewan Associates Ltd.

References

1. Cembrowicz R.G. and Krauter G.E., (1977), Optimization of urban and regional water supply systems. *Systems Approach for Development*, Ghonaimy N.A. ed., Pergamon Press

2. Goldberg, D.E., (1989), *Genetic Algorithms in Search, Optimisation, and Machine Learning* Addison-WesleyII.

3. Michalewicz, Z., (1992), *Genetic Algorithms + Data Structures = Evolution Programs*, Springer Verlag.

4. Savic, D.A. and Walters, G.A., (1997), Genetic Algorithms for the Least-cost Design of Water Distribution Networks, *ASCE Journal of Water Resources Planning and Management*, 123 (2).

5. Rossman, L.A., (1993), EPANET users manual, U.S. Environmental Protection Agency, Cincinnati, Ohio.

6. Savic, D.A. and Walters, G.A., (1997), Evolving Sustainable Water Networks, Hydrological Sciences Journal, 42(4), 549-564.

7. Mackle G., Savic D.A. and Walters G.A., (1995), Application of genetic algorithms to pump scheduling for water supply, in GALESIA'95, *Conference Publication 414*, pp 400-405, Institution of Electrical Engineers.

8. de Schaetzen,W., (1997), Genetic Algorithms for Pump Scheduling and Cost Optimisation in Water Supply Systems, School of Engineering Undergraduate Project, University of Exeter.

9. Schwab M., Savic D.A. and Walters G.A., (1996), Multi-objective genetic algorithm for pump scheduling in water supply systems. Centre for Systems and Control Engineering, Report 96/02 University of Exeter, U.K.

10. Thurley R.W.F., Savic D.A. and Walters G.A., (1997), The Application of Parallel Processing to GA based Optimisation of Water Supply Systems. CCWI Conference, Brunel University.

11. Halhal D., Walters G.A., Ouazar D. and Savic D.A., (1997), Water Network Rehabilitation with Structured Messy Genetic Algorithm, Journal of Water Resources Planning and Management, 123(3), 137-146.

CHAPTER 28

Application of Genetic Algorithms to Joint State and Parameter Estimation in Water Networks Under Set-Bounded Models of Uncertainty

M.A.Brdys *and* K.Chen

1. Introduction

Estimation of unmeasured flows and heads, parameters of pipes and other network element parameters based on available measurements and mathematical modelling of the network becomes a routine activity which is carried out on-line during network operation. Robust network states and parameter estimates are required for planning, decision making and operational control purposes. There exists an uncertainty in the estimation problem due to measurement errors and errors in the model structure. Also, values of certain external inputs to the system are not exactly known and the nodal demands can serve as examples of such inputs.

A traditional approach to modelling the uncertain factors utilises probability theory. The estimates are produced by minimising a selected criterion; typically the mean of the square of an estimation error. It is a common approach to model the uncertainty by employing Gaussian distributions. An exact statistical optimality is hard to achieve as the network model in non-linear. Even if the optimal estimates can be produced in the time allowed, their value is doubtful, as the probabilistic model is questionable regarding both the structure and the distribution parameters. This is very different from other application areas such as power systems. The situation is even worse regarding assessment of the estimation error. The statistical measure, which is the estimation error covariance matrix, often cannot be treated as sufficiently robust. Finally, one can end up, quite easily, with estimates whose value can not be robustly assessed.

An alternative approach to modelling an uncertainty for general estimation purposes was proposed in [15]. An excellent survey paper [16] covers the parameter estimation area. In this approach, bounded sets are used to describe the limits of unknown instantaneous values of uncertain quantities. The corresponding envelopes (tubes) constitute bounds on unknown trajectories. This a priori information is more natural and can be more easily available. The estimates are sets in which the unknown parameters and states are contained. The smallest sets bounding the estimated quantities that are consistent with the system model and the measurements available when the estimation problem is solved are the optimal estimates. They represent the tightest possible bounds on the unknown quantities. Once the set-estimates have been computed, the specific points can be selected depending on their future usage. If a high robustness is wanted, then special centres of the sets are calculated by minimising the maximum possible estimation error. Such point-estimates may be needed to support fully the actions or decisions to be chosen based on the estimates. A different selection is made if the system decision maker or operator is prepared to allow for a certain risk. Regardless of the choice of the point-estimate the error made can be always robustly assessed as the set-estimates provide guaranteed bounds on the unknown quantities. The approach is known as set-membership or set-bounded estimation.

An application of the set-bounded estimation to state estimation in water systems based on linearised models was reported in [2]. Only a static network was considered and bounded measurement error was the uncertain factor. The orthotopes were used to provide an efficient outer bounding of the exact set-estimates, yielding the intervals bounding the individual estimated variables. The ellipsoids instead of the orthotopes were used in [3]. In [4], [5] and [6] joint state and parameter estimation was formulated for a general dynamic water system with known structure and bounded measurement errors and the orthotopes were used for estimation purposes. Signomial programming was applied to solve the estimation problem. Both batch and recursive algorithms were proposed. Dedicated hierarchical estimation structures and algorithms were developed for a linearised quantity model with ellipsoidal bounding in [7] to cover the class of large-scale networks. A new class of the estimation problem solvers was derived in [8] based on piece-wise linear approximation of non-linear models of the network elements. The resulting estimation problem was formulated as a mixed-integer optimisation problem. Both λ and δ formulations were considered and the corresponding efficiency of the solver investigated. The estimation algorithm was applied successfully to the Neuhause water supply system in Thuringia, Germany. The approach was recently developed further to cover joint state and parameter estimation for integrated dynamic models of water quantity and quality [9].

In this chapter the joint state and parameter estimation problem for dynamic water supply and distribution network is considered and an improved formulation is presented. The uncertainty is due to modelling and measurement errors and it is modelled by employing the set-membership approach. Hence, the applicability of results presented in [4], [6] and [7] is extended to cover the errors in the model structure. The estimation is limited to the variables associated with water quantity (hydraulic model). An application of genetic algorithms for solving the estimation problem is investigated. The solver performance is illustrated using a simulation based on an example dynamic network.

2. Formulation of Joint State and Parameter Estimation Problem

It is rather rare that all hydraulic parameters are known and only the hydraulic states need to be estimated or that all the states are known and only the parameters require estimation. A realistic situation is that only certain states are measured accurately enough and only certain parameters are known. Hence, whether we like it or not, it may be not possible to estimate states and parameters separately.

Let us denote the hydraulic state and parameter vectors by $\boldsymbol{x}$ and γ, respectively. The state vector is composed of non-reservoir nodal heads $\boldsymbol{h}$, pipe flows $\boldsymbol{q}$, reservoir heads $\boldsymbol{h}_r$ and nodal demands $\boldsymbol{d}$.

Hence,

$$\boldsymbol{x} = [\boldsymbol{h}^T, \boldsymbol{q}^T, \boldsymbol{h}_r^T, \boldsymbol{d}^T]^T \tag{2.1}$$

The static part of the network hydraulic model is represented by a number of equalities relating the state variables and parameters for the network elements and describing connections between the elements [4, 10]. The equalities are described by non-linear functions. Let $\mathbf{F}$ denote the operator representing the static part of the model. Hence,

$$\mathbf{F}(\boldsymbol{x}, \gamma) = 0 \tag{2.2}$$

The operator $\mathbf{F}$ is not known exactly and only its approximate model $\mathbf{F}_m$ is available. The following holds:

$$\mathbf{F}(\boldsymbol{x}, \gamma) = \mathbf{F}_m(\boldsymbol{x}, \gamma) + \varepsilon(\boldsymbol{x}, \gamma) \tag{2.3}$$

The vector function $\varepsilon(\cdot)$ represents the error in the model structure and it is assumed that the bounds $\varepsilon_{m,l}$ and $\varepsilon_{m,u}$ on this error are known, so that

$$\varepsilon_{m,l} \le \varepsilon(\boldsymbol{x}, \gamma) \le \varepsilon_{m,u} \tag{2.4}$$

holds for all operational values of states and parameters.

The model can be used to bound robustly real state and parameter values as:

$$-\varepsilon_{m,u} \le \mathbf{F}_m(\boldsymbol{x}, \gamma) \le -\varepsilon_{m,l} \tag{2.5}$$

The network dynamics are described by:

$$\boldsymbol{h}_r(j+1) = \boldsymbol{h}_r(j) + \boldsymbol{A}_r\boldsymbol{q}_r(j) + \boldsymbol{A}_d\boldsymbol{d}_r(j) \tag{2.6}$$

where j denotes time step.

Not all heads, flows and demands are measurable. Let $\boldsymbol{h}_0^T, \boldsymbol{q}_0^T, \boldsymbol{h}_{r0}^T, \boldsymbol{d}_0^T$ denote vectors of the measured (observed) hydraulic states. Let z denote the overall vector of measured states. Thus,

$$z = \left[\boldsymbol{h}_0^T, \boldsymbol{q}_0^T, \boldsymbol{h}_{r0}^T, \boldsymbol{d}_0^T\right]^T \tag{2.7}$$

Notice that $z \subset \boldsymbol{x}$. The measurements are taken at $j = 1, \ldots k$, discrete-time instants corresponding to time steps of length Δt. The estimates are generated at the same time instants so that all new information available is utilised immediately.

The measurements available at time step k can be expressed as

$$\boldsymbol{Z}^m(k) = \left[z^m(1)^T, \ldots, z^m(k)^T\right]^T \tag{2.8}$$

The measurements are noisy, i.e.,

$$z^m(j) = z(j) + \varepsilon^m(j), \quad j = 1, \ldots, k \tag{2.9}$$

where $\varepsilon^m(j)$ is L_∞ bounded, i.e., $\varepsilon^m_{l,i}(j) \leq \varepsilon^m_i(j) \leq \varepsilon^m_{u,i}(j)$ for every component $i = 1,\ldots m$, of the vector $\varepsilon^m(j)$. The measurement equations (2.9) together with (2.8) constitute the *measurement information available at time step k.* As the actual measurement error vector trajectory over $\overline{1{:}k}$ is not known the Eqs. (2.9) are replaced by inequalities in which knowledge about the measurement error bounds is utilised as:

$$z^m_i(j) - \varepsilon^m_{u,i}(j) \leq z_i(j) \leq z^m_i(j) - \varepsilon^m_{l,i}(j)$$

for $j = 1,2,\ldots k$ and $i = 1,2,\ldots m$ (2.10)

The inequalities (2.10) constrain possible values of the measured states over time period $\overline{1{:}k}$. Denoting the vector of the state trajectories over $\overline{1:k}$ by

$$\boldsymbol{X}(k) = \left[\boldsymbol{x}^T(1), \boldsymbol{x}^T(2), \ldots, \boldsymbol{x}^T(k)\right]^T$$

we can abbreviate the measurement inequalities (2.10) as

$$\mathrm{M}(k)(\boldsymbol{X}(k)) \leq \mathbf{0} \tag{2.11}$$

where M is a suitably defined operator.

We also introduce operator m(k) in order to define the measurement inequality only at step k:

$$\mathrm{m}(k)(\boldsymbol{x}(k)) \leq \mathbf{0} \Leftrightarrow z^m(k) - \varepsilon^m_u(k) \leq z(k) \leq z^m(k) - \varepsilon^m_l(k) \tag{2.12}$$

The inequalities (2.5) applied at time steps j=1,..k produce the inequalities which constrain possible values of states and parameters due to a priori knowledge provided by the static network model:

$$-\varepsilon_{m,u} \leq \mathbf{F}_m(\boldsymbol{x}(j), \gamma) \leq -\varepsilon_{m,l} \quad \text{for } j=1,\ldots k \tag{2.13}$$

There are always available certain initial bounds on the states and parameters

$$\boldsymbol{x}_{min} \leq \boldsymbol{x} \leq \boldsymbol{x}_{max} \quad \text{and} \quad \gamma_{min} \leq \gamma \leq \gamma_{max} \tag{2.14}$$

For the sake of convenience these inequalities which represent *overall a priori knowledge* are abbreviated as

$$\mathrm{D}(\boldsymbol{x}(j), \gamma) \leq \mathbf{0} \tag{2.15}$$

2.1 Static Joint State and Parameter Estimation

At the time step k we shall define set $\Phi(k)$ of all state trajectories $\boldsymbol{X}(k)$ and values of the parameter vector γ which are *consistent* with the measurements gathered over time period $\overline{1:k}$ and a priori information:

$$\Phi(k) = \left\{(\boldsymbol{X}(k), \gamma) : \mathbf{D}(\boldsymbol{x}(j), \gamma) \leq \mathbf{0},\ j = 1,\ldots k \ \textit{and}\ \mathbf{M}(k)\boldsymbol{X}(k) \leq \mathbf{0}\ \right\} \tag{2.16}$$

In other words, $\Phi(k)$ is the *smallest set* containing all state trajectories and parameter values that are consistent with a priori information and the measurement data available at k time stage.

This set may be *empty*. If this happens, at least two conclusions can be drawn:

- There are *bad data* in the measurement data set which would indicate *sensor failure.*

- Modelling the structural errors is not correct which would indicate a serious error in the initial *model structure* or *changes in the network structure* during its recent operation due to, e.g., pipe burst or leakage.

It is extremely difficult to determine exact boundaries of $\Phi(k)$. On the other hand, the bounds on individual state variables and parameters rather than the overall set are needed for operational control purposes.

Hence, estimates of the unknown vectors of states and parameters are calculated at k time step as an orthogonal projection of the set $\Phi(k)$ on subspace $(\boldsymbol{x}, \gamma)$. As a result the orthotope bounding the estimated quantities $(\boldsymbol{x}(k), \gamma)$ is produced. The ends $x_i^{\max}, \gamma_i^{\max}, x_i^{\min}, \gamma_i^{\min}$ of intervals bounding the individual variables (uncertainty intervals) are computed by solving the optimisation problems:

$$\min(\max)[f_0(\boldsymbol{X}(k), \gamma) = x_i(k) \text{ (or } \gamma_i)]$$

$$\text{subject to} \quad (\boldsymbol{X}(k), \gamma) \in \Phi(k) \tag{2.17}$$

Note that although only the estimates at time step k are to be calculated it is important to take into account, as opposed to just state estimation, the a priori and the measurement information over time period $\overline{1:k}$, even when performing static estimation which does not consider the network dynamics. This is because the initial bounds (2.14) on the states and parameters are non-trivial constraints and the time-invariant parameters γ bridge all time steps through the network model inequalities (2.13).

An ellipsoidal approximation of set $\Phi(k)$ for static state estimation was considered in [3].

2.2 Dynamic Joint State and Parameter Estimation

Static estimation does not take into account the natural system dynamics, which are due to reservoir storage and can be described by Eq. (2.6). Incorporation of these dynamics may improve significantly the tightness of the estimates. Consider the reservoir equations over time period $\overline{1:k}$. The reservoir flow vector $\boldsymbol{q}_r(k)$ and the demand vector $\boldsymbol{d}_r(k)$ values at k time step which are to be estimated enter the Eq. (2.6) for $j=k$. Hence, this equation should be included in the set of equations used in formulation of the estimation problem at the k-th step. However, the reservoir head at $k+1$ time step is also present in this equation so that it will be automatically estimated as well, although it is not originally needed. This is in fact a prediction of the reservoir head vector value at the next time step and it will be shown in the sequel that this prediction is very useful for a recursive formulation of the estimation algorithm.

Similarly as in the static case we shall define set $\Omega(k)$ as the smallest set which contains all the state trajectories over $\overline{1:k}$ and parameter values consistent with the a priori and measurement information available at the time step k. Thus,

$$\Omega(k) = \Big\{\big(\boldsymbol{X}(k), \gamma, \boldsymbol{h}_r(k+1)\big) : \mathbf{D}(\boldsymbol{x}(j), \gamma) \le \mathbf{0};\ j=1,\ldots k; \quad \mathbf{M}(k)\boldsymbol{X}(k) \le \mathbf{0}; \quad \text{Eq. (2.6) hold for } j=1,\ldots k \Big\} \tag{2.18}$$

The dynamic joint state and parameter estimation problem is defined as:

$$\min(\max)[f_0(\boldsymbol{X}(k), \gamma, \boldsymbol{h}_r(k+1)) = x_i(k) \text{ (or } \gamma_i\text{, or } h_{r,I}(k+1)]$$

$$\text{subject to} \qquad (\boldsymbol{X}(k), \gamma, \boldsymbol{h}_r(k+1)) \in \Omega(k) \tag{2.19}$$

3. Recursive Algorithms

Formulation of static and dynamic estimation problems in the forms of (2.17) and (2.19), respectively, is not practical. One must consider the system relationships over all previous time steps, which makes computations extremely cumbersome in real time applications. A need for recursive algorithms is obvious. As the estimation problem is non-linear, its exact recursive form does not exist in general. However, it is possible to obtain good suboptimal recursive algorithms. It is worth mentioning that the quality of the recursive estimation algorithms can be easily improved, if it is necessary, by employing the concept of a moving measurement window. The new estimate is produced based on the previous estimate and the measurements contained in a window of suitably chosen length. If the window length is equal to one, that is if only the last measurement is used to modify the previous estimate in order to obtain the new one, an exactly recursive scheme is obtained. Our simulation study has shown that good results can be obtained using window lengths of reasonable size.

3.1 Static Recursive Joint State and Parameter Estimation

We shall define the set $\phi(k)$ which contains new information brought in at time step k. This information comprises the new measurement information and a priori information produced by network model at the *k-th* time step. Hence (see Eq.(2.12)), the set $\phi(k)$ can be described as:

$$\phi(k) = \left\{ (\boldsymbol{x}(k), \gamma) \text{: } \mathbf{D}(\boldsymbol{x}(k), \gamma) \le \mathbf{0} \text{ and } \mathrm{m}(k)(\boldsymbol{x}(k) \le \mathbf{0} \right\} \tag{2.20}$$

The set $\Phi(k)$ can now be expressed in a way that is suitable for the recursive formulation of the estimation algorithm (see Eq. (2.16)):

$$\Phi(k) = \Big\{ \big(\boldsymbol{X}(k), \gamma\big) : \big(\boldsymbol{X}(k-1), \gamma\big) \in \Phi(k-1);$$

$$(\boldsymbol{x}(k), \gamma) \in \phi(k) \Big\} \tag{2.21}$$

We shall also define the orthotopes $\Phi_x(k\text{-}1)$, $\Phi_\gamma(k\text{-}1)$ which are outer approximations of the projections of the set $\Phi(k)$ on the subspaces $\boldsymbol{X}(k\text{-}1)$ and γ, respectively. Clearly, these orthotopic outer bounding sets are produced by the estimation procedure at the $(k\text{-}1)$-th step. We are now in a position to define an outer approximation $\Phi^a(k)$ of the $\Phi(k)$ set which is suitable for the recursive estimation:

$$\Phi^a(k) =. \{(\boldsymbol{X}(k\text{-}1), \gamma) : (\boldsymbol{X}(k\text{-}1), \gamma) \in \Phi_x(k\text{-}1) \times \Phi_\gamma(k\text{-}1); \text{ and } (\boldsymbol{x}(k\text{-}1), \gamma) \in \phi(k)\}$$

In static estimation, the reservoir dynamics are not taken into account. The system state at time step k-1, that is $\boldsymbol{x}(k\text{-}1)$, does not affect the state at the next time step, $\boldsymbol{x}(k)$. The only connection between the time steps k-1 and k is that the parameters remain unchanged. Therefore, only the information about the set of parameters at time step k-1 needs to be brought to the time step k as a priori information about the parameters.

Hence, the recursive scheme for the static estimation problem at the k-th time step can be formulated as

$$\min(\max)\ [f_0(\boldsymbol{x}(k), \gamma) = x_i(\text{ or } \gamma_i)]$$

subject to $(\boldsymbol{x}(k), \gamma) \in \phi(k)$

$$\gamma \in \Phi_\gamma(k\text{-}1) \tag{2.22}$$

3.2 Dynamic Recursive Joint State and Parameter Estimation

We shall proceed as in static estimation and define set $\omega(k)$, which contains new information brought in at time step k. In addition to the static case, the reservoir equation taken at $j = k$ needs to be included in this set. Hence,

$$\omega(k) = \{(\boldsymbol{x}(k), \gamma, \boldsymbol{h}_r(k+1)) : \text{D}(\boldsymbol{x}(k), \gamma) \le \boldsymbol{0};$$

$$\text{m}(k)(\boldsymbol{x}(k), \gamma) \le \boldsymbol{0};$$

$$\text{Eq. (2.6) holds for j=}k\ \} \tag{2.23}$$

The set $\Omega(k)$ can now be described as

$$\Omega(k) = \{(\boldsymbol{X}(k), \gamma, \boldsymbol{h}_r(k+1)) : (\boldsymbol{X}(k\text{-}1), \gamma, \boldsymbol{h}_r(k)) \in \Omega(k\text{-}1);$$

$$(\boldsymbol{x}(k), \gamma, \boldsymbol{h}_r(k+1)) \in \omega(k)\} \tag{2.24}$$

Let us define the orthotopic outer approximations $\Omega_x(k\text{-}1)$, $\Omega_\gamma(k\text{-}1)$ and $\Omega_{hr}(k\text{-}1)$ of the projections of the set $\Omega(k)$ on the subspaces $\boldsymbol{X}(k\text{-}1)$, γ and $\boldsymbol{h}_r(k)$, respectively. All the sets are produced by the estimation scheme at time step k-1.

An outer approximation $\Omega^a(k)$ of the set $\Omega(k)$ which is suitable for the recursive estimation can now be defined as

$$\Omega^a(k) = \{(\boldsymbol{X}(k), \gamma, \boldsymbol{h}_r(k+1)) : (\boldsymbol{X}(k\text{-}1), \gamma, \boldsymbol{h}_r(k)) \in \Omega_x(k\text{-}1) \times \Omega_\gamma(k\text{-}1) \times \Omega_{hr}(k\text{-}1);$$

$$(\boldsymbol{x}(k), \gamma, \boldsymbol{h}_r(k+1)) \in \omega(k)\} \tag{2.25}$$

An estimation problem for the recursive dynamic state estimation at k-th time step is formulated as

$$\min(\max)[f_0(\boldsymbol{x}(k), \gamma, \boldsymbol{h}_r(k+1)) = x_i(\text{ or } \gamma_i \text{ or } h_{r,i}(k+1)]$$

subject to

$$(\boldsymbol{x}(k), \gamma, \boldsymbol{h}_r(k+1)) \in \omega(k)$$

$$\gamma \in \Omega_\gamma(k\text{-}1)$$

$$\boldsymbol{h}_r(k) \in \Omega_{hr}(k\text{-}1) \tag{2.26}$$

The orthotope $\Omega_{hr}(k\text{-}1)$ is the prediction of $\boldsymbol{h}_r(k)$ which is performed at time step k-1. This prediction is improved at the k-th time step using new measurement information to give the best estimate of $\boldsymbol{h}_r(k)$.

4. Solving The Estimation Problem by Genetic Algorithms

The optimisation problems that need to be solved during operation of the estimation algorithms are non-linear and non-convex. The local solutions are useless. In [4], [6] and [10] signomial programming solvers were used. The solvers were robust but applicable only to medium size networks. Mixed integer optimisation was applied in [8, 10] to piece-wise linear approximation of the optimisation problem to produce an approximate solution. Although significant improvement was achieved, clear limits on the problem dimension were vital if high accuracy of the estimates was required.

Genetic algorithms have been recognised as a new technology capable of solving difficult global optimisation problems [11]. A genetic algorithm (GA) is a computational model based on natural selection and the mechanisms of population genetics to solve optimisation problems [11]. GAs mimic the Darwinian evolutionary theory of survival and adaptation. In general, a GA maintains a population of individuals and a set of biologically inspired genetic operators defined over the population. Each individual corresponds to a point in the search space and is encoded into a binary string (chromosome). Three genetic operators are applied sequentially to the population: selection, crossover and mutation. The selection operator reproduces the part of the population with better fitness according to the linear ranking selection scheme [1,10]. The crossover operator swaps part of the chromosomes between two selected individuals. The mutation operator reverses the selected bit in a chromosome. This three part cycle is called a generation. The algorithm stops when a pre-defined number of generations has been reached or the whole population has converged to a certain point.

4.1 The GA Solver

For non-linear estimation problems in water supply systems (problems described in Section 3) a GA optimiser has been applied. Binary coding can be used. In the case of a pipe network each variable is assigned a binary code of finite length. The GA can provide a stochastic optimisation approach. There are two advantages of using GAs in water system network problems:

- GAs deal directly with a population of solutions at any one time. These are spread throughout the solution space, so the chance of reaching the global optimum is increased significantly.

- GAs use objective function or fitness information only, compared with the more traditional methods that rely on existence and continuity of derivative or other auxiliary information.

Dealing with constraints

Simple bounding constraints are the upper and lower bounds on each variable. This information is incorporated directly by using the bounds as the intervals within which the variables are encoded into binary codes. Once more, it is most preferable to supply as accurately as possible the initial bounds on each variable. Better initial bounds can avoid the computation waste of evaluating individuals that correspond to non-feasible solutions.

The GA assigns a penalty in each case when pressure violation or load unbalance occurs. The abstract values of the unbalanced nodal flows and the deficit of the pipe head-loss are multiplied by a large penalty number and added to the cost function. The GA uses the previously computed penalty if crossover does not occur. The penalty cost should be such that near-optimal non-feasible solutions are highly fit so that the optimum solution will be approached from both above and below the optimal objective values. Notice that there is no accepted methodology for combining the penalties.

The drawbacks of using the penalty functions are obvious. If one incorporates a high penalty into the evaluation of fitness, and the domain is one in which production of an individual violating the constraint is likely, one runs the risk of creating a GA that spends most of its time evaluating non-feasible individuals. Furthermore, it can happen that when a legal individual is found, it drives the others out of the population and the population converges to it without finding better individuals. The reason for this is that the likely paths to other legal individuals require the production of other illegal individuals as intermediate structures, and the penalties for violating the constraints make it unlikely that such intermediate structures will reproduce. If one imposes moderate penalties for violating the constraints, the system may evolve individuals that violate the constraints but are rated better than those that do not.

These problems become even more severe in the case of large network systems that are heavily constrained. This fact argues against using penalty functions.

One improvement proposed here is to apply penalty functions to the nonlinear constraints only. The linear constraints are taken into account by using a method similar to GENECOP by Michalewiz [12] where each individual of a generation corresponds to a solution that satisfies the linear network flow continuity law constraints. Only the pressure balance constraints are checked by taking them into account in the form of the penalty function. Alternatively, to improve the efficiency of solving the estimation problems with the GA, a shorter chromosome, including only reservoir heads and nodal demands can be used. The initial bounds would then incorporate all the measurements of reservoir heads and demands, and the initial information on the initial bounds of unmeasured reservoir heads and demands. The fixed values are treated as constant and are not included in the chromosome (e.g. fixed reservoir head and zero (pseudo-measurement) demands). The evaluation procedure runs a standard simulation program (e.g., EPANET [13]) and calculates the value of the estimated variable and the values of measured heads and flow corresponding to the given chromosome. Then $\mathbf{h}_o$ and $\mathbf{q}_o$ are compared against the measurement bounds. A penalty term is added to the fitness if $\mathbf{h}_o$ or $\mathbf{q}_o$ is outside its measurement bounds.

By this scheme, the length of chromosome and the objective function are highly reduced, hence the GA actions can be carried out more efficiently than the results of including every state variable and parameter in the chromosome and incorporating all the constraints in the original estimation problems into penalty terms.

The fundamental problem with the constraints is to find a natural (generic) way of handling them. This is a big, open problem that is yet to be solved. The penalty function approach is not totally satisfactory and the convergence performance function is not natural so that effectiveness of GAs decreases significantly.

4.2 Simulation Results

The joint state and parameter estimation algorithm was applied to an example system described in Tables 1 and 2. The system consists of 2 reservoir nodes (nodes 7 and 8), 6 non-reservoir nodes (nodes 1-6) and 7 pipes (pipes 1-7). Among the 6 non-reservoir nodes, nodes 1 and 2 are pure junction nodes, whose demand is therefore 0, whilst nodes 3-5 are demand nodes with base demands equal to 7, 5 and 5 l/s. Node 6 is a source node, taking water from outside the network; therefore the demand at this node is negative (base demand = -20 l/s). The two reservoirs supply water to the system. Reservoir 8 is a storage reservoir with variable head. Reservoir 7 is regarded as a fixed-head reservoir.

TABLE 1. SYSTEM NODE DATA INCLUDING RESERVOIRS

Node ID	Elevation (m)	Base Demand (m)	Max head (m)	Min Head (m)
1	100	0	150	100
2	100	0	150	100
3	100	7	150	100
4	100	5	150	100
5	100	5	150	100
6	100	-20	150	100
7	95	N/A	110.5	109.5
8	100	0	150	100

TABLE 2. SYSTEM PIPELINE DATA

ID	Head/Tail	Length (m)	Diameter (mm)	C	Max. Flow (l/s)	Min. Flow (l/s)
1	1 7	400	200	145	30	-30
2	2 8	400	250	100	30	-30
3	1 3	110	150	60	30	-30
4	1 4	650	300	50	30	-30
5	4 5	500	200	100	30	-30
6	2 4	1000	300	170	30	-30
7	2 6	1000	300	170	30	-30

The GAs were applied to the estimation problem of this small system to test their effectiveness in solving a bounded estimation problem. In this test, the measurements were:

Heads:

$h_1 = 109.283 \pm 0.16$ m

$h_4 = 109.2829 \pm 0.20$ m

$h_7 = 109.4 \pm 0.10$ m

$h_8 = 110.0 \pm 0.20$ m

Demands:

$d_1 = d_2 = 0$

$d_3 = 7.0 \pm 0.7$ l/s

$d_4 = 5.0 \pm 0.5$ l/s

$d_5 = 5.0 \pm 0.5$ l/s

$d_6 = 13.0 \pm 0.5$ l/s

The upper and lower bounds on nodal head h_2 were estimated. For comparison, the exact solutions were obtained by using other global optimisers (signomial programming [4, 6, 10]). The values were:

$h_{2,max} = 109.535$

$h_{2,min} = 109.125$

The system model had 6 nodal mass balance equations (d_1 - d_6) and 7 pipe headloss-flow equations (q_1-q_7). They were all incorporated into the objective function (fitness) in a form of penalty function.

In the GA problem, there were 6 double precision free variables (h_1, h_4, q_3, q_5, q_7 and d_4), each of which was encoded by a string of a length of 32 bits. Hence the total length of an individual was $6 \times 32 = 192$ bits. Each generation had 50 individuals. The GA which was dedicated for estimation purposes was developed based on public domain GA software packages GENEsYs [1] and GAUCSD [14]. It had the following features: *choice of different penalty functions*, *choice of penalty weights*, *DPE* (dynamic parameter encoding, see [14, 10]), *adaptive mutation, extinctive linear ranking.*

For each experiment about 25,000 evaluations were performed, taking on average 14 seconds on a SPARC station 5 (120MHz). The average evaluation time for one individual was about 0.4 ms.

Two types of penalty functions were employed. The first type was the absolute penalty function. Three weights, 10, 100 and 1000, were used. It was shown that different weights affect the convergence speed at the starting stage of the GA runs. But after about 500 generations, different weights converge and produce nearly the same final results.

Another type of penalty function is the square type penalty function. Three weights were used again but they produced exactly the same generation trajectories. An empirical conclusion is that the convergence speed of square penalty methods is generally faster than that of absolute penalty function methods. But absolute penalty methods can steadily improve the generation and are more reliable in obtaining a global solution.

Both the absolute and the square penalty functions can approach the optimal values sufficiently closely. It has been shown that the GA can find the global optimal solution of the error bounds with an acceptable accuracy (≤ 0.001) within a reasonably short time. Therefore, GAs could be a potential substitute for the signomial method if evaluation of the fitness function is cheap.

5. Conclusions

This chapter has considered set-bounded formulations of joint parameter and state estimation problems for water quantity. The recursive algorithms have been derived. Both the measurement and modelling errors have been taking into account. The non-probabilistic set-bounded approach to modelling uncertainty has enabled us to achieve wanted robustness of the estimates which is missing in the classical probabilistic approach. Genetic Algorithms have been used to design the estimation problem solvers. Preliminary promising results have been achieved which indicate that the GA type of solvers can compete with the signomial programming based solvers and the solvers utilising piece-wise approximations of the problem nonlinearities. Further work is needed to produce reliable and efficient software tools.

References

[1] Beck, T., 1992. 'A user's guide to GENEsYs', *Technical Report*, Department of Computer Science, University of Dortmund, Germany.

[2] Bargiela, A., & Hainsworth, G. D. 1989. 'Pressure and flow uncertainty in water systems'. *Journal of Water Resources Planning and Management*, (115), 2, pp. 212-229.

[3] Bargiela A. 1994. 'Ellipsoid method for quantifying the uncertainty in water system state estimation'. *In 'Proc. IEE Colloquium on Set-Membership Estimation'. pp. 10/1-10/3.*

[4] Brdys, M. A., & Chen, K. 1993. 'Joint state and parameter estimation of dynamic water supply systems under bounded uncertainty'. *In*' Integrated Computer Applications in Water Supply' (Ed. B. Coulbeck). Research Studies Press Ltd. **1**, pp. 335-355.

[5] Brdys, M. A., & Ulanicki, B. 1994. 'Operational Control of Water Systems: Structures, Algorithms and Applications'. Prentice Hall, New York, London, Toronto, Sydney, Tokyo.

[6] Brdys, M. A., & Chen, K. 1994. 'Joint state and parameter estimation of dynamic water supply systems under bounded uncertainty by using geometric programming'. *Proc. of the 10th IFAC Symposium on System Identification*, Copenhagen, **3**, pp. 331-336.

[7] Brdys, M. A., & Kang, C. Y. 1994. 'Algorithms for state bounding in large-scale systems'. *Int. Journal of Adaptive Control and Signal Processing*, **8**, pp. 103-118.

[8] Brdys, M. A., & Chen, K. 1995., 'Set membership estimation of state and parameters in quantity models of water supply and distribution systems', *Automatisierungstechnik, Oldenbourg Verlag*, **(43), 2**, pp.77-84.

[9] Brdys, M. A., & Chen, K. 1996. 'Joint estimation of state and parameters of integrated quantity and quality models of dynamic water supply and distribution systems', *Proc. of the 13th IFAC World Congress, San Francisco*, **1**, pp. 73-78.

[10] Chen, K., 1997. 'Set-membership Estimation of State and Parameters and Operational Control of Integrated Quantity and Quality Models of Water Supply and Distribution Systems'. *PhD thesis*, Birmingham University.

[11] Goldberg, D. E. 1989. 'Genetic Algorithms in Search, Optimisation and Machine Learning', Addison-Wesley, Reading.

[12] Michalewiz, Z., 1992. 'Genetic Algorithm + Data structure = Evolution Programs'. Springer-Verlag.

[13] Rossman, L. A., 1993. 'EPANET users manual', *United States Environment Protection Agency.*

[14] Schraudolph, N. N., 1992. 'A user's guide to GAUCSD 1.4', *Technical Report,* Computer Science and Engineering Department, University of California, San Diego.

[15] Schweppe, F. C. 1973. 'Uncertain Dynamic Systems'. Prentice Hall Inc.

[16] Walter, E., & Piet-Lahanier, H. 1990. 'Estimation of parameter bounds from bounded-error data: a survey'. *Mathematics for Computers in Simulation*, **32**, pp. 449-468.

Index